Learn about
Sexuality

By Jane Thomas

Learn About Sexuality
9780956894748

Published by *Nosper Books* 2020
www.nosper.com

Copyright © Jane Thomas 2020

To those who understand
the importance of differentiating
between reality and fiction
and to Peter
who has made this project possible.

Contents

Introduction to Learn about Sexuality	2
Men have typically led the research into sexuality	4
Alfred Kinsey's research findings (1948 and 1953)	6
Bill Masters and Virginia Johnson's research (1966)	8
Shere Hite's research findings (1976)	10
Rejection of research based on talking to women	12
The story behind the G-spot myth (1982)	14
Difficulties in assessing women's sexuality	16
Asking young women to define female sexuality	18
Providing sex information without political bias	20
Justifying evolutionary and biological precedents	22
Explaining men and women's sexual behaviours	24
Everyone achieves orgasm in similar ways	26
Topic: Human reproduction	29
Reproduction involves more than just intercourse	30
Diversity: our sex, our personality and our gender	32
How the male and female sexual roles differ	34
Why men feel inadequate over penis size	36
Why women feel inadequate about their bodies	38
Intercourse is the heterosexual lovemaking act	40
Intercourse needs to continue until ejaculation	42
Intercourse involves reproductive risk for women	44
Responsibility for contraception and abortion	46
The influence of religious beliefs on sexuality	48
Topic: Anatomy and development	51
Human sexual anatomy and development	52
The male erectile sex organ (or phallus)	54
The female erectile sex organ (or phallus)	56
The internal anatomy involved in reproduction	58
At puberty boys develop a reliable arousal cycle	60
Young men tend to focus on enjoying their arousal	62
Men tend to focus on opportunities for intercourse	64

At puberty girls develop a child-bearing capacity	66
Young women tend to focus on their attractiveness	68
Over time women often become focused on family	70

Topic: Responsiveness and orientation — 73

Sexual responsiveness and orientation	74
Responsiveness varies between individuals	76
Sexual responsiveness is a male characteristic	78
Characteristics of high sexual responsiveness	80
Factors that are believed to affect male responsiveness	82
Characteristics of low sexual responsiveness	84
Men cannot accept that women are unresponsive	86
Orientation is defined by who we are attracted to	88
Male homosexuality focuses on casual sex	90
Lesbianism focuses on longer-term relationships	92

Topic: Non-sexual intimacy — 95

Understanding the value of non-sexual intimacy	96
Sexual attraction and commitment to a relationship	98
Men's sexual satisfaction relies on having a lover	100
Sex is an emotional bonding mechanism for men	102
Men's sex drive can cause them to be insensitive	104
Ego means men overlook what women contribute	106
Women do not need to be like men to be valid	108
Women drive the need for dating and romance	110
The romantic pleasure a woman enjoys from sex	112
Platonic love is just as powerful as sexual love	114

Topic: Vaginal intercourse — 117

Intercourse is an act of mating and impregnation	118
Sex drive: a need to ejaculate through intercourse	120
How we know that women do not have a sex drive	122
Intercourse is totally defined by male responses	124
The receiver of intercourse need not be aroused	126
Women are naturally sexually passive with a lover	128
Women are often unsure about orgasm during sex	130
Women's orgasm claims do not result in more sex	132
How we know that the vagina is not a sex organ	134
Why women cannot orgasm through intercourse	136

Topic: Consensual sex — 139

Consent is vital even within loving relationships	140

The significance of nudity and being touched	142
Penetration is what makes sex erotic and taboo	144
Intercourse is a territorial act of male dominance	146
Male propaganda: saying women should enjoy sex	148
Sexual scenarios tend to be biased in men's favour	150
Sexual insults, bullying and habitual harassment	152
Domestic violence and emotional abuse in the home	154
Child sexual abuse, incest and paedophilia	156
Sex without consent is rape regardless of intent	158
Topic: The sexual mind	161
Some people enjoy abstract eroticism and fantasy	162
An arousal trigger is either an object or a concept	164
Understanding a man's need for erotic turn-ons	166
Only men are aroused by the prospect of sex	168
Men are aroused by seeing and stimulating genitals	170
The erotic pleasure a man enjoys from sex	172
Women make conscious effort to respond sexually	174
Women fake orgasm to reassure men's sexual ego	176
Why couples don't discuss female arousal	178
How we know women do not orgasm with a lover	180
Topic: Masturbation to orgasm	183
How anyone achieves orgasm when they are alone	184
How men masturbate themselves to orgasm	186
Educated men masturbate more than other men	188
How women masturbate themselves to orgasm	190
Women's fantasies are sexually explicit scenarios	192
The kind of stimulation that leads to orgasm	194
How we know that female masturbation is rare	196
We (not a sex toy or lover) cause our own orgasm	198
Women only orgasm when alone not with a lover	200
How we know that female orgasm is uncommon	202
Topic: How orgasm is achieved	205
Orgasm is a one-off release of sexual tension	206
Orgasm is an instinctive response to erotic stimuli	208
Arousal is psychological and arises in the mind	210
The mental focus required to achieve orgasm	212
Mental arousal combines with a thrusting instinct	214
The male psychology of seeing a lover as a sex object	216
Similarities between men and women's responses	218

Women mistake emotional sensations for orgasm	220
How we know that someone has had an orgasm	222
Differences between men and women's responses	224

Topic: The sex industry	227
The sex industry focuses on male gratification	228
Prostitution generally involves men paying for sex	230
Women are not respected for being promiscuous	232
Sex as a competitive sport and erotic entertainment	234
The sexual politics of women competing over men	236
Women attract men by sexualising themselves	238
Women are often disappointed with casual sex	240
Women have varying degrees of sexual willingness	242
Misunderstandings over how orgasm is achieved	244
Sexual behaviours compensate for responsiveness	246

Topic: Committed relationships	249
Men and women's perspectives on relationships	250
The misconceptions that arise from pornography	252
Sex as a bargaining chip in loving relationships	254
The misunderstandings behind sexual dysfunction	256
Premature ejaculation and erectile dysfunction	258
Anorgasmia, preorgasmia and vaginismus	260
The role of relationship therapists and counsellors	262
How a man can have relationship sex more often	264
How a woman can interest a man in having sex	266
Why couples struggle to communicate over sex	268

Topic: Sexual pleasuring	271
How to make the most of sexual pleasuring	272
Sexual techniques that may pleasure a man	274
A man wants a partner to make love to his penis	276
How a couple can bring variety to intercourse	278
Sexual techniques that may pleasure a woman	280
A man needs to make sex exciting for a woman	282
Only some men are motivated to offer foreplay	284
Sexual pleasure is defined by sociable activity	286
Why women do not orgasm from cunnilingus	288
Sexual pleasure need not always focus on orgasm	290

Appendix	293
Why sex education is vital today more than ever	294

The idea that women are naturally aroused with a lover	296
The idea that intercourse should cause female orgasm	298
About Jane Thomas, the sex researcher and educator	300
Jane Thomas's unique approach to sexuality research	302

This book accompanies www.LearnAboutSexuality.org. The book replicates the text on the site (as at 2020).

There is so much involved in a discussion of sexuality that any text is obliged to limit its scope. Learn About Sexuality focuses on topics that are rarely covered elsewhere. The author has written about the issues associated with sexuality that she feels most qualified to comment on.

The author sincerely apologises for any possible bias in her work given she is a heterosexual woman. The book focuses firstly on female sexuality in an attempt to rectify erroneous beliefs and secondly on heterosexuality because it is relevant to most people and has the reproductive precedent.

Introduction to Learn about Sexuality

Our society provides no sex education. The magazine articles, we glance at occasionally, regurgitate the same old wives' tales. We rely on so-called sex experts not because they have special knowledge or experience but just because so few people are willing to talk about sex in public. Despite the universal silence from women on sexual topics and even though faking is a catchword for women reassuring men's ego, no one questions the bravado. Most women are silent to avoid conflict. Some are politically astute enough to say only what will benefit them. Many women feel threatened by unrealistic male expectations that they cannot possibly fulfil. Others are either too frightened, ignorant, inexperienced or embarrassed to question. This embarrassment suits those who make money out of sexual ignorance.

Incredibly it is assumed everyone has the intellect, experience and emotional detachment needed to understand sexuality. It is assumed that because most people have sex, everyone understands what they are doing and why. This is like saying that since we all have to eat, of course, everyone has a thorough knowledge of nutrition and the necessary culinary skills to prepare a healthy meal. An objective researcher is very different to the uninformed consumer, who bases their opinions on their interpretation of their own experiences.

No one ever talks honestly and explicitly about their sexual experiences. Our so-called sexual knowledge is based almost entirely on erotic fiction. Our confidence in our ignorance is reinforced by the bravado of others. But this is a closed loop. We all repeat and assume what everyone else repeats and assumes. Yet everyone has the impression that we know all there is to know.

A comprehensive sex education should expose the emotional beliefs that cause many people to prefer sexual ignorance over sexual knowledge. Men are typically intent on confirming their fantasies, which constitute a justification for sex. Some women insist on being portrayed in way that is attractive to men. The highly emotional nature of sex makes it difficult to accept facts and logic even when these indicate that our intuition is wrong.

Understanding sexuality includes a discussion of sexual anatomy, reproduction and responsiveness. Everyone has a phallus but only a man can enjoy the pleasures of penetrating a lover. Men orgasm much more commonly and more frequently than women. Men associate sex with erotic pleasure while most women associate sex with a relationship and family.

Understanding sexuality includes a discussion of consent, the mating act and the value of non-sexual intimacy. Sex is foremost about the mating act we see in Nature. Intercourse is a demonstration of a man's virility and his arousal cycle (from erection to ejaculation). Women typically need to feel an emotional attachment for a lover before sexual activity feels appropriate.

Understanding sexuality includes a discussion of our enjoyment of fantasies, masturbation and how orgasm is achieved regardless of gender and orientation. Very few women have the ability to respond to erotic stimuli in a way that allows a woman to access her subconscious arousal. Responsive women discover orgasm by focusing on fantasies during masturbating alone.

Understanding sexuality includes a discussion of intimate relationships, the sex industry and sexual pleasuring. For men, intercourse is an erotic act that provides their sexual release and pleasure. Some men engage in foreplay to extend their own arousal. A woman may interpret male lovemaking as a demonstration of a man's sexual admiration and his commitment to her.

Learn About Sexuality presents the precedents for responsiveness and explanations for men and women's behaviours. It puts our sexuality in perspective relative to the rest of Nature, especially mammals and primates. A sex education includes interpreting the research that has been done. We can use men and women's sexual behaviours and factual evidence to assess these findings. By applying a little common sense, we can appreciate some of the issues that led to the wrong conclusions. We need to take into account sexual politics as well as the fantasies and assumptions of sexual ignorance.

If it is to be trusted, sex information should present both the negative and the positive aspects of sexuality in a constructive way. Sex education needs to present an unbiased picture of the different perspectives of men and women, heterosexuals and homosexuals, in such a way as to fairly represent both sides. Sex information should be objective and clearly expressed (avoiding slang and medical jargon) to gain as wide an audience as possible.

Learn About Sexuality differentiates between the behaviours that women employ (to arouse men) and orgasm, which occurs (when the erectile organ is stimulated) as an instinctive mental response to erotic stimuli. The book and website provide parents, teachers, adults and children with the appropriate material to build an understanding of some of the sexual issues associated with intimate relationships that may arise throughout our lives.

Despite all the supposed support for sex education, there is little in practice. We cannot legislate for sex education in the sense of insisting that everyone agrees on the facts and logic involved. Education depends on an individual's ability to accept the conclusions of others. Regardless of our own personal experiences, anyone can benefit from a sex education. It helps protect us from being intimidated or confidence-tricked by others in sexual scenarios.

The scientist who investigates sexual behaviour seems under especial obligation to make his findings available to the maximum number of persons, for there are few aspects of human biology with which more persons are more often concerned. (Alfred Kinsey)

Men have typically led the research into sexuality

Sigmund Freud, the Austrian psychologist (1856 to 1939), was the first scientist of note to talk of female sexuality. Freud's methods were based on observation rather than science. He treated women for what was believed to be repression of their natural sexual urges. In those days, few couples in the population were aware that women were capable of orgasm. Nevertheless, Freud invented the term vaginal orgasm, as if such a response was possible.

Most young boys first discover orgasm by masturbating. But as they mature, men prefer the erotic pleasures of intercourse. Freud dismissed clitoral orgasms as immature because of the male experience. Unlike male masturbation (which involves the same anatomy as intercourse), female masturbation (to orgasm) involves stimulating the clitoris (not the vagina). No one saw any contradiction in suggesting two quite different sources for female orgasms. Mental arousal instinctively motivates us to stimulate the phallus. But men want women to respond to the stimulation of intercourse.

No one thought that Freud, as a man, might be unqualified to pronounce on how female orgasm is achieved. Men have always been confident to assert how women should respond sexually and women tend to accept male opinions. Embarrassment prevents women from challenging what they are told. The reason women can't make sense of the explanations for their sexuality is that men have defined it for them. Men have instinctively chosen to portray female sexuality in terms that suit their own purposes. Men propose theories and assume they are correct because of women's silence. But silence does not constitute proof. This issue is core to heterosexual society because of the symbiotic relationship between men and women. The inducement of support for a family incentivises women to agree with men.

Men have traditionally lead sex research but they only fund research that backs their own interests. The male quest to understand female sexuality is evidence of men's dissatisfaction with women's sexuality as they find it. They want to find ways of encouraging women to be more interested in sex. The goal of sexology would seem to be to educate women in their role of providing male pleasure. This is a political battle rather than a scientific one.

Women wrote books about topics they felt qualified to write about such as cookery, housekeeping, child-raising and even childbirth. They did not write authoritative books about sex. Even today, women lack the authority and the motivation to put men right about their own sexuality. Men's lack of objectivity over female sexuality is never acknowledged. If sexology were a science, women's sexual experiences would be accepted for what they are.

The response of orgasm evolved millions of years ago. Nothing new can be discovered as such. We can only document the facts and use logic to explain women's sexuality as we experience it. If women were responsive (as men are), these phenomena would be well understood. There would be no need for researchers to tell us what generations of heterosexuals have missed.

The fact that no one discusses erotic turn-ons in the context of female sexuality is evidence that women are not aroused as men are. The focus is always on stimulation techniques. Either new anatomy (such as the clitoris) or new areas (such as the G-spot) are suggested in a never-ending search for the magic button that will guarantee female orgasm. But regardless of the anatomy men stimulate, we do not solve the issue of how to arouse women.

An unfortunate by-product of research that involves talking to women is that unrealistic orgasm claims are given credibility just because they have been recorded by researchers. Any man can observe how his female partner behaves during sexual activity. Nothing changes just because someone puts on a white coat. A scientific understanding of human sexuality involves reconciling what people say with what they actually do. It includes understanding how anyone becomes erotically aroused. Researchers need to establish the physiological and psychological mechanisms that account for orgasm. This includes understanding how a person's mental response to erotic turn-ons can make it possible for genital stimulation to cause orgasm.

Everyone seems to assume that erotic fiction is the equivalent of holy scriptures rather than fictional stories aimed at arousing and entertaining. Researchers must challenge what they are told. Instead of promoting orgasm claims, researchers should promote ideas for how couples can enjoy erotic pleasure and emotional contentment over decades together. Researchers need to abandon their personal opinions based on ignorance, prejudices and assumptions. They should approach sexuality with an open mind, ready to accept the facts and conclusions before them. They should establish how women can enjoy sexual activity alone and with a lover, by appreciating eroticism, and how they can be encouraged to explore a variety of sex play.

Individuals and institutions fight for scant resources. Theories are promoted on the basis of sensationalism rather than credible evidence. Those who can conjure up an attention-grabbing headline, regardless of any facts or logic, get noticed. Sex research that produces unpopular conclusions is ignored. Sexologists should welcome different perspectives and encourage active debate. Sex is a subject on which every adult feels entitled to have an opinion, however uninformed. We all think our personal experiences and personal opinions qualify us to know better. No wonder we have so little sex research!

Considering the importance which sexual problems have in the practice of psychiatry, medicine, psychology, and counselling of every sort, it is disconcerting to realize what scant bases there have been for over-all statements that have been made in this field. (Alfred Kinsey)

Alfred Kinsey's research findings (1948 and 1953)

Alfred Kinsey and his colleagues held private interviews with over 10,000 people. His team classified people according to sex, age and education level. They then produced tables to see if there were any correlations between sexual activity and personal characteristics. Kinsey used the frequency of orgasm (responsiveness) as a measure of sexuality. His work was unpopular for highlighting women's much lower responsiveness. The reports were co-authored by four men. This, in itself, was evidence of women's much lower interest in sexual matters and their lack of authority compared with men.

Kinsey's team acquired an unprecedented knowledge base, which enabled them to objectively assess a person's sexual experiences. Kinsey's work was unpopular because people were offended by its explicitness. He provided statistics for men and women's total outlet (defined by the incidence of orgasm) including masturbation, coitus, extra-marital affairs, homosexual activity and sex with prostitutes. Kinsey's work provides us with the most comprehensive data there is on sexuality. There has been no research since that has come anywhere close to the detail and thoroughness of his work.

Kinsey's report on male sexuality was published in 1948 followed by the female report in 1953. The five-year gap was due to the controversy over his conclusions on female sexuality. His research covered a period of more than 10 years (between 1938 and 1948), which allowed time for some of the more reticent individuals to be persuaded to contribute. This approach ensured the research samples were representative of the general population. Kinsey spoke to over 5,300 men and 5,940 women (white Americans). He indicated that it was likely that both race and culture influence a person's sexuality.

Around 10% of the women in Kinsey's sample acknowledged that they had never had an orgasm in their life. Many women (30% of Kinsey's sample or around 1,800 women) openly admitted that they were never or rarely aroused. Despite such a large proportion of the female population being unresponsive, other women's orgasm claims were accepted at face value. As a scientist, Kinsey was obliged to document the orgasms women reported with a lover. Kinsey challenged these orgasm claims because he found that the frequencies with which couples had intercourse correlated closely with the man's responsiveness. If women had orgasms with a lover, their responsiveness would also have a similar impact on intercourse frequencies.

Kinsey's report focused on orgasm in an attempt to draw objective conclusions. This approach provided interesting insights into male sexuality because when a man is stimulated genitally, orgasm is usually a given. Male orgasm is easily identified because it is accompanied by ejaculation. But there is no proof of female orgasm. Female orgasm is more subjective and relies on a woman's testimony. If a woman says "I might have had an orgasm once", this is not evidence of orgasm. A person knows for sure if they have an orgasm. Orgasm does not occur spontaneously. For adults, orgasm is the result of a person consciously bringing their mental arousal to a climax.

Kinsey found that men were on average up to 6 times more responsive than women. For men under 30, orgasm frequencies were 3 times per week on average. He found that women orgasm around once every 2 to three weeks on average. Women's orgasm frequencies through masturbation and lesbian sex were both sporadic and infrequent. It was only with a male lover, that women claimed to have orgasms in line with male orgasm frequencies.

Even with these doubtful orgasm claims, Kinsey concluded that very little of women's overall sexual activity ever resulted in orgasm. To the public, it was a revelation that women were capable of orgasm at all. Only 20% of women (in Kinsey's sample) masturbated regularly. Yet Kinsey concluded that women achieved orgasm most reliably through masturbation alone. Women, who masturbated, were successful 95% of the time. Kinsey used masturbation as the basis for understanding the physiology of female orgasm.

Kinsey's work was publicised on television and he sold many books. But few people are interested in academic non-fiction on a topic as sensational as sex. Research (in any field) naturally ages as time passes. The difference is that in other fields, research is continually updated. No further work was done to either confirm or correct the original research. Kinsey highlighted the role of the clitoris in female orgasm. But this information is just as unpopular today. Sexologists continue to promote fantasies about women's sexuality rather than the facts. Any woman who raises the issue of a lack of orgasm is unpopular with her own sex because by highlighting her experience, she calls into question the orgasms other women claim to have.

The findings from this statistical sex research were not accepted even when first published. The researchers were subjected to verbal abuse, character assassination and the marginalisation of their work. The approach of asking women to document their experiences was simply dropped. It had not provided the results that were wanted. Specifically it challenged the emotional beliefs of the general public and the sexology profession, which relies on support from a sexually ignorant public in order to make money. Consequently, there is no sex research programme (of any significance) in any institution anywhere in the world today. Modern day research focuses on obscure and tangential issues that hold little interest for the public. There is no research into the big issues involved in understanding human sexuality.

The validity of extending generalizations derived from a study of any sample depends, fundamentally and unavoidably, upon the representativeness of that sample. (Alfred Kinsey)

Bill Masters and Virginia Johnson's research (1966)

William Masters and Virginia Johnson observed volunteer couples having intercourse in the laboratory. Female orgasm was simply assumed to occur as a result of intercourse. This laboratory-based approach was much more popular than Alfred Kinsey's complex statistical approach and has remained the predominant model. The public is easily impressed by people who wear laboratory coats, assuming that they must be applying scientific principles. By observing sexual activity, scientists appear to provide empirical evidence.

Their sampling technique made no attempt to be representative of the general population. Their approach involved selecting women who believed they had orgasms from intercourse. The objective was political rather than scientific. The implication was that if it can be shown that one woman thinks she has an orgasm from intercourse then every woman can be convinced that she should orgasm through intercourse. This research was popular because it promoted vaginal intercourse as a means of pleasuring women.

Masters and Johnson accepted Kinsey's conclusion that the clitoris was the female sex organ and source of female orgasm. They simply assumed that the clitoris was indirectly stimulated during intercourse. They suggested that the area of skin around the clitoris is stretched or pulled as the penis thrusts into the vagina, thus providing enough clitoral stimulation for orgasm. Later Shere Hite suggested this stimulation did not cause orgasm in most women.

Virginia Johnson started out as Bill Masters' assistant. Given she was not his professional equal, she would have lacked the authority to challenge his views. Later they married. Given she was involved in a sexual relationship with him, she could hardly be deemed an objective researcher. Neither would she be the first woman to mistake emotional sensations for orgasm.

Masters and Johnson are famous researchers but no one reads their book today. Unlike Kinsey and Hite, Masters and Johnson's work produced no detailed research findings. Anyone who reads their book will find it difficult to identify any scientific conclusions drawn from their work. Their analysis, being vague and lacking objectivity, has little impact on modern sexology.

Scientists (who are typically male) assume that a woman must have had an orgasm simply because her body returns to its normal state once sexual activity ceases. There are many physiological changes that occur in the human body during sexual activity. Such changes are observed in other mammals, both male and female. But only the male provides evidence of orgasm. Rather than ask women, modern researchers use machines to prove that a woman has had an orgasm. They measure increases in electrical impulses, blood-flow or vaginal secretions that they assume are evidence of arousal even though these women may not be conscious of any pleasure.

Regardless of what we call such phenomena, they do not prove that women experience sexual pleasure in the way that men do. Researchers ignore the role of psychological arousal in women's accounts of orgasm because so few women consider it necessary. This is clear evidence that they have never experienced erotic arousal. For men, the arousal process is trivial but few women ever discover how their minds might respond to erotic stimuli.

Our body responds to a fight or flight situation by producing adrenaline. Adrenaline in the bloodstream increases our heart rate and rate of breathing in anticipation of exertion. In a sexual situation, a male animal potentially anticipates a struggle if he needs to subdue a female into accepting intercourse. A female is potentially in a flight situation. Both of these fight and flight situations cause the increased blood flow necessary for arousal.

But only a man is conscious of being erotically aroused. Likewise, even with orgasm we may not always experience pleasure. For example, if a man ejaculates then he must have had an orgasm because orgasm is the trigger for ejaculation. But there may be no accompanying psychological pleasure. The quality of the orgasm we have, our sexual satisfaction, is primarily linked to the effectiveness of the erotic stimuli that cause our mental arousal. A new sexual fantasy may be particularly effective as well as having a new lover, engaging in more adventurous sex play or having sex in different situations.

Sex research is not considered a priority in our society partly because of the taboo but also because no one has been able to convince society that there is a scientific way of analysing such an emotional topic. For political and emotional reasons, men are motivated to establish that women can enjoy intercourse (this is equated to being able to orgasm from the activity) just as men do. Any research that supports intercourse as a means of providing female orgasm is promoted. Research that contradicts that belief is ignored.

People often object to old sex research and they suggest that more modern research must exist. They don't seem to appreciate that if such research existed then they would know about it. Sex research of any consequence is likely to be headline news. But it is in fact very rare. This is because facts are very unpopular when they challenge people's beliefs about how sex should work. It is noticeable that people object much more often to any research that promotes the role of the clitoris. Research that promotes intercourse, such as Masters and Johnson or the G-spot proposal, are never denounced by anyone. This is not just because of men's biological need for regular intercourse. It is also because women associate the positive aspects of sex with marriage and family, which rely on offering a man regular intercourse.

Women, on the other hand, can become physically aroused (increased blood flow in the reproductive organs) without becoming psychologically aroused even in the slightest. (Robert Weiss)

Shere Hite's research findings (1976)

Shere Hite's work was a thesis produced for her doctorate in sexuality. Her research had much lower funding than Kinsey's and so was more limited in scope. Hite circulated a lengthy questionnaire in the US through women's magazines and to passers-by on the street in the early 1970s. Shere Hite's sample was not selected in a way that would make it representative of the general population. So the percentages cannot be applied to all women. Women's accounts of orgasm were less reliable, being written anonymously on a form rather than given via personal interview as Kinsey's research was.

Hite decided to ask women how and when they experienced orgasm. She found that women, who were confident about orgasm, referred to masturbation much more than to any sexual activity with a lover. Kinsey had also noted that women's experiences of masturbation provided the most convincing accounts of female orgasm. Unlike Kinsey, Hite's work had political bias. Just as Masters and Johnson wanted to show that women orgasm through intercourse, Hite hoped to show that women use clitoral stimulation to orgasm with a lover. But she failed to establish this. Although four fifths (82%) of her sample said they could masturbate to orgasm, the same techniques were not as effective with a lover. Only 44% of the women in her sample said they could orgasm regularly with a lover by stimulating the clitoris manually. Only 42% could orgasm through oral stimulation. In other words, the number of women who conclude that clitoral stimulation does not cause orgasm with a lover outnumber the women who think it does.

Both Alfred Kinsey, and later Shere Hite, noted that with no man present (when masturbating or having sex with another woman) women use clitoral stimulation. They didn't take into account the fact that women often engage in sexual activity without ever achieving orgasm. Men and women approach sexual activity with different levels of arousal. This is the key reason why the clitoris does not respond with a lover. They assumed that the clitoris should respond exactly as the penis does. The penis and the clitoris develop from the same genital tubercle in the foetus. But the amount of development is much greater for the penis. The penis protrudes from the body. Whereas the clitoral organ (containing the corpora cavernosa) is internal to the body.

The anatomical evidence for the clitoris as the female sex organ is overwhelming. By suggesting that women might stimulate the clitoris with a lover, researchers are encouraging women to say they do. There was no evidence previously that heterosexuals (of either sex) had any interest in the clitoris. Researchers did not appreciate the issue of arousal. If clitoral stimulation caused female orgasm with a lover, the clitoris would not be ignored as it currently is. Both Kinsey and Hite used percentages to measure incidences of female orgasm while rates of male orgasm are usually 100%.

In Hite's sample of women, 30% said that they could orgasm regularly through intercourse alone by using a hands-free approach. They found a position for intercourse that maximised the clitoral stimulation they obtained from intercourse. But why would anyone engage in an act that only provides indirect stimulation? We can see from the male experience that men need penile stimulation to be direct and continuous. It doesn't make sense to suggest that women need less stimulation than men do. Intercourse provides neither sufficient nor the right kind of stimulation to cause female orgasm.

Hite proposed that some women are successful with orgasm with a lover (while others are not) because they take conscious steps to obtain clitoral stimulation. If this were the case, there would be much more awareness of the role of the clitoris in the population. It is nonsensical to suggest that researchers can discover something by talking to a small sample that millions of couples have not discovered over millennia. If men knew techniques to help women achieve orgasm reliably, the details would spread like wildfire.

One of the problems with suggesting that female orgasm occurs through masturbation, is that very few women masturbate. Most women are clearly not interested in masturbation because of the disgust they show towards men's masturbatory activity. Most women are embarrassed by any reference to fantasies or explicit clitoral stimulation, which is associated with porn. Women who promote the clitoris and masturbation on the web are clearly providing turn-ons for men. They imply that they use the same techniques with a lover. They are evidently unaware that there is no research to support the idea that clitoral stimulation works with a lover. Hite's work is the only research we have and that indicates that most women think it is not possible.

Shere Hite commented on the women who are confident to brag about the orgasms they experience with a lover. She also mentioned that women were often unsure about the orgasms they thought they were supposed to have. This was evidence of the political and emotional incentive for women to claim to orgasm in the sociable context that pleases men. By specifying the anatomy (suggested by the researchers) women can sound more convincing.

Kinsey concluded that educated women were less responsive than other women. Education (having a creative imagination) may make the use of fantasy more likely. It does not reduce responsiveness. Educated women have the confidence necessary to challenge male fantasies. Some women know they do not orgasm with a lover because they appreciate that orgasm is a significant and identifiable phenomenon that provides sexual pleasure.

... the idea that it is a man's role to 'give' the woman an orgasm during intercourse. ... this idea also often puts the man in a no-win situation since the information he has been given - that thrusting during intercourse should bring a woman to orgasm - is faulty. (Shere Hite)

Rejection of research based on talking to women

The value in using statistical sampling techniques (that attempt to ensure that the sample is representative of the general population), is that the finding can be applied to a much bigger population than the original sample. However, conclusions can only be extended to the population if the research is based on individuals who are selected in a way that creates a representative sample.

Today experts quote from Alfred Kinsey's work by saying that 10% of women never orgasm by any means. They also quote from Shere Hite's work by reassuring us that only 30% of women orgasm from intercourse. No one explains why the rest of their research findings are ignored. By asking women about orgasm, both Kinsey and Hite revealed some of the reality of women's sexuality. These findings challenged male beliefs about how and when women should orgasm. So the approach was quickly abandoned.

Given the lack of precedents for female orgasm elsewhere in the animal kingdom, we need strong evidence to support the human phenomenon. Kinsey found that women who engaged in sexual activity alone (masturbation) were successful in achieving orgasm 95% of the time. But he found that only two out of every five women (40%) who engaged in sexual activity with a lover (intercourse) said it was possible to orgasm three times out of four (75% of the time). The rest found orgasm to be less reliable and a considerable number did not believe that orgasm was possible with a lover.

A problem with surveys and simple 'yes/no' questions is that there is no way of knowing if someone knows what they are talking about. Once you have had an orgasm, not only do you know that you have had one but you also assume that anyone who has not had an orgasm, knows that they have not had one. But it is much more difficult to be sure about a lack of orgasm.

When researchers ask, "Do you orgasm from intercourse?" the very act of asking the question implies that 'yes' is a legitimate reply as if such a phenomenon is known to be possible. Some women reply: "Well I'm not sure if I have ever had an orgasm, perhaps once or twice." The researcher says, "OK what percentage would you say – perhaps 10% of the time?" She says, "OK yes perhaps 10% of the time." Another woman says, "Yes I think I do sometimes but not always." "Do you think perhaps 75% of the time?" "Yes maybe 75% of the time." These statistics are a measure of women's uncertainty about orgasm and not a true orgasm frequency. Success rates are never used to categorise male orgasms. A man just has an orgasm - period.

It is unlikely that women who say orgasm is impossible with a lover are mistaken. It is much less certain that women, who think they might orgasm, are not mistaken. Researchers need to take human psychology into account. Men equate claims of female orgasm to women wanting sex. Women in turn want to be attractive to men. A woman who admits to not having an orgasm with a lover is considered to be frigid, unloving and sexually dysfunctional.

Imagine a room full of women. You ask each of them: "Do you achieve orgasm from intercourse?" The first woman says "No". The second woman says "Yes" and so on. What conclusion would you draw? The answer is that you can't draw any firm conclusion at all. The result is inconclusive because it is very clear that women don't know. But this is why you are asking the question in the first place. If women knew, no one would have to ask.

Shere Hite's research was based on a sample of 3,500 women. Around half of these women said that they "never or rarely orgasm from intercourse". People are often unaware of their own ignorance. Others are reluctant to admit they don't know the answer. It's just human nature. Given a question with two possible answers even if women are just guessing, the result would be a 50:50 split given a large enough sample. That's how probabilities work.

Modern sex research makes no attempt to indicate the relevance of findings to the whole population. There is no justification of the qualifications of the researchers, of the political or scientific aims of the funders of the research or of the way in which the sample is selected (whether it is representative of the general population). Findings from tiny samples are promoted as if they apply to everyone. We hear women eulogising about vibrator orgasms. But this is not a statistical sample. Women who never buy a vibrator or buy one and find it does nothing for them are never heard. This is the difference between personal opinions and sex research based on statistical sampling.

People who talk about sex do so to promote their own presumed sexual expertise. Women boast about orgasm and men claim to give women orgasms. Some enjoy the bravado of intimidating others. Most people say nothing to avoid being criticised or attacked. Authoritative sex research needs to tap into the silent millions to obtain a more balanced picture of human sexuality. This is, in part, why Kinsey and Hite were ignored. Their findings conflicted with popular beliefs, which are based on erotic fiction. It is almost impossible to encourage any kind of objective discussion of sex.

Some people suggest generalisations are useless because they are not always true. For example we can say that, on average, men are taller than women. This is a generalisation but it is also a fact. Generalisations can be useful if we understand that there are exceptions. Statistical research is useful because it gives us an idea of what activities or experiences are usual. But having an experience that is different to the average, doesn't make us abnormal. Even rare characteristics can be quite normal for the individuals who have them.

A G-spot orgasm requires penetration, which just so happens to be the way most guys prefer to get off. (Elizabeth Kiefer)

The story behind the G-spot myth (1982)

In the 1980s, Beverly Whipple and John Perry were teaching Kegel exercises to women with urinary stress incontinence. They identified a patch of tissue that can be felt through the front wall of the vagina, directly behind the pubic bone that they suggested might cause orgasm in some women. They published a book with Alice Khan Ladas: The G Spot: And Other Discoveries about Human Sexuality. The authors were not sex researchers.

The G-spot was named after Dr Ernst Gräfenberg, who wrote about the area in 1950. This was clever thinking because it implied symmetry between the sexes. Men were known to experience intense pleasure from stimulation of the prostate gland. But the anatomical parallels are erroneous. Women do not have a prostate gland, which helps explain their lack of interest in anal sex. Both homosexual and heterosexual men can obtain intense pleasure from anal stimulation, which is also used when a semen sample is required.

Kinsey and Hite highlighted the indisputable arguments for the clitoris as the equivalent of the penis. Thereafter, researchers tried suggesting that the vagina can still respond because the clitoral organ is adjacent or connected in some way. The fact that men need much more direct stimulation for orgasm is overlooked. Men are highly motivated to engage in intercourse. So men define female orgasm in terms of intercourse. This has nothing to do with facts or logic. A belief in vaginal orgasms is vital to men because it represents a means of justifying regular intercourse. The G-spot succeeded for this reason. It provided political and emotional incentives for women, who know nothing of orgasm, to claim to orgasm in a way that pleases men. For women who assume they orgasm as men say they should, research that suggests vaginal stimulation causes orgasm gives their claims authenticity.

Sexologists seem to assume that we already know everything there is to know about sexual function. They are content with the explanations they have. They busy themselves with embellishing current beliefs, adding a few minor details here and there. They work their way through the alphabet as they come up with new spots within the vagina walls in an endless quest to explain the female response to intercourse that they hope for. But this kind of stimulation could never cause orgasm. Orgasm is achieved by massaging the blood within the corpora cavernosa of the aroused erectile sex organ. No one provides theories to explain how male orgasm occurs. To do so would highlight that women have equivalent anatomy as men and that women also might be capable of a similar response, not through stimulation supplied by men, but from stimulation that women are themselves motivated to provide.

Men can only engage in sexual activity when they are aroused (have an erection). No one wants (nor is it usually comfortable) to continue stimulation once orgasm has been achieved. But given women provide an orifice, the principle is much less evident for women's sexuality. There is no point during intercourse at which a woman refuses to oblige a man in attaining the goal of intercourse, male ejaculation. Men satisfy their needs (based on territorial instincts) by ejaculating into a vagina. The ejaculation of sperm into the vagina is the key reproductive event and it is critical that it should be achieved regardless of a woman's need for erotic stimulation.

The G-spot was invented in 1982. But if the G-spot truly existed, it would have been discovered by heterosexual couples themselves rather than scientists. Heterosexuals reproduce by engaging in intercourse and yet in over 200,000 years of evolution, homo sapiens did not discover the G-spot. This is the political nature of sexology, which provides political ammunition for people's emotional beliefs. It has been hugely popular despite the research being challenged as inadequate and being disproved by sexologists.

The only sexual anatomy that men and women have in common is the phallus (penis or clitoris). The male glands (including the prostate) develop from ducts that waste away in the female. As a result, a woman has very different internal reproductive anatomy to a man. So women do not ejaculate as men do. Similarly, the vagina (including the anterior wall) develops from ducts that waste away in the male. If women were capable of orgasm through stimulation of any part of the vagina, such a response would need to have evolved separately from the male orgasmic capacity. Yet there is no biological justification for women ever having an orgasm by any means.

In 2010 Andrea Burri did some research at Kings College, London. There was no physical examination. There were 3,000 women, pairs of identical and non-identical twins, who completed a survey. Among other questions, they were asked if they believed they had a small area on the front of the vagina that was sensitive to deep pressure. The study (the biggest of its kind to date) concluded that the G-spot as a well-defined area did not exist. Despite appearing in the Journal of Sexual Medicine, the findings have had little impact compared with the sensational success of the original theory.

Other areas of science involve proposing theories that are tested and supported by substantial evidence before being accepted. Yet the G-spot (which was never described as a theory) continues to be promoted despite widespread cynicism and contrary evidence. It could never apply to all women because the samples involved were so small. Yet the G-spot is talked of as if every woman can benefit from knowing about it. The G-spot has been universally accepted despite the endless quest for couples trying to find it.

... the mysterious G-spot ... I found it irresponsible to claim the existence of an entity that has never been proven, using in some cases a cohort of just 30 women worldwide. (Andrea Burri)

Difficulties in assessing women's sexuality

Our understanding of female sexuality must reflect what real women are physically and emotionally capable of. The advantage of a realistic approach is that couples can build on what is practically achievable rather than hanker after an impossible fantasy. Men stress about what they can do or say to get a woman into bed. So they are frustrated when a date does not result in sex. An experienced woman knows that any relationship with a man involves an on-going commitment to offer regular sex. So although it's only one time, it's usually the first time out of many. A man more or less assumes that the arrangement is on-going. This makes the first time a much bigger decision.

Women who claim that orgasm is easy are clearly talking about sensual experiences within a loving relationship. They assume that romantic and emotional interpretations of sexual activity can substitute for a knowledge of the physiological facts. Women represent an educational challenge because they are not nearly as curious as most men are about sexual phenomena. Female arousal is not a conscious phenomenon so women lack the experience of what a response to erotic stimuli feels like. Mental arousal motivates us to stimulate the phallus instinctively in a way that causes orgasm.

Yet researchers ask women in the general public about the stimulation they use to achieve orgasm. How do they expect to discover something from the public that they do not know themselves? If female orgasm occurred routinely with a lover, all heterosexuals, both male and female, would know not only the anatomy but also the erotic turn-ons required. The problem with researching female orgasm is that women cannot provide information that they do not know themselves. Rather than conclude the obvious (that women have no experience of arousal), men assume that women are too timid or embarrassed to reveal details of the erotic turn-ons that they use.

Most women have no idea how orgasm is achieved. So when researchers ask women about arousal and orgasm, they get confusion not science. The more women are told that they should orgasm the more confusion there is. Women who are shocked or disgusted by eroticism are assumed to orgasm simply because they engage in intercourse. Women are asked simple yes-no questions such as "Do you orgasm?". Due to ignorance of what orgasm feels like, women can ascribe the word orgasm to almost any sensation, emotional or sensual, that they experience with a lover. Anyone who can orgasm knows the anatomy, the kind of stimulation and the erotic turn-ons that they need.

Men's sexuality is straightforward in the sense that men naturally focus on the mating act. Men are motivated to engage in intercourse because of the pleasures of thrusting, the release of orgasm and the satisfaction of ejaculation (the reproductive event). Men assume that women should obtain the same pleasure from intercourse that men do because they want women to be amenable to intercourse. Most women never stimulate themselves so they only time their genitals are stimulated is when they are with a male lover.

Any research that focuses on responsiveness is likely to conclude that female sexuality is inferior to male. But the behaviours some women employ makes their sexuality much more flexible than male sexuality. Men engage in sexual activity with the simple goal of enjoying their own pleasure and sexual release. Women can be much more generous as lovers. They offer a lover an opportunity for sexual release through penetration. Due to a lack of arousal, women can continue sexual activity for longer and with many consecutive lovers (e.g. in prostitution). Some women enjoy providing male erotic turn-ons and they use conscious behaviours to facilitate male orgasm.

Images and stories of women, apparently enjoying sex, abound in fictional media. Even a responsive woman, who has the experience of orgasm through masturbation doubts the inevitable conclusion from her own experience. But it is much more difficult for women who never experience orgasm. They have nothing to replace the fiction with. Most women conclude that these fictional experiences must be true for some undefined other women. At the same time, the sexual ego and bravado cause others to conclude that it is all a hoax. But this private conclusion is never promoted.

Men need genital stimulation and a mental focus on eroticism to achieve orgasm. Most women never experience orgasm so they don't understand this. Women claim to orgasm from nipple stimulation, belly-button stimulation and even brushing their hair. This ignorance over female orgasm is compounded by men who will believe anything just so they can convince themselves that women want sex. Men are fascinated by any account of female orgasm no matter how unrealistic. Inadvertently, Kinsey's research fuelled the belief that women are capable of orgasm from breast stimulation and multiple orgasms simply because a few women claimed to have them.

Researchers try to identify the anatomy involved in orgasm but they don't specify the kind of stimulation involved. What is not appreciated is that responsive women use a similar stimulation technique to men and stimulation must be continued up until orgasm. Both sexes use a rhythmic motion (squeeze technique) that massages the whole sex organ from outside (fingers) as well as inside (pelvic muscles). There are limits to how and when orgasm can be achieved by anyone. If a man can't do it then a woman can't either. We are limited by the responsiveness with which we are endowed.

Even Sharon Stone admits that she did women a disservice in 'Basic Instinct' by suggesting that they could reach orgasm in about 30 seconds flat. This is just not how the female body works, and anyone who suggests otherwise is either a good actress, deluded or blessed by the gods. (Marina Muratore)

Asking young women to define female sexuality

Young women are naturally impressed by men's greater confidence. They are full of romantic illusions and curiosity. They have the inexperience and the optimism of youth. It's easy for a woman to give a man the pleasure he wants. Young women can't understand why older women recommend modesty and restraint. They enjoy the novelty of being popular. Young women ignore older women's advice, assuming that they resent the fact that men are aroused by younger women. Ultimately, young women are looking for a supportive mate. Meanwhile, they might as well enjoy being admired.

Young women anticipate sex must be amazingly pleasurable because their families and society try to protect them from it. They may hear about sexual pleasure through erotic fiction. They overlook the possibility that fiction is not always a true reflection of reality. Nor do they perhaps appreciate the significance of the fact that pornography and prostitution are both financed by male interest. This ignorance is further compounded because no one is willing to state the obvious conclusion that sex is primarily a male pleasure.

Just as young people continue to smoke (despite knowing it can kill), women are tempted to try sex (with all its risks) because of the implication that adult maturity is involved. They assume there must be some pleasure involved. Otherwise, why would adults do it? In truth adults, just like teenagers, do many stupid things. They do them to be accepted by their social group. They don't always act wisely because they hope to be admired by others. Some people do completely crazy things because they think they are supposed to.

Young women are easily tempted to provide the sex that men want out of ego and because they are flattered by the attention they get from men. This is very natural. More experienced women appreciate that men promote their own sexual interests. As they age, by acquiring status or wealth and through education, women gain confidence and they accept that they expect other things from a relationship in exchange for offering regular intercourse. Mature women often feel under less pressure to provide men with sex.

Many men like to encourage young women to talk about orgasms that reflect male fantasies because they find such talk arousing. Some women enjoy boasting about orgasm because they learn that men admire them when they talk of orgasms. But encouraging women to refer to random emotional and sensual feelings as orgasm, causes confusion and distress for many others who use the term orgasm to describe a significant release of sexual tension.

Many young men see sex as a sport where women are trophies rather than people with emotional needs of their own. Fathers are well aware of this and try to protect their daughters from irresponsible men who have little concern for the reproductive risk women are exposed to in the name of love. Young men focus on obtaining their sexual release through intercourse. Women never experience this drive, or the frustration (when not available) or the release (when achieved). So women interpret men's interest in them (at least initially) as being the same platonic interest that women feel for a lover.

In the presence of women, men can be embarrassed by pornographic images, knowing on some level that most women are offended by this crude and unrealistic portrayal of their sexuality. Some men support censorship to protect women's sensitivities. Similarly, men may shelter their female relatives from the sexually graphic male mind. Men assume that the women they are attracted to differ from other women (such as female relatives). No man is attracted to every woman. Men naturally focus on young and attractive women for reproductive reasons. There has to be a mechanism that causes this to happen. The mental process of sexualising women helps ensure that heterosexual men are aroused by women (rather than by men or children).

Women's conscious responses with a lover are driven by social attitudes. In the past it was considered unseemly for a woman to cooperate with intercourse. The idea that a woman might enjoy the activity put pressure on a man to continue intercourse for longer than he could. This is evidence that women's responses with a lover involve conscious behaviours rather than spontaneous sexual responses. No one can suppress their responsiveness.

Most people, who are capable of rational thought, can figure out that sex is not a biological necessity for a woman. In Western society, the fact that women are naturally sexually passive (just as most men are naturally sexually proactive) has been quashed by a political desire to promote modern women as men's sexual equals. Kinsey's revelation (1950s) that women are capable of orgasm led to those with political motivations dominating public opinion and subverting common sense as well as science. Sexual ignorance in the media and easy access to pornography have all exacerbated this situation.

Research has tried to establish the anatomy involved in female orgasm. Researchers have proposed a variety of theories but none of them has been unanimously confirmed by couples in the general population. The fact that we have had to research this basic information is evidence that women are nothing like as responsive as men are (especially with a lover). It is inconceivable that women would not know what anatomy was involved if they routinely masturbated to orgasm. It is equally inconceivable that men would not know, if women responded to the point of orgasm with a lover. No research was necessary to establish the penis as the male sex organ.

Sexuality is shaped by culture and history. For example, a hundred years ago a woman who loved sex could be regarded as being mentally disturbed, whereas today if you don't love sex you could end up being diagnosed as dysfunctional. (Bella Ellwood-Clayton)

Providing sex information without political bias

Most adults would probably agree on the need to educate children about sex. But it is much more difficult to obtain consensus on what children should be told. No one is confident about what children should be told because of the contradictions, the harassment, the manipulation, the deceit and the exploitation. There are many sources promoting fantasies but few providing factual information. Exploitative images and misleading sex information abound. Schools have very few resources to draw on. Given the rejection of the research findings, all we have are personal opinions. It is difficult to find two people who agree. The facts and findings are typically in direct conflict with the emotional and political beliefs many adults have.

We can demonstrate an unbiased view by explaining:

- The biological and evolutionary precedents for responsiveness;
- How and why men and women's sexual behaviours differ; and
- How orgasm is achieved regardless of sex and orientation.

Girls deserve a rational account of men's emotional needs including an understanding of men's sex drive to ejaculate through intercourse. Men's behaviours cannot be explained in terms of the romance that women enjoy. It's equally impossible to explain the concept of consent without being honest about the very different rewards men and women obtain from sex. Sex education needs to differentiate between fantasy and fact so that women have an account of female sexuality that doesn't make them feel exploited.

Boys deserve a rational account of women's emotional needs including an understanding of why most girls hope for an emotional connection before they are willing to have sex. Women's behaviours cannot be explained in terms of the eroticism that men enjoy. Teenage boys need to understand that penetrative sex involves responsibilities and a need to respect a lover.

The fact that sex information is so wrong today reflects the fear that dominates the topic: fear of ridicule, fear of failure, fear of knowledge and fear of the truth. We tell children to be honest. Yet in the adult world men and women lie, swindle and cheat. Men kill, rob and rape. Women are less openly aggressive but they're hardly saints. Nevertheless, when it comes to sex, we suggest that no one ever embellishes, exaggerates or fabricates stories. Most men think the joys of sexual pleasure should be promoted. While most women want to inform youngsters of the many dangers of sexual activity.

Anyone who tries to talk about sex in public, quickly picks up on the negativity that surrounds the topic. The fact that there is a sex positive movement implies there are negative aspects to sex. What are these? Why do they arise? And what can be done to address (rather than ignore) them?

Our sexual experiences cover a broad spectrum of situations that cannot possibly be 100% positive for everyone all of the time. Inevitably there are disappointments and regrets. If we never discuss these disadvantages, we are not presenting an honest view of sex. Sex is not always loving or erotic.

Promiscuity, when carried to extremes, often does not provide emotional happiness. Most parents instinctively shelter their children (even boys) from sex. They hope a son will overcome the temptations of eroticism and settle down with a nice girl to raise a family. Men are motivated by the erotic turn-ons needed for arousal and by the orgasm that arises from stimulating consistent anatomy. Women lack similar explanations for their presumed motivation and yet it is implied that women enjoy the same pleasure as men. Sexual pleasure is often associated with sex outside relationships. Most people are confused if carnal lust is mentioned in the context of marital sex.

There are massive holes in the logic surrounding our beliefs about women's sexuality. We are so accustomed to fiction being promoted as fact that we simply accept it. Movies for general release (mostly produced by men) portray women's sexuality as men think it should be. Some women accept unrealistic portrayals of female orgasm (through nipple stimulation, vaginal penetration and cunnilingus) because they increase women's attractiveness.

Sexologists promote their theories on female orgasm as if they are gospel that can never be questioned. No one challenges these theories nor is there any supporting evidence for them. They appear to be unaware of the benefit of an alternative point of view. The sexology community is regulated by organisations that ensure members promote messages that are acceptable to the political activists. Any sexual references are general rather than explicit so as not to offend anyone. Educators insist that consent is vital and yet they confuse the message by simultaneously promoting sex as a mutual pleasure.

There is no research or any evidence from society to support the male fantasy that women enjoy the same physical gratification from sex that men do. Prostitution has always involved men paying for the erotic pleasure they enjoy from women's bodies. Likewise lap-dancing bars, striptease shows, pole-dancing bars and pornography are all aimed at a male audience. Few women would participate even if they were paid. The pleasure men enjoy from sex encompasses much more than orgasm. Nevertheless, as soon as society learned of the possibility of female orgasm, it was used to justify women's motivation for engaging in both casual and marital sex. Yet most women clearly only ever engage in sexual activity within a loving relationship.

Sexual histories often involve a record of things that have hurt, of frustrations, of pain, of unsatisfied longings, of disappointment, of desperately tragic situations, and of compete catastrophe. (Alfred Kinsey)

Justifying evolutionary and biological precedents

Human sexuality does not stand alone. It is part of a wider picture of the sexuality of all other lifeforms. Even plants have male and female parts and reproduce sexually (the new life has characteristics from both parents). The male is the more active part and is proactive in fertilising the female. The female part is fairly static and has the reproductive function of producing the new life. Biological precedents provide crucial evidence for human sexuality. Precedents include the evolution of the erectile sex organ, the male arousal cycle (from erection to ejaculation) and women's reproductive function.

We share our ancestry with all life on earth. More recently we have ancestors in common with mammals and primates. Mammals have been around for about 225 million years. Primates appeared about 55 million years ago. If a characteristic, such as female orgasm, doesn't exist in these two groups we need to be able to explain how the human female evolved such a capability. In other mammals, masturbation is primarily associated with males. Other male mammals masturbate less frequently than human males and less commonly to orgasm. Some female mammals do stimulate their genitals but, since they do not ejaculate, it is difficult to establish that they ever orgasm.

Only male orgasm is needed for reproduction. In mammals, the male generally initiates the mating act. A male is motivated to mate because he is aroused by an attractive female. Within the primates, the male initiates his own genital stimulation and a partner's. Some females stimulate a male or allow him to stimulate them genitally. This is a behaviour rather than a sign of responsiveness. There are no biological precedents for female orgasm.

Every embryo has a structure (called the genital tubercle) that becomes the phallus (clitoris or penis). The clitoris is the homologue of the penis. The clitoris has no role in reproduction. The vagina, however, plays a crucial role. For impregnation to occur, a man must ejaculate into the vagina. The male and female internal reproductive organs develop from different foetal glands. For the vagina to be involved in female orgasm, male and female responsiveness would have needed to have evolved via totally different routes. Male orgasm is a fundamental response of the human body (since it is critical for reproduction). If women experienced a similar response, we would expect it to be the result of a similar physiological process. Nervous excitement in the brain (sexual arousal) causes blood to flow to the phallus.

While male orgasm (co-incident with ejaculation) is 100% vital to men's reproductive capability, female orgasm has zero impact on women's ability to conceive. It would be very strange if female orgasm were common because it plays no part in human reproduction. The anatomical precedents indicate very clearly that orgasm is achieved through anatomy that parallels the male (the clitoris) rather than anatomy that complements it (the vagina). Even responsive women orgasm sporadically and infrequently (certainly not daily).

Men often conclude that women are sexually repressed. No one explains why only girls are affected by this social pressure. An obvious answer is that girls are impregnated. Rather than being repressed, it's just common sense. The proposal was that the invention of reliable contraception (primarily the contraceptive pill) would cancel out the effects of millions of years of evolution (from well before homo sapiens) and cause intercourse to become for women exactly what it represented for men: an opportunity to enjoy erotic pleasure, arousal and orgasm. It is not possible for women to evolve a sex drive almost overnight just because they have reliable contraception.

A man's key reproductive priority is to maximise his ejaculations (into a vagina) and increase his chances of procreating. Male responsiveness arises because male orgasm triggers ejaculation of sperm. Women's top reproductive priority is to find a mate who will be dedicated to protecting and supporting her through the long process of bearing and raising a child.

A man gives through his role as protector (where a man supports the family) and defender (where a man risks his life). Families depend on men for protection. But men are inclined to take risk. This means that men often represent the greatest threat to women and children in the first place. Most of the time men have little interest in women, so when a man notices her, a woman is complimented especially if he is successful. If a woman sees an advantage in having a man's protection, she may be motivated to please him.

Women may flirt to indicate their amenability to a man they admire. This is a conscious behaviour and not a sign of sexual arousal. Women have learned that when they offer intercourse, some men can be generous in return. So women have an incentive to offer intercourse regardless of their own pleasure. If a woman depends on a man's willingness to fight or earn, it is difficult for her to complain when he wants the intimacy obtains from sex.

Women need men for two reasons. A woman needs a man to protect her (against other men) and to support her while she raises children. Most animals (carnivores) only kill to eat. Men (and other male primates) kill their own kind. Women have needed to find a capable man to protect them. The reward a woman needs to offer to her protector is regular intercourse. Other female mammals raise their young alone (with no assistance from the male). Human offspring need a mother's care for much longer than other animals because of the complexity of the human brain. In modern times, a woman still needs support from a man (otherwise parents or society) to raise a child.

Outside of the human species, orgasm is infrequent and possibly absent among females of most species of mammal. (Alfred Kinsey)

Explaining men and women's sexual behaviours

Men and women behave very differently in sexual scenarios. Key behaviours include male promiscuity, women's sexual passivity and women's focus on relationships. We use behaviours to enhance the way others see us. This has nothing to do with responsiveness. Women use behaviours more than men do. Some people try to enhance the perception others have of their sexual amenability, sexual experiences or responsiveness (by using bravado). Men focus on sexual opportunities. Women focus on attracting a supportive partner. These behaviours provide crucial evidence for human sexuality.

Behaviours are more strongly influenced by sex than by orientation. This is because our sex, but not our orientation, affects our responsiveness. Some behaviours are determined by our responsiveness. Others are a result of conscious decisions resulting from our personality or culture. Sexual behaviours include enhancing attractiveness, being sexually proactive and being willing to pleasure a lover. We can differentiate between groups, such as men and women or gays and heterosexuals, according to their behaviours.

Men's behaviour with a lover reflects their responsiveness. Men's focus on obtaining the turn-ons and stimulation they need, men's proactiveness (including initiating sexual activity) as well as their refusal to continue sexual activity once they have ejaculated are all evidence that men orgasm with a lover. Women's behaviour with a lover reflects their lack of responsiveness. Women's willingness to assist with male orgasm (rather than achieve their own), female sexual passivity, and women's ability to continue sexual activity until male orgasm are all evidence that women don't orgasm with a lover.

Men initiate most heterosexual activity including dating and intercourse. Men seek out sources of eroticism to enjoy their own arousal. The vast majority of men masturbate regularly. Men's bravado involves boasting about the number of sexual opportunities and partners they have had. Men may exhibit perversions and deviant behaviours. Men can be paedophiles. Men may have fetishes. Only men can perpetrate sexual assaults and rapes.

Men instinctively know they have the greater sexual need. Men need to pursue and date women. If women were keen, it would not be a male conquest. Young women, flattered by men's advances, think they are being clever by giving men what they want. But a woman needs a strong character to stand up to a man's highly persuasive tactics. The difference, between a lady and a tart, is that a lady keeps her legs crossed. Ladies are respected; tarts are not. When a man pressures a woman, he knows that she does not want sex in the way that he does. Some women are too timid to say no. Others hope that by offering sex they will gain some advantage, or just love.

Men learn that women can be persuaded into bed when they are inebriated. This is because alcohol suppresses women's natural reluctance. It's called inhibition because of the assumption that women should respond as men do. Whereas, in truth, the key emotional reward (when a woman loves a man) involves giving pleasure. Women can choose not to participate in sexual activity because they don't have a sex drive and because they do not obtain any particular pleasure from sex. This is not inhibition, in the sense of repressing natural urges. Women don't have sexual urges in the first place.

Once a man finds a lover, he may be motivated to protect a woman who provides him with so much pleasure. Women look for this protection as a form of emotional reassurance. Men look for reassurance through sex. A woman uses intercourse to keep a man dedicated to her. This female behaviour together with male responsiveness are crucial to reproduction.

Kinsey noted that many people were reluctant to have their sexual histories known for fear of the consequences. Human society loves gossip of a sexual nature but our interest is judgemental and critical rather than enthusiastic and supportive. In extreme cases people are victimised for their sexual habits. Even men punish other men (gays for example) because they feel safe that their own sexual preferences can be hidden within a social marriage. It is women who are at the core of the negativity over sex. Wives and girlfriends rarely engage in shameful sexual behaviour. Heterosexual women consider intercourse to be acceptable because it can be justified by their family goals.

A woman offers her body to a man to give him the pleasure he wants but she may feel embarrassed by her passive role. When a woman leaves a man's bedroom, she can feel awkward on encountering another woman. Mothers often dislike the idea of teenage (or adult) children having sex in their home. The idea of sexual activity is offensive to them unless it is linked to the commitment of a serious relationship. Women are more willing to accept intercourse (with all its risks) as a loving-making act because it leads to family. Yet men want intercourse more frequently than is required for reproduction.

A man can be made to feel ashamed of his sexual activities (by a woman for example) but he feels no natural shame because of the pleasure he enjoys. Once she is married, a woman engages in sexual activity in the privacy of her own home. There are no observers and her participation can be implicit rather than being explicitly acknowledged to the world. This reflects the shame many women feel over the trade between offering sex and having a family. Women's embarrassment over sex derives from the sexual trade. Having the facts of their sexuality is critical to women gaining some of the confidence men naturally have to face the world with their heads held high.

Males are much more inclined, and females are less inclined to discuss sexual matters with other persons. (Alfred Kinsey)

Everyone achieves orgasm in similar ways

Orgasm is a primitive response of the human body. It is achieved through an identical mechanism regardless of gender and orientation. The key characteristics of orgasm include: mental arousal must precede stimulation, stimulation focuses on massaging the blood flow within the corpora cavernosa of the phallus and stimulation ceases once orgasm is achieved.

People often focus on physical stimulation techniques when talking about female orgasm. The psychological aspects of erotic arousal are rarely acknowledged. Male arousal may seem automatic. But even men need some kind of mental stimulation, a fantasy or turn-on, to arouse them. Women rarely understand the need for mental arousal, which is typically omitted from their orgasm claims. It is assumed that women are aroused just as men are but this assumption is backed by no evidence (women censor all forms of nudity) and no logic (female arousal is not required for reproduction).

Equally it is often mistakenly proposed that female sexual arousal depends on emotional criteria. This misunderstanding arises for a variety of reasons. First, women tend to associate sexual activity with a loving relationship. Second, many women are uncomfortable with the kind of explicit eroticism that causes arousal. Third, women cannot account for any erotic turn-ons.

Orgasm is a response involving genital stimulation as an instinctive response to mental arousal. Just as men and women (or gays and heterosexuals for that matter) experience responses such as hunger or anger in the same way, they must experience orgasm similarly. In the 1950s when the public first learned of female orgasm, there was great excitement that women might be capable of the same sexual response as men. Male orgasm involves a mental focus on eroticism and a rhythmic massaging of the phallus from start to end. Yet female orgasm has come to be associated with emotional factors and a variety of physical stimulation techniques applied to inconsistent anatomy.

There are differences in the orgasm techniques that men and women use. But it is not logical to suggest that a person of one sex achieves orgasm in a different way to another person of the same sex. So, for example, lesbians must use the same orgasm techniques as heterosexual women. This is because our minds and bodies respond in similar ways according to sex. Our orientation does not affect our responsiveness or how orgasm is achieved.

Female masturbation is associated with lesbians because of the masculine connotations of the clitoris. But responsiveness varies among women, gay and straight, just as it does among men. Gay women do not masturbate any more commonly or more frequently than straight women. The anatomy involved in orgasm must be consistent for all women of all orientations whether they are alone or with a lover (regardless of their lover's gender).

We need to contrast the different stimulation men and women obtain from various sexual activities: masturbation alone, oral sex and intercourse. Each of these involves consistent penile stimulation for a man. But both the anatomy and the stimulation technique are very different for women.

The phallus (penis or clitoris) is the only erectile organ of the body. Within the phallus are the corpora cavernosa that fill with blood when a person is mentally aroused by stimuli of an erotic nature. This process is almost automatic in young men but requires specific conscious focus for women.

Sexuality includes both conscious behaviours and responsiveness. In terms of reproduction (intercourse replicates the mating act that is so rewarding for the male), a woman has to employ conscious behaviours to complement male responsiveness. But a woman's enjoyment of her own responsiveness parallels the male experience. This is because the anatomy and mechanism involved in achieving orgasm are the same for everyone. The brain must first respond positively to erotic stimuli so that blood flows to the erectile organ. Only once the penis or clitoris is tumescent, does orgasm become possible. Very few women ever experience this instinctive response to eroticism that makes it possible for a woman to access her subconscious arousal and achieve orgasm. This is why women continue to be silent on sexual topics.

Kinsey noted that some women masturbate by lying face down and thrusting in a way that is typical of male mammalian copulatory activity. Women achieve orgasm by emulating the male (not the female) role in intercourse. Once the clitoris was identified as the source of female orgasm, couples were told to include clitoral stimulation in their lovemaking. The clitoris was added as an optional extra and never replaced the vagina. Men still wanted vaginal penetration regardless of female orgasm. But if clitoral stimulation caused orgasm with a lover, heterosexuals would have discovered the clitoris themselves. They would not have needed to learn about it from researchers.

There is no logic to the beliefs people have about how women are believed to achieve orgasm with a lover. We know that these orgasms are fictional because even a man, who is much more responsive, could not orgasm in the ways that are suggested for women. For example, to orgasm from intercourse a woman must orgasm within time constraints set by her lover's responses of erection and ejaculation. Even a man cannot orgasm on demand within precise time limits. In addition, no one (certainly not a man) continues the stimulation that caused their orgasm once they have had an orgasm. Men's need to believe that women will always be amenable to offering intercourse and women's desire to be attractive to men (to get what they want from relationships) mean that no one has any desire to question these anomalies.

Rhythmic pelvic thrusts during sexual activity are among the distinctive characteristics of the class Mammalia. (Alfred Kinsey)

Topic: Human reproduction

Reproduction involves more than just intercourse

Sexuality is about reproduction. But human reproduction involves much more than intercourse. The distinct male and female roles are apparent from nature. The female produces the egg and the male fertilises it. We are all a product of genes from one man and one woman. A man has a protruding phallus (penis) and a woman has an opening between her legs (vagina).

When a man is erotically aroused, his penis becomes firm and erect. This makes penetration possible. After a man inserts his penis into a woman's vagina, the pleasure of thrusting causes him to orgasm. Orgasm is a peak of sexual pleasure that triggers the ejaculation of semen. Semen contains millions of microscopic spermatozoa (sperm for short), together with other glandular secretions. The sperm are created in a man's testes throughout his life in a continuous process. The act of ejaculation (where semen is produced from the end of the penis) causes the man's genetic material to be transferred to the woman. After ejaculation, the penis returns to its usual flaccid state.

A woman ovulates on a monthly cycle as a result of a hormonal and subconscious process. A woman can engage in intercourse without being erotically aroused. So there are no psychological stimuli that cause female arousal with a lover. Equally, the circumstances of sexual activity with a lover are not conducive to a woman achieving orgasm. The only requirement, in order to be impregnated by intercourse, is that a woman must have recently ovulated. Compared with the significant time and effort a woman invests in pregnancy, breastfeeding and raising a child to adulthood, intercourse represents a relatively small part of women's total reproductive function.

Conception occurs inside the woman's body after a man has ejaculated into her vagina. When one of the sperm joins with an egg (the egg and sperm nuclei fuse) inside the woman's body, a new life is conceived. Once the egg is fertilised, the combined cells divide and multiply rapidly to form a zygote. The zygote attaches itself to the wall of the uterus (womb) and the placenta starts to form. The placenta is an organ that provides the growing cells with oxygen, water and nutrients as well as removing waste products. After about 4 days, the zygote consists of 32 cells. At this point it is called an embryo. After 9 weeks when the body has completely formed, it is called a foetus.

After conception, the baby grows inside a woman's womb until it is mature enough to be born. This period of gestation, called pregnancy, lasts around 9 months. It's a simple principle of what goes up, must come down. During childbirth, the baby comes out of the mother's abdomen via the birth canal. The vagina, together with the rest of the birth canal, accommodates a baby's head and body during childbirth. This is why the vagina is insensitive to the relatively insignificant stimulation provided by the penis during intercourse.

Problems with pregnancy are common and include ectopic pregnancies, miscarriages and still-births. Miscarriages occur when a woman loses the child she is carrying before it is mature enough to survive outside the womb. Miscarriages are common and can occur at any time during pregnancy. Childbirth is dangerous. Even with medical assistance, childbirth can be life-threatening for the mother and the child. Various pain-relief methods are available. There are three stages of labour: dilation of the cervix (neck of the womb), the baby passing from the uterus to the outside via the birth canal and the placenta detaching from the wall of the womb. If a natural delivery is not possible, then the baby is extracted by Caesarean delivery (C-section).

A woman's breasts enlarge during pregnancy. For the first few days after birth, her breasts produce antibodies to protect the baby from infections. When her milk first comes in, a woman's breasts feel very tender and are susceptible to mastitis until the swelling subsides. A mother's breasts (mammary glands) produce milk so that she can feed the baby until it is weaned onto solid food. This allows for bonding between mother and child.

Reproduction is much more crucial that we ever acknowledge. If women stopped having babies or men stopped producing sperm, the human race would be extinct within a hundred years. Even today, it is hard work for one parent to raise a child alone. Most people only plan a family once they have a supportive relationship that is compatible with raising children to maturity. Women continue to be much more involved in the daily care of children than men typically are. Some male animals even eat their own offspring, if they aren't protected by the mother. This nurturing instinct arises because the young are a product of the mother's own body. This devotion to their children motivates women to provide the regular intercourse that men need.

Men have sexual needs they hope a lover will satisfy. A man's view of relationships is short term. He thinks of a lover when he has an erection. A woman's love is constant. Women look for platonic (caring and affectionate) love. Women have nurturing instincts because they need to be motivated to care for children on a daily basis. Women are looking for evidence that a man is sincere rather than just using them as a sexual outlet. Men should be affectionate without always expecting sex. If a man ignores a woman's need to feel appreciated (admired and respected) and her need for affectionate companionship, she sees this as evidence that he doesn't care about her.

... the average female marries to establish a home, to establish a long-time affectional relationship with a single spouse, and to have children whose welfare may become the prime business of her life. Most males would admit that all of these are desirable aspects of a marriage, but it is probable that few males would marry if they did not anticipate that they would have an opportunity to have coitus regularly with their wives. (Alfred Kinsey)

Diversity: our sex, our personality and our gender

Sexuality includes our sex, our personality and our gender. The reason we have two sexes is for diversity. Some people like being different. They like the attention they get and they may take steps to differentiate themselves from others by dressing or behaving differently. Others have no choice in being different from others and they may resent being treated differently. We need to be sensitive to remarking on people who are different. We should consider how we would feel if we were excluded for being different.

Sex determines a person's biological status as male or female. Sex is defined by biological facts: chromosomes, balance of hormones as well as internal and external anatomy. No one can change their sex. We cannot acquire a reproductive function different to the one we were born with. Men produce spermatozoa from their testes. Women produce eggs from their ovaries.

Sexual differentiation is a process that ensures most of us are born either male or female. We have either testes or ovaries. Rare exceptions are intersex babies, who display physical characteristics of both sexes at birth. They have a vagina, but no clitoris, because their phallus is a penis. **Intersex** is a congenital anomaly of the reproductive and sexual functionality. In the US, one in 100 births involves a baby that is neither male nor female. The clinical recommendation for intersex babies is to raise them as girls, with surgery to feminise the appearance of the phallus. In the US, one or two births in 1,000 result in surgery to normalise the appearance of the genitals.

Gender is a person's feeling of identification with being male or female. Gender, typically described in terms of masculinity and femininity, is a social concept that varies across different cultures and over time. Gender identity is concerned with a sense of belonging. From an early age we want to be identified according to our gender. We align our personal preferences with specific characteristics. Most girls align themselves with a personal presentation that enhances their attractiveness and an accommodating demeanour (smiling and docile). Boys align themselves with a practical personal presentation and an assertive demeanour (competent and serious).

From a young age most children want to be identified as the sex they were born even if they do not always behave in ways that are stereotypical for their sex. Gender is a concept that is influenced by culture, social class and race. Gender refers to the behaviour and presentation that are considered male or female in one social group but may be viewed otherwise in another. In the workplace, women (but not men) can have long hair while men (but not women) must wear a necktie. This inequality between the sexes is rarely challenged. Men are much more constrained than women. Behaviour or dress that is acceptable in a woman is disapproved of in a man. Such attitudes are at the root of the gender issues in society today. But they are not directly linked to sexuality in terms of a person's responsiveness or their motivation to engage in sexual activity. Both of these are defined by our sex, which is determined before birth. A few people have a strong emotional objection to being identified as their biological sex. Such people are statistically rare in the population but they are highly vocal in drawing attention to themselves.

A woman cannot become a man because a woman lacks a phallus capable of penetration. But a person, who is born male, can have surgery and hormone treatment to transition to a female appearance. **Transsexuals** are biological males who identify with feminine personality traits. With the availability of modern surgical techniques and more acceptance of gender variations, men can opt for surgery to feminise their genitals. They cannot change their genes nor can they acquire female reproductive capabilities.

Transgender is a term for people whose identity, expression, behaviour or general sense of self does not conform to what is usually associated with the sex they were born in the place they were born. It is said that transsexual is a matter of the body, while transgender relates to the mind. A transgender man does not change his sex but he wants to be treated as if he is a woman.

Some heterosexual men like to dress in women's clothes, which is called cross-dressing. Some men are aroused by the feel of clothing or by dressing in women's clothes. A man who has a clothing fetish is called a **transvestite**. Men's sexual behaviours are driven by their own arousal. Women may wear masculine style clothing for social or political reasons (not erotic arousal).

Homosexuals who dress in women's clothes are called **drag-queens**. Drag is clothing and makeup worn on special occasions for entertaining. Some men like to dress as women to communicate their femininity, which is defined by their submissiveness (amenability to being penetrated by a lover) and their willingness to please a lover (by putting his orgasm before their own arousal).

Gender stereotypes are generalisations. Each of us is a unique individual. There is a range of personality types in both sexes. We don't have to change our sex to be ourselves. A man can wear make-up, put on a dress and even have his testicles removed. But he is still male. Most people like to be able to identify the sex of a person. Men pose a potential threat to others because of their desire for penetrative sex. This is the main reason that it is important to know a person's sex. Women are not capable of penetration so they are not motivated (as men tend to be) to obtain sexual gratification from others. This means that women are trusted in intimate situations where men are not.

No one who knows how remarkably different individuals may be ... would conceive of erotic capacities (of all things) that were basically uniform throughout a population. (Alfred Kinsey)

How the male and female sexual roles differ

Primitive life, such as bacteria, reproduce asexually. But most animals and plants reproduce sexually. Offspring inherit genes from both parents. Even in plants, the process for enabling the male gamete to join with the female gamete is engineered by the male reproductive part of the plant. There is competition between male gametes because only one fuses with the female gamete. This is essentially the biological definition of male and female.

Single-sex organisms fertilise their own eggs. The male is a later evolutionary development. Early single-sex organisms evolved a phallus. Then over eons, the development of the phallus varied according to the metabolic rate of the individual. The more proactive individuals impregnated the more passive ones. The female phallus is internal rather than being a functioning phallus.

The female continued to be a reproductive being. The only difference (compared to the single-sex organism) is that a female must be amenable to being impregnated. The male, instead of producing eggs, now has to fertilise a female in order to reproduce. So the male has to be a more active being. The sexual process is orchestrated and controlled by the male. Orgasm is a result of a mindset that is intent on being the penetrator in sexual activity. Psychological arousal relies on identifying with the male role in intercourse. This explains why female masturbation is so rare in the general population.

Responsiveness (the ability to respond to the point of orgasm) is part of male reproductive function. For reproduction to occur, a sperm cell (from the man) must join with an egg (from the woman). This involves:

- A man having an erect penis (male arousal);
- A man being motivated to penetrate a vagina (male sex drive); and
- A man being motivated to thrust until ejaculation (male orgasm).

Male and female sexualities are not the same. They complement each other. Heterosexuality involves a symbiotic relationship between men and women. A man's reproductive role is to maximise his opportunities for intercourse. Women's sexual role is to provide a man with his sexual release by cooperating with intercourse. This is the emotional bonding mechanism that keeps men tied into relationships with women. Women's focus is to establish an affectionate relationship that motivates a man to support a family.

Sexual differentiation involves more than anatomy. Male and female brains respond very differently. There are differences in behaviour between the sexes even in very young children. Various chemicals, including hormones, control emotional and sexual response. Men respond to erotic stimuli while women need emotional stimuli to offer the regular intercourse a man needs.

Even in male homosexual relationships, one man often assumes a dominant role as penetrator and the other a more submissive role as receiver. So gay men need to use behaviours before they pair up to indicate whether they are dominant or submissive. Fairly naturally a more dominant male is less sensitive to the needs of a partner. A more submissive male is more ready to accept bad behaviour from his partner because he obtains some emotional reassurance from his partner's stronger drive and personality.

Men are more autonomous and emotionally detached than women. Many men have a strong drive to take on challenges, to venture far from home and to strive for control through money or status. Men's needs are easily satisfied through sex. Men have little interest in the emotional aspects of relationships (daily comfort, affection and companionship) that women value. A man is proactive because he is looking for sexual release. A man is obliged to approach women until he is accepted. A man is attracted to a woman by his genital response (sexual arousal) to her body, her behaviour and personality.

Heterosexual women's sexuality involves:

- A motivation to make themselves attractive to men;
- A willingness to facilitate male orgasm through intercourse; and
- A longer-term desire for companionship and family.

None of these involve a woman's arousal and orgasm. They depend on women's conscious decisions and sexual behaviours rather than responses. The female sexual role is much more passive due to a woman's lack of responsiveness. Her lack of sexual motivation means that she can use social criteria to assess a man's suitability as a mate (an imperfect process at best). Ideally a woman chooses a mate on the basis of more objective criteria such as his apparent dedication to her and his willingness to provide for the family.

A woman is in the position of having to choose from those men who present themselves. She does not experience a genital response to seeing her lover's body. Unlike a man, she does not choose a lover on the basis of behaviours such as his amenability to responding to a lover or his willingness to provide erotic turn-ons. Many erotic stimuli that men enjoy are repugnant to women. She is attracted to men who appear to care, who reassure her emotionally by their confident behaviour or who excite her in an intellectual sense with their personal drive. Women are strongly tied into their relationships, especially with their children. This makes negotiation with a man difficult. A woman cannot insist that a man demonstrates the caring behaviours she values or that he provides her with the affectionate companionship that she hopes for.

The average male ... has a greater need than most females have for a regular and frequent sexual outlet. (Alfred Kinsey)

Why men feel inadequate over penis size

Men's sexual role (after impregnating women) is to protect the family. In an aggressive situation a man must be physically large and muscular to intimidate an opponent. In a political situation he must be assertive and competent enough to impress an adversary. A man has more natural authority than a woman has. On the other hand, men are more of a threat.

Variations in nature often have a normal distribution, with most (70%) measurements falling around the average and relatively few measurements falling either side. According to a paper published in the British Journal of Urology International (2015) the average erect penis is 13.12 cm (5 inches). Out of 100 men, only five have a penis longer than 16 cm (6 inches). While only five out of 100 men have a penis smaller than 10 cm (4 inches).

It's unlikely that statistics relating to penis size are accurate. A man only has an erection when he is aroused, which is a private situation. It is difficult to imagine how anyone could measure erect penises in sufficient numbers to provide reliable statistics that could be extended to the whole population. Any research relying on men's own measurements would be suspect given the challenges of measurement and men's desire to exaggerate penis size.

The maximum penis size is likely to be limited by the depth of a woman's vagina. There would be a reproductive disadvantage to having a penis longer than a woman can accommodate. Many men have a penis that is larger than is needed for reproduction. A penis can be a weapon. The bigger it is the more damage it can do. Rape causes damage to a woman's internal anatomy and can kill. Consensual intercourse may involve a man using some restraint.

The testicles hang down from the body because sperm production is optimised at 2 degrees lower than body temperature. If the scrotal temperature rises, a man's fertility may be reduced. When flaccid, the penis is much smaller than its maximum size. In cold temperatures the penis shrivels to nothing. The testicles and penis are retracted into the body for protection. Men prefer to display an erect penis and may be embarrassed to show their flaccid penis. Most men (maybe 70%) have a penis that is small when flaccid but increases in size when erect (a grower). Other men have a penis that increases little in size when erect but is larger than average when flaccid (a shower). These men have an advantage in the changing room.

For men, there is no subject more taboo than penis size. Size is an issue given men's desire to impress. The first issue is a natural competition of virility between men. A man hopes his erect penis will impress others, particularly a lover. A man's penis is a token of his masculinity. Men never want to be laughed at and no one is intimidated or impressed by a small penis. Some men have a tiny penis that never becomes fully erect. They can still have a high sex drive. They can enjoy vaginal penetration and thrusting a much as any man. Regardless of size, a man is proud of his erection because of the pleasure it provides. A man's penis is the core of his sexuality and his masculinity. This contrasts with women's disinterest in the clitoris.

Women may have a phallus but they do not have erections. Women only witness a man's erection primarily immediately before having sex. But erections occur at any time, especially in the presence of an attractive woman. Young men often have a bulge in their pants that can be inconvenient and uncomfortable. If women notice, they laugh out of embarrassment. There are no obvious signs of female arousal, which is largely subconscious and therefore works quite differently to male arousal.

Men are quick to assert their superiority over women in every respect. Yet when it comes to sex, men happily accept being outstripped by women. Men assume that women have the same sex drive and feel the same intensity of arousal as men. They don't think it's odd that women never complain of sexual frustration. The implication is that the pleasures of penetrating a lover are insignificant when compared with the pleasures of female orgasm. It's as if having such a magnificent organ, like the penis, counts for nothing.

Men assume because their penis gives them so much pleasure that it must also give a woman an equal pleasure. Unfortunately there is very little erotic pleasure for the receiver of intercourse. The biological precedent for achieving orgasm (among mammals) is based on rhythmic pelvic thrusting. The key pleasure of intercourse is experienced by the penetrating male. A man should treat his lover like someone he wants to make love to and not just a body he thinks he has a right to ejaculate into. A man should work on being attractive to his partner and amenable to providing for her emotional needs. He should think about how he could be less sexually demanding.

Men often ask about penis size. They then go on to assert that they have a large penis. Men assume incorrectly that intercourse is more pleasurable for a woman if a man has a bigger penis. A woman feels little from intercourse regardless of penis size. If women wanted to be penetrated with a large penis, they would use this criterion as a means of choosing a mate. Luckily for many men, women have little interest in the size or other characteristics of a man's genitals. If a man has a small penis, a woman is probably no more disappointed than a man might be when a woman has tiny breasts. A lover's anatomy is not the most important aspect of loving someone. Anyone who feels inadequate over their body probably suffers more than their lovers do.

... men come to the sexual experience with only his porno-sex-ed and general socialization – ergo pleasing a woman means: 1) A big penis 2) Lasting a long time during intercourse 3) Making her orgasm. ... Instead many women want an emotional connection, intimacy and feeling nurtured. (Trina Read)

Why women feel inadequate about their bodies

Given women's dislike of genitals, many of the terms for the female genitals come from men and are considered obscene by women. Rather than refer to explicit anatomy, most women prefer to gesture and make vague references to 'down there'. We can use 'pussy' for girls as the equivalent slang to 'willie' for boys. A woman's clitoris is much less evident than a man's penis. Men are, in any event, more intent on penetrating a woman's vagina.

A girl has a vulva, including clitoral glans, labia and vaginal opening. The mound at the front covered in pubic hair is the mons pubis. From front to back there is first the clitoris, next the urethra (opening for urinating), then the vaginal opening, the perineum (bridge of skin) and the anus at the back.

Women buy magazines that display women's bodies. Women compete with each other to attract male attention. Women are not interested in male nudity. What have they to gain? A man needs to be erect (which is totally up to how attractive he finds a partner) before anything can happen. When he is erect, it makes no difference whether a partner is aroused or not. He just needs a woman who is amenable to him demonstrating his arousal cycle.

A woman's sexual role focuses on what happens before intercourse. She needs to attract a man and arouse him sufficiently so that he wants to have intercourse with her. Men like to admire their lover. Heterosexual men get used to the admiration being one way. A woman accepts male compliments but she feels no obligation to return them. She accepts that a man needs to be attracted to her. But also, she is not aroused by observing male nudity.

Women approach sexual encounters from a social perspective. They focus on their looks because they know that men admire good-looking women. If a man makes little attempt to keep in shape, wear fashionable clothes and maintain an attractive image, a woman may consider this to be disrespectful. Heterosexual men should respect women's desire for an attractive partner.

Humans get competitive when comparing themselves with others. Women compete with each other over looks. So a woman is just as likely to judge other women foremost by their looks rather than their achievements. In general, we tend to assume that more is better than less and that big is better than small. A man is not sexier because he is more responsive than average. Nor does having a bigger penis than average make him a better lover. Similarly, a woman is not sexier because she is more attractive than average.

Advertising uses images of semi-nude and seductive-looking women to promote products of all kinds. High budget movies, digital photography and the internet, promote images of women that are enhanced to maximise attractiveness. Women feel under increasing pressure when they compare themselves with these unrealistic images. We cannot all look the same. We are meant to be unique. Brazilian women have surgery to have their breasts enlarged. Japanese women have surgery to increase the size of their eyes. Rich women around the world diet, have face lifts, botox and liposuction.

Attractiveness is defined in terms of fashion and is not absolute. The emphasis on young women is not down entirely to men. Indirectly women reinforce this prejudice because of the drive young women have to attract a mate. The way our bodies are viewed depends on our reproductive capacity. A woman has a limited period when she is fertile. After that, she may be less desirable to men. A man does not have the same limitation. As long as he can get an erection and ejaculate, he can still have children. Even an old man may have the resources to support a younger woman with her family goals.

Women assume that men are looking for all the glitz and glamour that women appreciate. Most men simply want a woman who is attractive and willing to offer intercourse. Male sexual performance is crucial to intercourse. A woman's performance relies on providing male turn-ons such as faking her arousal and orgasm. Some men expect this as a matter of course. A woman's use of sexual behaviours contributes to her attractiveness. From a sexual perspective, men admire a woman's sexual attributes rather than her personality and pretty face. Many men prefer a plump woman to a thin one. Men often like a partner with fuller breasts and larger buttocks because these aspects of women's bodies are a natural male erotic turn-on.

Some women claim to orgasm from nipple stimulation. But the female nipple, like the male nipple, cannot provide an orgasm when stimulated. Women routinely touch their breasts with no sexual response. Women do not have orgasms from breast feeding. Men can enjoy nipple stimulation because they experience whole body tumescence when sexually aroused. In societies where women routinely show their breasts, men are not aroused by them. It is only when men associate nudity (including breasts) with sexual activity that they are aroused on seeing them. This explains why in the past (when everything else was covered) men were aroused by a woman's ankle.

A woman who is flat-chested may feel just as insecure as a man who has a small penis. Finding a partner has much more to do with matching personalities than being stunningly attractive. It's about appreciating what we value in another person and about valuing the love another person feels for us. We cannot all be blessed with amazing looks but, hopefully, we have other qualities that compensate. There is someone out there for each of us.

According to some estimates, over 40 million women have some problem with sexual desire and excitement. But if there are tens of millions of women complaining that their libidos aren't up to snuff, who are the normal ones?
(Joan Sewell)

Intercourse is the heterosexual lovemaking act

When a man and a woman are attracted to each other, intercourse feels very natural. This is no coincidence. The male and female body fit together to allow a sexual coupling. The mating position used by other mammals is rear entry (doggy position). Women tend to feel humiliated by this subjugated position. Most societies use the missionary position (man facing the woman). It is more acceptable to women, being less explicit. A woman enjoys upper body lovemaking but her lack of response is evident so it encourages faking.

Both male and female sexuality contribute towards reproduction. Throughout their lives, men focus on the eroticism that causes their arousal while women focus their lives on caring for a family: the consequence of sex. Men have a genital focus while women focus on upper body lovemaking. Women enjoy the platonic emotions of nurturing love, companionship and affection. They also employ behaviours to attract and retain a man's interest.

Heterosexual men assume that what pleases them must please a woman equally as well and heterosexual women accept whatever stimulation a man offers. This causes endless confusion, when coupled with the belief that women must orgasm through such activity. It would be convenient for all, if men and women had a mutual enthusiasm for intercourse. But (beyond the initial curiosity) women have little interest in the basic act of impregnation.

Men are always hassling women for sex so they know that women are less enthusiastic. But any realistic information is suppressed for fear of putting women off sex. Women are told that they should enjoy sex. Due to a lack of confidence in sexual matters, when women don't respond as men want them to, they tend to accept that there must be something wrong with them.

A woman cannot be impregnated every time she engages in intercourse. Each month a woman has a few days in which she can become pregnant. Once she is pregnant, a woman cannot be impregnated again until after she has given birth. The maximum frequency with which a woman can reproduce is once every nine months. There is no biological reason why a woman should want intercourse more than a few times in her lifetime.

Some couples experiment early on with different positions. But they usually resume missionary style intercourse, which involves least effort for a woman. Women's lack of erotic arousal, the upper-body contact (kissing and caressing) as well as the diffuse stimulation of intercourse mean that women experience consensual intercourse as a lovemaking act. Intercourse demonstrates a man's sex drive and admiration for a woman's body (his ability to be aroused by her) and his virility (his ability to impregnate her).

Men's sex drive causes them to see intercourse as an erotic act. Men enjoy trying more explicit positions, which allow them to observe penetration. The disadvantage of the missionary position is that a man cannot see the genital action. Men like positions that allow them freedom of movement and the ability to control their own stimulation through thrusting (not woman on top). Just as men are aroused by observing their own erect penis during masturbation, they also enjoy seeing their penis enter a lover's body. Women are not aroused by such sights, which they consider to be obscene.

Men's proactive role is a natural consequence of their erotic arousal. Men can enjoy the erotic turn-ons of interacting with a lover as well as obtaining sexual release through penetration. Given her lack of erotic arousal with a lover, a woman has no incentive to be proactive in sexual activity of any kind unless she enjoys pleasuring a lover. Most women are unwilling to engage in manual or oral contacts. Women assume that it is men's role to drive sex.

Modern political pressure on women to seem to be men's sexual equals has led to more couples having sex in daylight or with the lights on. This favours men's enjoyment of intercourse as an erotic act. A disadvantage for women is that their lack of mental engagement is more visible to a lover. Men's increased awareness of the possibility of female orgasm has made faking commonplace as a means of facilitating male orgasm. The need for a woman to be more involved in lovemaking has contributed to emotional bonding.

In a primitive society, an attractive woman has little choice about offering sex to men. Her choice is to have many lovers (whoever cometh) or to choose one man to fight the others off. It is in a woman's interests to choose one man who she likes and trusts. She has no need for sexual release but she does want a lover's protection. Her sexual loyalty makes it more likely that a man will agree to support any children resulting from the sexual activity.

The vast majority of heterosexual activity focuses on intercourse because of men's sex drive. The idea that women experience orgasm in circumstances separate to what men want is alien to many people because of the way they experience sex. Women exist very happily without sex but if they want a relationship with a man, they know that sex is expected. A woman hopes that by offering a man the short-term pleasure of sexual release, she will obtain his love, respect and support for her family goals. A woman demonstrates her love by allowing a man to obtain his sexual release from her body. A man loves a woman who provides for his sexual needs. A man's gratitude motivates him to protect and support a family. Women accept this trade instinctively. Women offer sex over the longer-term because they identify a man as a worthy mate as well as an affectionate and supportive companion.

Women's top 5 turn-ons. 1. Romance 2. Commitment 3. Communications 4. Intimacy 5. Non-sexual touching (Allan and Barbara Pease)

Intercourse needs to continue until ejaculation

A man is biologically motivated to impregnate a woman through an on-going process of demonstrating his virility (as a potent male who may be in demand from other women). Ejaculating into a lover's body is the natural conclusion to the male arousal cycle. A man needs intercourse to dissipate accumulated sexual frustration and to feel a complete sexual satisfaction. So heterosexual activity will always focus on men's arousal cycle, from erection to ejaculation. Men are highly sensitive about their ability to achieve and maintain an erection as well as to engage in sexual activity without ejaculating too soon.

Women's bodies are relatively inert, so they have no experience similar to the male erection. The first time a woman encounters an erect penis is when she is a virgin. A woman comes to accept that once a man has an erection, he also has an urgent desire for intercourse that she is expected to satisfy. For a woman, sex involves investing in her lover's pleasure with no payback. She is also expected to reassure a man that he is pleasing her. This is the authority of male sex drive, which is reinforced by women's embarrassment over sex. Even mature and sexually experienced women never challenge the male view. Men's sex drive means that the only female perspective that prevails is when women say what men want to hear. Every generation of young women assumes they should respond as men tell them they should.

Intercourse is trivial for women in the sense that they are indifferent to it. Women can cooperate easily enough with men's desire for intercourse by leaving the initiative to the man. Once a man has started thrusting into her, he is unlikely to stop until he has ejaculated. A woman accepts that she needs to remain in position until her lover has obtained his sexual release. Intercourse may be effortless for a woman but emotionally and erotically she feels little. Women need emotional factors (which rely on having an affectionate and appreciative lover) to enjoy the romantic aspects of sex.

Eventually, men do seem to want a conclusion to their thrusting. Some women use vocal accompaniment or assist with penile stimulation by moving their hips (in time with his thrusting action) so as to reduce the time needed for intercourse. If a woman anticipates a man's build-up, she can assist by providing the turn-on he needs to achieve orgasm. Some women time the sound accompaniment of their faked orgasm to coincide with male orgasm.

Men's challenge is to enjoy the pleasure of thrusting for as long as they can before they feel compelled to ejaculate. It suits a man that intercourse does not require female arousal. He does not need to wait for a lover to be aroused. A man can engage in intercourse whenever he has an erection. Likewise, men do not want a woman to orgasm easily. If she did, she would cease to be interested in further stimulation. Male orgasm ends a man's ability to stimulate a lover through intercourse. But men define female orgasm to suit themselves. The idea that female orgasm has occurred communicates a woman's approval (erotic feedback) of a man's efforts to please her. Because women provide an orifice rather than a phallus, a man knows that according to his definition of what it represents (evidence of female approval), female orgasm does not end sexual activity. Conveniently a man can continue intercourse until ejaculation (the reproductive event).

A responsive woman who has already experienced orgasm alone, is shocked when she first has intercourse. Intercourse is so totally different to masturbation. There is no erotic mental arousal. During masturbation a woman's mind is completely absorbed in the action of a fantasy. She has no awareness of the real world around her. She experiences arousal and orgasm in a very surreal, private and personal situation. But sexual activity with a lover has none of this subconscious self-absorption. A woman's mind is fully conscious all the time. Even the kind of activities that she might use in her fantasies are devoid of any erotic significance when she is with a real lover.

In the early days, a man's sex drive seems like a demonstration of love because he spends companionable time with a woman. Over time, sex becomes a functional expectation. It becomes obvious that a man is focused on satisfying his own sexual needs. A man is oblivious to how a woman feels about supplying his sexual relief. Without any affection, a woman feels like a sexual relief tube. When intercourse ends, a woman's satisfaction derives from her relief that the man has achieved his release. She is free to get on with her day. She doesn't have to offer sex until the next time. In long-term relationships this obligation never goes away. It is always in the background.

If we are to understand men and women's sexuality, we must never forget that Nature wants us to engage foremost in intercourse. Male sex drive and women's lack of responsiveness with a lover both work towards this goal. Women can engage in sexual activity indefinitely because they are not aroused with a lover and so not focused on achieving their own orgasm. This makes women much more flexible and generous lovers than men tend to be. Men have power in relationships because their sex drive and their desire to enjoy their own erotic arousal dictate what happens during sex. The only proactive role available to women is assisting with male orgasm. Heterosexual relationships depend on women providing the body orifice and the erotic turn-ons (even if only an attractive body and passively amenable disposition) that men need to obtain a satisfying sexual release. Women obtain their rewards in the wider relationship with a loving partner.

Orgasms are elusive. Most women don't have one every time (or maybe even most times) they hit the sheets. Plenty of surveys—and likely your own bedroom experience—verify that. (Anna Davies)

Intercourse involves reproductive risk for women

Men tend to focus on sexual pleasure so we often equate sexuality to responsiveness. Orgasm is certainly one erotic pleasure that motivates a person to initiate sexual activity. But sexuality is, in fact, foremost about reproduction. Pleasure is merely a by-product. Given the key role of intercourse in male sexuality, it is tempting to assume that it must have a similar role in female sexuality. Unfortunately, this does not follow. The vagina is a reproductive organ but thrusting into it provides male orgasm. For the purposes of reproduction, only men need to be motivated to engage in intercourse. Female orgasm occurs outside the reproductive process.

A man's key reproductive role is impregnating a woman. A woman's key reproductive role is bearing children. Most of us base our understanding of sexuality on this reproductive view because of how we experience sex. Male responsiveness aligns with a man's reproductive role because male orgasm is the trigger for ejaculation (which is the key reproductive event). So we assume that female responsiveness must also align with women's reproductive role. Men assume that because reproduction involves a woman being penetrated, she must thereby experience arousal and orgasm. Such a situation would be very convenient for everyone but wishing doesn't make it so. We need to consider the very different overhead for men and women in terms of the consequences of engaging in intercourse (the mating act).

As a result of intercourse, a woman can be obliged to carry a man's progeny in her uterus for 9 months. After this time, the social responsibility for raising the child is clearly hers. A woman is expected to care for a child on a daily basis until it can fend for itself. Without the protection of reliable contraception, few women would volunteer for unprotected intercourse. Women naturally avoid intercourse. Many of the world's children are born because of an act that a woman may not welcome or that is forced on her.

For a man, intercourse is risk free. There are no consequences. A man's best chances of passing on his genes involve having a biological drive to impregnate any attractive woman regardless of circumstances. But if women behaved as men do, our species would not have been so successful reproductively. For a woman to successfully reproduce (raise a child to adulthood), she needs to choose both the man and circumstances conducive to raising children. Before the 1960s there was no reliable contraception. A woman potentially risked pregnancy every time she engaged in intercourse.

Throughout history, married women have spent their whole lives either pregnant or breastfeeding. Women commonly died in childbirth. So women paid for intercourse with their life. If she was unmarried, a woman was blamed for bringing a child into the world without a father to pay for its upbringing. Unless she has some reassurance that a man will support her in raising a child, no woman is likely to risk pregnancy without a fight. This conscious ability to avoid intercourse with an unsuitable mate is incompatible with being erotically aroused by a potential partner and having a sex drive. A woman makes a conscious choice to offer regular intercourse to a devoted man who is willing to support her through years of child-raising.

Once reliable contraceptive became available, it was assumed that women would be free to enjoy the same pleasure from intercourse that men have always enjoyed. It was proposed that women would behave as men do. This has not happened. Men still need to date women before there is likely to be any sexual activity. Most women will only offer sex in the context of a committed and loving relationship. Men also continue to be the ones who propose. A marriage proposal represents a man's offer of financial support.

Certainly, there are women today who are willing to have sex for no particular reason other than ego. But women's motives are different to men's. Women are not intent on their own pleasure but rather on what they might obtain by providing male pleasure. Reliable contraception cannot change women's instinctive responses that have evolved over millions of years. Sexual responses do not change over decades. Only women's sexual behaviours change as fashion dictates and because of improved policing.

Men want intercourse for the erotic pleasure they enjoy from it. This is not just sensual and emotional pleasure. It is crude lust. Men need sex regardless of the risks, which are not just confined to getting a woman pregnant. Both hetero- and homosexual men risk their careers, political future or public censure. Others have risked death or severe punishments (especially gay men) to obtain penetrative sex. This is the power of a strong sex drive that motivates some men to take considerable risk to obtain the sexual release they can obtain from another person's body in a way that women never do.

Most women are only willing to offer intercourse when they are attracted to a man in such a way that they feel amenable to sex. This amenability is emotional and romantic rather than erotic. When a woman loves a man, she enjoys giving him pleasure. In the days before reliable contraception and maintenance payments, if a woman became pregnant she had no choice about offering sex to obtain a man's on-going support. So the emotional factors that make women amenable to sex only need to operate in the early days of relationships. These romantic factors may work later on if a woman obtains rewards from the wider relationship that compensate her for investing passively or actively in her sex life. Men provide for women's material needs but they are often less sensitive to women's emotional needs.

Being a woman is a terribly difficult task, since it consists principally in dealing with men. (Joseph Conrad)

Responsibility for contraception and abortion

The (contraceptive) pill, taken on a daily basis by a woman, contains hormones that stop her ovaries producing eggs. A condom, worn by the man over his penis during intercourse, prevents semen entering the vagina. A woman can wear a rubber diaphragm over her cervix (neck of the uterus). A woman can also have a coil inserted by a doctor, which prevents sperm entering the uterus. The morning after pill, which may prevent her getting pregnant, is taken by a woman the day after having unprotected intercourse.

Sterilisation involves rendering a person infertile (incapable of reproducing). In a woman, the fallopian tubes are cut. This prevents an egg descending into the womb and being fertilised. In a man, the tubes from the testes to the penis are cut. This prevents sperm being added to his ejaculate. In either case the surgery is irreversible and therefore it is a serious decision to make.

A woman is easily identified as a mother. If the father is absent or unknown the shame falls on her and the child. Men are not so easily identified or put in a situation where they have to take responsibility for the consequences of unprotected intercourse. Even with the availability of reliable contraceptives, parents still protect their daughters more than sons. Marriage laws exist to ensure that men accept responsibility for the consequences of intercourse.

Before the availability of reliable contraception, intercourse inevitably led to pregnancy. Marriage is a social obligation aimed at ensuring that men pay for the families that result from the regular intercourse they want. Marriage is also a legal contract. A woman marries in order to secure the financial and possibly the practical support she needs to raise children. A man marries in order to secure a sexual asset or perhaps to secure socially advantageous family connections. Some men use infidelity to get the erotic variety they need. Other men are content with marital intercourse over decades. Women hope for love, respectability and support for their family goals. Although a woman tries to attract a man, she waits for him to propose marriage before considering the attention he pays her to be a sign of love rather than lust.

Fathers appreciate that their daughters do not have the carnal instincts of young men. Most girls hope for love and they tend to feel used after a one-night stand. For boys, a variety of lovers adds to the erotic enjoyment. Lust arises from male arousal, which is a physical rather than an emotional response. Because of their sex drive and regular arousal, men view intercourse as an erotic act, which they rarely connect with reproduction. The pleasures of the flesh refer to the gratification a man obtains from sex.

If a man experienced platonic love for a woman, he would be just as concerned about the risk of pregnancy as a woman is. He would be concerned about the risk she takes of becoming pregnant and he would take precautions or abstain from intercourse to ensure her welfare. But male sex drive means that men want intercourse regardless of the consequences.

Even with reliable contraception, there are occasions when a couple is caught unprepared. Men are unwilling to use a condom because it reduces their pleasure. Some women make bad decisions (they are persuaded by irresponsible men to risk pregnancy) and the result is an unwanted pregnancy. Even though it takes two people to make a child, women continue to be held responsible for unwanted pregnancies, abortion and for a child's daily care. Women have to make sure they protect themselves by using reliable contraception such as the contraceptive pill. Men usually get away scot-free but if they are caught, they may have to pay substantial financial compensation. Some women, both today and in the past, also exploit men by using pregnancy to obtain money or a marriage proposal.

For centuries only married women were encouraged to engage in intercourse. In the absence of reliable contraception, a woman inevitably becomes pregnant when she has regular intercourse. The contraceptive pill means women can have intercourse without risking pregnancy. But even the pill is not 100% effective (if a woman forgets to take it). When women become unintentionally pregnant, they are offered abortion as a solution. Abortion is an issue connected with the freedom women now share with men to be sexually active without the need for a supportive relationship that would allow them to raise the children resulting from their sexual activity.

Abortion laws vary considerably between countries. A woman often needs both the father's and a doctor's consent. Most European countries give a woman the unconditional right to have an abortion within the first 15 weeks of pregnancy. Shame and fear of reprisal often cause women to delay getting help. Many women are ignorant of the symptoms of pregnancy or the cause. A woman, who has allowed a man to impregnate her, gets little sympathy.

Abortions are used by women when contraception fails. Safe, legal abortions performed by qualified practitioners are rarely associated with any fertility risk. Most women return to their pre-pregnancy fertility immediately following the abortion procedure. Most doctors who have relevant experience of women undergoing the procedure, conclude that the psychological effects of abortion are positive and serious adverse effects are rare. Women who make their own clear decision about abortion generally find it a health enhancing experience. Having an abortion is not inherently traumatic. However, every step in the process of accessing abortion services can be made traumatic for a woman because of how she is judged by others.

... no matter what she says, how much she likes sex and all that jazz, if she is literally being penetrated by you ... then her emotional and mental well-being will always be involved as well. Always. (Alice Carter)

The influence of religious beliefs on sexuality

Each culture has its own set of values. Some people consider these beliefs to be more important than others. While we are children, our parents make choices for us in the belief that they are for our benefit. Once we are adult, we can decide on our own values. Research indicates that both the cultural and the religious beliefs we hold, influence the way we express our sexuality. Traditional moral standards have always condoned promiscuity in men but required that a woman had to be a virgin on her wedding night. Marriage traditionally involved a man paying for an unsullied (chaste) sexual asset.

Someone who has never engaged in penetrative sex is called a virgin. Female virginity is valued by men because of the territorial nature of male sexuality. Men are attracted foremost to timid women because men want control in sexual situations. Men prefer an inexperienced lover so that they can focus on sexual activity that they enjoy. An inexperienced woman is more likely to accept whatever a man offers without question because she has no expectations from other men. Men dislike being compared with other men.

In some religions and cultures, a man is allowed to have many wives. The words monogamy, bigamy and polygamy all refer to how many wives a man has. It is embarrassing for women to be viewed as such an obvious sexual asset. Women rarely have sex with more than one man at a time. Women are unfaithful when their current relationship is emotionally unfulfilling or when they hope to improve their lifestyle with a more successful man. Women who are financially independent, often decide that a relationship with a man is not worth it. The sexual overhead is onerous over decades.

Men can volunteer to be sperm donors and their semen is offered to women who cannot or don't want to conceive by natural means. Test-tube babies are conceived in an artificial environment. But the developing embryo must then be implanted into a woman's womb. Science can replace the male role, but not the female role, in reproduction. Test tube babies must develop in the womb and are born like other babies. Women, called surrogate mothers, volunteer their wombs in return for payment. This has enabled people such as gay men and lesbians to have a baby that has one of the partner's genes.

Human beings kill millions of animals every day but we place a spiritual value on human life. Religious beliefs about conception and the creation of human life attribute a soul to a zygote only a few seconds old. Many people believe abortion (for any reason) is morally wrong. Abortion has only been possible relatively recently in our history. Making life and death decisions, that used to be left to Nature, can be equated to playing God. In some cultures, even rape is not considered sufficient reason for a woman to have an abortion.

Women associate sex with a loving relationship and family. Women are not capable of experiencing the erotic pleasure of sexual activity as men do naturally. So women tend to be offended by references to genitals and fantasies. A person who doesn't enjoy eroticism is not consciously choosing to be inhibited. It's just the way they are and most likely they are happy to be that way. They just don't have the benefit of enjoying the pleasure of responding positively to eroticism. People who object to suggestions for enjoying sexual pleasure have rarely experimented themselves by exploring pleasuring beyond intercourse. They cannot imagine that they would enjoy more adventurous sex play and so they believe that no one else should.

Pornography, prostitution and strip bars all attract male customers. Anyone who engages in activities outside the socially acceptable is described as a sexual pervert. Women are primarily responsible for this negativity over sex. Women never experience the sexual urges that men do, so they tend to consider them sordid and crude. This is why pornography is censored in every society around the world. Women's dislike of explicit eroticism causes some men to feel guilty about their natural sexual urges. Most people want to be seen to conform to the social norm. Men can also be highly competitive. No one else can ever understand the erotic pleasure we enjoy from our sexual experiences. They are personal to us. Given women's universal disinterest in sex, we can conclude that the majority of people (including many older and less responsive men) are not sexually motivated.

Anyone who is responsive (capable of orgasm) naturally has a positive response to eroticism. A positive response means we enjoy the feelings we experience when our minds are aroused by specific erotic stimuli (personal to each individual). Anyone who lacks a response to eroticism cannot appreciate the mental turn-on of sex. They question the purpose of sexual activity outside a relationship or other than as a demonstration of affection (lovemaking). They may seek a moral or a spiritual justification (such as tantra) for sex. Women, much more than men, look for justifications for sex. Few women ever experience erotic arousal and naturally question their role.

Once someone has experience, such as masturbation or gay sex, there is little difference between the religious and the unbelievers. So religious beliefs only deter people from gaining experience in the first place. Religious men engage in sexual activity much less frequently than other men. Inevitably celibacy and abstinence are much more appealing to those with low responsiveness. Some men never or rarely have sex. Their sexual arousal is never strong enough to overcome the obstacles in finding a partner who is willing to offer them an opportunity for penetrative sex. But these men usually masturbate.

It is easier to abstain from sin when one is not physically or psychologically endowed with the capacity – or with much capacity – to sin. (Alfred Kinsey)

Topic: Anatomy and development

Human sexual anatomy and development

Sexuality is about appreciating the human body and sexual anatomy. We should understand the function of the male and female genitalia as well as the changes that occur throughout our lives. It is also useful to know what kind of stimulation may be pleasurable or is involved in achieving orgasm.

The step of evolving two sexes was inevitable because of the huge advantage that sexual reproduction provides. Sexual reproduction involves combining gene pools from two parents and allows more rapid development of genetic diversity. Lifeforms can adapt more quickly to changing environments. Those individuals with a more advantageous set of genes reproduce and survive more successfully on average than those who are less advantaged. Many organisms reproduce by using this method, called natural selection.

Many plants and animals reproduce sexually. Animal reproduction requires insemination of a female by a male. The corresponding transfer of genetic material in flowering plants in called pollination. The male genetic material is mobile and plentiful. The female genetic material is fairly static. The male part (even in plants) is the active agent that effects the reproductive transfer. After fertilisation, the embryonic cells (formed from egg and sperm cells) divide and grow within the female reproductive anatomy or part of a plant. This standard definition of male and female is used throughout nature.

The reason we have genitals is because we have two sexes: male and female. Sexual reproduction involves combining genetic material from two parents. Every human embryo develops a pair of gonads. The sex chromosomes determine whether the gonads in the embryo become the testes (for a boy) or the ovaries (for a girl). The gonads become centres for the production of genetic material (eggs or spermatozoa). A girl is born with her genetic material: immature eggs. Once the testes of a male foetus start producing androgens (male hormones such as testosterone) they drive further change, which is concluded at puberty. This process is called sexual differentiation.

There are relatively few anatomical differences between the sexes. We can have one body part, for example head and heart. We can also have two, for example eyes, legs and lungs. There is symmetry even in our sexual anatomy. A woman has two ovaries and a man has two testes. Both sexes have nipples but a man never develops the mammary glands that form the female breast.

We all start with the building blocks for both the male and the female reproductive organs. Regardless of sex, we have Wolffian and Müllerian ducts. Development of our internal reproductive anatomy depends on hormones produced by the testes (or not in the case of a female). In most foetuses only one set of reproductive ducts (male or female) develops. A process called atrophy inhibits the development of the superfluous anatomy.

In a boy the Wolffian ducts develop into the male reproductive organs. The male ducts form the vas deferens (that connects the testes to the penis) as well as other tubes required for ejaculation of semen. In a female these ducts waste away. Women cannot ejaculate because their equivalent organ (the clitoris) does not have these tubes. Nor do they have equivalent male glands.

In a girl the Müllerian ducts form the female reproductive organs. The female ducts form the vagina, which leads into the womb (uterus) where the foetus develops before birth. In a male embryo these Müllerian ducts disappear. This is clear anatomical evidence that the vagina (anatomy that is not present in the male) is not involved in orgasm, which is a nervous system response common to both sexes. Male ejaculation is the only justification for orgasm. Female orgasm is a hangover from how the sexes have evolved.

Unlike most of the internal reproductive anatomy, the phallus is not an either-or option. Every foetus has the same rudimentary phallus, called a genital tubercle. Therefore it is impossible to determine the sex of a foetus until after 14 weeks. This erectile organ is responsible for orgasmic response. The phallus (erectile sex organ) is identically positioned for men and women. The penis is largely external and highly visible especially when erect. The clitoris is largely internal and only the tiny glans is visible. Women's arousal is subconscious so most women are never aware of having a clitoris.

We all use the same mechanism to achieve orgasm regardless of gender and orientation. The penis and clitoris are easily reached by the hands, which makes self-stimulation (masturbation) possible. The phallus develops to a different extent depending on the hormones sent out by the testes (or not in the case of a girl). The genital tubercle undergoes significantly more complex development in a boy. The labioscrotal folds of the embryo become the scrotum (for a boy) and the labia (for a girl). Women's genitalia (clitoris and labia) are anatomically equivalent to men's genitalia (penis and testicles).

Girls and boys have equal amounts of androgens until the age of 7 or 8. At puberty levels of androgens (male hormones) rise markedly in boys but less so in girls. Women have much lower levels of androgens than men, including testosterone (involved in libido and responsiveness). Boys and girls also have equal amounts of oestrogens. At puberty the levels of oestrogens increase abruptly in girls but only slightly in boys. Women's levels of oestrogens are much higher than men's are. There is a steep increase in male responsiveness at adolescence but female responsiveness is relatively rare.

... the reported levels of the 17-ketosteroids in the human male differ from the reported levels of the 17-ketosteroids in the human female in a manner which more or less parallels the differences which we have found between the median frequencies of orgasm at various ages in the two sexes. (Alfred Kinsey)

The male erectile sex organ (or phallus)

A man's sex organ (penis) is separate from his internal reproductive anatomy (testes and glands) but also integral. The penis has three main functions.

Firstly men use their penis to urinate (but only when flaccid). Urine and semen both pass down the urethra, the tube which extends through the length of the penis. When a man has an erection, the muscles at the base of the bladder contract and close off the urethra so urine cannot be released.

Secondly the penis is the male sex organ. When a man has an erection, his penis becomes highly sensitised and pleasurable to touch. The erect penis juts out from the body at an angle of approximately 45 degrees. When a man's mind is focused on erotic stimuli and he massages his erect penis, he can usually orgasm easily. A man feels strong pelvic muscle contractions and highly pleasurable sensations of sexual release both in his mind and body.

Thirdly the penis acts as a reproductive organ. The male reproductive organs include the penis, the testes and various glands (including Cowper's gland and the prostate). Male orgasm triggers the ejaculation of semen, which contain a man's spermatozoa (sperm). Intercourse is an activity that facilitates male ejaculation of semen. The sperm (from the testes) pass from the penis (via the vagina) into the uterus to meet the egg (produced by the ovaries). The penis and the vagina act as reproductive conduits during intercourse. When a sperm cell and an egg fuse, a new life is formed.

Many mammals, including most primates, have a penis bone (bacula) that facilitates penetration. Females have an equivalent bone in the clitoris. Humans appear to be unique in having blood flow to the genitals, which in the male is trapped and causes the erection that makes penetration possible.

The post-adolescent penis is designed so that it can become capable of penetration. The penis consists of erectile tissue, connective tissue and skin. It has a shaft, which has a core of erectile tissue, containing a specialized arrangement of arteries within a matrix of connective tissue. Two cylinder-shaped chambers (called corpora cavernosa) run the length of the penis (either side of the central urethra tube). When these spongey chambers fill with blood, the penis becomes rigid and increases in size (both in width and in length). This creates an internal strength and rigidity that is far greater than would be possible if a hollow tube were filled to an equivalent pressure.

The corpora cavernosa are encased in a sheath of tough fibrous connective tissue (Bucks fascia). Between this sheath and the overlying skin is a layer of elastic connective tissue that allows the skin of the penis to move freely along the shaft. The skin, which is slightly darker in colour than the rest of the body, is loose and folded while the penis is in a flaccid state. A circular fold of skin, commonly called the foreskin (or prepuce), extends forward to cover the glans, which is the bulb at the end of the penis. At birth or during early childhood, the foreskin may be removed (this custom is probably due to hygiene issues) in an operation called circumcision. The penis and clitoris extend far back into the pelvis between the muscles of the lower abdomen.

When a man is aroused, his brain sends messages to the nerves in the penis causing the arteries to relax and blood to flow in. The resulting pressure causes the penis to expand, which compresses the veins that normally allow the blood to drain away. Once the blood is trapped, a muscle within the corpora cavernosa sustains the erection. An erection is reversed when the muscles contract and stop blood flowing into the corpora cavernosa. It is common and quite normal for the penis to be curved (sometimes sideways). There is no detrimental effect on either reproduction or on sexual pleasure.

Orgasm is possible without ejaculation. But ejaculation is always preceded by an orgasm. Ejaculation relies on a trigger. There is no physiological event other than orgasm that could trigger ejaculation. The sensations that accompany orgasm vary considerably depending on the physical and psychological (erotic or emotional) circumstances that give rise to orgasm.

Some male prostitutes can climax five, six or more times per day regularly over many years. Even with such high frequencies, although the quantity of ejaculate is lower than usual, a little semen is always produced. Around three quarters of men do not ejaculate with any force. Their semen is merely exuded from the glans. Other men may ejaculate semen over distances of a few inches or even a few feet (very rarely up to even a meter or more!).

Orgasm is a vital aspect of male reproductive function. The pleasure provided by orgasm triggers ejaculation and starts the reproductive process. Achieving penetration and ejaculation are key to men's sense of emotional well-being. Most men identify with a masculine image that gives them control in sexual scenarios. Men need this control, not only to obtain their sexual release, but also to fulfil their biological imperative to impregnate a female.

A penetrating male attracts a lover by impressing her (or him) with his confidence (his ability to maintain a strong erection and enjoy extended thrusting activity with a lover). This dominant nature is matched by the more passive nature of a receiving partner who has a lower responsiveness. Some heterosexual men worry that enjoying anal penetration is a sign of being submissive, perverted or gay. Men's inhibition over enjoying anal penetration arises because they associate being a receiver of intercourse with the subordinated role that women naturally assume in heterosexual activity.

The relaxed penis can be any size, depending on ambient temperature.
(Antony Mason)

The female erectile sex organ (or phallus)

In the absence of testosterone, the genital tubercle forms the female phallus, called the clitoris. The clitoris consists of the glans and the internal organ. The clitoral glans is located just above the vaginal opening. Most of the clitoris (the body or shaft) is internal. Just below the mons pubis (that is covered with pubic hair) are the lip-like external structures of the vulva (just below the prominent bone). The labia majora (on the outside) are larger and surround the delicate labia minora (on the inside), which are smaller. They provide protection for the clitoral glans, the urethra and the vaginal opening.

A woman's sex organ (clitoris) is separate from her internal reproductive anatomy (ovaries, uterus and vagina). The sole function of the clitoris is to be a sex organ. Unlike a man, a woman has separate anatomy for urination (the urethra), reproduction (the vagina) and orgasm (the clitoris). These three functions are all combined for a man and provided by the penis. The female anatomy is more highly evolved (because each part of anatomy has only one function) but a man's anatomy is more practical and convenient.

The sex organ (penis or clitoris) is the only erectile organ of the body. When a person is aroused (their mind responds positively to eroticism), the brain causes an increase in the rate of blood flowing to the genitals. Our physical arousal, which involves increased blood-flow in the corpus cavernosa causes swelling to varying degrees, called tumescence, of the sex organ (or phallus).

The clitoris is largely an internal organ. Only the tiny glans (or bud) is visible externally. The glans tends to be hidden by the labia majora and pubic hair. The glans is covered by a clitoral hood formed in part by the fusion of the upper part of the two labia minora. The body of the internal clitoral organ has two corpora cavernosa that are smaller but analogous to those of the penis. When aroused these tissues are engorged with blood. After orgasm has been achieved, the excess blood is released back into the circulation.

The clitoris is the homologue of the penis but the two organs develop to a very different extent both before birth and at adolescence. The body of the clitoris consists of two parallel corpora cavernosa of erectile tissue (which may increase to over 2 inches when aroused), smooth muscle and connective tissue (collagen and elastin) surrounded by a fibrous sheath (tunica albuginea). But the clitoris doesn't have the same mechanism for trapping blood (a muscle within the corpora cavernosa) that the penis has. The clitoris becomes tumescent (swollen) but it does not become erect (rigid) as the penis does. This explains why women are largely unaware of this much lesser physical arousal. When masturbating, a responsive woman needs to use quite extreme (surreal) erotic fantasies to access her subconscious arousal.

It is very evident that men are sensitive to stimulation (capable of reaching orgasm) because of the erection they have due to blood flowing into the penis. Without this arousal, men are incapable of orgasm. The clitoris has equivalent structures (corpora cavernosa). It is inconceivable that these would not have the same function in a woman as for a man. It is equally inconceivable that women could have evolved a quite different mechanism (separate from the male) for a sexual response as primitive as orgasm.

However, the clitoris is never rigid and so it lacks the extreme sensitivity of the penis. Since neither the clitoris nor female orgasm are involved in reproduction, women do not experience the acute arousal that men do, from responding to real-world erotic stimuli. A woman may be indifferent to gentle stimulation of the glans (over the hood) but due to hypersensitivity she can also feel discomfort, or even pain, if stimulation is too aggressive. If a woman stimulates her glans without any accompanying mental arousal, there is no pleasure. The clitoris is not an external phallus that can be used to impregnate another person. Consequently, women do not have a sex drive.

Even responsive women do not obtain the same sensational pleasure from clitoral stimulation that men enjoy from penile stimulation. Mental arousal (by focusing on surreal fantasy) and physical arousal (tumescence) provide only mild pleasure. The key pleasures of female masturbation involve the pelvic contractions and the sensation of releasing sexual emotions at the end.

Female orgasm is a miracle for two reasons. Firstly, we usually only evolve functionality for a specific (life-critical) purpose. Secondly, we also lose characteristics that have no useful function. Male orgasm triggers ejaculation but female orgasm has no role in reproduction. Female orgasm is a hangover from how the sexes evolved. As an internal organ, the clitoris has much less significance for a woman than the penis has for a man. The clitoris is the source of female orgasm, which provides a woman's own personal pleasure.

In younger women there is little externally discernible swelling of the clitoral organ. But in mature women, during periods of subconscious arousal, increased blood-flow can cause the internal clitoral organ to swell. If a woman places her three middle fingers over her vulva, she can feel the top of the pelvic bone. If she then runs her fingers down towards the perineum, she can feel a tingling sensation of the clitoral glans with her index finger. The swollen pubic area is noticeable both to the eye and to touch (by pressing down either side of the labia majora). Clitoral tumescence is not a sign of mental arousal nor does it help with orgasm. The main benefit of clitoral tumescence is an increased sensitivity in the pelvis during intercourse.

The shaft of the clitoris may average something over an inch in length. It has a diameter which is less than that of a pencil. (Alfred Kinsey)

The internal anatomy involved in reproduction

Our sex is determined by chromosomes. A man has an XY chromosome and a woman has an XX chromosome. There are other combinations (involving three chromosomes) but the Y chromosome is associated with being male. A boy inherits a Y chromosome from his father. The father's genes (not the mother's) determine the sex of a baby. Every foetus has a pair of gonads. The sex chromosome determines whether they develop into ovaries or testes, which produce hormones and gametes (sperm or egg cell).

A man's internal anatomy includes the penis, testes, epididymis, seminal vesicles and prostate gland. The testes (inside the testicles) are the male gonads. They are 4 to 5 cm long and 2.5 cm in diameter. The testes produce male gametes (sperm), containing genetic material. Sperm are produced regularly from the testes throughout a man's life (called spermatogenesis). A man's sperm are tiny (relative to the size of the egg) and mobile. There are millions of them (versus only one egg) so they are more dispensable. Sperm cover some distance to reach the egg. The testes are also endocrine glands, which produce testosterone. The testes are located below the penis within a pouch of skin (a sac) called the scrotum. The testes are outside the body and so cooler than body temperature, which is necessary for sperm development. The testes are suspended by the spermatic cords and are highly vulnerable.

The epididymis is a system of ducts that receive immature sperm from the testes. Its function is to develop immature sperm and to store mature sperm. The vas deferens are two more fibrous and muscular tubes through which sperm pass from the epididymis to the urethra. Seminal fluid is produced during ejaculation by the seminal vesicles, the prostate and Cowper's (or bulbourethral) gland. Nutrients in the fluid keep the sperm alive and mobile.

There are two seminal vesicles. Each 7.5 cm sac is lined with a mucous membrane, which secretes a pale fluid (containing sugars) to provide energy for sperm cells. This fluid makes up about two-thirds of semen. Tubes leading from the seminal vesicles, join the vas deferens to form the ejaculatory duct. Each ejaculatory duct empties into the urethra. The prostate is a firm muscular gland about the size of a chestnut, located near the internal opening of the urethra within the pelvic cavity. During ejaculation, the prostate produces a milky, alkaline fluid containing enzymes that increase sperm motility. Cowper's glands are located at the base of the penis. During sexual activity, these glands secrete an alkaline fluid which helps neutralize acidity from urine in the urethra and acidity in the vagina.

A woman's internal anatomy includes organs and structures that promote the production, support, growth, and development of female gametes (egg cells) and a growing foetus. The ovaries are gonads, which produce female gametes (ova or eggs). Ovaries are also endocrine glands, producing the hormones progesterone and oestrogen, which are sex hormones that govern early development and contribute to the menstrual cycle. There is one ovary on each side of the womb. Each ovary is about 4 cm long and 2 cm wide. The ovarian ligament attaches it to the uterus while a suspensory ligament attaches it to the pelvic wall. A woman's genetic material (called ova) contains nutrients for the foetus and so is relatively large. These eggs are released one at a time from the ovaries on a regular monthly schedule from puberty until just after a woman's last period (called the menopause) in late middle age.

During ovulation, an ovum is dispensed from an ovary's surface. The Fallopian tubes transport the egg cell from the ovaries to the uterus (womb). Fertilization typically occurs in these tubes. The fallopian tube, or oviduct, is about 10 cm long. Once released, ova travel through the fallopian tube to the womb. The fallopian tubes lead into the upper part of the womb, one on either side, while the lower part of the uterus leads down into the vagina.

Also called the womb, the uterus is where a developing foetus resides during pregnancy. The uterus is a hollow, thick-walled, pear-shaped muscular internal organ (a duct) that is located in the pelvic cavity between the bladder and the rectum. The cervix is the lowest part of the uterus and leads to the vagina. Both the cervix and the vagina are internal reproductive organs that are largely without nerves. A woman cannot easily identify the anatomy stimulated by intercourse because the sensations are diffuse. Nevertheless, women who claim to orgasm from intercourse say this anatomy is the origin of their orgasms. Ligaments hold the upper part of the uterus in suspension; the lower part is embedded in fibrous tissue. When an egg is fertilized, it embeds itself into the uterine wall and develops. During pregnancy the uterus expands. After childbirth, the uterus shrinks back to its normal size.

The vagina is a fibrous, muscular canal leading from the cervix (opening of the uterus) to the external portion of the genital canal. It is part of the birth canal. The mouth and vagina have characteristics in common. Both are susceptible to thrush (a fungal infection), being warm and moist. Thrush causes an itchy feeling in the vagina. Women may assume that these infections arise because they have done something improper. This is not the case. Women should wash between their legs thoroughly at least once a day as well as after defecating. Cystitis, an infection of the bladder, causes a stinging sensation in the bladder and is accompanied by an urgent need to urinate. Medication can alleviate the symptoms and eliminate the infection.

There is a great deal of anatomic and clinical evidence that most of the interior of the vagina is without nerves. A considerable amount of surgery may be performed inside the vagina without need for anesthetics. (Alfred Kinsey)

At puberty boys develop a reliable arousal cycle

From a young age, many boys already demonstrate a more active and outgoing personality than most girls. Boys enjoy physical activities such as sport where conversation is minimal. This gender difference is apparent before the onset of adolescence and is not attributable solely to hormones. The changes at puberty are not limited to physical changes. There are emotional and social impacts. There is likely to be competition between boys for opportunities for physical intimacy with girls, uncertainties about approaching the opposite sex and possible concerns about homosexual feelings. Both sexes have a desire to be accepted as part of the social group.

The male sex organ is easily identifiable because boys hold it when they urinate. The proper name for a boy's willy is penis. There are many slang words for the penis including cock, dick and prick. The penis and testicles increase in size at adolescence and boys become sexually active. During puberty, hormones cause boys to experience sexual arousal. They feel excited when they think about a person they are sexually attracted to. Men have an arousal cycle that starts with erection and ends with ejaculation.

Boys can have erections as early as 8 or 9 years old. Instead of being flaccid (or limp), the penis becomes very firm (stiff or hard) and juts out from the body at an angle. Slang words for an erection include a stiffy, hard-on and boner. The average position for men of all ages is just above the horizontal. 15-20% of men carry the penis at 45^0 above the horizontal while 8-10% have an erection tight against the body. A young boy can hold an erection for longer and at an angle tighter to the body on average than an older man.

Kinsey observed that boys, who have sexual experience, may be capable of orgasm at a young age (half by 7 and two-thirds by 12 years old). But many fewer boys experience early orgasm in the general population due to lack of sexual opportunities. Until they start ejaculating, these early orgasms tend to be sporadic. Less than 1 per cent of boys (0.81%) ejaculate without any genital contact in pre-adolescence. Fear, apprehension, shock or surprise can all produce nervous system responses. Other emotional stimuli and non-sexual physical stimulation may also cause an early one-off ejaculation.

At puberty a boy's mind naturally focuses on his penis and its responsiveness. Some young men can become erect many times throughout the day. Boys enjoy the visual stimulus of nude pin-ups from adolescence onwards. Girls are not aroused by male nudity in the same way. Men are expected to cover their genitals to avoid offending women. Boys do not spend time imagining the social context of marriage and family as girls do.

Testosterone is produced by the testes and the ovaries. Testosterone is involved in the development of the male reproductive organs before birth, and the development of secondary sex characteristics at puberty. Prior to puberty, boys and girls have the same levels of testosterone. A boy's testosterone levels rise significantly (30 times more than before) in puberty, which causes physical changes in the body and also emotional mood swings. Males usually have much higher levels of testosterone in their body than females. When levels of testosterone are high enough, the testes start producing sperm, the penis and testes increase in size, the voice deepens, the chest and shoulders broaden and facial hair starts to grow. Testosterone is a factor in a man's sex drive and can cause severe acne during puberty.

The first sign of male puberty is usually accelerated growth of the testes and scrotum with reddening and wrinkling of the scrotal skin. Pubic hair growth begins around the same time. The stimulus that triggers accelerated penis growth, also causes the seminal glands and the prostate to enlarge and develop. These glands and the prostate are situated close to the testicles (testes) and contribute 60% and 40% respectively of the seminal fluid.

Most boys (90%) ejaculate for the first time between the ages of 11 and 15. The start of male adolescence is defined by the age at which a boy has his first ejaculation. First ejaculation occurs about a year after the beginning of the accelerated penis growth. Semen is a creamy liquid that contains sperm (the genetic material needed to make a baby), which are produced by the testes. Semen passes via the urethra (the central tube of the penis) to the outside. Ejaculation (of semen) and male orgasm are two separate phenomena. It is possible for a young boy to orgasm without ejaculating. But once a boy reaches adolescence (assumed to coincide with a boy's first ejaculation) he most normally ejaculates every time he has an orgasm.

Sources of first ejaculation are masturbation (two-thirds), wet dreams (in an eight of the cases), vaginal intercourse (one boy in eight) and homosexual contacts (one boy in twenty). Initially male arousal occurs as a response to hormones. Over time boys come to associate their arousal with psychological stimuli (erotic turn-ons) that are explicitly sexual in nature. They also become increasingly reliant on specific penile stimulation to achieve orgasm.

Some boys ejaculate when they are asleep. Wet dreams are most common (71% of men) between the ages of 21 and 25 when the highest average frequency is about once in three weeks (0.3 per week). By the age of 50 only a third of men have sex dreams, which do not average more than four or five a year. Both masturbation and sex dreams are more common among the educated because they depend on a man having a creative imagination.

Erection ... is practically a daily matter for all small boys, from earliest infancy ... Slight physical stimulation of the genitalia, general body tensions and generalized emotional situations bring immediate erection, even when there is no specifically sexual situation involved. (Alfred Kinsey)

Young men tend to focus on enjoying their arousal

Men are valued for their physical strength, their practical skills and their personal confidence (leaderships skills). Young men increase their muscle mass at puberty by 50% more than young women do. The male territorial drive (to establish and defend territory or status) consumes more of a man's time and energy than his sex drive ever does. Men focus on their own pursuits rather than being motivated to care for others. Once a boy becomes sexually responsive, he also develops a degree of emotional insensitivity. A man enjoys fantasies that boost his arousal and promote his sexual ego. Male ego (arrogance or assertiveness) is vital to men's role in defence and in sex.

From puberty onwards, boys are fascinated by their penis: the way it grows and is pleasurable to touch. They learn that their appreciation of eroticism can take them from arousal to orgasm. The average white male ejaculates for the first time around the age of 13 years 10½ months (13.88 years). The more responsive young men wake up each morning with an erection. They may have spontaneous erections throughout the day as sex-related thoughts occur to them or simply as a result of seeing someone they are attracted to.

When he is aroused, a boy's penis becomes erect and hyper-sensitive so that it is very pleasurable to touch. The whole length of the penis is sensitive and massaging it creates waves of highly pleasurable sensations in the brain. The harder the erection, the better the feelings. A blow job or hand job make the feelings more exquisite. Initially some boys stimulate their penis (called masturbation) because they enjoy the sense of release when they ejaculate. Later most men have a strong urge to engage in penetrative sex (intercourse).

Even as virgins, boys are aroused by the prospect of sexual activity with a lover. They may masturbate by imagining an opportunity for intercourse. They imagine the sexual attributes, genitals and behaviour of a partner. They do this through buying pornographic magazines or watching porn movies. Some boys enjoy comparing notes on the sexual attributes of the opposite sex and their chances of manoeuvring a girl into a sexual situation. This is a chase situation where the man is the predator and the woman is the target.

As boys approach adolescence, they identify with other male adults. The idea of approaching a woman and penetrating her becomes a natural goal. Intercourse feels like an adult activity because of the challenge and subsequent reward of persuading a partner to accept penetration. Boys naturally feel proud of their newly acquired ability to penetrate a lover. A man's challenge is to find a sexually amenable partner and to succeed in persuading them into a sexual situation. A man has to take all the risk of negotiating a sexual situation and endure the humiliation of rejection. This process is even more risky for homosexual men. They have to approach other men who may not be as gentle as women are in rejecting their sexual advances. Nevertheless, a man's sex drive compels him to take these risks.

Male arousal is very evident. Men find it difficult to ignore the sensations that accompany their arousal. A man's erection is highly visible and identifiable. He is also acutely aware of the sensation of the increase in blood-flow to his penis. Finally, his mind is highly focused on an opportunity for sexual activity. Some men are happy to share their fantasies with any woman who will listen. Many men enjoy sharing their fantasies with a lover.

Male changes at puberty include the shoulders broadening and the chest cavity increasing in capacity. The voice box develops so that the tenor of a man's voice is lower than a woman's voice. A boy's voice breaks relatively late in adolescence. The change in pitch is a result of the enlargement of the larynx and lengthening of the vocal cords, caused by the action of testosterone on the laryngeal cartilages. The Adam's apple, thyroid cartilage that protect the larynx, causes men's voices to deepen. Male mammals often use a loud call as a means of establishing authority. There is also a change in quality that distinguishes the voice of both men and women from that of children. This is caused by the enlargement of the resonating spaces above the larynx, as a result of the rapid growth of the mouth, nose and upper jaw.

Many men have a heavy growth of hair on their face, chest, arms and legs. Armpit hair appears on average some two years after the beginning of pubic hair growth. In boys, facial hair begins to grow at about the time that the armpit hair appears. The remainder of the body hair appears later. Men's hips are narrower and their buttocks are smaller than women's. On average men are taller and more muscular but they have less body fat than women.

Personal hygiene becomes more important as hormones cause hair growth and increased sweating. Most men shave their facial hair daily and they need to wash regularly as well as use deodorants. Pubic and underarm hair in both sexes have a smell, which is intended to be attractive to a potential mate. We tend to cover up these natural odours with artificial scents. If a man is careless about hygiene, sweating causes an unpleasant body odour (B.O.). There is a discharge from the penis that accumulates and may become infected if not cleaned. A boy needs to pull back his foreskin and clean the discharge from his glans regularly. Mothers do this for young boys until they can do it for themselves. Circumcision helps to avoid infection and involves cutting the skin that attaches the sheath of the penis to the glans. Circumcised men may experience slightly different physical sensations from intercourse.

... physical changes in the adolescent boy usually proceed as follows: beginning of development of pubic hair, first ejaculation, voice change, initiation of rapid growth in height, and, after some lapse of time, completion of growth in height. (Alfred Kinsey)

Men tend to focus on opportunities for intercourse

Sex may not be the only reason men seek relationships with women, but it is the key reason. Men's sex drive focuses them on obtaining opportunities for intercourse. Given married men's complaints about low intercourse frequencies over the longer-term, sex is clearly much less important to women. The romantic and emotional factors that naturally motivate a woman to offer sex, only operate at the beginning of relationships when men are devoted. Foremost, women offer sex because they know it is expected. Women feel obliged to offer sex in exchange for a man supporting a family.

Men's goal when engaging in sexual activity is simple. Men want to enjoy their own arousal by close contact with a lover's body and enjoy various forms of penile stimulation. Ultimately their goal is to obtain the sexual release of ejaculating into a lover's body. A man is acutely aware of his sexual needs (and his frustration when those needs are not met). The strength of male sex drive makes men selfish in obtaining what they want and oblivious to women's perspective. Marriage provides the most reliable source of regular intercourse because most wives know that their husbands need sex.

Women send out mixed signals that are very confusing for a man. They display their bodies in ways that arouse men. But their behaviours are also timid and reluctant. So men often have no idea whether a sexual advance will be accepted or not. If he gets it wrong, he gets a slap across the face. If he gets it right, a woman returns his kiss. So the first kiss is a test. After that, a man has to find out what a woman's morals are. Some women may be happy to proceed directly to sex. Others may want to spend more time continuing with a platonic but affectionate relationship that falls short of sex.

Mothers have difficulty controlling their sons from a young age. Boys grow up knowing that women can be persuaded and coerced. A man admires a woman's docility, her sensitivity and her compassion. Even though heterosexual activity is clearly motivated by male arousal, men ensure that sex is always promoted as a universal and mutual pleasure. Men don't want to admit that sex is one-sided in case they lose out on sexual opportunities.

A dog chases a ball because the ball represents a small animal. A dog is a carnivore and has natural instincts to chase animals to eat. Similarly a man is attracted to a woman because of the way she looks or moves. His sex drive (urge to penetrate) motivates him to want to mate with her. But what does a woman want to catch, overpower and dominate? Women are clearly not aroused by nudity of a potential lover or by sexual opportunities as men are.

When a carnivore lines up its prey you can see the tension. A bird flutters and rustles. The cat is mesmerised by the sight and sound of its prey. The predator sways on its haunches as it stares with fixed concentration at its prey.

It's thinking about how it can succeed in catching the bird. Then the cat tenses in anticipation. It springs forward and pounces on its prey, holding it down grasping the throat and clamping tight until it has subdued or killed it.

It's not that men are incapable of platonic love. But men's sex drive puts penetrative sex at the centre of their adult life. A man feels loved when his sexual needs are satisfied. Their sex drive causes men to prey on women. A man is attracted by a specific woman who catches his attention. His other senses shut down as his mind focuses on the intense arousal that he feels from observing her. He imagines her naked and what intercourse would feel like. He decides on a strategy to approach her and try to charm her into bed. Men assume that women are sexually motivated even though they also accept that their role is to be the initiator and driver of sexual activity with a lover.

A man has to initiate his sexual advances against the background of women's social natures. It isn't easy. Risk of rejection is high but (depending on his sex drive) a man is compelled to try. Most men need some kind of invitation before they risk rejection. A man may wait for a woman to indicate her amenability or he may hint and wait for a reaction. Men mistakenly assume that women use the same criteria as men for their relationships. Men assume women are looking for sexual satisfaction. For a woman, sex is a social experience that can be (at its best) sensual and emotional. For these factors to operate, a woman needs a lover who appreciates the romantic aspects of relationships. A woman hopes for a lover who is companionable and charming. Foremost, women are looking for men who are good providers.

The male dilemma is how to negotiate sexual opportunities. This relies on a partner's amenability. Women have the opposite dilemma. They feel constantly under pressure to provide the regular sex a man wants. Marriage involves a man agreeing to limit his sexual opportunities elsewhere in exchange for regular sex with his wife. Relationships are primarily for a woman's benefit since they are a requirement for family life. A woman needs to offer intercourse to keep a man committed to supporting her family goals.

Biologically speaking, men are fancy free. They can live their lives quite happily without ever needing to take responsibility for their children. Some men avoid relationships with women by relying on casual sex, especially in their younger years. Young men accept the overhead of supporting a woman because of their desire for regular sex with the same partner. Men are rarely motivated to take on the daily care of the children that result from their desire for regular intercourse. If a man leaves his wife for another (often younger) woman, he rarely takes his children with him. Men focus on their own goals and prefer to engage in active pursuits rather than care for others.

The frequencies of marital intercourse are two or three times as high as the intercourse of the single male. (Alfred Kinsey)

At puberty girls develop a child-bearing capacity

From a young age, most girls demonstrate a more passive and timid personality than most boys. Girls often focus on social activities rather than physically active play. This gender difference is apparent before puberty. Women need to deal with men who can be ruthlessly aggressive. Women have evolved a survival strategy of being more passive and cooperative. Men tend to disrespect this female amenability, which is considered a weakness in men. To be motivated to care for children, women need certain characteristics. Foremost, they need to be less driven than men are about following their own pursuits. Secondly, they need to enjoy nurturing others.

At puberty a girl's body starts producing oestrogen and progesterone, which cause physical changes and often have an impact on emotional responses including depression. Oestrogen causes the breasts to grow. In girls the appearance of the breast bud is the first sign of puberty, though the appearance of pubic hair precedes it in about one-third. Growth of pubic hair begins at 12.3 years of age on average. The uterus and vagina both develop simultaneously with the breasts. The labia and clitoris also enlarge. The fallopian tubes also develop. At the same time, the way the body stores fat changes, which makes a woman's waist, hips and buttocks more curvy.

Female adolescence focuses on the development of reproductive function rather than responsiveness. The age of first menstruation ranges from 9 to 25 years. The median girl's periods start at 13. The early cycles are irregular and do not include ovulation. A period lasts around 5 days each month and involves losing the cell lining of the womb (more like gelatinous clots than liquid blood) that builds up each month in preparation for pregnancy. Regular ovulation does not begin until sixteen to eighteen years of age. After puberty, oestrogen and progesterone control the menstrual cycle including ovulation and periods. A girl's growth is complete by 15.8 years old.

Most women ovulate anywhere between Day 11 and Day 21 of their cycle, counting from the first day of the last menstrual period (LMP). Women use sanitary pads or tampons to absorb the blood. Some women spend days in bed with stomach cramps and have pre-menstrual tension (PMT), which can make them bad-tempered. Other women experience no period pains at all. Tampons have lessened women's self-consciousness over menstruating.

A woman has a life-time supply of eggs within her body from the day she is born. After puberty, a woman ovulates automatically (without conscious awareness). One mature egg is released from an ovary each month. After the egg is released, it moves down into the fallopian tube where it stays for about 24 hours. A woman can conceive (if sperm are present from a recent ejaculation) during that time. If the egg is not fertilized during that time, the egg disintegrates and menstruation (blood flow) begins 2 weeks later. A woman can be impregnated any time she has intercourse. A man only needs to ejaculate into her vagina (or close to it). Sperm can sometimes enter the vagina if a man ejaculates just outside. To know the days when she is fertile, a woman needs to keep a temperature chart. Few women do this and so they tend to assume that they may conceive any time after their period ends.

The opening to the vagina lies between the urethra and the anus. A woman should wash (with soap) the pubic hair either side of her labia majora (outer lips or skin folds). As a woman ages, the skin either side of her labia majora becomes wrinkly and slightly baggy, very similar to the skin of the scrotum (the equivalent male anatomy). There is no need to clean inside the more delicate labia minora (inner lips). A man's anus is isolated to the rear but a woman's is close to her vaginal opening. Many women think genitals are dirty. They will not touch their genitals even in the shower. So they never insert a finger into their vagina. There is nothing inherently unclean about the vagina. A man urinates from the end of his penis, which allows him to direct the urine stream away from his body. A woman likes having soft toilet paper even for urinating because when she urinates, her public hair gets wet.

Female anatomy is more susceptible to infection than the male because of the proximity of the orifices: urethra, vagina and anus. A woman should wash between her buttocks and anus separately by reaching her hand down behind. She can insert a finger into the vagina to check for discharge. Some of these are healthy while others arise from infections such as thrush. These discharges can mark underwear, which women tend to find embarrassing. A woman considers her monthly period to be an unhygienic and distasteful body function that is often associated with unpleasant smells. She hides any view of her menstrual blood flow from others, including her lover, because she considers the whole process to be very unattractive. For this reason, women are appalled by some men's fascination with women's underwear.

A boy has experience of arousal well before he comes to his first sexual encounter. Most boys also know the pleasures of orgasm and ejaculation. But a girl has none of these experiences. Very few girls masturbate. Those who do, are unaware that the artificial mechanism they use when alone (surreal fantasies) does not work with a lover. If women were aroused with a lover, they would also be aroused by images of nudity as men are. There are no real-world erotic stimuli that cause female arousal, which is largely a subconscious phenomenon. So women identify sexual activity with negative phenomenon such as ugly genitals and smelly discharges. This contrasts with the much more positive male experience based on their erotic arousal.

... the capacity to reproduce is not synonymous with the capacity to be aroused erotically and to respond to the point of orgasm ... (Alfred Kinsey)

Young women tend to focus on their attractiveness

A girl first becomes aware of herself as a sexual being when men start commenting on her breasts. The breasts develop from around 12.4 years. Beast development signals a woman's reproductive maturity. A girl should wear a supportive bra to avoid getting stretch marks. It is perfectly normal for a woman's breasts to be different sizes. The nipple stands erect when cold. Otherwise the nipple may be inverted, particularly in young women.

Most men are not aroused by pre-adolescent girls who have figures similar to boys. Breast development is a clear sign that a girl has become a woman. Women have wider hips than men and their buttocks are larger. A woman's pelvis is wider than a man's as it is adapted for childbirth. One consequence of a wider pelvis is that women's hips may sway as they walk. Women wear high heels in part to accentuate this movement, which men find attractive.

Women often wear makeup because it is expected, for example, for their job or on formal occasions. But most women wear makeup to feel better about themselves. We are all guilty of judging other people. We judge men on their status and women on their looks. Women are more critical of a woman's appearance than men are. By enhancing their attractiveness, women send out messages that they are seeking approval. This marks them out as vulnerable, which is attractive to men, especially the bullying kind. So women make themselves victims of sexual abuse simply because of their own sense of inadequacy. Any woman who doesn't enhance her attractiveness is assumed to be a man-hater as if vanity is a compulsory aspect of heterosexual women's sexuality. Some women don't see the need to wear makeup. They prefer to be themselves and save the time and money of wearing makeup. A man is good enough as he is, so why can't a woman be? So much for equality!

Men like young women for their lack of sexual experience. A man assumes that timid women will be more easily persuaded to accept his advances. A woman assumes a man is attracted to her because she is pretty and has a good figure. Women enhance their attractiveness by accentuating their vulnerability and docility (precarious shoes, long hair and big baby eyes). Women never develop coarse hair, skin and firm muscle tone as men do. Apart from having breasts and wider hips, they still look much like children.

Men sexualise women as part of their arousal process. Breasts, for example, take on a sexual significance. Girls react to male lust for their bodies with embarrassment and even shame. Women think their genitals are dirty because of the crude urges they evoke in men. Some girls develop a negative view of themselves. Anorexia and bulimia are nervous disorders that occur because a girl has a distorted view of her body. A woman's body naturally lays down fat (for breastfeeding) so girls may be reacting to these changes.

Male puberty causes men to have a new curiosity in their own genitals and also in any opportunity to observe nudity in others. Female adolescence does not include this sudden and intense increase in responsiveness that boys experience. Adolescent girls talk of the man they might marry one day and the children they hope to have. Once she has a boyfriend, a girl may contemplate the longer term. This contrasts with boys who are much more short-term in their thinking and who often want to keep their options open.

Young women are curious in a social (rather than an erotic) sense in anticipation of their first experience of intercourse. A girl is not aroused by nudity or by anticipating sexual activity as boys are. Without romantic love, sexual activity seems crude and impersonal. Intercourse is an adult activity for a woman because she risks pregnancy. By offering sex, women obtain other rewards from men. A woman can easily offer intercourse but if she gets pregnant, it's solely her fault (not the man's). A woman needs the social maturity to understand men's drive to enjoy their own physical gratification.

But as she matures, a girl comes to appreciate a more romantic view of sex. When in love, a woman responds to a man's admiration of her attractiveness and his sexual desire to possess her. A woman wants a strong man (both in character and competence) to admire her and enjoy her company (not dominate and patronise her). Women see the world from a social, rather than erotic, perspective. Women like a man for his experience and the security he can provide. A woman wants a man who is competent enough to protect her and provide for a family. Having a lover (and children later on) increases a woman's sense of personal confidence and emotional security.

Even a responsive woman has very similar responses to other women. She cannot fully understand men's responses (because she does not experience them) but she can empathise with men's enjoyment of eroticism because she uses her own form of eroticism when masturbating to orgasm. But sexual activity with a lover is primarily a male pleasure. It does absolutely nothing for a woman even if she is responsive when masturbating alone. Sex involves a woman allowing a man to touch and penetrate her most private anatomy in an act that she considers taboo. To offer sex, a woman needs to love and trust a man. Sex involves a serious emotional commitment for most women.

Some women enjoy the reassurance of being admired by men. They may interpret this emotional neediness as a sex drive. Some women use their bodies to gain favour with men) to obtain an advantage at work or elsewhere. As they age men worry about impotence. Women worry about looking old. Young women take centre stage but older women are of interest to no one.

Thus, between adolescence and fifteen years of age there were 78 per cent, and among other teenage girls there were 53 per cent who were not reaching orgasm in any type of sexual activity. (Alfred Kinsey)

Over time women often become focused on family

Female mammals are involved in grooming, feeding and affectionate play with their young. Female mammals are always smaller and more nervous than males. This anxiety keeps women at home and close to their children. Women gravitate towards men who can provide protection and lifestyle through earnings or status. Many women consider the tasks of raising children and providing a home the most important achievement of all. Family provides a continuity to the cycle of life and security for old age.

Women have value in society for three main reasons. Firstly, they are valued as a sexual asset by men. Secondly, they are valued as bearers of children. Thirdly they contribute to society by caring for children, the disabled and the elderly. Men rarely do this work, which is undervalued and has little status. Society honours men's achievements, not because women's contribution is not valued but, because we rely on men for defence and survival. A woman's sexuality determines the course of her life much more than a man's does. A man's sexuality involves occasional pleasure. Women continue to earn less than men because of their dedication to the family.

Reliable contraception has freed women from the obligation to have children. Yet most women continue to disadvantage themselves in the workplace and make themselves dependent on a man so that they can raise children. This is the symbiotic relationship between men and women that makes human reproduction so successful. Women's desire for family may not as urgent as male sex drive but it is vital to reproduction. Men assume they have special privileges because they support the family financially. But most men work regardless of any relationship. Women also work and support the family by dedicating their daily lives to others in practical ways.

Given women represent around half of any population, they should have no difficulty in obtaining equal rights with men. But only a minority of women want these rights and they have to fight against other women's attitudes just as much as against men's. Political activists insist that women can be just as independent and adventurous as men. Of course, they can. But few want to be. Most women are amazed to see a woman do more than cook, clean and care for a family. Any woman who works alongside men, has to be strong enough to assert herself against a majority of men. Most women are happy to settle for a more traditional role. This is natural. Against this background of timidity, men (and a few women looking for male approval) suggest that every woman is just as adventurous and as motivated by sex as men are.

We all have different personalities. We also have different emotional responses (that make relationships more rewarding) and personal confidence (that motivates us to succeed through our own achievements). In general, men do while women talk. Women think that men single them out for bad behaviour. The truth is that men treat everyone badly. The women's liberation movement involves women's attempts to negotiate with men for special treatment. This demand for special privileges only further convinces men of their own superiority. When a woman is providing a man with a sexual outlet, she can insist on this special treatment because she makes it a condition of the relationship. Some men undoubtedly understand this concept much better than others. Many men are quite oblivious to the female perspective and also to any feedback they receive from their partner.

A man has a biological need that makes intercourse hugely attractive to him. A woman does not have the same need. Sexual activity in general is repulsive to her. Initially women offer sex for a loving relationship. But over time as their needs are ignored, they continue to offer sex out of compassion. They recognise their partner's sexual needs. Ultimately, women have to fall back on their desire to keep the family together, to continue to offer sex to a lover who does nothing to respond to their needs in the wider relationship.

A woman may be able to persuade a man to support her goal of raising a family but she wants to keep control of the family and have the responsibility for ensuring that her children get the best care. Men are happy to let women have this role so that they can focus on their own talents that bring them the emotional reward of social status and personal achievement. A man spends his life with work colleagues and other strangers. He focuses on the goal of making money. Men remain much more independent of the family, taking on travel far from home, more challenging and risky enterprises and are consequently still able to earn more and enjoy the privileges that brings.

Women always define themselves in male terms. Women tend to support men's endeavours rather than initiating their own. So men call the shots. It is this lack of initiative, their unwillingness to take risk and inability to focus one hundred percent on a selfish goal that disadvantages women. These are the characteristics that make men super-rich entrepreneurs and leaders in society. Of course, a few women do achieve these goals but they are rare.

If women were expected to die in battle, most of them would simply refuse. In this respect women's self-esteem is higher than men's. Many men do not appear to put much value on their own life and the quality of it. Many women consider leading and fighting to be male goals that are irrelevant to women's lives. They positively choose to spend their lives focused on affectionate companionship in the home. Most women prefer sharing their lives with those they love. A woman's relationships define her idea of quality of life.

A woman doesn't want sex for the same reasons a man does. A woman enters a new relationship looking for romance and love. Sex comes as a consequence. (Allan and Barbara Pease)

Topic: Responsiveness and orientation

Sexual responsiveness and orientation

Sexuality is about responsiveness and orientation, both of which are determined before we are born. Among the genes we inherit from our parents are those that determine responsiveness and orientation. Any child can potentially be born homosexual. Likewise, we are all born with varying degrees of responsiveness. Responsiveness is a measure of the frequency with which a person's mind responds positively to eroticism in such a way that causes arousal (blood to flow to the sex organ). When we focus on enjoying our mental arousal, in conjunction with stimulating the phallus, sexual tension builds until it is released as nervous energy, called orgasm.

There are three key aspects to responsiveness: biological, emotional and intellectual. The most important aspect is biological since this is the physiological response. All men orgasm (with varying frequencies) because male orgasm is the physiological trigger for the ejaculation of semen. Ejaculation is a male glandular emission related to men's territorial instincts to dominate and fight for possession of resources. Male mammals mark out their territory by spraying glandular emissions over landmarks to deter competitors. Female mammals do not exhibit these territorial behaviours.

Human reproduction depends on a man impregnating a woman through intercourse. Sexual activity is crucial to men's sense of emotional well-being. Most men engage in regular sexual activity throughout their active lives. Most (but not all) men enjoy masturbation and fantasies. The need for regular penetrative sex with a lover is emotionally significant to men (important to their state of well-being). The term emotionally significant has nothing to do with the emotional aspects of intercourse women may enjoy. Orgasm and sexual activity do not have the same importance for women. As a result of women's sexual psychology, the clitoris does not respond with a lover. Women are not aroused by real-life triggers such as body parts as men are. Even a responsive woman enjoys orgasm alone as an occasional pleasure.

No one teaches us how to orgasm. We discover orgasm because we have the capability. Orgasm is a significant response that we definitely realise we have had. Naturally we are pleased when we have our first orgasm but we don't rush out to tell our parents or our friends about it. Our instincts tell us (if the general embarrassment over sex doesn't) that orgasm is a personal experience. Even later on, our enjoyment of orgasm is a private pleasure. Those who truly orgasm (men for example) don't typically boast about it.

Like sneezing or coughing, the triggers for orgasm are the same regardless of gender and orientation. After adolescence, a responsive person discovers that when they think about erotic scenarios, blood flows to the sex organ. This physical arousal motivates a responsive person to massage the sex organ and discover orgasm. Clearly, those who object to eroticism have never experienced arousal. Sexual phenomena (such as masturbation or gay sex) hold little interest for us until we discover that we enjoy them personally.

The ability to respond to the point of orgasm is an instinctive response of our mind and body that we either have or do not have. This ability varies considerably between individuals. Science does not take sides or blame anyone for the way things are. Science is about presenting the facts without judgement. We can't help being the way we are. Men are intended to be responsive; women are not. That is how we have evolved because of the way that sexual reproduction works. Female orgasm is an evolutionary anomaly that is evidently very rare. It is only comparatively recently that we have learned of its existence from scientists (Kinsey). If female orgasm were common, no one would need to discover it. It would be taken for granted and, like male orgasm, no one would have any interest in discussing it.

Our orientation is defined by who we are attracted to, for example, the same sex or the opposite sex. Most people are heterosexual, which means that they are attracted to people of the opposite sex. Some people are attracted to people of their own sex. When this is exclusive (they are never attracted to the opposite sex) we say that they are homosexual. A person, who engages in sexual activity with people of either sex, is called bisexual. Being gay (homosexual) is completely normal and accepted in most societies today.

There is a biological precedent for heterosexuality because intercourse is the basis for reproduction. But our sexuality is much broader than a purely reproductive function. Although it is usual for people to be heterosexual, it is not abnormal for someone to be attracted to a person of the same sex either exclusively or just occasionally. We have no choice over our orientation. We do not become gay because of the people we associate with or because of the way our parents raised us. Orientation is not a life-style choice. Our orientation (whether we are aroused by or amenable to sex with a lover of the same or opposite sex) is innate (we were born that way).

Sexual orientation is just one aspect of ourselves. Orientation does not change how we are as human beings, our personalities and talents. Men are more likely to identify their orientation because men are responsive. Most men deduce their orientation during puberty because of the fantasies they have. Orientation is less significant to women because of their lack of responsiveness. Many women never have sexual fantasies. A woman may feel different to other women but not understand the reason why. Lesbians often marry and have children before realising years later that they are gay.

Far from being a disorder, low libido is just the natural state of affairs for many women. (Bella Ellwood-Clayton)

Responsiveness varies between individuals

We have no conscious control over our responsiveness. Our ability to enjoy eroticism is an instinctive and subconscious response. Our responsiveness is a factor of our sex and the way our mind works. All men are responsive to some degree. Research indicates that there is a huge range in responsiveness (orgasm frequency) for both sexes that defines normal. Even extreme frequencies can be completely normal for the individuals that have them. Yet orgasm is referred to as if everyone is capable of the same frequency.

Responsiveness is the ability to respond to an erotic trigger (an erotic thought or a visual stimulus). We are each born with an ability to respond to erotic stimuli to varying degrees. If we are responsive (most men but only a few women), our mind responds to specifically erotic stimuli. We do not choose to be responsive or unresponsive. It is just the way we are. Orgasm is a response of the mind and body that we cannot control consciously. Orgasm arises as a subconscious response when the circumstances are appropriate. Once our minds are aroused, we supply the correct stimulation instinctively.

Regardless of the stimulation supplied (a vibrator is not the right kind), orgasm does not occur as if we are just pressing a button. This is because orgasm relies on the brain responding to eroticism in a specific way. Orgasm works like other physiological responses, such as sneezing. It occurs sporadically. There is a stimulus. We cannot know for sure exactly when, or even if, we will sneeze. We cannot make ourselves orgasm on demand. A man may ejaculate spontaneously if he is highly aroused, young or inexperienced. But women never orgasm spontaneously. Female responsiveness is more noticeably sporadic because of the infrequency.

Responsiveness works like a capacitor. Sexual tension accumulates slowly over time. Tension builds in the nervous system (like electrical potential) and is released in a burst. A man needs some time to recover from a sexual release before he can realistically contemplate another orgasm. He knows from experience that orgasm is not as pleasurable until some time has passed since the last one. Only a few boys can orgasm many times in a row with only minutes in between. A younger and more responsive man can be aroused (at least once) with little rest between a first orgasm and a second. Most older men and less responsive men need at least a few hours between orgasms.

A woman needs much longer. A young woman may be able to orgasm twice in a row with only half an hour between. But more typically she waits for 12 hours (early morning or late at night) before trying again. The only reason she has for thinking that orgasm might be possible is the idea appearing in her head. This is quite random and not related to any real-world triggers. Female orgasm relies on subconscious mental and physiological processes.

A man is aware of his arousal because he is acutely aware of having an erect penis, which is highly sensitive to touch. But the clitoral organ is never rigid. It is internal to the body, so women are unaware of any tumescence. A woman's mental arousal (that leads to orgasm) must always be consciously generated. Even a responsive woman has to focus intensely on surreal erotic fantasies before she becomes aware of her arousal. Men, as they age or when alone, may also have to work at arousal depending on their responsiveness.

Responsiveness refers not only to the frequency with which we orgasm but also to the average time a person needs to reach orgasm. The more responsive a person is, the more frequently they orgasm and the less time they need for orgasm. Men orgasm after an average of 2 minutes of intercourse. Research indicates that women take 4 minutes to masturbate to orgasm. Climax with a lover takes around 10-20 minutes. A woman may be aroused by the implicit turn-on of the stimulation her lover is supplying.

Responsiveness reflects a person's total orgasm frequency both alone and with a lover. Men are much more responsive than women ever are. Even responsive women only ever orgasm by masturbating alone. Being unresponsive (rarely or never having an orgasm) is completely normal for women. Research indicates that 10% of women have never had an orgasm in their whole lives. Another 20% admit that they rarely orgasm. So a total of 30% of women readily acknowledge that they do not respond erotically.

Responsiveness does not arise because an individual has some special knowledge or techniques. This is not a conscious choice. So a woman who is unresponsive, cannot learn to masturbate. Responsiveness is a characteristic of the brain we are born with. A responsive person discovers orgasm because the sensations of tumescence (increased blood-flow) motivate them to stimulate their genitals. Once the clitoris is tumescent, a responsive woman can orgasm by focusing on specific aspects of eroticism.

We are motivated to satisfy a need, for example hunger, only when we are conscious of it. Once we have reached the climax of our fantasy, we do not want to start all over again. A person feels sated, not just physically, but also mentally. We need some time to pass so that we can approach a sexual opportunity with a fresh mind. Even for men there is a range in sexual interest. Research reveals that when a man leaves his wife for a younger woman, the novelty causes him to be more sexually initially. Over time his responsiveness (and sex drive) returns to what it was before (normal level).

Like many other physiologic functions, erotic response depends upon a remarkably fool proof mechanism. When one reaches the limit of physiologic endurance he no longer responds erotically. He is no longer capable of erection and finds little incentive to force the situation. (Alfred Kinsey)

Sexual responsiveness is a male characteristic

Male orgasm is not directly linked to reproduction, but ejaculation is required. The function of male orgasm is to trigger the ejaculation of sperm. Some small boys may orgasm (as a one-off) without ejaculating but after adolescence, orgasm always triggers ejaculation. Apart from orgasm, there is no other physiological event that could account for ejaculation. Ejaculation is physical and orgasm is psychological. A man can enjoy both as separate phenomena. Male orgasm rewards a man for ejaculating and potentially impregnating a female. Faking female orgasm is also used as a reward for men. The negative reaction most women have to eroticism is evidence that few women are responsive. Female responsiveness operates at a much lower level than male responsiveness, which is very apparent and immediate.

Responsiveness is a male characteristic. Very few men orgasm infrequently. Most young men are capable of frequent ejaculation, especially with a lover. Intercourse is an act that is intended to facilitate male orgasm. Sexual frustration arises as the come-down effect of the adrenaline rush (of being repeatedly aroused) not being released by the sensations of release and reward. The physical symptoms can be very strong sensations including trembling and feeling weak at the knees. The nearest comparable sensation is the hangover you have after drinking too much alcohol the day before. A man may feel depressed and tired as well as feeling very short-tempered.

Males of all species have an instinct to mate that females do not have. A man's sex drive to engage in intercourse involves both the reproductive event of ejaculation and the pleasure of orgasm. There is a biological reason for men to have an urgent need to engage in regular intercourse. Orgasm is part of the male reproductive function but it has nothing to do with female reproductive function. By suggesting that orgasm is equally significant to women's sexuality, it is as if we are denying the nature of men's sexuality.

Everything that makes a man male, his responsiveness, his sex drive and his enjoyment of sexual pleasure are all supposed to be exactly replicated in women. What then is the point of being male? Men would be the equivalent of women but without the ability to gestate and give birth to offspring. It's as if men's sexuality has no purpose. Nature ensures there is a balance. Male and female sexuality make different contributions. If they both had the exact same function and sexual role, there would be no point in having two sexes.

Responsiveness involves an instinct to penetrate another person's body (a responsive woman uses fantasies to focus on penetration). Only a person who is born male (with penis and testes) can reproduce by ejaculating into a vagina. So only men have a sex drive. The role of penetrator in intercourse involves substantially more pleasure than that of the receiver. Only relatively unresponsive men or women offer a male lover the pleasure of penetration.

Our responsiveness is determined at birth and is primarily a male characteristic. We cannot learn how to become sexually responsive. It is not possible to teach someone how to orgasm. Masturbation clinics encourage women to feel better about their bodies. When a woman feels better about her body, she may be more amenable to intercourse. Needless to say, there is no need for masturbation clinics for men (nor for responsive women).

Men accept that women have to be pursued, which they attribute to female timidity or modesty. Women don't have the responsiveness that motivates men to enjoy short-term pleasure. Men usually make the first move in dating scenarios, which puts a woman in the position of turning down the men she is not attracted to. Women's motivation to engage in relationships comes from a much longer-term desire for affectionate companionship and family.

Female responsiveness has no biological justification. Female orgasm occurs sporadically and infrequently. Very few women are responsive. Research indicates that female orgasm is associated with women's solitary masturbatory activity. A responsive woman generates her arousal consciously by focusing on eroticism. As a result of clitoral tumescence, she instinctively massages the increased blood-flow within the clitoral organ and thrusts to orgasm. Female arousal is subconscious, so women are rarely aware of it.

Female orgasm is rare because it involves no reproductive advantage for women. As a parallel example, some birds are flightless despite having wings. Women may have a phallus but they have largely lost their responsiveness. The clitoris is capable of becoming tumescent but it is never erect, which is what makes the penis so sensitive to stimulation. The corpora cavernosa, which are within the shaft of the penis, are within the internal clitoral organ.

Every man is responsive to varying degrees because responsiveness is a characteristic that defines him as a male. Once boys reach adolescence (defined by first ejaculation) they remain sexually active until old age. Kinsey found that men are sexually active (alone or with a lover) throughout their lives. Kinsey found that women were sexually active only when they had a sexual partner. Women who are single, widowed or divorced can exist perfectly happily for decades without engaging in any sexual activity of any kind. Clearly women do not have the same sexual needs that most men do.

By 15 years of age, 92 per cent of the males have had orgasm, but at that same age less than a quarter of the female have had such experience; and the female population is 29 years old before it includes as high a percentage of experienced individuals as is to be found in the male curve at 15. (Alfred Kinsey)

Characteristics of high sexual responsiveness

As a boy grows into a man, he sees men bragging about their assumed success in providing a woman with amazing sexual pleasure. He sees men comparing notes on the sexual attributes they appreciate in a lover. He sees issues arising because of voyeurs, peeping Toms, men who assault and rape women. He can identify with these behaviours because of the urges he experiences. The evidence for male responsiveness is very clearly available in society. So a man does not feel isolated or alone in his sexual experiences.

A boy can observe how women behave very differently. He notices that his older female relatives (including his mother) may be outspoken about their dislike of eroticism. He sees his younger female relatives (also his sisters) being silent and modest about sex. He experiences women who object to the crudeness of male sexual urges. He can see women in the population who object to flashers, to men groping them, to men pressing their erections against them in the bus or subway. But confusingly he also sees images of women in more appealing situations (such as pornography) who are apparently just as enthusiastic as men are about sexual activity with a lover.

The precedent from Nature is clear. Male mammals are often solitary. They fight other males for breeding rights and they engage with females primarily to mate. The female has little choice in the matter. Men enjoy talking about turn-ons because doing so causes them to become aroused. Men enjoy the sensations of their own arousal. Men enjoy sharing fantasies with a partner or a potential partner. Women do not do this. Female arousal has always been a mystery. Rather than accept that women are not aroused, we are persuaded that women must be aroused by some inexplicable mechanism. Men do not boast about orgasm, which ends their sexual pleasure. Some men delay ejaculation with a lover for as long as possible in order to enjoy the sensations of intercourse. Others (especially younger men) approach sex more strongly focused on ejaculating to release accumulated sexual tension.

The male territorial instinct to mark out territory with glandular emissions motivates men to continue thrusting until ejaculation. Male mammals (much more than females) desire and offer oral stimulation of the genitals. A man's sex drive motivates him to initiate intercourse, which (after the first time) is further positively reinforced by his experience of the pleasures of intercourse. Penetrative sex allows a man to obtain relief from sexual frustration, by releasing sexual tension. He can enjoy the physical gratification of thrusting and the ego of territorial conquest and dominance.

Heterosexual activity is driven by male arousal. Men's needs are obvious and men focus on getting what they need. Men want regular sex and they don't need a relationship to enjoy it. Men are aroused by a lover's body and by sexual opportunities. A woman can easily provide male turn-ons, which revolve around a display of sexual anatomy (especially offering a partner penetration) and sexual invitations. Men usually orgasm easily with a lover.

The key characteristic of responsive individuals (men) is that they are highly motivated to stimulate their erectile sex organ (penis). Men are also easily aroused by opportunities to penetrate a body orifice. The anatomy involved in male orgasm is very evident not only because men have erections when aroused. Men are motivated to stimulate their penis regardless of the sexual activity that they are involved in. Intercourse, fellatio and male masturbation all focus on stimulating the penis. Men can also enjoy anal stimulation but this does not usually lead to orgasm without simultaneous penile stimulation.

Highly responsive individuals focus on their own arousal and orgasm. They do not engage in sexual behaviours that involve providing erotic turn-ons for a lover. A man's interest in his penis comes from his regular sexual arousal. His interest in a lover's genitals comes from his sex drive. A man's instinct to initiate sexual activity with a lover, by displaying his erect penis, communicates his desire stimulate his penis by engaging in intercourse.

Some animals (notably birds) mate for life. But there is no evidence to indicate that men are naturally monogamous. In fact, all the evidence points the other way. Not all men are promiscuous but most men are tempted by promiscuity. Some men see sex as a simple pleasure rather than an activity to be limited to one person for life. For a man, intercourse with an attractive woman is not a misdemeanour. It is just Nature taking its natural course.

Women are not offended that gay men are not attracted to them. So why do men assume that lesbians hate men? Men are looking for a partner who is amenable to penetrative sex. They assume that any woman who doesn't want intercourse must be frigid, a man hater or a lesbian. A man needs an erection (to be sexually aroused) to be willing to offer sex but he assumes his partner will always be amenable. Erotic fiction is based on the male view because women take little interest in eroticism. But men only support sources that show women apparently enjoying sex. Men want to believe that real women love sex too. They just ignore all the publicity over sexual abuse and rape.

Men appreciate the physical: their own body, the body of a lover and physical interaction with a lover. Men are not motivated to spend significant amounts of time with those they love. They prefer following their own pursuits. They may only think of a partner when they need a sexual outlet. If a man only ever touches or kisses a woman because he wants to initiate sexual activity, she may come to resent the transparency of this behaviour.

The idea of 'no-strings attached' sex is very attractive to most men, gay or straight. (George Michael)

Factors that are believed to affect male responsiveness

Factors that affect men's orgasm frequencies include their age, the age at which they reached adolescence, as well as their level of education and whether they feel constrained by the judgement of religious teachings. Frequencies of sexual activity vary but almost all men (92%) orgasm quickly and easily through masturbation as well as through intercourse (research indicates that men orgasm 100% of the time with their wives). Even by the age of 60, male orgasm frequencies have not fallen to the lower female level.

Age is by far the most significant factor in male performance. Men are most sexually active in adolescence. Men's responsiveness decreases with age because male orgasm depends on the physical process of maintaining an erection. Both the firmness, angle of erection and length of time an erection can be maintained, all reduce gradually over decades. Male impotence is relatively rare until old age. At 70 years of age only 27% of white Americans are impotent but by 80 this has increased to 3 out of 4 men. The continuing amenability of a man's sexual partner is doubtless also a factor as he ages.

Responsiveness including erection, ejaculation of sperm and the associated orgasm trigger are all key aspects of male sexuality. When boys first start ejaculating, they have the highest responsiveness of any time in their lives. Initially boys orgasm spontaneously as a result of a variety of stimuli such as fright and shock. But over time men become dependent on penile stimulation as well as some form of fantasy or mental erotic stimulus to be able to orgasm. Boys who become adolescent first (before 12 years of age) tend to have the highest orgasm frequencies throughout their lives. Having a creative imagination has a positive correlation with responsiveness. Boys with a high IQ (intelligence quota) are often those who reach adolescence first.

Male responsiveness gradually declines from adolescence onwards so that few men masturbate regularly by the age of 50. This is natural given the erotic turn-ons available with masturbation (typically images of nudity) are much less arousing for men than having a real-life sexual partner. Similarly the turn-on of penetrative sex in reality is much greater than any sexual fantasy. As men age, the frequency of their early morning erections decreases. The angle of elevation of the erect penis, which varies considerably between individuals, also reduces as a man ages. In addition, the time over which a man can maintain an erection reduces from an average of over one hour in the late teens to an average of around 7 minutes for 66 to 70-year-olds.

Research indicates that the vast majority of men focus on achieving orgasm as quickly as possible. Most men are interested in a woman's sexual attributes and her sexual willingness. Typically less educated men prioritise their own relief over the quality of the experience. Such men prefer to head straight for intercourse rather than offer a sexual partner any foreplay. Female partners of less educated men can enjoy being the object of a man's desire without needing to do very much or fake a response. A man takes what he needs and he's not interested in what a woman gets out of it. Less educated men enjoy their own pleasure rather needing to imagine a lover's arousal.

Some (often less educated) men are more reliant on a biological response that has nothing to do with the mind enjoying erotic stimuli. They need intercourse for sexual release and may need a greater variety of partners to maintain the eroticism of the act over decades. Such men use masturbation alone as a source of sexual relief much less than more educated men. Research indicates that the men with the highest overall orgasm frequencies throughout their lives are the less educated. Men respond most readily to sexual activity with a lover rather than when they have to use their imagination by masturbating alone. So it makes sense that less educated men (who masturbate less but have intercourse more) might have more orgasms.

Even though sex drive causes men so much frustration, they wouldn't be without it. Men would never want to take a contraceptive pill (which affects hormone levels) because they wouldn't want to have either their personal drive (that they often need to achieve higher earning levels) or their sex drive reduced. A high metabolism is evidenced by how physically active we are. In general men are much more active than women. Men's minds are also much more sensitive to erotic and aggressive urges. There are few outlets for men's natural aggression and drive, which may explain porn addiction. The adrenaline rush of combat that is intent on killing can be compared with sexual arousal. Watching movies with hand-to-hand fighting provides an outlet for men who have no other opportunity to express these male emotions. Sport can also represent an alternative outlet for the physical exertion of hunting, fighting an adversary as well as engaging in intercourse.

If men lived solitary lives like other male mammals, they would be much less sexually active. Male arousal occurs in response to being in the physical presence of a potential partner or seeing images of attractive nudity. It is the primate custom of living in communities which has caused men to evolve a higher responsiveness. Sex has become a recreational pleasure for men as the human brain has increased in complexity and with the ready availability of erotic turn-ons because of their regular close physical contact with women. The increasing financial independence of women is likely to have a negative effect on men's access to amenable partners. In the past women have been dependent on men's earnings and so more willing to offer the sex men need.

... the boys who become adolescent first (by 11 years of age) have, on an average, about twice as much sexual outlet per week as the older-adolescent boys have during their early teens. (Alfred Kinsey)

Characteristics of low sexual responsiveness

Research indicates that single women are not nearly as promiscuous as single men. Most men engage in sexual activity, even if it is only masturbation, on a regular basis from adolescence to old age. Many women can live quite happily without being sexually stimulated for weeks, months and even years.

Unlike a boy who finds many examples of others of his sex who enjoy eroticism, a responsive woman is completely isolated in her sexual experiences. She finds no other women who appear to share her enjoyment of erotic fantasies and masturbation. It is as if her experience doesn't exist. Women appear to universally accept the male view of their sexuality. But a responsive woman knows that all the suggestions for how women are supposed to orgasm with a lover, do not work. If she is brave enough to ask other women, they react with anger and defensiveness. They are offended that anyone should challenge their text-book experiences, which they have been told they should have. They cannot explain how they achieve mental arousal or the stimulation technique and anatomy involved in their orgasms.

When a responsive woman observes other women, she sees very little evidence for all this presumed female responsiveness. Women universally ensure that sexual references are avoided in their presence by showing their displeasure in non-verbal ways. A responsive woman sees older women's expressions of disgust and younger women's silence. She sees the superficial innuendo and sexual bravado that a few women use to intimidate others. Despite all the bragging about orgasm, women's behaviours do not provide any evidence of sexual responsiveness. Women talk about love and relationships. They never refer to erotic turn-ons. Women tend to be offended by any form of eroticism and never comment on sexual pleasure. They only ever talk about reproductive health, dating and relationship issues.

The key characteristic of an individual who has a low frequency (or non-existent) erotic response to sexual activity (typically women) is that they are sexually passive with a lover. Women do not focus on obtaining the physical stimulation they need for orgasm because they do not experience sexual arousal with a lover (so stimulation is pointless). Neither are women motivated to stimulate a lover explicitly (manually or orally) because they are not sexually aroused by real-world erotic stimuli such as a lover's genitals.

The sudden increase in responsiveness that boys experience during adolescences changes their attitude towards genitals. Teenage boys develop an interest in their own genitals because of the pleasure of their own arousal. They are also fascinated with the genitals of people they are attracted to and with opportunities for penetrative sex. Girls do not experience this sudden increase in responsiveness, so women think of genitals as smelly and dirty because they are associated with toilet activities. The vagina is a moist orifice similar to the mouth. Before putting a penis in her mouth, a woman expects a man to wash it. This contrasts with intercourse, when she has little interest in a man's hygiene. To women, the vagina is out of sight and out of mind.

Women provide male turn-ons, such as referring to their presumed arousal (as if women respond exactly like men), for various reasons. They provide turn-ons for fun, for ego (vanity), to obtain favours and to assist with male arousal (which speeds up sex and makes their job easier). If women were truly aroused, they would be motivated to enjoy their own turn-ons (as men do). Also men, rather than search endlessly for the mysterious anatomy that might cause female orgasm, would routinely provide female erotic turn-ons.

When a woman provides fellatio or moves her hips during intercourse, a man may assume that her motivation for doing so is because she is aroused. In truth a woman does this to please her lover (or because she is paid). Alternatively, women can provide turn-ons such as faking their own arousal and orgasm. Women also wear attractive lingerie or engage in offering more explicit invitations. Some women (but by no means all) may allow a lover to stimulate them in various ways depending on what their lover finds arousing.

Women talk of their desire to display their bodies as being part of their sexuality. They are correct that is part of female sexuality but it is a passive behaviour. It has nothing to do with women achieving their own arousal and orgasm. The active response comes from a man responding to what he sees. This conscious behaviour initiates male arousal and therefore intercourse.

Young women hope that a man can give them an orgasm because of the fiction spread by men hoping to get women into bed. Some women may enjoy using their bodies to give pleasure. Women obtain more pleasure from sensual touching than from genital stimulation techniques. They hope a lover will engage in the more romantic (loving, affectionate and companionable) aspects of relationships. A woman's top concern on having sex is not her own orgasm but that a man should care about her as a person.

Women can be openly affectionate, touching and kissing friends of either sex without any sexual implications. It is much more difficult for men to engage in the same kind of innocent non-sexual intimacy because men often have sexual motivations when making physical contact with other people. Women connect emotionally to people for significant periods of time as a result of their nurturing instincts. Women use sex to get what they want: money, marriage or family. Men accept this implicit trade just as much as women do. This is the symbiotic relationship between men and women.

"He's just using me for sex," we whine self-righteously. And what are we using him for? A wedding ring? His sperm? (Valerie Harris)

Men cannot accept that women are unresponsive

Men's experience of women is based on their observation of their lovers. Couples, even in long term relationships, do not discuss the details of sexual pleasure. As with orgasm, pleasure is more or less assumed. Men observe that some women have little response to stimulation. Yet others, even if only in pornography, appear to have a dramatic response to being stimulated in any part of their anatomy. Women often receive rewards for pleasing a man. Yet men cannot believe that some women employ behaviours to please men. Even if a man denies any personal experience of unresponsive women, he knows that they exist because of the men who ask about pleasuring a woman and the women who ask about female orgasm. Men try to explain these different experiences in terms of responsiveness because that is how men experience sex. They describe women as being dysfunctional (unloving) or normal (aroused). Men can happily explain women who appear to respond in terms of responsiveness but they cannot explain why some women do not.

Women feel very little physical stimulation from intercourse and certainly not internally. There is only a slight impact on the external genitalia but this thumping of a man's groin into her vulva is not pleasurable. Men's focus tends to be genital (e.g. cunnilingus) rather than sensual caressing of the whole body and the affectionate kissing that a woman appreciates. Men are lucky. The penis is both a reproductive organ and a sex organ. Unfortunately, the same is not true for the vagina. The vagina complements the penis but only for reproductive purposes. Men desperately need a lover to be enthusiastic about engaging in intercourse because of their sex drive.

Men can't have babies because they don't have women's reproductive biology. Everyone accepts this logic because men don't want babies. But men do want women to have orgasms as and when they do. So the logic that women don't have men's reproductive biology is not accepted. Sexual politics motivates adults of both sexes to promote the idea that women should orgasm from stimulation of their reproductive anatomy (the vagina).

The only proactive sexual role available to women is to assist with male orgasm. This behaviour is consciously motivated, rather than a response to eroticism. If a woman cares about a man, she may appreciate that his sexual release is critical to his emotional happiness. Women also provide turn-ons to reduce the time they have to invest in sexual activity. By co-operating with intercourse, a woman provides both the erotic (because a man assumes his lover is aroused) and physical stimuli that help achieve male orgasm sooner.

Many men insist on believing that women offer sex for their own gratification. Men call it ego but it's deeper than that. It's a self-absorption that comes from having a sex drive. It is a determination to believe that the receiver must be obtaining the same pleasure as the penetrator. This is the key misconception that supports men's political pressure on women to provide sex. A woman gives because she wants to. Women give willingly or not at all. Coercion, pressure and bullying all work against a woman's love. Men don't seem to want love. They just want to feel good about themselves.

Every woman on the planet could wear a sticker saying: 'I'm not interested in sex' and men still wouldn't get it. A woman could hit a man over the head with a club hammer to convey to him the strength of her conviction that she is truly not interested in sex. He still wouldn't get it. Such is the nature of male sex drive. This male trait of ignoring all forms of feedback, both subtle and obvious, means that men fail to read the signs women give them, not just on sex, but on all aspects of relationships. Men's ability to be impervious to any form of feedback handicaps them in their relationships with women.

A man's sex drive is not affected by issues in the wider relationship. If a woman behaves badly towards a male partner, he may be upset. But men enjoy sex regardless of any relationship. As soon as a woman puts on a short skirt and spreads her legs, a man is likely to forget any resentments he has. The pleasures of intercourse are enough to cancel out all other concerns. But there is no equivalent of a short skirt for a man. A woman does not benefit from the same kind of easy arousal that a man does nor does she enjoy the same erotic pleasure from intercourse. A lover's behaviour towards her is much more significant for a woman than it tends to be for a man.

Women offer sex because they empathise with a man's needs. If a woman is in the mood, providing a man with the sexual pleasure and release that he needs can be fun. What is selfish is a man's need to believe that a woman does this because she wants it for her own pleasure. It is the denial of the female perspective that is insulting. Men refuse to accept that women offer a partner sex to demonstrate their love. It is the greatest gift a woman can give.

Men's prime interest in sexual knowledge focuses on how women can be encouraged to be more enthusiastic about intercourse. Men cannot relate to the emotional drivers that women need to enjoy sex. This confusion between arousal (which relies on erotic stimuli) and amenability (which relies on emotional stimuli) is due to ignorance over how orgasm is achieved. If men accepted that women are not capable of orgasm with a lover, maybe they could start focussing on the real issue. Men need to provide some of the emotional factors that make women more willing to provide the sex that men want. Men need to put their erotic fantasies to one side to get what they want.

Studies have shown anywhere from 55% - 80% (If not more) of women fake orgasms. Yet ask any man on the street and they think they are handing out orgasms like a bag of peanuts on an airplane. That math is not adding up people! (Stephan Labossiere)

Orientation is defined by who we are attracted to

The genes that cause us to be homosexual arise in random individuals throughout the population. Homosexuality is a completely harmless and natural orientation for anyone to have. For those people who are gay, homosexuality is quite normal. There is a misconception (particularly among women) that being gay is a lifestyle choice and the result of a conscious decision. No one chooses to be gay. It is just the way they are.

Research indicates that some people engage in sexual activity with same sex partners just once in their lives, perhaps as a form of experimentation when they are young. Others are embarrassed that they are aroused by people of the same sex and consciously take steps to avoid homosexual contacts. Others are not exclusive about the gender of the person they have sex with. They can enjoy sex with people they are attracted, to regardless of gender.

Some men are aroused by both sexes and many men (37%) have had at least one gay encounter that ended in their own orgasm. Many of these are one-offs or sporadic. There is a social bias in favour of heterosexuality but some men may enjoy the proactiveness and explicitness of homosexual sex play. Bisexual women enjoy physical intimacy regardless of their lover's gender.

Orientation is determined by the gender of the people we are emotionally attracted to or who we are aroused by. Men's orientation depends on explicit turn-ons: specifically, male or female anatomy. Given women are not aroused by real-world triggers such as a lover's genitals, their orientation is determined by those they form an emotional connection with. Even a responsive woman, who can orgasm alone, is not responsive with a lover. So a woman may choose to live with another woman without ever having sex.

A woman is called heterosexual because she is willing to be a receiver of vaginal intercourse. Some women are able to provide this or are forced to do this in exchange for money. But most women need an emotional connection before they are amenable to offering men sexual opportunities. A woman is called lesbian because she is never motivated to offer a man intercourse for any reason. Instead, she forms emotional attachments to women. But she has exactly the same sexual responses as a heterosexual woman. She is not aroused by body parts or by sexual activity with a lover.

Women are attracted to a female partner because of her lack of responsiveness. This means that a female lover understands the value of a non-sexual emotional connection. Many women conclude that men are like animals. Men are like male mammals just as women are like female mammals. Women see people as social beings. Women obtain emotional rewards from enjoying affection and companionship with a lover. Women enjoy the non-sexual intimacy, of spending companionable time, that goes with sex. Women's love for a partner is based on their nurturing instincts.

Few people object to lesbians, who are viewed as slightly odd but harmless. It is men's desire for penetrative sex that makes gay men a sexual threat. People often wonder what lesbians do in bed. This is a result of the heterosexual focus on intercourse, which is driven by the male responses of erection and ejaculation. Lesbians may engage in thrusting activity to mimic the activity that they see promoted in society or in the belief that they should.

Two people of the same sex cannot engage in vaginal intercourse so gay people are obliged to use more explicit genital stimulation. Heterosexual society hides behinds the respectability of intercourse, which is justified by our reproductive biology. Yet men want intercourse much more frequently than can be justified on reproductive grounds. Most of the time, couples have sex to enjoy sexual pleasure or to support emotional bonding.

Parents may not want their children to be gay because they hope their children will have families and be part of normal society. Gay men are often victimised and threatened by heterosexual men. Today some gay couples decide to adopt or have children that have one of the partner's genes. Many heterosexuals believe every child (regardless of orientation) should have heterosexual parents. This is the biological and social precedent but other parenting issues may be much more critical to healthy child development.

Gay men see women purely as social (rather than sexual) beings and so they are not aroused by them. There must be some mechanism that causes heterosexual men to see women as sex objects. Similarly, a paedophile's brain causes him to see children as sex objects. Homosexuality is becoming much more accepted in society. Gays may choose to come out by admitting their orientation to family and friends. Women typically get on well with gay men. Gay men often have the social skills that women appreciate. Some men have mannerisms that we call effeminate because they are more typically associated with women. Effeminate men are not necessarily homosexual.

It is a misconception that gays look or behave differently to straight people. But our orientation does not affect our character, our personality or abilities. Some people naturally have mannerisms that are associated with being gay. There is no guarantee that a butch woman is lesbian or that an effeminate man is gay. As people, gays are no different to anyone else but they may choose to differentiate themselves by dressing or behaving in certain ways.

... there are a great many males who remain as masculine, and a great many females who remain as feminine, in their attitudes and their approaches in homosexual relations, as the males or females who have nothing but heterosexual relations. (Alfred Kinsey)

Male homosexuality focuses on casual sex

Kinsey found that only 50% of the men in his sample were exclusively heterosexual. Many men (46%) were attracted towards other men even if only as a one-off experience. Around 10% of men at some time in their lives have predominantly homosexual relationships for a period of a few years. Highly sexed and uneducated men are more likely to engage in gay sex.

Many heterosexual men feel no animosity towards gay men. Kinsey noted that the men who were most bitterly opposed to gays often belonged to the social class with the highest occurrence of homosexual behaviour. A man who is bisexual has a choice. He can suppress his homosexual urges (no doubt believing such feelings are shameful) because he is also aroused by women. He may conclude that every man should be able to do the same. But around 4% of men are exclusively gay. They are only aroused by men.

Some people assume that people choose to be gay as a kind of lifestyle choice. It is ridiculous to suggest that men have made themselves victims of bigotry and persecution throughout history merely on a whim. It's understandable that women might think this way but men fully understand the strength of male sex drive that cannot be repressed. Homophobia is largely down a certain kind of heterosexual man, who disrespects men (and women) for being a receiver of penetrative sex. This is one of the greatest crimes against humanity that has been perpetrated in the name of beliefs about the sanctity of vaginal intercourse. Women may use their family goals to justify sex but men's sexual needs involve more than creating a new life.

Young men (regardless of orientation) have disadvantages when it comes to being a good lover. They can only enjoy a few minutes of thrusting activity (through intercourse) before they are obliged to ejaculate. Young men ejaculate quickly due to a youthful responsiveness and inexperience. Experience helps with lead-ins and reduces awkwardness with a new lover. Experience teaches us how to generate a comfortable atmosphere for enjoying sexual pleasure. We learn how we can suggest sexual activity and vary the pace. We learn what we enjoy ourselves and what a lover may enjoy.

Men's physical gratification is based on sexual pleasure rather than the emotional rewards women enjoy by pleasing a lover. Young men, both gay and straight, are inclined to focus sexual encounters on penetration and thrusting to ejaculation. They approach sex with an ego that means the sexual attributes of a sexual partner are a trophy to be boasted of. They are easily flattered when someone agrees to have sex with them. A man's desperation to find a partner may lead him to accept a low quality of sexual experience.

Many young men (regardless of orientation) start out by looking for quantity over quality of interaction. They measure their relationships in terms of a lover's sexual attributes and see no value in knowing them as a person. Even if gay men theoretically agree to open relationships, they are notoriously jealous. If a man wants an open relationship it is often a sign that he is just notching up lovers. If a man stops allowing lust to cloud his judgement, he may make different sexual decisions. Loving, passionate sex can be much more fulfilling than a one-night stand with someone who has no technique.

Having sex with someone tells you little about the person. It is a good idea for anyone to get to know a person before getting involved sexually. Taking time to choose a partner who is a good match (of personality, values and interests) and investing in that relationship, can make male homosexual experiences much more rewarding. This doesn't necessarily mean being a couple for life but just building a relationship of substance that lasts for years rather than months. The quality of sex can be vastly improved by having sex with someone who is a decent and likeable person. Good sex involves finding a partner who you can experiment with, explore and discover what you like. The quality of sex is more pleasurable with emotional intimacy.

Casual sex, even with protection, is always a risk. Being the penetrator may seem straightforward but we are not talking here about jamming a rod into a hole. A penetrator needs to use some sensitivity and respond to feedback. Verbal communication is often necessary. The person being penetrated can cooperate and give feedback to accommodate the penetrator's thrusting action and make it more erotic and sexually rewarding. This co-operation verges on consent and often represents the line between pain and pleasure.

A gay man must always protect himself, including using condoms and lubrication. Many of the tissues involved in penetrative gay sex are sensitive and tear easily. The golden rule of sex is: if it hurts, then stop doing it. If something does not feel good, it should not be done. Sex is about pleasure, both what we give and what we receive from a lover. There are many ways to give and receive sexual pleasure. No one should ever feel pressured to engage in penetrative sex especially if both lovers are not enthusiastic. Sex between men need not always include penetration. Fellatio is often a more reliable way to give and receive pleasure without any risk of injuring anyone.

Gay men are often highly promiscuous. Research indicates that a high proportion of gay men have sex with many different men and 22 per cent have had more than ten partners. Men do not have the limitation that women (regardless of orientation) have of needing an emotional relationship to feel good about offering sex to a partner. Research indicates that only 29 per cent of lesbian women have sex with more than two partners and only 4 per cent who have had more than ten partners. Lesbians are rarely promiscuous.

Many of the (homosexual) males had been highly promiscuous, sometimes finding scores or hundreds of sexual partners. (Alfred Kinsey)

Lesbianism focuses on longer-term relationships

Only 2% of women are exclusively gay (half as common as male homosexuality). The average age to come out is 17 years old for gay men but 40 years old for lesbians. Responsive women may be able to deduce their orientation from their erotic fantasies. Our responsiveness is related to our sex and has nothing to do with our orientation. Lesbians benefit from having similar levels of responsiveness as their lovers. Also being women, they are not so intent on genital stimulation, penetration and any need for orgasm.

Women engage in intimate physical activity with a lover primarily as a bonding mechanism and to demonstrate affection. We may call these sexual in the sense that the emotions cause women to offer sexual activity to a partner for whom they feel an emotional attachment. With a lover there is the opportunity to explore their body and to allow them to explore our body. The sensations of being touched by another person are different to when we touch ourselves. There is also the psychological thrill of knowing that a lover wants to touch us and the trust involved in wondering what they will do next.

Lesbians may enjoy undressing for a lover or removing a lover's clothing. They may caress a partner's erogenous zones with their hands or tongue. Women like to engage in displays of affection, such as prolonged kissing, hugging or other forms of touching. Women's breasts are clearly related to reproductive function. But because of male interest, breasts are often considered to be sexual even by women themselves. Besides creating maternal feelings, breast and nipple stimulation may also decrease a woman's anxiety and assist with emotional bonding (trust between lovers).

Lesbians have the advantage of being women themselves who are attracted to other women. They may have an above average knowledge of female sexual anatomy. With no penis requiring urgent attention, gay women can focus on sensual pleasuring rather than genital stimulation. Lesbians can be more relaxed about exploring pleasuring without the pressure to achieve their own orgasm. Lesbians use fingering (manual stimulation) to massage the genitalia. A woman may finger herself (clitoral glans, the labia and the outer portion (the entrance) of the vagina). Genital fingering may be mutual.

We tend to equate sex to intercourse because of men's sex drive. Women do not have the same biological drive to penetrate a lover that men have. Female masturbation involves an instinctive thrusting action similar to the male role in intercourse. A responsive woman achieves orgasm alone by using fantasies and by stimulating the internal clitoral organ. But these masturbation techniques are incompatible with sociable activity. Lesbians may play act intercourse because they have the impression that this is what sex is about. But there is no sexual arousal and certainly no orgasm involved.

Non-penetrative sexual acts between women are called tribadism. They are also referred to as frottage or dry humping. This may be achieved in a number of positions, including missionary, woman on top or doggy style. It involves a woman rubbing her vulva against her lover's vulva, thighs, stomach or other body part. Such general stimulation does not cause orgasm. It may be accompanied by fingering of the clitoral glans or penetration with a dildo.

Lesbians may assume (as others do) that heterosexual women respond to intercourse because they are aroused by male genitals and vaginal penetration. But a woman's genitals and her ability to respond to stimulation are identical regardless of orientation. No woman has a drive to be impregnated. What is bewildering for everyone is that a tiny minority of politically motivated individuals use their views to intimidate the majority. But millions of other more rational people who may disagree, say nothing.

Lesbian sexual activity is dictated by the motivation of the two partners involved who may (quite naturally) not be especially proactive. A woman may provide fingering from behind, massaging of erogenous zones as well as introducing a dildo or vibrator into the vagina or anus. Lesbians can also make use of bondage or other BDSM activities. Cunnilingus is a common practice among those lesbians who engage in sexual activity. Oral stimulation of the anus is less often practised. For deeper vaginal or anal penetration, a strap-on dildo or other sex toys are used by the more sexually adventurous.

Given most women are unresponsive, we can define a heterosexual woman by her desire to attract male sexual attention. Lesbianism may simply indicate a preference for female companionship. A woman's orientation is determined by the sex of the people she feels emotionally attached to. Lesbians can live together without having sexual relations. Lesbians are often intent on gaining political and social acceptance of their sexuality. Lesbians do not talk of turn-ons or sexual pleasuring any more than any other women.

The lack of orgasm women experience (that no one likes to admit to) is often attributed to incompetent male lovers. Yet some (more imaginative) men are much more motivated to explore a lover's body and discover how it might respond to stimulation than any woman ever is. It is suggested that men do not know what anatomy to stimulate. This is hardly men's fault since the problem could be easily solved if women told men what to stimulate. It is also asserted that lesbians have more orgasms than heterosexual women. But explicit explanations for how lesbian women achieve arousal (as a response to erotic turn-ons) and any reconciliation of lesbian lovemaking techniques with the kind of stimulation that might cause orgasm are noticeably lacking.

It should be emphasized, however, that a high proportion of the unmarried females who live together never have contacts which are in any sense sexual.
(Alfred Kinsey)

Topic: Non-sexual intimacy

Understanding the value of non-sexual intimacy

Sexuality is about our emotions and how we feel loved in our relationships with others. Although sex is often described in terms of eroticism, many people also look for emotional rewards. If we grow up within a family, we have a sense of connection with those around us. Children need their parents to care for them and to take an interest in them. When adults love someone, that sense of emotional connection has to be generated from zero. Men feel loved because they enjoy regular intercourse. Men's post-coital gratitude makes a woman feel needed. Women assume that men respond as they do.

Everyone has emotions but the sexes express their feelings in different ways. Most women cry when they are upset, angry or frustrated. Female responses are considered weak or effeminate (because of the debilitating effect women's emotions have on them) and are disapproved of in a man. For many men, facing fear can be exhilarating because of the adrenaline rush. Women are more likely to be paralysed by fear rather than be propelled into action. Men can live quite happily in functional environments devoid of emotional attachments. But women's lives focus on their relationships. Most women want to share their lives with people they care about. This is why women are often less motivated to work in paid employment than men are.

Women enjoy non-sexual intimacy with a lover, which has nothing to do with nudity or genital stimulation. It relates to the companionable time a couple spends together sharing platonic interests and demonstrating caring behaviours. When we care about another person, we have their interests at heart. We make effort for them and we consider their feelings. We feel valued when they give us what we need emotionally. Men's obsession with sex, means they rarely relate to these aspects of relationships because their sexual needs swamp all other concerns. Naturally men assume women must respond just as they do. The result is that neither sex understands the other.

Men talk about work, sport and women (as objects of arousal). Women talk about family, fashion and relationship issues. Men talk for strategic reasons. Men meet up to network, create business contacts and opportunities and to find out information. Of course, some women also do this but most women get together for emotional reasons. They look for reassurance from others, comfort and support. Most men do not relate to this kind of communication.

To many women, communicating about their feelings is natural when they are intimate with someone. But men are often uncomfortable about sharing their feelings. This is an instinct based on competition between men. Men instinctively avoid showing weakness and thereby opening themselves up to attack. For this reason, many heterosexual men dislike discussing emotions.

Men tend to put work priorities before the demands of a relationship. In women's eyes, this is not love as they experience it. To a woman, love involves wanting to spend every moment with someone. But women accept men's different priorities because of the need to support the family. To men, work represents a means of competing with other men for status as well as a means of attracting a woman (as a result of their ability to support a family). A man feels justified in working all day or all week before turning up at home and expecting his wife to be instantly amenable to sex. A man's emotional needs are satisfied within minutes. Men mistakenly assume that by satisfying their own sexual needs, they have also satisfied a woman's emotional needs.

Sex is a much more emotional experience for a woman than it ever is for a man. Women have a strong sense of personal privacy because they are not aroused. Sex involves a woman giving up this autonomy over her own body. Men find this difficult to understand because they want a lover to stimulate them. A woman offers sex for decades because she recognises that regular sexual activity is important to a man. This is what many women in long-term relationships call love. Women have to give through sex. Men need to give back in other non-sexual ways. Women's emotional needs are much subtler than male sex drive. A man needs to understand what is important to a woman. A woman hopes that a man cares about her enough to please her.

Just as a man has no control over what arouses him, a woman has no conscious control over the factors that cause her to feel an emotional attachment. Both responses arise subconsciously. So we can decide that it would be sensible to be attracted to someone who is rich, talented or good-looking. But attraction is based on factors that are most advantageous for successful reproduction and survival. They have evolved over millennia. We are attracted to people who fulfil our emotional needs. Men look for rewarding sexual activity while women like to feel protected and cared for.

Men are primarily attracted by a person whose anatomy and behaviour arouses them. Men may come to love those who interact with them sexually because of the erotic rewards of intercourse. Women are attracted to someone who reassures them emotionally by being physically strong (even aggressive), a good provider or just a kind person. Women come to love those who support them and care about their welfare. The love we feel comes from the reassurance that we obtain either from sex (for men) or from feeling that a lover cares about us in a wider sense than sex (for women). Women want affectionate companionship, communication and support.

... it's time to talk about what most men could initiate more of, and that is non-sexual intimacy. ... It involves any kind of intimacy that isn't centered around sex. It can include making time to talk, cuddling, engaging in fun activities together, and so on. (Stephan Labossiere)

Sexual attraction and commitment to a relationship

Especially in the early days of a romance, both sexes can feel an electric thrill from touching, hearing or seeing a lover. We have a desire to be physically close and to hold them. For women this is an emotional thrill but for men, the desire is genitally focused and includes sexual arousal. When we are young, the novelty of these adult emotions can result in tremendous emotional highs and lows. If we feel overwhelmed by such emotions, confiding in someone we trust may help us keep our feelings in perspective.

We refer to personal chemistry meaning that we naturally feel at ease with someone and that we are attracted to them. We identify with the sound of their voice, how they look and how they express themselves. Speed-dating tends to work because we assess people within a few seconds of meeting them. We are attracted to others even when we are just friends. Some people have platonic relationships with the opposite sex. Others lose interest in such friendships unless they become sexual. Some people only want sex with a person they love. Others are motivated by lust. Some people find it easy to demonstrate affection. Others are more reserved about showing affection.

Sexual attraction describes the male response. Erotic arousal causes a man to feel intimate with someone. A man has no conscious control over his response. He cannot choose not to become aroused. He can only ignore or act on the urge to make a sexual advance. As soon he has an erection, a man has a desire for intimacy. He doesn't need to know personal details before he can enjoy a sexual encounter. So men don't usually need a lead-in to sex. Gay men can agree to have sex, within minutes, of meeting. Straight men do not have the same freedom because women's responses are emotional.

Men learn that women do not appreciate direct sexual approaches. A man is likely to get his face slapped or to be reported for sexual harassment. Men seduce women by admiring them in a platonic way (without revealing their sexual urges), by being an interesting companion, respectful and socially amenable. Specifically, men do not display their bodies or make sexual invitations. Women tend to be wary of any male approach, no matter how it is disguised, because they learn that men are just looking for sex. A woman needs time to get to know a man and assess him as a potential partner. She only agrees to sex once she feels attracted to him in an emotional sense.

A man is attracted by a woman's body and her behaviour. Men interpret female timidity as amenability. If a man pays a woman special attention, she may assume that he is attracted to her. This is particularly true as a woman ages because her vanity is flattered, especially from younger men. So men have to be careful not to imply that they are intent on a sexual relationship.

Women value their relationships as an emotional necessity. They hope for a partner who contributes enthusiastically to their intimate time together: sharing a sense of humour, interesting conversation and affection. Most women are attracted to decent men with kind faces and reassuring voices. A woman wants a man to protect her and who is competent enough to support her. She also hopes for an affectionate companion to share her life with.

Some couples document their relationship by having a legal marriage ceremony. A core concept within marriage, whether a couple has religious beliefs or not, is that once married the couple is sexually loyal to each other. A wedding can be a way of communicating the new relationship to the wider family. A big celebration (as well as being enjoyable) may emphasise the responsibility involved in making a long-term commitment to each other. Not everyone wants to get married. Some couples decide to have children without getting married. Some couples don't want to have children. In some cultures, a child may feel embarrassed to have unmarried parents. There is also considerable taboo over a child being the result of an illicit affair.

Splitting up a family home is typically extremely upsetting and inconvenient. So sometimes adults continue in unhealthy relationships. They may want security and continuity. They may believe their partner can't help being how they are. There is always the hope that the situation will improve. They are afraid of change or of being alone. They may not be able to find alternative accommodation. Many couples, especially if they have children, try to stay together. If a couple is always arguing, it is often better to end a bad marriage. A couple may separate initially and then divorce, which legally ends their marriage. Couples divorce for many reasons. Key reasons are sexual differences and financial problems as well as incompatible personalities.

One woman can only have a finite number of children. But a man can potentially impregnate a (different) woman with every ejaculation (many hundred times in a lifetime). Men are naturally promiscuous because of the pleasure they enjoy from sexual encounters and because promiscuity maximises their chances of passing on their genes. Monogamy is primarily in a woman's reproductive interests. Most men are attracted primarily to young women. This is a biological (subconscious) preference that means that fertile women are targeted. Men are rarely attracted to much older women. Women experience platonic love. They can marry much older and relatively unattractive men because the social and emotional factors they look for, work just as well with older men. Women are attracted to men who will support them. They are reassured by men's confidence and robustness.

... there seems to be no single factor which is more important for the maintenance of a marriage than the determination, the will that that marriage shall be maintained. (Alfred Kinsey)

Men's sexual satisfaction relies on having a lover

The key purpose of sex is to effect reproduction, which is done via intercourse. So men's sexuality has to include a need to engage in sexual activity with a partner. Male responsiveness is required for intercourse to be possible and their orgasm triggers the reproductive event (ejaculation of sperm). Women's sexuality does not have the same need for a lover. Female responsiveness has nothing to do with the reproductive process. From a reproductive perspective, a woman only needs to be willing to co-operate with men's desire for intercourse. Most women only agree to do this in combination with a loving relationship and, typically, support for a family.

A man's arousal is caused by the presence of an attractive partner, especially one who dresses or behaves in a way that is intended to attract male attention. A man is aroused by a lover's body, their genitals and their behaviour. As they reach old age, most men stop masturbating before they stop engaging in intercourse. The real-world erotic turn-ons of a lover's body and the pleasure of penetrative sex, cause men to experience much stronger arousal than they do by imagining the same situation during masturbation alone.

A man is dependent on a woman's body both for his arousal, for his sexual release and for the satisfaction of ejaculating into a vagina. But a man does not fulfil the same role for a woman. Being unaroused means that a woman is merely a bystander. Intercourse is the male equivalent of female masturbation except that a man needs a lover to enjoy his best orgasms. If a man knows that his lover masturbates, he should respect her solitary pleasure. Allowing a responsive woman the space to enjoy orgasm is a way of compensating her for the many times that only the man has an orgasm.

Many men travel away from home for their work. They do this willingly because they are less attached to their family relationships. In these circumstances, a man is exposed to many erotic turn-ons that may arouse him. This includes attractive potential partners who may be sexually amenable. Some men give into temptation and have extra-marital affairs. But many men remain sexually loyal. So when they have to, many men appear to be able to do without sex fairly happily sometimes for weeks at a time.

It's possible that sex drive, rather than being an irresistible sexual urge, depends on the availability of a willing partner. Men expect to have regular sex with their partner. This expectation means they are frustrated when their partner is physically present but not sexually willing. The expectation comes from women's general amenability and willingness to keep men happy. Women are pressured by the acceptance of regular intercourse as a marital duty, attitudes in society that women should provide for the needs of others and, of course, male propaganda that women should enjoy intercourse.

The wonderful thing about sex (compared with artificial highs) is that there are no addictive aspects. But sex does rely on having an amenable partner. This is the issue of consent. A physically stronger man can insist on intercourse with a woman if he catches her alone. This is why young women have only been able to move about safely very recently in our social history.

Even though a man has to seduce or persuade a woman into having sex, he cannot accept that she may see the activity in a different light. This is equivalent to a carnivore assuming that his victims want to be eaten. It is clearly the lot of vegetarians, herbivores and smaller carnivores to be eaten by larger carnivores. But most animals fight for their lives. Likewise, a woman fights off unwanted suitors. She needs to find a man attractive as a mate and be assured of his protection before she wants to mate with him.

Having a good time for a woman involves a nice meal, perhaps a movie and some pleasant companionship. A man can also appreciate such activities but only once he has had the opportunity to release the sexual tension he has accumulated throughout the day or week. A woman doesn't experience this sexual need or consequent frustration. She doesn't need orgasm in the way a man does. It's very evident to most women that men want sex for their own pleasure as well as the relief they obtain from the sexual frustration that builds up when they are frequently aroused without access to penetrative sex. Women see evidence of men's gratitude in terms of their willingness to pay.

Swinging used to be called wife swapping. It is still an activity that is driven by men with women supporting. Men enjoy the opportunity for intercourse with multiple partners. Women just enjoy being admired. As with all forms of casual sex, swinging focuses on intercourse and male orgasm. Rich men around the world maintain wives and mistresses. Some very rich men have hareems. References to women's sexual role in providing male pleasure can be embarrassing for those women who work alongside men professionally.

Heterosexual men are never put in the position of being treated like a sexual commodity. The closest analogy is when a man of European race calls a man of African race 'boy'. We feel humiliated when we are patronised by an arrogant person who considers themselves to be naturally superior. When a man sexually appraises a woman's body, she is frustrated because she cannot retaliate by treating a man in the same way. Women (even lesbians) are not aroused by anatomy as men are. Women experience emotional (not erotic) attraction towards a lover because they feel a nurturing affection for a lover. Women have no need for sexual activity of any kind. But providing sex for an appreciative lover may cause some women to feel emotionally rewarded.

It wasn't until I actually got married that I realized that, day in day out, this man I was now committed to dating every single day of my life also wanted sex (nearly) every day of his life. (Joan Sewell)

Sex is an emotional bonding mechanism for men

For men, sex is like a magic pill that makes the world seem more positive. Some men look to women as a distraction from everyday life. Sex represents an escape from the real world into fantasy. Sex can also be a form of male entertainment. Sex does not fulfil the same function for women. A man commits to a relationship with a woman who offers him more regular sex than he can get elsewhere. If women offered sex readily to any passing male, then men would have no reason to settle for one woman. Sex is the bonding mechanism that makes relationships possible. Men need to be incentivised because of the temptations of promiscuity. Women are motivated by the emotional rewards of family life, including affectionate companionship.

Once a man has found a woman who offers him regular intercourse, he may be motivated to legalise the arrangement. Not all men want to limit their sexual options. For some men, the excitement of the chase and the novelty of a new partner, make the hard work worthwhile. But a man needs a regular sexual outlet and this is obtained most easily by engaging in a relationship with one woman. Although sexual release is a physical need, men also often have a need to feel loved and appreciated. Of course for some men, marriage does not stop them looking for sexual opportunities elsewhere.

Men clearly want more than orgasm from sex, otherwise they would masturbate and be done. Men are not motivated by orgasm itself, which ends their enjoyment of engaging in intercourse. They enjoy the erotic rewards of thrusting into a lover's body. Men obtain an optimal release from penetrating and ejaculating into another person's body. Men do not have the same emotional reassurance women have of being needed. Once a man chooses a mate, he feels emotionally fulfilled because of the promise of regular sex given his acceptance as her lover. He considers his love for her to be special because it involves his admiration of her body in return for his enjoyment of his own sexual arousal and thrusting, followed by his ejaculation and orgasm.

Orgasm does not encapsulate all the erotic, sensual and emotional pleasures that men enjoy from sex. Yet orgasm is used to encapsulate all of women's sexual pleasure. A man assumes that a woman is satisfied and that she appreciates his performance. Men hope a woman will confirm their prowess as a lover. Orgasm is used as a token of a female approval. A man wants to feel that a woman appreciates his desire to penetrate her body and that she enjoys a similar pleasure. Women offer sex because they know it's expected.

Even if a woman's behaviour is unenthusiastic, a man can still convince himself that she is enjoying some undefined aspect of the activity as long as her very evident disinterest is not openly acknowledged. Unless a woman puts on a performance, a man has no way of knowing that she has been pleased by his lovemaking. Men notice that women do not initiate sex and that they wait for intercourse to finish. Men complain about these female behaviours but they still insist that sex provides an equal pleasure in order to justify sex. Women do not show signs of obtaining sexual release or post-coital gratitude as men do. Men suspect that pleasure is all theirs because of these signs. So men are always asking how they can pleasure a woman.

Women don't tend to worry about pleasing a man because men's pleasure is usually very evident. Men's satisfaction in ejaculating as well as their post-coital gratitude for a woman providing them relief from frustration provides plenty of proof of pleasure. A woman does not need reassurance from sex because she is reassured by a man's admiration of her body. A man's erection is a clear indication of his appreciation for a lover. A woman's body does not provide such clear erotic feedback. A woman needs to provide explicitly erotic feedback during sex by her behaviour or by what she says.

For a woman, sex is a social activity. But for a man, intercourse represents the culmination of his arousal cycle that is commenced many times throughout the days or weeks and concluded only when he has intercourse. Intercourse is a male activity that men orchestrate. A man's performance is vitally important to him and he doesn't want to be judged by a woman. Men insist on the fantasy that women are aroused by a large penis or long intercourse because it increases the importance of their own role in the act.

If women want relationships with men, then they have to accept that satisfying a man's need for intercourse is an integral part of that relationship. Women are initially drawn to men because they are flattered and feel emotional reassurance because of the protection they obtain when a man is interested in their welfare. A man is instinctively motivated to protect a lover as a source of regular intercourse. A man's sexual admiration may result in a woman feeling reciprocal emotions (love) for him. She is emotionally attracted to having a companionable relationship with him. Over the longer-term, women's desire for family also ties them into relationships with men.

If men just wanted intercourse, they could pay a prostitute. Some men see sex as a form of mutual exchange. A man wants a woman to be proactively engaged in the sexual activity that is so important to him. A man wants an engaged sexual partner. While a woman wants a man to be interested in her thoughts and concerns. A man who takes his camera on a date is like woman reading book during sex. A woman wants an engaged social partner. We don't feel appreciated if our lover is not giving us their full attention when we are occupied with activities and communication that are dear to us.

To a husband, sex is about right up there on the list with eating and breathing. Can he survive without it? Yes, but it's not fun at all. Sex is to the man, what talking/communication is to the woman. (Gerad Harris)

Men's sex drive can cause them to be insensitive

Men's sex drive motivates them to take the sexual initiative. Men are foremost attracted to body parts but they also like a lover who is sexually amenable, which means passive rather than asserting her own needs. Women give sex as a means of demonstrating affection. When a woman feels emotionally attracted to a man, she willingly offers sex. Anyone who is the receiver of intercourse appreciates respect from the penetrating male.

Men assume sex equals emotional intimacy. Men have sex to feel validated. The penetrator has most of the pleasure. When a man is aroused, he automatically assumes that a woman is equally aroused. This not so, even if she is in a relationship with him. The receiver only has the reward of giving pleasure, which is greatly reduced if the penetrator is disrespectful. Over time men take a partner for granted and assume that sex is an automatic right. Within a relationship, a woman needs a lover to demonstrate that he is willing to give her the affectionate companionship that she appreciates.

Men respect each other on the basis of power: brute force, money or status. The male role of protector gives men a sense of superiority over women. Men call their male companions 'ladies' as an insult. The implication is that rather than being robust and strong men, they are weak and feeble women who need to be indulged with special privileges. This male arrogance and self-absorbed interest in their own sexual performance angers women. If a man is offensive, a woman will often fall silent. Women notice such things. But men assume someone will assert their opinion if they disagree. A woman expects a man to respect the common courtesies. Most women discontinue relationships with men who are consistently insensitive or disrespectful.

Men might not be so arrogant if someone was constantly hassling to penetrate their orifices (mouth or anus). Men disrespect those (women and gay men) who offer a lover an opportunity for penetrative sex. Yet homosexuality involves much more of a mutual exchange than heterosexuality. Unlike gay men, heterosexual men never have to reciprocate by offering to be a receiver of intercourse (this is the advantage of heterosexuality). Men respect foremost the biological role of being the penetrator. This attitude recognises that the penetrator takes his satisfaction and pleasure in penetrating a lover's body and thrusting until ejaculation.

The only people who talk of sexual pleasure are men. The only women who talk about sex in public are being paid to do so. Men like to assume that silence equals happiness. Women harbour resentments towards men. We see this in the sexual harassment charges. Men resent women's eternal sexual reluctance that they can't understand. This confusion can turn into strong resentment, and even anger, that men then sometimes take out on women.

Men would not be so happy if (instead of their heterosexual pornography) society was full of pouting and seductive-looking men posing in revealing underwear in suggestive poses. Nor would men enjoy close ups of male genitals and unrealistic portrayals of male sexual performance. Women are expected to be immune to parallel images of their own sex. Some women find it offensive that women's breasts and vaginas are displayed so freely everywhere on the internet. It's certainly not an erotic turn-on for women.

Men need intercourse regardless of women's amenability, so they are naturally insensitive to the female perspective. A predator cannot afford to feel compassion for its prey. A carnivore only eats meat. Someone has to die. Male sex drive works similarly. A man cannot afford to empathise with women's perspective. Otherwise he would lose out on sexual opportunities and the human race might die out. A man depends on intercourse to release sexual tension so his devotion is selfish. Women tell men all the time, both verbally and by the way they behave, that they do not want sex as often as men do. But men don't take any notice. This is how men must be, to fulfil their sexual role. It doesn't make men bad people but it isn't right either.

Consequently, a man is offended by sexual rejection regardless of any logic. Even if a woman has recently given birth, a man cannot accept that having a penis thrusting into the birth canal, could not possibly be pleasurable. A woman needs at least six weeks to recover from childbirth (longer if she had a Caesarean). Medical staff should support women by explaining the trauma of giving birth and recommending an abstinence from sex in the early days after childbirth. A woman is often coerced into offering intercourse simply because she empathises with a man's apparent emotional need. Yet men appear incapable of empathising with women's physical pain or discomfort.

A man's desire to display his erect penis is usually limited to a partner. Most men learn that women dislike explicitly sexual phenomena. Men hide signs of their sex drive from women to avoid the embarrassment of women's disgust. Most men prefer to be accepted by a woman in order to enjoy the best sexual pleasure and release. A few men enjoy pressing their erection against women in a crowded place or flashing their genitals to women in public. Women's expressions of rejection are natural given that intercourse (from the perspective of the basic animal instinct) originates from a male assault. Pornography also portrays women shrieking or screaming, which can confuse some younger men who may assume that such behaviour reflects how real women experience arousal. Whether men heckle, flash or assault women, they seem satisfied with women's reactions of disgust, anger or embarrassment. It does not deter them. A man is simply after a response.

Overall, men were more likely than women to be sexually active, report a good quality sex life, and be interested in sex. (Lindau and Gavrilova)

Ego means men overlook what women contribute

Prostitutes must have more sexual experience than even the most promiscuous of men. But a prostitute is never called a great lover. Men attribute all the skill and the effort of intercourse to themselves rather than to a woman. Men assume that women are merely the ungrateful recipients of the amazing sexual pleasure that men work so hard to deliver. Men's arousal and their sex drive causes them to focus on their own performance.

By offering her body to a man to ejaculate into, a woman can guarantee that he will have an orgasm. Yet a man never thanks a woman for giving him an orgasm. The man is the active partner in intercourse, so it is assumed that he makes his own orgasm as well as giving a woman an orgasm from the same activity. Men want to believe that they are doing something to a woman that causes her to respond in some way. But the origin of this expected response is based on an assault scenario rather than consensual intercourse. This is one of the key misunderstandings about the role of intercourse and specifically women's erotic response to intercourse rather than having to use conscious behaviours to produce the effect that men crave. This is the taboo and deceit of sex, which pressures women into faking to reassure men's ego.

Men are convinced that they provide women with amazing pleasure. Women say nothing. It's a waste of time telling men how women feel because men simply don't understand. In reality, sex involves women making effort for men's sake. Women are told that they should enjoy providing men with sexual pleasure and the emotional reassurance that he needs. But this duty can never be acknowledged because a man is offended.

The key problem with men thinking that women obtain a similar pleasure from sex is that they fail to engage on the romantic factors that women need to feel amenable to intercourse. Men think that they can behave however they want and still get the intercourse they want. Sex is a male pleasure. A woman is more likely to offer a man sex when she gets the emotional rewards from the relationship that she wants (based on affectionate companionship).

For a woman, any sexual activity with a lover (especially penetrative sex) is the most intimate act anyone can engage in. She feels vulnerable and it takes a great deal of trust. Offering her body to a lover can be slightly humiliating for a woman (and incredibly boring) because of her full consciousness of her situation (without erotic arousal). Sex for a woman is an invasion of privacy, messy, slightly disgusting, tedious, uncomfortable, embarrassing and mortifying. This is the power of a woman's love that enables a woman to overcome these instinctive feelings. Men seem to think that no matter how they behave that a woman should always offer sex, as if it's male right. A woman doesn't feel loved by this scenario. She feels used for male pleasure.

Even very pleasant men have a way of asserting their will and they often expect a woman to agree with them. Many women simply can't be bothered to fight all the time. But men need to be aware that such behaviour makes it very unlikely that the relationship will ever be communicative. The best sex is enjoyed over the longer term when a couple develops honest and open forms of communication. This can only be done if both lovers have a degree of flexibility in attitude and a willingness to accept a lover's point of view.

A woman's cooperation with intercourse can be much more constructive than mere passivity. She may contribute to male gratification by offering additional stimulation or turn-ons such as implying a response. These behaviours benefit women because men tend to be generous to women who please them sexually. A woman accepts the risks of intercourse to give pleasure to a man she loves or to incentivise him to pay the family bills.

Although men may admire a woman who presents herself attractively, they rarely acknowledge the conscious effort she makes to play along with male fantasies and to respond lovingly and erotically to intercourse. A man sees his own role as core to intercourse. He assumes that a woman obtains an equal pleasure from intercourse or if not, that she should. Women cannot help being unaroused any more than men can help being regularly aroused.

If a woman wants children, it obviously makes sense to have the support of the father. But even without children, a woman wants to enjoy the companionship of a man who is an interesting companion and who cares about her. Having a relationship with a man involves offering regular intercourse. A man will not be loyal without regular sex. This is still true today and explains why women feel obliged to provide the sex men need.

Men travel away from home for weeks at a time without complaining about the lack of sex. It is only when they have a partner available that men expect sex on a regular basis. Many women feel pressure to keep those they love happy. Some women have a strong sense of emotional (caring) obligation to provide the intercourse a man needs, regardless of their own personal happiness. Over time, men come to think of sex as a relationship right. The message for women is: don't be so soft. Expect more in return from a man.

Men subsidise a woman's lifestyle in return for obtaining regular intercourse. Most men are happy to do this, seeing their ability to provide for a woman and a family as key to their own sexuality. Their earning ability gives men control in relationships. But men's need for regular intercourse gives women control. These two factors balance each other in a rewarding relationship.

So what turns her on? ... A man who makes her feel 'safe' and treats her like she is a vital part of his very existence, and not just a favourite sperm dumpsite. (Yangki Akiteng)

Women do not need to be like men to be valid

Sex educators think women need to be educated about masturbation and the clitoris. Yet no man ever needs to be told about masturbation and the penis. No one considers that this behaviour (of not masturbating) might be quite normal for women. We do not orgasm because we are given information. A responsive woman does not need to be told about the clitoris. She discovers it naturally by herself as a result of mental arousal. If a woman is unaware of her clitoris, it is because she has never experienced erotic arousal and consequently has never discovered how to masturbate to orgasm. This is evidently the case for the vast majority of women worldwide.

Sex educators tell girls that they will orgasm just by stimulating their genitals. They obviously don't appreciate that orgasm results from enjoying erotic turn-ons. Arousal depends on a person's mind being able to respond to erotic stimuli. Mental arousal causes tumescence of the phallus (penis or clitoris), which motivates us to supply the correct stimulation instinctively. The clitoris was not discovered by heterosexuals. It was identified by scientists who observed that women masturbate by stimulating the internal clitoral organ (by rubbing over the glans and either side of the labia). Despite all the publicity, heterosexuals continue to show little interest in the clitoris.

By providing incorrect information about the clitoris, women spread sexual ignorance about women's ability to orgasm, especially with a lover. It is a misguided to think that promoting the clitoris will make any difference to any woman who does not already appreciate its role. The only impact will be that some men who hope to pleasure a female lover may explore oral or manual stimulation of the clitoral glans (if a woman allows him to). It is also wrong to imply that stimulation of the clitoral glans (which is what they are referring to when they talk of the clitoris) provides amazing erotic pleasure.

Men pressure women to maximise their sexual opportunities, which is understandable given their sex drive. Female sex educators patronise other women out of ignorance and the desire to make money, which is much less forgivable. There is no 'should' about sexual pleasure. When it is suggested that young women should be encouraged to enjoy sexual pleasure, the idea is strongly opposed by many mothers. Mothers know from experience that women do not obtain the same pleasure from sex that men do. Mothers don't want their daughters to get pregnant while providing male gratification.

The evidence for female responsiveness comes, not from one woman's orgasm claims, but from the behaviour of women in the general population. A few women boast about orgasm because they like the attention. They enjoy feeling superior by intimidating other women. Advice is given on the basis of theory rather than personal experience. Personal confidence comes from knowing the facts; not from putting on a show of false bravado. They can't explain anything in the real world with confidence. Telling women that they should be able to do something, that they are clearly incapable of, undermines women's self-confidence. Sex educators reflect the male view of sex, by implying that women should respond as men do. They promote pornography and swinging, for example, as if women experience arousal as men do. This makes it even more difficult, than it would be if such misinformation did not exist, for men to understand why a woman would ever object to sex. A man assumes that his partner is unusual. Women who promote sexual fantasies make us all feel isolated in our sexual experiences.

Unresponsive women defend their right to define orgasm any way they want. They believe this empowers them in some way. They give no thought to the women who are made to feel inadequate by these orgasm claims. When a woman admits a lack of orgasm, she is told to find another man. It's as if we are telling girls they should approach life as an endless quest for a man who can 'make them orgasm'. There is little concern voiced over the risks of pregnancy, sexual disease and the emotional upset that go with promiscuity. There is a view that adults only ever engage in sexual activity that ends with their own orgasm. The idea that women enjoy giving pleasure (typically when there is an emotional connection) doesn't appeal. It's not macho enough.

Feminist educators tell young women that they should be less intent on pleasing men. Just exactly what does everyone think women have been doing since the dawn of time? Girls are advised to be sexually daring and self-confident. This sends contradictory messages to girls. Are they supposed to be promiscuous or should they aspire to a mutually caring relationship? Pornography and erotic fiction give young women the impression that they are supposed to enjoy activities like oral sex. Some girls feel pressured into offering fellatio and are coerced into anal sex. Men enjoy these genital techniques and they hope (in their fantasies) that women will provide them.

Women think they will be respected for claiming to be the same as men. We are respected for being honest and having the courage to stand up to others. Women need to educate men. Women have different emotional responses and life goals. Women are good enough as they are. We will never be able to protect girls, if we are not honest about what they can expect from sex. Women on the internet are not looking for erotic turn-ons (such as images of male nudity) or opportunities to enjoy orgasm. Girls need to appreciate this. Any woman who wants intercourse, can find it easily enough. Women only advertise because they are trying to make money out of men.

And yet, too many folks choke on the fact of innate gender differences in libido. Feminists equate a lower sex drive with inferiority. Feminism equates a vigorous libido with a healthy, even dominant ego. (Joan Sewell)

Women drive the need for dating and romance

Without sex, there may be friendship between adults but there is little physical intimacy. Heterosexual women are dependent on men to provide this sense of connection with another adult. Platonic love is caring and affectionate. Sexual love (or reciprocating sexual love) can be more intensely emotional in the beginning. Women experience this emotional reward initially from a man's evident but typically unspoken post-coital gratitude.

A woman is not amenable to intercourse on first meeting a man. Her amenability grows as she gains confidence that a man's devotion may last beyond a one-off opportunity for intercourse. Women indicate their amenability by accepting male advances and by not contradicting male fantasies. A woman likes having a man's attention. A woman expects a man to show her the same respect he shows his boss. She hopes he will want to impress her as much as he wants to impress his colleagues. She hopes he will be as motivated to spend time with her as he does with his male friends.

In a new relationship a woman enjoys the novelty of being admired through sex. Women naturally respond with affection (hugging and kissing) when they love someone. A woman in love enjoys the emotional sensations of dancing with a lover. But men are easily aroused when in close physical contact with an attractive partner. The intense sensations of their arousal prevent men from appreciating these more platonic aspects of attraction.

A mother responds to her child's need for her by developing an emotional attachment. This motivates her to care for the child. Men do not experience the same bonding mechanism. A woman responds to a man's devotion (based on his sexual needs) in a similar way. A woman feels loved because of the pleasure a man enjoys from her body. These emotions are not sexual (involving arousal and orgasm) but they are just as vital to a woman feeling emotionally connected to a lover as the sexual emotions that a man feels.

It would be strange indeed if the negative aspects of sex that men never (or rarely) experience had no impact on how women view sex: the trade in child brides and sex slaves, abortion, prostitution, sexual assault and rape. If women are assumed to enjoy the same pleasure from sex that men do, nothing makes sense. Women are just as keen on romance and marriage as they ever were, despite their supposed sexual liberation. Yet men have never needed emotional factors to enjoy their sex lives. The issue of consent is a nonsense if we say both sexes want the same thing. It's as if the world has gone mad in a drive to promote sexual equality regardless of common sense.

Men judge women primarily on their attractiveness and amenability to intercourse. Women cannot base their relationships with the opposite sex purely on sexual criteria as men can. So they must be less sexually driven.

Women have to be much more careful about assessing a partner's character. Unless she is trading sex for money, most women need some lead-in to sex. It is not just a question of attraction. Women need to feel safe so that they can trust a man enough to be intimate. This is because there are some very dangerous men who prey on women. Some men will attack, rape and even kill a woman. Men don't have this contradiction in their dealings with women. In order to survive, women must be more socially mature than men. Women take longer than men to choose a lover because they hope for more than good looks. Men need an attractive lover who is amenable to regular intercourse but women hope for a decent, caring and companionable lover.

The secret of male courage is to act and not think too much, otherwise doubt and fear set in. It doesn't help men be good defenders, if they are always empathising with the enemy. However this instinct doesn't help men when it comes to their relationships with women. A woman wants to understand a man's motivations, his values and morals. This is self-defence. A woman wants a lover who is loving, interesting and has a sense of humour. Throughout a relationship a woman needs a man to communicate his motivations so that she can trust that he doesn't take advantage of her love.

Most women need to feel an emotional connection before sex feels appropriate. This emotional connection arises when a woman is attracted to a man who she can see is motivated to care for her. Women do not experience sexual arousal as men do. They have a different mechanism that generates a sense of intimacy. Women are attracted to men who take an interest in them. This is not a conscious trade. It is a subconscious response to feeling admired, which reassures a woman that a man will protect her.

A man's interest in a woman arises primarily from his sex drive, at least in the first instance. Young women may assume that male admiration is evidence of a man's eternal love. This is not always true. A more astute or experienced woman may delay showing her approval to find out if a man's intentions are for the longer term. Men seem to value sex more if they have to work for it. It seems as if sex that is obtained after a struggle feels more like a conquest to a man than if a woman just lays herself out before him.

A woman looks for the attention and caring behaviours in a man that she hopes reflect his dedicated sexual devotion to her. She accepts compliments silently. She is not gushing with gratitude because she knows that a man enjoys the arousal he obtains from her body. She reserves her gratitude for the times when she wants something from him. The test of a man's devotion is his amenability to providing the things that she wants from the relationship.

Tell her she's important to you. For a woman to feel the desire for sex, she needs to feel loved, adored and significant. (Allan and Barbara Pease)

The romantic pleasure a woman enjoys from sex

In modern times we talk of sexual partners but in the past, heterosexuals more often talked of lovers. Women do not think of sex in terms of the erotic turn-ons and genital stimulation as men do. Women think of sex in terms of a man's sexual passion in romantic scenarios. A man's desire is communicated in his sense of purpose, the firmness of his kiss and his touch on her body. His desire to penetrate her body is very evident. Intercourse is an act of carnal desire that satisfies a man's sexual needs. It becomes an act of love when a man takes a woman's emotional needs into consideration. When a man shows his admiration for a woman by sensual caressing and kissing as a demonstration of his affection, intercourse becomes a lovemaking act. But this all relies on a woman accepting a man as her lover.

Sex acts like a barometer in relationships because, if a woman feels loved and appreciated, she may offer a man the sex he needs. A woman has emotional needs just as a man does. But these emotional needs are not met through orgasm. Some women define their emotional needs in terms of orgasm because this is how men relate to intimacy. Women try to express the sense of connection they feel from sex. This is an attempt to be taken seriously by men who define all adult intimacy in terms of sexual responses.

A woman allows a man to make love to her. She has a choice so it's not about being dominated. It's about allowing, inviting and welcoming. This emotional reward is much stronger than simply going along with what a man wants. A woman can enjoy a sense of longing, wanting to be loved, enjoying being desired sexually. She wants to matter to him so that he will care for her. She lets him penetrate her body for his own physical gratification. An affectionate female lover enjoys giving pleasure when a man pleases her in other ways. Her reward is his gratitude for sexual release. Men show this gratitude by subsidising a woman's lifestyle and pleasing her in other ways.

Men are driven by their sexual responsiveness. A man is attracted to someone who arouses him sexually. A woman falls in love or she comes to love a man, if he is devoted to her. But a woman's platonic love does not mean that a man will return her love. If a woman is attracted to a man, she can only hope and dream. Romance involves passive anticipation that has no appeal for men. Women enjoy romance and the poignant emotions a woman feels when she discovers that a man, she loves, reciprocates her love.

A man's emotional reward is the sexual pleasure he enjoys with a lover. A woman's emotional reward is the male devotion that results from providing a man with the sexual release he needs. When a woman is attracted to a man she admires, she is flattered that he wants intercourse with her. She feels emotionally exhilarated by the idea that he is aroused by her body. She accepts that this male devotion includes a desire to engage in intercourse.

When a man is attracted to a woman, he assumes that she has exactly the same responses that men do. He doesn't appreciate that women have quite different emotional responses. This may be because the male sex drive causes men to convince themselves of a partner's amenability or because men objectify people who arouse them. Men fail to appreciate that women want a relationship and not sex (directly). Equally women fail to appreciate that male sex drive means men have very different sensations to women's platonic (not involving genital arousal), romantic and emotional responses.

When a woman is affectionate with a man, he interprets this as a desire for sexual intimacy. This is because he is aroused by her physical proximity and he assumes that she responds sexually in the same way. But her demonstration of affection is purely platonic and is not sexually motivated. This is why many women stop being affectionate over time because they learn that men interpret any demonstration of affection as a lead-in to sex.

When a man dedicates time to showing an interest in a woman and demonstrating that he cares for her (beyond sex), a woman may be motivated to demonstrate her affection. A woman ideally hopes for a loving partner to enjoy sharing affection and intimate communication. She enjoys the emotional reassurance of having a lover's support and protection. She takes pride in his achievements and enjoys the reflected glory from his success.

In the early days of a romance, sex is only a small part of the quality time a couple spends together. Men may be devoted in a new relationship but after years together, the novelty wears off. Men tend to become engrossed in their daily pursuits over time and sex is taken for granted. In the past, women were tied into relationships because of their dependence on men for support. Men have been slow to encourage women in the workplace, in part, for this reason. In modern times, women look elsewhere for the emotional love they want. They turn to their children, to friends or to a new, more devoted lover.

Genital stimulation is important to men but it has little emotional value for women due to their lack of erotic arousal. Given sexual pleasuring involves women passively accepting what men offer then, in truth, men's efforts to arouse women are just about men trying to balance the rewards of sex in ways that appeal to them. True emotional rewards involve what we are motivated to ask for. Men need to listen to what women want, which rarely involves any kind of sexual contact. It more often involves relationship issues such as open communication, more honesty and genuine caring behaviours.

Women leave men, not because they are unhappy with what he can provide, but because they are emotionally unfulfilled. (Allan and Barbara Pease)

Platonic love is just as powerful as sexual love

When sexual performance is discussed, the sexual ego, bravado and general unpleasantness that is so often displayed is due to insecurities. Everyone wants to be admired, to be thought normal and preferably to be a good performer. But orgasm is a personal pleasure. It has nothing to do with providing pleasure for another person. Men are turned on by the idea of female arousal and orgasm because they need to feel that a woman appreciates and responds to their efforts during lovemaking. But achieving our own orgasm has nothing to do with the effort we need to make to please a lover. These are two quite separate things. A woman can easily please a man through sex but a man needs to demonstrate that he cares for a woman.

Men are attracted to people whose bodies arouse them. They need to ejaculate through penetrative sex to obtain the physical gratification that may give them a sense of intimacy with another person. So men promote sexual love. They think that love between adults should always be sexually motivated because that's how they experience it. Yet many men disrespect the women they have sex with. Other men use sex to humiliate others. Men treat women like sex objects by refusing to take them seriously at work. In the extreme, a few violent men even assault women and cause serious injury or death in their selfish pursuit of the territorial conquest of intercourse.

Sexual love arises from the gratitude a man may feel when he enjoys physical gratification with a lover. Sexual love involves a man focusing on his own pleasure rather than responding to a lover's needs. This kind of love only lasts as long as a man is enjoying regular sex. So sexual love is not as long-lasting as platonic love that is based solely on affection. Women do not have an arousal cycle. Nor do women experience sexual frustration or a need to engage in intercourse or any other sexual activity. Women do not need to achieve orgasm with a lover, in order to make an emotional connection.

Men assume platonic love is inferior for being sexless. They think that an unresponsive person might as well be dead. If a man spends time on romantic dinners or money on gifts, he no doubt appreciates that his efforts are not going to help arouse a woman. A woman appreciates these things because they are indications that a man cares about her welfare. This is the kind of platonic love (companionable and affectionate) that women value.

A woman sees a man foremost as a social person. Women do not love men for their sexual attributes. Women love men who they can rely on for moral and practical support. Women feel cared for because of the sexual love that men have for them. But this doesn't make women's love sexual. Women can enjoy feeling needed, admired and desired. Women can also enjoy pleasing a male lover by offering him regular sexual release through intercourse.

For women, the sense of emotional connection, the loving emotions and caring about someone else are achieved differently. For women, sex is not about functional biology but about caring feelings and emotional connection. Women can be more relaxed about enjoying sexual contact than men because sexual activity is less functional and needy. Lesbians are likely to benefit most from this female approach to sensual and emotional pleasuring.

Given their lack of arousal with a lover, sex is meaningless to women as an erotic activity. Women focus on platonic love, which relies on emotional intimacy that builds up over time by a person being consistently caring. Platonic love is about affectionate companionship and showing consideration for a lover. Women's ability to care for a partner means that relationships involving women (heterosexual and lesbian) last much longer than relationships involving only men (male homosexual relationships), which focus on erotic pleasure, impromptu scenarios and a variety of lovers.

Women alone have little reason to embark on intimate relationships with other adults. Male sex drive is the trigger that initiates most adult sexual relationships. This may explain why lesbians often delay starting sexual relationships. If women behaved like men, adult relationships would be much shorter than they are. Women's willingness to offer intercourse cements the relationships that men initiate for sexual reasons. Women's desire for affectionate companionship allows heterosexual and lesbian relationships to endure beyond the initial passion and novelty of casual sex.

Women's emotional bonding mechanism must be sufficiently enduring to motivate them to care for children over decades. This bonding mechanism stems from women's nurturing instincts and has nothing to do with sexual rewards. The same instincts motivate women to provide what a male lover needs. Men's emotional bonding mechanism is much weaker, allowing them to leave the family to pursue their own interests. Men love their children but very few men devote their whole lives to raising them. The opportunity to engage in intercourse is a key factor in motivating a man to return home.

Women get emotional payback in other (non-sexual) ways. Women obtain emotional rewards from demonstrating affection and by caring for a lover. Men never experience these significant emotions, which is a loss they cannot appreciate. As with responsiveness, we only know what we experience personally. Women experience a nurturing love. Women want to share their lives with a companion who is interesting to be with and who is interested in them. Women see love as being about giving not taking. Women are motivated by their nurturing instincts and the opportunity to care for others.

Sex is only one way in which people give and receive love, so although it is very important, it is not the only way to develop or express intimacy. (Jonathan Lenbuck)

Topic: Vaginal intercourse

Intercourse is an act of mating and impregnation

Sexuality is about the act of mating. Humans do not have sex simply in order to reproduce. We also have sex to enjoy pleasure (recreation) and intimacy, which creates the emotional bonding that keeps couples committed to each other over the years needed to support a family (deferred reproduction).

For most animals, a male fertilises a female by making a quick insertion. Only mammals employ an extended thrusting technique. There is no obvious advantage to the extra time male mammals take to mate. This inefficiency is no doubt due to the pleasure the male obtains from thrusting and possibly also to the increase in the human brain's imaginative capacities.

Intercourse refers to interaction between two or more people e.g. social intercourse. To have sexual intercourse means to engage in sexual activity with a lover (as opposed to masturbatory activity alone). Both 'to have sex' and 'to have sexual intercourse' often refer to vaginal intercourse. To avoid any confusion, the more specific term 'coitus' may be used for intercourse.

Sexual activity that involves being the receiver of an erect penis (into the mouth, vagina or anus) is inherently more risky for the receiver. When a man inserts his erect penis into another person's orifice, he does not have his body invaded in the same way. Fellatio cannot be taken by force because of the threat of the receiver's teeth. But both vaginal and anal intercourse can be an act of violation because a person's anus or vagina is easily penetrated by an erect penis. The penetrating male has the pleasure of penetrating and ejaculating into an orifice. Anticipation of this pleasure (that women can never experience) is what we call male sex drive. For the receiver, any form of penetration involves providing rather than receiving pleasure.

We can differentiate between three distinct categories of sexual activity. First there are **manual contacts** where we use our hands (or fingers) to stimulate (massage) the sex organ (called masturbation). Masturbation can be used with a lover but less commonly to the point of orgasm. Any activity short of intercourse used to be called petting and was popular in the days before the availability of reliable contraception. A man's optimal sexual release is obtained through thrusting to ejaculation, so intercourse typically concludes heterosexual activity. Some men enjoy extending their arousal by engaging in non-coital activities prior to intercourse. Hence the term: foreplay.

Secondly there are **oral contacts** where we use our mouth or tongue to kiss or stimulate (by licking, sucking or kissing) the sex organ (called oral sex) or other parts of the body. Oral sex performed on a man (called fellatio) is much more common than oral sex performed on a woman (called cunnilingus). Cunnilingus is associated with lesbians and pornography.

Thirdly there are **genital contacts** where a man penetrates a lover's body (called intercourse or penetrative sex) with an erect penis. Vaginal intercourse involves a man's erect penis penetrating a woman's vagina. Heterosexuals and, more commonly, homosexual men also engage in anal intercourse (also called anal sex) where an erect penis penetrates a lover's anus. Anyone may use a dildo or vibrator to penetrate a lover's vagina or anus. Women can use a strap-on dildo to penetrate a lover (called pegging).

In the presence of an attractive potential partner, men accumulate sexual tension as a result of constant arousal. This pressure can be released by masturbation but ultimately relies on penetrative sex. Intercourse is an act that requires the penetrating male to be aroused (erect) but not the receiver. If women were consciously aroused (as men are) they would focus on the clitoris. This would work against reproduction, which relies on a penis ejaculating into a vagina. For this reason women are not aroused as men are.

We can differentiate between three approaches to intercourse. The vast majority of intercourse is defined by a man's sex drive. A man holds his erect penis between his lover's legs to find the entrance to her vagina. The man then thrusts rhythmically into her vagina as the woman kisses or caresses him allowing him the time he needs to ejaculate. Vaginal intercourse provides women with almost no physical stimulation or erotic arousal. Women offer intercourse to a lover because it involves them in very little explicit sexual activity and because they know that it is expected. Compared with foreplay, vaginal intercourse involves a woman in much less effort. A woman only needs to allow a man to penetrate her vagina and thrust until ejaculation.

Secondly there is intercourse that is preceded by foreplay. Foreplay is primarily provided by the man. Research indicates that men with a creative imagination tend to enjoy eroticism, fantasy, masturbation and foreplay more than others. Men's enjoyment of eroticism (male turn-ons) may be the result of having an active creative imagination. Other men (especially when young) prefer to get straight to intercourse rather than spend time on erotic turn-ons. Eroticism is defined by male turn-ons that fall short of coitus itself.

Thirdly there is fantasy-style sex as portrayed in erotic fiction that is characterised by the proactive role of the woman. The woman initiates sexual activity, encourages the man to stimulate her and provides facial expressions and vocals that assist with male orgasm. Some women feel obligated to provide at least some of this performance for a lover either because they think it is expected or because they want a more proactive role.

It is the constant complaint of married females that their husbands are ... primarily concerned with genital stimulation ... It is the constant complaint of the married male that his wife ... does not tactilely stimulate his genitalia. (Alfred Kinsey)

Sex drive: a need to ejaculate through intercourse

Male sex drive arises from the build-up of sexual tension (through regular arousal). Men may be able to relieve tension to a degree by masturbating. But ultimately intercourse provides the most satisfying way for men to release their sexual emotions. This is a natural consequence of our reproductive biology. There is no point in men having erections unless they are also motivated to impregnate women. A man engages in intercourse in response to an instinctive urge but his mind focuses on the pleasure of penetration. If a man has a lover, he is likely to be more acutely aware of sexual frustration in his partner's presence, when intercourse is not available, because he anticipates both the pleasure of thrusting and obtaining release.

For someone to have a sex drive there must be a trigger that generates an urge to engage in intercourse. Sex is natural for a man because the urge to engage in intercourse comes from his own body. Successful reproduction relies on the penis being an external erectile organ. Most men must also be motivated to penetrate a vagina (rather than an anus). Finally men must be aroused primarily by fertile women (who are capable of being impregnated).

A man is incentivised to engage in intercourse because of his erection (his arousal is triggered by the presence of a partner). He is motivated to enjoy the erotic pleasure of penetrating and thrusting into a lover's body. He has a territorial instinct to deposit semen inside a body orifice (the vagina). Women cannot have the same urge by definition. They do not have an erect organ to penetrate with. The clitoris is only ever tumescent (rather than rigid) and is largely an internal organ. So women never experience an urge to penetrate another person's body with an aroused sex organ. Nor are they aroused by such opportunities. So women have no comparable experience.

A sex drive involves a motivation to initiate intercourse. Men's motivation is based on the male mating act we see in Nature. Penetrative sex completes a man's arousal cycle (from erection to ejaculation) in a way that maximises the satisfaction a man obtains. Men enjoy the pleasure of penetrating a lover and the sexual release of orgasm. Intercourse involves much more risk for women and, very importantly, it has absolutely nothing to do with female orgasm. Firstly, the vagina is the wrong anatomy. Secondly, if stimulation is intended to cause orgasm then it must continue until orgasm is reached. But the stimulation of intercourse only lasts as long as a man can keep thrusting.

There are many triggers that cause male arousal throughout the day. This constant rearousal causes intense sexual frustration for many men if they have no opportunity to release sexual tension by ejaculating through intercourse. If women had a sex drive then they would also suffer all the difficulties and discrimination that men do. They would be persecuted for acting on their sexual instincts. We would see women charged with sexual abuse and assault in the same numbers as men. We would see women heckling men in the street and constantly hassling a lover for penetrative sex.

Some women do experience a residual thrusting instinct. When little girls engage in masturbatory activity, they lie face down with their hands between their legs and thrust with their hips. This is the instinctive mammalian thrusting action that we see when a male dog dry-humps. But there is a difference. The male dog is responding to a reproductive urge to ejaculate into a female. We can say that his behaviour is focused. If he had the opportunity, he would engage in the mating act for real. A girl can never have this opportunity. A girl's behaviour is a subconscious reflex that is a hangover from how our anatomy evolved. Her behaviour is unfocused. She cannot penetrate anyone so she can never be the penetrator in the mating act. Little girls do not orgasm because female orgasm relies on using adult fantasies.

The suggestion that a woman can ask a man for a massage instead of intercourse or that a woman can end intercourse when she tires of it are evidence of women's ignorance over male sex drive. Women are pressured into sex (or raped) because they don't understand the strength of men's sex drive. Male sex drive is a biological instinct not based on logical thinking. A drive is an irrepressible urge to achieve penetration regardless of the challenges or consequences and with no concern for others. To women this seems immoral because they have no comparable experience. A man's sexuality is selfish because of his need for sexual release. This is how males have evolved. Men's enjoyment of erotic stimuli defines their quality of life.

Women think that a sex drive is just about saying that sex is wonderful. Men don't contradict this belief promoted by some women (those who are selling sex or enjoying the attention they get) because men like to support any evidence that might indicate women are just as sexually willing as men are.

Women need to understand that male sex drive is an urgent sexual need. And men need to understand that for women it isn't. Understanding that women don't have a sex drive is valuable for men. Men can free themselves from feeling inadequate about their inability to arouse a woman. Women are naturally emotional rather than sexual. No matter how hard a man tries he is never going to please her sexually in the way that she can please him.

If a man is truly intent on rewarding a woman for the pleasure she allows him to enjoy from her body, he should give some thought to the non-sexual activity and caring behaviours that he could provide in order to please her.

The fact is - and it's a big one - across every culture and every eon it's been shown in myriad ways that women are far less sexually driven than men. (Joan Sewell)

How we know that women do not have a sex drive

Women's dislike of eroticism means that men learn to keep their responses to themselves. Men's embarrassment over communicating their sexual needs (due to the disgust women express over sexual urges) contributes to the confusion over female sexuality. Women can claim to have a sex drive because men never explain in explicit and graphic detail what it means to have a sex drive. Women gain the impression that a sex drive is just a nice feeling. So while male sex drive is associated with explicit and crude (in women's eyes) erotic turn-ons, the equivalent female phenomenon, called libido, has a much softer and emotional image. Women need to feel in the right mood to offer a partner sex. This behaviour relies on women's emotional amenability. It has nothing in common with the male sex drive.

A drive involves both positive and negative emotions. It is also difficult to ignore. This is the biological imperative. It is triggered by physical proximity or virtual images of an attractive potential partner. Negative feelings arise from the sexual frustration that arises when the need cannot be satisfied by intercourse. If we want something badly enough, we can convince ourselves of anything. Although men typically initiate sexual activity, they still convince themselves that women want sex. Women are blamed for encouraging men because their bodies provide a pleasure that men want. It is difficult for women to understand because there is nothing they need that badly. We all need air to breath, water and food but none of these depend on another person. Women have only recently been free to move about society because of modern laws that protect them against assault. This freedom of movement is a right for any woman in a civilised society. But that does not mean she has the right to roam about half-dressed without ever encountering difficulty.

In society, men are obliged to contain their sexual urges. But when law and order disappear, some men are willing to take their pleasure by force. This is called sexual assault and rape. But a woman cannot force a man to provide intercourse. No one can evolve a need that they cannot satisfy reliably. We only have a drive to engage in activity that we can control. A person must be able to respond to a drive by obtaining what they need to satisfy it. The idea that women need a loving partner to enjoy sex, is evidence that women look for emotional rather than erotic rewards. Some men like to imagine that women obtain gratification from sex because it helps with their own arousal.

Men assault women, they suffer sexual frustration and they are proactive lovers (motivated to obtain their own sexual release). Men don't do these things on a whim. Men do them because they experience a strong biological drive to engage in intercourse with a degree of urgency that cannot be ignored. Women do none of these things because they lack a sex drive. The fact that the contraceptive pill has increased women's sexual amenability is evidence that men and women are different. Men have always had a sex drive regardless of the availability of reliable contraception. The survival of the human race has depended on the persistency of men's need for intercourse. The timidity of most young women is incompatible with having a sex drive.

An activity that relies entirely on male motivation does not equate to a woman having a sex drive. The only attractive force is from the mind of an aroused man towards a vagina as a repository for his semen. A man's mental arousal causes increases blood to flow to his penis. A man is highly conscious of his penis because of the acute sensations of having an erection. The clitoris is never erect, which is why few women have any interest in the clitoris. Female arousal is subconscious. The vagina is only ever stimulated when a man thrusts into it. Once he has an erection, a man is typically motivated to penetrate another person. A man admires a woman's buttocks because of his desire to penetrate her vagina. A woman never experiences an urge that causes her to focus on a man's pelvic region. A woman is not motivated by any physiological stimulus to engage in sexual activity of any kind even alone.

No one can have a drive to be penetrated by a penis or any other object. Neither can we have a biological drive for someone else to do something to us. A heterosexual man has a drive to ejaculate into a woman's vagina. But a woman cannot have a biological drive for a man to ejaculate into her vagina. If women had a drive to be penetrated by an erect penis, we would see them running around eager to impale themselves on the first erect penis they saw. Women don't do this. Instead, they are inclined to run in the opposite direction if they see an erect penis. Intercourse with an unknown lover not only involves a risk of pregnancy but also provides no emotional rewards.

A man is aroused when he wants to engage in penetrative sex, which is when he has an erection. So men assume that if a woman is willing to engage in intercourse, she must be equally aroused. Women don't have erections. Having an orifice to offer a lover has nothing to do with arousal. Anyone can provide a mouth, a vagina (women only) or an anus for a male partner to penetrate. These orifices are not sex organs. No matter what kind of stimulation or for how long it is applied, the receiver will not have an orgasm.

Many men travel away from home for extensive periods. They never give a thought to their partner's needs in their absence. Women's needs are for affection and companionship, which they obtain from others. Most women are happy to look after their children. But if the wider relationship with their partner has broken down (emotional intimacy has been lost) some women may look for another lover to obtain the emotional rewards of feeling loved.

When I hear sexperts on TV give advice about how to help women with their "dysfunctional sex drives" I get suspicious that we're all feeding into the convenient male fantasy of the sexually voracious woman. (Joan Sewell)

Intercourse is totally defined by male responses

Men have much more confidence over sexual matters than women because sex revolves around male responses. A man's arousal motivates him to initiate sexual activity. His desire for penetration ensures that he wants to obtain sexual opportunities with a partner. His erection makes penetrative sex possible. But his orgasm ends his interest in engaging in further activity.

When a man wants to ingratiate himself with a woman, he buys her flowers. At some level, men seem to accept that women look for emotional rewards from relationships. He may even buy her a sexy nightdress as a hint that he would like to see her wearing it. He does not display himself in provocative underwear as an erotic turn-on. If a woman buys sexy underwear for a man, it is a hint that he should improve his clothing style not a hint that she wants to play with what's inside the underwear. Yet a man assumes that a woman has sex because she is aroused to the point of orgasm. A woman offers sex when she loves a male partner but, at the same time, she knows it's expected.

We can differentiate between a person's physical capability to participate in sexual activity and their emotional amenability. A man's physical capability to engage in intercourse depends on his ability to obtain an erection. This occurs as a result of his mental response to erotic phenomena such as sexual opportunities or nudity of an attractive partner. Even if a man reaches orgasm by other means, such as oral sex or masturbation, an erection is still required. This is because mental arousal always precedes orgasm. But a woman can always participate in intercourse (even if she is unwilling). The only variable is her emotional amenability (which depends on a relationship).

Intercourse provides the psychological arousal and the physical stimulation that a man needs for orgasm. Men's speed-to-orgasm depends on the familiarity of the situation and behaviour of their partner including any turn-ons they may provide. Once aroused, any difficulties a man may have reaching orgasm may be due to a lack of enthusiasm from a female lover or because he lacks confidence with a stranger (for example with a prostitute).

Before we attempt orgasm, we need to appreciate how to achieve arousal. For a man, this usually occurs fairly spontaneously. A man's arousal causes his penis to become erect and makes penetration possible. Women are assumed to be aroused as men are by the prospect of intercourse. Heterosexual men always assume the role of penetrator and thereby obtain the penile stimulation. The penis is stimulated by penetrating and by thrusting into a lover's body. Most heterosexual men object to assuming the role of the receiver of (anal) intercourse. Intercourse stimulates a woman's reproductive anatomy rather than the anatomy that is equivalent to the penis.

Men's arousal cycle (from arousal to ejaculation) is most satisfactorily completed by engaging in intercourse. This makes a woman's role mandatory from the male perspective. A man cannot understand why a woman wouldn't want intercourse whenever he capable of providing it.

Intercourse could never provide both partners with an orgasm because the stimulation of intercourse only lasts as long as a man has an erection. The amount of stimulation (length of time) a person needs to orgasm depends on their mental state of arousal. A man cannot predict the timing of his orgasm any more than a woman can. Even if a woman could respond to intercourse as men hope, she would not be able to orgasm at the same time as her lover. Women never reach a point where they can no longer offer intercourse. An orifice can always be penetrated so it cannot be a sex organ.

When we say that a couple slept together, we mean that they had intercourse. The natural assumption is that if a man and a woman share a bed it is very likely that they had intercourse. This is because men are easily aroused just from the thought of a woman (possibly semi-naked) lying in close proximity to them. There is absolutely nothing a woman can do to make intercourse happen. Intercourse relies on a man having an erection. A woman's role is simply to arouse a man and cooperate with intercourse until he ejaculates.

The function of sexual activity with a lover is clearly penetration and reproduction. But only the male is capable of penetration. The traditional justification for marriage was to allow a couple to raise children and to minimise promiscuity (which leads to exploitation of women, unwanted pregnancies and sexual disease). Yet most men want sex much more frequently than is needed for reproduction. In order to have a family, couples only need to have intercourse a handful of times. Intercourse frequencies are determined by a man's sex drive. Ejaculating into a vagina has a special emotional significance for men. Intercourse completes a man's arousal cycle and gives him a sense of satisfaction and emotional well-being.

Women are shamed for being sexually unwilling and so causing men to look elsewhere. Yet some men are much more sexually demanding than others. A women's sexual reluctance depends on the state of the relationship, her own willingness to explore sex play and her partner's sensitivity to recognising her lower interest in sex. In our society, women's sexual amenability is typically assumed in direct conflict with the issue of consent.

Just as in the human animal, and even more often than in the man animal, petting among the other mammals is primarily, although not exclusively, male activity which is directed toward the female. As in the human species, it is the male which is more likely to be aroused psychologically and usually before he makes any physical contact. (Alfred Kinsey)

The receiver of intercourse need not be aroused

Alfred Kinsey concluded that female masturbation provided the most convincing evidence for female orgasm. Kinsey found that lesbians and responsive women had orgasms on average around once every 2 to 3 weeks. Even though they did not obtain the correct stimulation (of the clitoris), women who claimed to orgasm from intercourse reported higher orgasm frequencies. These correlated with the male partner's responsiveness, which caused Kinsey to question whether these women were truly having orgasms.

There are two distinct roles in penetrative sex: the penetrator is a man who penetrates (with an erect penis). Then there's the person being penetrated (the receiver). The receiver can be either male or female. Homosexual men engage in anal intercourse. The vast majority of heterosexual activity is based on intercourse that ends with male ejaculation. Intercourse relies on the male penetrator having an erection and the amenability of the receiver. Women's amenability to intercourse is a conscious behaviour and has nothing to do with responsiveness. The stimulation of an orifice (mouth, vagina or anus) does not result in orgasm for the receiver. If the penetrator uses a dildo, then they don't orgasm either (even this obvious fact is disputed by some women).

If a penetrating male loses his erection, a partner's disappointment is due to missing an opportunity to enjoy the sensual and emotional pleasures of being penetrated. The situation would be alleviated if the receiver was willing or able to offer alternative activity that focused on their own arousal and orgasm. But this may not be an option (especially for a woman) because the receiver is typically the less responsive partner. Anyone, who is willing, can offer an orifice and engage in penetrative sex as a receiver. Given it is always available, offering an orifice is unconnected with a person's state of arousal.

Anyone who offers penetrative sex to a lover is not aiming for their own orgasm. They are offering that opportunity to a lover. The receiver enjoys giving pleasure, of being the object of desire and the sensations of being penetrated (even though such sensations do not cause orgasm). Being penetrated is an intimate experience. There is considerable trust involved. An orifice can be penetrated by an erect penis even if a receiver is unwilling.

Ironically, despite the risk of pregnancy, women are inclined to accept intercourse over other sexual activity because it involves them in so little effort. Just as they prefer not to see genital action, women also prefer to remain largely oblivious to what is happening in their pelvic region. They also prefer vaginal intercourse over anal intercourse partly because there is no physical sensation. Women's lack of responsiveness makes anal sex a much less interesting prospect than for homosexual men. The possible pleasure of stimulation does not compensate a woman for the taboo and her hygiene concerns. Other reasons for women to avoid anal intercourse include the need for the couple to communicate, for the man to control his thrusting instincts and for a woman to reconcile her natural instincts to reject the practical realities of engaging in messy and explicit genital activity.

Men's responsiveness causes them to focus on exploring any stimulation that may be pleasurable with little regard for issues of personal hygiene. Homosexual men, being both givers and receivers of anal intercourse, are more likely to understand the need for a cautious approach. But also anal intercourse is expected between gay men and so needs little discussion. Even when heterosexual men do engage in anal intercourse, they may still prefer to ejaculate into the vagina. This is very natural given the male sex drive.

A woman's willingness to offer sexual pleasuring depends on:

- Her personality and the extent of her personal generosity;
- The quality of the wider relationship or other rewards that she obtains from the relationship; and
- Her level of sexual experience and whether she is informed about the techniques described in erotic fiction.

In other mammals, mating only occurs when the female is in oestrus because this is when she can be impregnated. Oestrus causes female animals (such as cows) to be more amenable to being mounted. Even quite unattractive women can offer intercourse as a means of enhancing their appeal to men.

Some women have a strong aversion to the idea of engaging in sexual activity of any kind. Some never experience the emotions that are generated when a woman falls in love. These emotions make a woman more amenable to offering intercourse. Women who never engage in intercourse cannot reproduce and so their genes do not contribute to future generations. This is how Nature ensures that women are amenable to intercourse. But women only need to be amenable a few times in a lifetime to be able to reproduce.

A woman is aware of her sexual obligations because of attitudes in the society around her. But there are also emotional pressures. A woman knows that she has to offer regular sex to keep a man interested in a relationship with her. Some women can acknowledge this consciously. Others simply respond to male demand. A woman learns that a man's behaviour and attitude towards her improves when he gets sex. When she offers sex, a man responds with affection. When she doesn't, he is moody and bad-tempered.

If you are a man whose partner is less interested in sex than you, start paying attention to your friendship. Many women are wired this way—they can't get turned on unless they feel close to you. (Michele Weiner-Davis)

Women are naturally sexually passive with a lover

Imagine a woman who responds like a man. She is highly aroused from the start. She strips her lover naked to see his genitals. She caresses and kisses her lover's body from head to toe. She makes love to his penis and provides amazing oral sex. Where would the human race be now if women behaved like this? Most men would ejaculate before they ever got to intercourse.

A woman is naturally in the position of something sexual (especially penetration) being done to her. A woman cannot penetrate or impregnate a lover. She can only be penetrated and impregnated by a man. In the early days, novelty means a man's arousal is automatic so a woman can enjoy being the object of his desire without needing to contribute much. She can feel pampered rather than needing to act the concubine who is focused on assisting with male arousal. This also explains why rape fantasies are popular with women. It's important here to distinguish between the reality of rape (a brutal act) and the fantasy of being taken by a man (an act of submission).

Passive acquiescence is such an accepted female behaviour that no one ever questions why only men admire a lover's sexual attributes and are proactive about providing genital stimulation. Most women do neither of these things. Given their lack of erotic arousal, women have no agenda of their own on approaching sexual activity with a lover. Moreover, a woman has little interest in knowing the explicit details of the stimulation a man provides. Women simply accept or reject the stimulation men offer. A woman closes her eyes and lets a man explore her body to the extent she feels is proper.

When heterosexual couples engage in intercourse, the man takes hold of his erect penis, locates the vaginal entrance and inserts his penis. Unless a woman is providing male turn-ons by showing sexual initiative, she does not generally touch her lover's penis with her hands or take an active role in initiating the stimulation of intercourse. This is evidence that men (rather than women) are motivated by the stimulation of intercourse. Even with anal sex, for both homosexual and heterosexual couples, the penetrating male tends to take control of the stimulation of his own sex organ. The receiver of intercourse has a much lower motivation due to the reduced pleasure.

We say that a man makes love to a woman. We do not say that a woman makes love to a man. Men's acute erotic arousal on approaching a sexual scenario focuses them foremost on penile stimulation. A man does not make love to a prostitute because her consent has already been agreed. Lovemaking implies non-genital activities such as loving talk, caressing, stroking, kissing and massaging of the breasts, buttocks and other erogenous zones. Lovemaking is an activity a man uses, especially with an inexperienced woman or in the beginning of a relationship, as a lead-in to intercourse.

Women rarely dictate sexual activity with a man. Even prostitutes provide what a male client asks for. Some women may initially explore a lover's body to give pleasure. But over the longer term, women lack the motivation to be sexually proactive because they are not aroused. A woman naturally adopts a support role of accepting the pleasuring a man offers based on the arousal he enjoys from exploring her body. The easiest role for a woman is to cooperate with intercourse for just as long as a man takes to ejaculate.

Men assume it is their role to provide a woman with the orgasm she cannot give herself. Yet this is fallacious thinking because orgasm occurs as a result of stimulating the tumescence caused by our own mental arousal. Men are proactive because they are aroused. If a woman was similarly aroused with a lover, she would be motivated to obtain her own stimulation. Women's sexual passivity, which results from their lack of arousal, allows a man to assert his own sexual needs. Intercourse provides for male release and optimises reproduction but has nothing to do with achieving female orgasm.

Men's sex drive provides a much greater motivation (in the short term) for initiating intimate interaction with others. Men accept failed attempts as a natural aspect of being male. But if a man doesn't want sex with a woman, it is difficult for her to persuade him. A woman learns that if a man doesn't find her sexually attractive, there is often little point in her approaching him. This must, in part, explain why women are much less inclined to approach men in addition to the fact that women do not have the same incentive that a man has to make a sexual advance (of enjoying erotic arousal with a lover).

When sexual activity is focused on achieving orgasm, it naturally ends once orgasm achieved. This is the clearest evidence we have that women do not orgasm by engaging in intercourse. There is no point at which a woman puts a stop to intercourse. An orifice is always available by definition. So intercourse always ends with male orgasm, which is the trigger for ejaculation. Ejaculation of sperm into the vagina is the goal of intercourse, which is a reproductive act. The pleasure a man enjoys from intercourse is what motivates him to pursue women, persuade them into a sexual situation and, once aroused, achieve vaginal penetration and thrust until ejaculation.

Initially a man may offer pleasuring other than intercourse but over time men focus increasingly on intercourse because women do not respond positively to other pleasuring. Women tend to reject manual stimulation of the clitoris, which is far too sensitive. Many women are disgusted by the idea of oral sex. Even if a woman does allow her lover to stimulate her clitoris with his tongue, she feels almost no sensation and little pleasure. Women's lack of responsiveness ensures that sexual activity focuses on intercourse.

... the female is generally less responsive than the male erotically, and for that reason ... less often takes the initiative in any sex play. (Alfred Kinsey)

Women are often unsure about orgasm during sex

If intercourse caused female orgasm, there wouldn't be a mystery that needed researching in the first place. Any scientific account of female responsiveness has to be able to explain why female orgasm was such a secret for so long. The fact that women are capable of orgasm was highlighted by scientists. If female orgasm occurred easily with a lover, it could not possibly have remained a secret as it did. Kinsey noted that many couples had no idea that women were even capable of orgasm. Female orgasm has always been a mystery and most women that realise it is elusive with a lover. Yet researchers accept women's orgasm claims verbatim. The way such claims are welcomed is more appropriate for religious beliefs than for science. The evidence for female sexual pleasure comes from real women in the general population initiating and being enthusiastic about sexual activity with a lover.

Women rarely specify the anatomy involved in female orgasm. Less educated women assume it's the vagina because couples' sex lives equate to intercourse. Also less educated men spend less time on foreplay. Educated women (or their partners) are more likely to have heard of the role of the clitoris in female orgasm. No wonder then, when researchers ask about women about orgasm, that some of them claim to orgasm in these ways.

Women think they are supposed to orgasm with a lover through vaginal or clitoral stimulation (or both) but there are no research findings to support this assumption. Whether women explain their orgasms in terms of the vagina or the clitoris, it makes little difference. Researchers assume that women must participate in sexual activity because of their own arousal. Yet few women admit to having erotic fantasies or reading erotic fiction. The urge to engage in intercourse comes from a man's body. Sex is something that men do to women. Women's view of sex is emotional rather than erotic.

Women are often left to provide sex education. Women focus on warning children of the problems associated with sex, including sexually transmitted diseases. They talk about reproduction, including pregnancy and contraception. Women are not so comfortable talking about sexual pleasure, which is considered to be a personal topic. Most men prefer to talk of eroticism rather than the reproductive facts. But men are easily aroused by talking about sexual pleasure, which could be embarrassing. Sexual pleasure tends to have immoral overtones, being associated with the sex industry and is often considered an inappropriate topic for education. Marital sex is more respectable but is rarely described in terms of erotic turn-ons and orgasm.

Women could provide young people with the research findings relating to female sexuality. They don't do this for a number of reasons. Firstly, few women are interested enough in sexuality to read very widely. So women tend to be uninformed about sexual issues. The research findings tend to conflict with erotic fiction and popular beliefs (sexual ignorance). Women lack confidence in their own experiences to know which to believe. Finally, men never want to promote the fact that intercourse is solely a male pleasure.

While men talk of sexual pleasure openly and willingly, women's silence is assumed to indicate their satisfaction. Once intercourse ends with male ejaculation, a man is presumed also to have satisfied his lover. A woman is believed to orgasm from intercourse at some undefined point. No one can explain the anatomy or the turn-ons involved. For men, it is clear (because they have erections) that they need to be aroused before attempting orgasm. But women are never demonstrably aroused so they can claim to orgasm without needing to account for the mental arousal that would cause orgasm.

Men engage in intercourse to release the sexual frustration that arises as a result of their regular arousal. It is unthinkable that a man would engage in sexual activity and walk away unsatisfied. His arousal ensures his orgasm. Women never reach a state where orgasm becomes inevitable (even alone). Women may be frustrated because of the unrealistic expectations that have been set for female orgasm with a lover. But women never experience an urgent need to obtain sexual release. They never suffer sexual frustration.

Intercourse is a mating act. The purpose of intercourse is to facilitate male orgasm and ejaculation of semen into the vagina. Female orgasm is not involved in this reproductive process. Women are only capable of orgasm because of how the sexes have evolved. Men and women have different internal reproductive anatomy but we each have a phallus. Responsive women who have the ability to respond positively to eroticism, stimulate the internal clitoral organ in an instinctive thrusting motion when they are alone. Women masturbate to enjoy orgasm rather than to satisfy a sexual need.

Women do not respond to real-world erotic stimuli (such as nudity) that indicate an opportunity to penetrate another person. They don't have sufficient responsiveness to experience orgasm as reliably as a man nor an urge to penetrate (sex drive). The clitoris does not provide the same pleasure that the penis does. Women have a smaller, less responsive phallus and a residual thrusting instinct. A few women are able to achieve orgasm by emulating the male role in intercourse. Psychologically this puts them in the position of being the male penetrator. Female arousal is largely subconscious. The mental mechanism a woman uses to access her arousal is therefore fairly obscure. A woman has to use surreal fantasy where she effectively (in psychological terms) assumes the proactive role of penetrator.

Sexual double standards that favour pleasuring men continue to prevail. But I also believe women often think they are having an orgasm when in fact they are not. (Nicole Prause)

Women's orgasm claims do not result in more sex

Let's imagine, for a moment, that men and women experience the same level of responsiveness (orgasm frequency). Even so, responsiveness varies between individuals. There would inevitably be times when one lover or the other wanted more sex. There would be many complaints from women of all ages that they were not getting enough sex. This does not happen.

The willingness of some women to provide male turn-ons, by suggesting that male fantasies are a reality, make it difficult for couples to find answers. The fact that women do not respond as men think they should, makes sex taboo. Some women provide turn-ons that are directed towards getting what those women want. This is sometimes called prick-teasing because a woman's objective is rarely to provide male gratification but typically only to titillate. A woman's breasts sustain a baby and her vagina satisfies a man's sexual needs. A woman can feel loved because she is needed by those she loves. A woman may enjoy using her body to provide a man with the release he needs.

Alfred Kinsey found a correlation between male responsiveness and the age at which men became adolescent (defined by a boy's first ejaculation). Men who became adolescent before the age of twelve were about twice as responsive (their orgasm frequencies were twice as high) as men who became adolescent at a later age. Kinsey found that once men married, they masturbated less because they had intercourse with their wives instead. In other words, a single man has complete control over his total sexual outlet but a married man depends on a partner's amenability for his sexual outlet.

Any two people are likely to have different levels of responsiveness. So married men's intercourse frequencies should be affected by their wives' responsiveness. This is not the case. Kinsey was surprised to find that the frequency with which couples had intercourse varied according to the man's sex drive. Kinsey noted that there was exactly the same correlation between age of adolescence and orgasm frequency for married men as for single men. Couples have intercourse with frequencies that depend solely on a man's responsiveness and that have nothing to do with a woman's responsiveness.

Kinsey also found couples have intercourse with a regularity that is not matched by any other activity that women engage in. He found that women orgasm through masturbation or lesbian activities only once every 2 to 3 weeks. So it is highly unlikely that women can orgasm by any means every time a man has one because of their lower responsiveness. Kinsey found that young couples had intercourse on average between two and four times a week. This frequency slowed down over the years in line with the gradual decline in male responsiveness. By the age of forty intercourse frequencies for the average couple had dropped to about once a week on average.

Kinsey met some couples who lived in rural areas and had intercourse four times a day every day of the week. It is unlikely that modern lifestyles allow couples to have sex this frequently today. But even in the 1950s such frequencies were unusual. Most couples undoubtedly hover around the once a week mark. This is logical since the weekend offers more opportunity for companionable activities. Women who claim to orgasm are no more amenable to intercourse than other women. Nor do they initiate intercourse more than women who know orgasm is impossible. All the eulogising about sex and presumed enthusiasm for sex, does not lead to more sex for men.

Some women refer to masturbation just to be fashionable but they have no interest in discussing explicit details. Women often dislike erotic detail and yet arousal is caused by explicitness. By refusing to give details, women defend their ignorance. Women who boast about orgasm with a lover dismiss masturbation as inferior. They are confident to do so because they know that men focus on women's sociable responses. They obviously don't appreciate that the research indicates they have never had a real orgasm. No woman is called dysfunctional for not masturbating. Female orgasm with a lover is political because of men's desire for women to be sexually willing.

The anatomy, the physical stimulation and the erotic turn-ons needed for male orgasm are evident not only a man but also to his lover. By contrast, women's responses are not such that men can divine the turn-ons and stimulation involved. That doesn't stop men trying to guess. It is suggested that some women can orgasm from intercourse because of the proximity of the clitoris to the vagina. This is like saying that if a man's testicles are stimulated, he will orgasm due to the proximity of the testicles to the penis. Reproductive organs, such as the testes and the vagina, cannot cause orgasm. This kind of flawed argument is typical of the endless guessing regarding the anatomy in attempts to explain how women could orgasm from intercourse.

These suggestions all come from men because few women are interested in their own sexuality. Men's motivation is the ego behind the idea that a man gives a woman an orgasm. Women rarely discuss female orgasm except for those who compete for male approval. The sensations of intercourse are vague and diffuse. So the anatomy involved, in the orgasms women think they have, could be attributed to anatomy anywhere within the pelvis. The anatomy involved in a true orgasm is easy to identify. If women masturbated to orgasm, they would know for sure what anatomy was involved. If women had orgasms from activity with a lover, then their partners would also know.

Read all the sex surveys you want but you still won't really know what other people do in bed because what people say and what people do are two totally different things. (Tracey Cox)

How we know that the vagina is not a sex organ

Orgasm is a primitive and fundamental response of the human body because male orgasm triggers ejaculation, which is vital for reproduction. Male orgasm involves the brain (which responds to erotic stimuli by increasing blood flow to the genitals) and the penis. The penis and the clitoris develop from the genital tubercle in the foetus. They are equivalent organs. Women are only capable of orgasm because they have the remnants of a phallus.

The ducts that form the vagina in a female foetus waste away in the male. If the vagina was a sex organ, women would have needed to evolve a completely different mechanism (separately from the male) for responding erotically. It is highly unlikely that the vagina could ever have evolved as a sex organ in women alone. The implication is that women evolved a responsiveness that has no reproductive function and no useful purpose of any kind. We only evolve functionality for reproductive or survival reasons.

It is assumed that a woman can orgasm one time from vaginal stimulation and another from clitoral stimulation. Alternatively, it is assumed that some women need clitoral stimulation while others need vaginal stimulation. Either way, the implication is that women have evolved two quite different routes for achieving orgasm. No one ever provides a rational explanation for how a physiological mechanism can vary between women and from one occasion to the next. Nor do they explain how such a mechanism could have evolved. One of the problems is that no one explains the exact mechanism by which even male orgasm is achieved. So, in our ignorance, we are easily persuaded by all kinds of non-scientific assumptions that do not make any logical sense. Orgasm occurs as a result of specific physiological responses.

We have sensitivity in external anatomy that helps protect our bodies from injury. The vagina evolved from primitive egg ducts and (like all organs that are internal to the body) has little sensitivity. Research indicates that only the outermost portion (entrance) of the vagina and rectum have any sensitivity. The vagina is part of the birth canal. The intense climaxes women report during childbirth come from peaks of sensation as the baby's head stretches the vaginal entrance (often tearing the skin). This sensation can be replicated by the hand (called vaginal fisting) but not by the penis (regardless of size).

Anatomy such as the vagina, which is essentially a cavity, could never be a sex organ. A cavity can always be penetrated. Once orgasm is reached a person desists from further stimulation. But there is no point at which the vagina can no longer be penetrated. This is the clearest anatomical evidence that the vagina is not a sex organ. A cavity is made to hold something. In the case of the rectum, it is faeces. In the case of the vagina, it's semen. Neither of these organs is erectile. Mental arousal causes blood to flow into the penis and clitoral organ (the corpora cavernosa), which makes orgasm possible.

Intercourse involves the penis (a phallus) entering the vagina (a cavity). There is limited opportunity for the penis to stimulate the vagina in any way because it is relatively long and thin, while the vagina is like the inside of a balloon. The only possibility is that the penis jabs or pokes at the walls of the vagina. This is not the kind of stimulation that causes orgasm. Stimulation (aimed at orgasm) needs to massage the blood-flow within the erectile organ.

There is no requirement for someone who is the receiver of an erect penis to be aroused. The receiver offers a body orifice for a penetrating male to ejaculate into. The mouth is the most sensitive of all body orifices but men appreciate that giving oral sex cannot not cause orgasm. They probably also know that being a receiver of anal intercourse does not cause orgasm. It is only female anatomy that is ascribed an imaginary sensitivity. Unresponsive women have no incentive to question these emotional beliefs. Women who never orgasm cannot easily refute men's fantasies about their responsiveness.

Women never contest these myths because of their general embarrassment over sex, their uncertainty over their own arousal and their desire to please men sexually. Most women are unresponsive and so they don't appreciate that orgasm is achieved by stimulating specific anatomy. To a responsive woman (once she has been given names for her internal anatomy), it is just as obvious that the clitoris is the source of her orgasm as it is to a man that the penis is the source of his. Mental arousal that arises from focusing on specific erotic concepts, indicates to us the anatomy that needs to be stimulated. Anyone who has ever been aroused can identify their sex organ.

The hymen is a small flap of skin that covers the entrance to the vagina (in most but not all women). When the hymen is broken there may be a little blood and some discomfort. Before the days of tampons, women's hymens were broken the first time they engaged in intercourse. This is clear evidence that women did not masturbate by inserting objects into the vagina. In modern times when women use tampons to absorb their menstrual blood, they do not obtain any sexual pleasure from inserting tampons into their vaginas. If women had orgasms from inserting objects (such as an erect penis) into the vagina they would seek this kind of stimulation themselves. Yet research has indicated that women who masturbate stimulate the clitoris and the labia majora. Specifically, the only women who engage in vaginal stimulation are those who are told by men that they should orgasm by stimulating the vagina. Clearly, they have never had an orgasm in their lives.

There is, however, no evidence that the vagina is ever the sole source of arousal, or even the primary source of erotic arousal in any female. (Alfred Kinsey)

Why women cannot orgasm through intercourse

Male orgasm through intercourse is crucial to human reproductive biology.

(1) Intercourse is totally defined by male responses

Intercourse is a demonstration of the male arousal cycle, from erection to ejaculation. Intercourse is only possible once a man has an erection and it comes to an end once he has had an orgasm (the trigger for ejaculation of sperm). A woman cannot determine the length of time intercourse will last. No one, not even a man, can orgasm from stimulation that lasts for a period of time determined by a lover. To achieve orgasm reliably, we must be able to ensure that stimulation continues until orgasm and preferably not beyond.

(2) Orgasm ends sexual activity that is focused on achieving it

When we masturbate, we cease stimulation once orgasm has been achieved. This is a basic characteristic of orgasm. It is also evidence that orgasm has occurred. When any sexual activity is aimed at achieving orgasm, it ends once orgasm has occurred. This is why men lose interest in all sexual activity once they have had an orgasm. If women were as responsive as men, then for about half the time sexual activity would end with a woman's orgasm. But if women behaved in this way, men would not be able to satisfy their need to ejaculate into the vagina and reproduction would be adversely affected.

(3) Orgasm cannot be defined to suit the individual

Orgasm is a basic physiological response of the human body so it is not possible for one individual to have a unique response. A few women boast about orgasm, which is easy but doesn't explain why men pay prostitutes, as well as assault and drug women, to get sex. These male behaviours cannot be explained by saying that women are as sexually amenable as men hope.

(4) Women need more time to orgasm than men do

Men masturbate to orgasm within a minute or so. Intercourse may be more rewarding but the stimulation is more indirect so it takes longer. Most men (three-quarters of them) orgasm on average within two minutes of initiating intercourse. A woman is assumed to be able to engineer her orgasm to occur within this two-minute window. Yet research indicates that women need 4 minutes to orgasm alone and 10 to 20 minutes or longer with a lover.

(5) Women orgasm much less frequently than men do

Orgasm does not occur like pressing a button. Each person experiences orgasm with a specific frequency. Women orgasm on average once every two weeks regardless of age. Men orgasm much more frequently than women. It is not possible for a woman to orgasm every time a man does.

(6) A woman cannot obtain the correct stimulation with a lover

The position a woman assumes to allow penetration of the vagina is incompatible with how female orgasm is achieved. During intercourse a woman lies on her back and cooperates with male thrusting, by spreading her legs and gyrating her hips to assist with stimulation of the penis. To achieve orgasm, a woman lies face down and massages down over the glans with her fingers, while thrusting her hips and tensing her buttock muscles.

(7) Women need emotional factors to be amenable to intercourse

The emotional environment of rape is certainly very different to consensual intercourse. But the physical stimulation of rape is not so radically different. Rape involves a man thrusting into a woman's vagina with his penis. It is not possible for an act that causes women so much distress to also cause arousal. Women need emotional factors to be amenable to offering intercourse. Consent would not be an issue if intercourse caused female orgasm.

(8) For a woman, intercourse is a loving rather than an erotic act

Men are aroused by intercourse regardless of relationship factors. This is because an erotic stimulus causes arousal regardless of emotional circumstances. Intercourse is only erotic from the point of view of the male penetrator. Intercourse, from the female perspective is merely an act of impregnation. There is no reason why women should ever be aroused even with a lover, so women are not aroused by real-world triggers as men are.

(9) Women are meant to be unresponsive with a lover

Male arousal is crucial to reproduction because a man must have an erection to make penetration possible. But an orifice, such as the vagina, can always be penetrated regardless of a person's state of arousal. Women's reproductive role is to cooperate with intercourse until a man ejaculates semen (containing sperm) into her vagina, which is the reproductive event. If women could orgasm through their own efforts (from clitoral stimulation) or if they were motivated to stimulate a lover (by hand or by mouth), intercourse would be less likely and reproduction would be less successful.

(10) Female orgasm has no role in human reproduction

The function of male orgasm is to trigger the ejaculation of sperm. This is how a man's genes (within the spermatozoa) are transferred to the women's body. A woman is impregnated if sperm are present at a time when she has recently ovulated. An egg fuses with a sperm to create a new life. Ovulation occurs automatically so female orgasm plays no role in reproduction.

The vagina has no anatomical structure that can cause orgasm. (Vincenzo and Giulia Puppo)

Topic: Consensual sex

Consent is vital even within loving relationships

Sexuality is about the choices we make to explore our sexuality both alone and with a lover. The way in which we express our sexuality should show consideration towards others. Everyone should be free to make their own sexual decisions without undue influence. We have the choice to remain a virgin or to be celibate. We should respect other people's sexual decisions. Ideally sex is an emotional or erotic pleasure rather than being an obligation.

Sex education should discuss sexuality in a coherent and consistent way. We must explain how intercourse can equate to lovemaking on one occasion and rape on another. For example, date rape involves a more passive female role than usual and a more proactive male role. But it is essentially the same as any other intercourse. So why do women object so vehemently? And why are men so desperate that they need to drug women? A man initiates and proactively engages on sexual activity with a lover because of his sex drive. A woman merely accepts or rejects a man's sexual advances. Consent is about the receiver's right to control when and with whom they have intercourse.

We need to be able to explain why men can love women and yet also be a threat. Before puberty, most children play with their own sex friends. Adolescence brings men and women together but it is men who actively seek women out. Women are pursued. Women need to be wary of strange men for their own protection. Women's behaviour of displaying their bodies to obtain platonic admiration acts as a bait. Sex is a game that women try to play but they need to understand the risks of dealing with younger men's sex drive. Our society is full of male violence and the victims are often women.

Men are typically physically stronger than women and children. So the law protects these two vulnerable groups. Most societies have laws that make it illegal for children under the age of 18 to engage in sexual activity (either with an adult or another under-age person). Sexual scenarios are very different for a woman, especially if she is inexperienced or has a new lover.

Consent is not about responsiveness or even mutual pleasure. Women are not aroused by sexual activity with a lover at any age. But by the time they are adult, women have gained an appreciation of what they want from men. Consent is more about a person having the social maturity and life experience to understand the consequences of engaging in sexual activity. An adult is assumed to have the experience and confidence to make their own sexual decisions and, if they are unwilling, to stand up to anyone who puts pressure on them (emotional or otherwise) to engage in sexual activity.

A woman is assumed to have the maturity to understand the risks associated with sexual activity. A woman is expected to know that intercourse may result in her becoming pregnant if she doesn't take precautions (use a contraceptive). A woman learns how she can use sex to obtain a man's emotional commitment to her. Women interpret male devotion as love in the way they experience it. Men's love is conditional on obtaining a woman's consent to regular intercourse. Similarly most women, especially if they want a family, will not stay long with a man who cannot support them financially.

A man may realise that a woman is less sexually driven (than he is) because of her lack of enthusiasm or because she takes steps to avoid sex. As long as this apathy goes unacknowledged, a man can continue to obtain intercourse from a woman on the basis that she does not object. Many women are far from enthusiastic about sex but they rarely object explicitly. During sex, a man explores a woman's body within the limits set by her tacit approval.

One of the issues with consent is that women tend to passively accept sexual activity that men initiate. Men are proactive because of their arousal. Unhealthy relationships are where people use intimacy, sex or a show of affection to get what they want: to manipulate, to exploit or to control. Women have much less control than men have. This explains why women are less enthusiastic about casual sex than men are. A few men are violent and abusive towards women. Some men have deviant sexual behaviours.

Women do not know if a man will be dangerous or just a nuisance. So any man is a potential threat, regardless of whether he is likely to make an advance (even if he were attracted to a woman). This is a shame for the many men who go about their business without hassling women at all. Most men engage in friendly conversation first and then look for a sign (encouraging feedback) that a woman is attracted to them before they make any advance.

Different women are rewarded to varying degrees by love, ego (of being popular with men) or financial benefits (that men offer a sexual partner). But most women want a man who demonstrates caring behaviours and respects their need for affectionate companionship, before they offer regular sex. They are also looking for a man who is willing to support their family goals.

Traditionally marital intercourse has always been a fully condoned (even encouraged) sexual activity even by the strictest of religions because of men's need for regular sexual interaction. An implicit assumption of marriage is that a woman consents to intercourse with her husband. A wife's refusal to consummate the marriage (by offering intercourse) is grounds for annulment. Regardless of her relationship status, a woman retains her rights over her own body, including what she does with it and what a lover can do with it. When it comes to sexual decisions, we should only do what we are comfortable with and not what others (even a lover) tell us we should do.

In marriage the male more or less assumes that coitus is his privilege, and the law confirms him in this interpretation. (Alfred Kinsey)

The significance of nudity and being touched

Private parts refer to the anatomy that we may want (or be required) to cover up. Private parts include the buttocks, the genitals and the female breasts. Girls are discouraged from showing their panties. Boys learn to keep their penis hidden. It may be considered indecent to show too much bare flesh. Parents often think it is inappropriate for their children to see adult genitals or even a hint of sexual activity. But there is no reason why children should be harmed by nudity. Children should know what adult nudity looks like.

People wear clothes to keep warm and protect the body. Nudity tends to generate a great deal of curiosity in both sexes. Nudity can be embarrassing because our bodies are all so different. Differences in physical appearance can cause us to feel insecure and embarrassed. As we age, we may be embarrassed by the effects of aging or by having a less than perfect body.

Many women prefer to keep their clothes on to avoid the attention they inevitably get from men. Female modesty is due to women's lack of confidence over their bodies. Women do not want to be judged by men, who can be highly critical and insulting towards women they don't find attractive. Media images of young women with perfect bodies enhanced by computer technology cause women to feel that their bodies are ugly. But men enjoy a variety of different female body shapes, breasts and genitals.

Nudity is not always aimed at arousing anyone. Men need sexually explicit images to assist with orgasm without a lover. Pornographic images involve close-up shots of genitals, typically a penis penetrating an orifice. Censorship exists to limit the distribution of images that offend women. Some images use clothing to accentuate female anatomy such as breasts or buttocks. Sexual come-ons may be implied by a woman's facial expression or what she says. Other images of nudity are simply tasteless or lacking in human dignity.

Censorship restricts the portrayal of the nudity to protect the dignity of the individual. Women often feel exploited because someone else is aroused by their nudity. Men rarely express the same concern perhaps because men see themselves having more control over their sexual choices. Also a man is rarely in the situation where someone else is using his nudity for arousal.

Children should know that other people (usually family) can touch them but never in inappropriate ways. They also need to understand that nudity is not always acceptable. This does not mean that they should be ashamed of their bodies. With those we love, in the family, among friends, nudity may be acceptable as long as everyone is comfortable with this. But we are expected to abide by the social conventions of the society in which we live. Many people feel very uncomfortable unless they are conforming to social norms.

When we touch another person, it is a tentative sign of trust. It may be an invitation or an offer of further intimacy. There are cultural differences. What is acceptable in one culture or family may be unacceptable in another. Different personalities are also more inclined to touch others in daily life. Customs about what is believed to be an appropriate demonstration of intimacy within and outside the family, vary considerably between cultures.

Most people avoid touching other adults out of respect for individual privacy. Inappropriate touching refers to someone who attempts to touch another person on or in the vicinity of their private parts. No one is obliged to allow another person to touch them however innocently. Even children feel awkward, as well as a sense of shame, if they are touched inappropriately by an adult (besides a parent), regardless of whether the intention is sexual. Laws have become draconian in some areas (gyms and swimming pools). The law treats all adults of both sexes, and even the parents of the children being observed, as a potential threat. There are still no laws to protect a child who receives one-to-one instruction from an adult (e.g. piano lessons).

Two adults may touch each other in neutral body zones (such as on the shoulder or arm) without any implication of intimacy. They can also kiss on the cheek as a show of friendship. When a couple engages in mouth-to-mouth kissing it may be a petting activity but more often it occurs between couples already in a sexual relationship as a precursor to sexual activity. Often there is some cursory touching of more intimate body parts as a lead-in to increased sexual intimacy. This is especially true where couples dance.

Women enjoy more platonic forms of general body touching that may be used to communicate affection. Women can touch others of either sex without anyone assuming that they have sexual motives because women are not aroused as men are by nudity and physical interaction with others. When a woman touches a man, it is to demonstrate affection. So when a woman is angry, she doesn't want her lover to touch her. She doesn't want him to have the pleasure of her body because he has upset her. She remembers each occasion when a man offended her as evidence that he does not care for her.

Men don't obtain the same platonic emotional rewards from relationships that women do. Intimate touching for men is strongly associated with sexual activity because men are aroused by a lover's body. A man often touches a woman as a precursor to intercourse. Men typically want a lover to stimulate their genitals. The desire for genital stimulation is a characteristic of male responsiveness but is only relevant once a boy has reached adolescence. Women do not experience the same erotic reward from genital stimulation.

Women often complain that their husbands never touch them unless they want sex. (Michele Weiner-Davis)

Penetration is what makes sex erotic and taboo

Penetrative sex (both anal and vaginal intercourse) has a special role in our concept of eroticism. Penetration by a phallus is key to our view of what sex is about. Both sexes may be aroused by the concept of either being the penetrator or being penetrated regardless of sexual orientation. Both men and women can use an artificial phallus to simulate penetration as a turn-on either for themselves or for a lover. Both sexes can be penetrated by a phallus or dildo but only a man can penetrate a lover with his own sex organ. Even without arousal, the receiver of penetration (by finger or dildo) can experience the sensations of allowing another person to be so intimate.

Penetrative sex involves a penis penetrating another person (vagina or rectum) and thrusting until ejaculation. Only the giver (not the receiver) has an orgasm from intercourse. Sexual activity need not equate to intercourse but when it does the penetrator needs to be highly considerate of his lover. A woman is obliged to cooperate with intercourse for as long as a man needs to ejaculate. A woman has to remain in position until a man has finished. Women accept this instinctively and because of the authority of male sex drive. A man's needs, including ejaculating into a vagina, are very evident. Women's ability to continue sexual activity indefinitely is due to lack of arousal. Their amenability is due to their instincts to care for those they love.

Intercourse provides a man with the sexual release he needs. It is generally accepted that a person (male or female) needs to be at least 18 years old before they can deal with this world of aggression and sexual pressure generated by men. Women cannot understand why men find such a mundane and repetitive act (of a penis thrusting into a vagina) so fascinating. Men can't understand why women are so offended by sexual references.

Intercourse relies on a man's sex drive to penetrate another person's body (vagina or anus). Penetrative sex (intercourse) is core to what we consider to be sexual and erotic. Penetration represents the most dangerous, most taboo and yet most exciting of all sexual activity. Any mating act is a male conquest. The female is subjugated (dominated) in sexual terms. Women rarely appreciate eroticism because it is naturally defined from a male perspective.

Intercourse makes perfect sense to a man. A man's sexual role is to impregnate a woman. A woman's role is much less obvious. Sex is something that is done to a woman. Nothing in a woman's mind or body motivates her to want intercourse. In consensual intercourse a woman accepts her lover's attentions by cooperating with intercourse and facilitating male orgasm. When in love, a woman may reciprocate by demonstrating her affection.

A man doesn't need an experienced lover to obtain the release he needs from intercourse. Men target young women because they are more easily flattered into being sexually amenable. Young women enjoy being admired as long as men are respectful. But over time they realise that men's focus is the pleasure they obtain from ejaculating into a woman's vagina. Men are motivated by their own pleasure rather than emotional feelings for a lover.

Young women especially often put up with pain and discomfort to provide a man with the regular intercourse he needs. A woman's vagina may not be adequately lubricated for intercourse to be comfortable. The first rule of sexual pleasure is: if it hurts, don't do it or if it's painful, stop doing it. Young women may need to use a water-based lubricant. The action of a man's groin pounding into a woman's vulva can also cause damage by squashing the delicate skin of her labia. A man should vary his thrusting technique and may need to back off intercourse for a while until a woman has healed up.

If women wanted intercourse as men do, they could make money easily. Sexual harassment and rape are common, not only because of male sex drive, but also because women routinely reject men's sexual advances outside a loving relationship. If women wanted sex, they would walk around naked all the time and display themselves for male appreciation. Women are modest about covering up their private parts because they know men are aroused by them. Women take steps to avoid sex. Sexual assault is common and even men are propositioned by gay men. But a man can hope to fight off an attack if necessary. Women carry weapons in case they are attacked.

Anal intercourse is much less popular among heterosexuals than among gay men. Women have a natural dislike of genitals but even more so, of the anus, which they regard as massively taboo. In any context, women have a strong preference for cleanliness and hygiene. Vaginal intercourse is messy enough but even the idea of anal intercourse is quite abhorrent to most women. Vaginal intercourse has a moral justification (since it is required for reproduction) and so it is a much more socially acceptable sexual activity. Consequently, anal intercourse is associated mainly with male homosexuals.

Women's lack of arousal with a lover means that they have little reason to explore sex play. Some women invest in sex play out of curiosity and to please their lover. Vaginal intercourse requires much less skill on the part of the penetrator since the vagina is designed to be easily penetrated by a penis. Ironically, women also prefer the lack of stimulation provided by vaginal intercourse because it is less explicit erotically. A woman can be oblivious to what a man is doing to her sexually because she can feel nothing from penetration. Both male sex drive and women's preference to leave all the stimulation of sexual activity to a man, naturally assist with reproduction.

Heterosexual contacts occur more frequently because they are facilitated by the greater submissiveness of the female and the greater aggressiveness of the male. (Alfred Kinsey)

Intercourse is a territorial act of male dominance

In a society where men and women raise families together, intercourse is presented as a lovemaking act. But by looking at Nature we can see that mating is an act of male assault. By depositing his sperm in a woman's body, a man potentially forces her to bear his progeny. A woman responds to rape with loud vocal and strenuous physical objections, which involves most adrenaline (and so is most exciting) for a man. Consensual intercourse is an artificial scenario where a woman lets a man potentially impregnate her.

In consensual intercourse, the natural turn-ons of a resisting partner are absent. A woman feels no erotic arousal and little physical sensation. But if she lies inert during intercourse, a man feels unappreciated. Men put pressure on women to provide a simulated response to intercourse. A woman may feel obliged to provide the body movements and noises that make intercourse erotically rewarding for a man. A man interprets this cooperation with intercourse as a sign of female arousal. But this is clearly a conscious behaviour that is used by some women when they choose to.

Intercourse begins with a man's arousal because it relies on a man having an erection. Intercourse comes to an end with male orgasm and ejaculation because a man loses his erection. This is why male performance (the ability to become aroused and orgasm) is critical to heterosexual activity. Female performance has come to refer to women's skill at providing male turn-ons.

Men are inclined to portray sex as a male conquest. The woman's role is belittled. Hence why sex is often demeaning for women. We can see from Nature that the mating act is a territorial act of male dominance that subjugates the female. For men, intercourse is foremost an erotic act, not necessarily a loving act. In our society men are shamed for being dominant (violent and bullying) and women are shamed for being submissive (timid and modest). Yet these natures lie at the very heart of human reproduction.

Some men approach sex with an egotistical attitude as if a woman represents nothing more than a territorial conquest for them before they move on to the next. The implication of male sexual bravado is that women are just helpless victims. Men tend to condone male infidelity but not a woman who cheats. They assume a woman has no sexual agenda of her own. Some women enjoy the ego of a man desiring them even as a one-off occasion.

Men boast about sexual conquests as if women are objects rather than people with minds and choices. They laugh at women's embarrassment or anger at being treated in this way. This male behaviour causes women to conclude that sex is an experience that men gain from at women's expense. This is why women often demand respect. Men talk about "giving her one" as if it's a form of punishment. The word bitch is used for female animals but when a man says to another man "You can be my bitch" he is reflecting the attitude of the dominant and penetrating male. Women are sullied or violated by intercourse whereas men have proven themselves by winning something. These attitudes reflect a man's assessment of his own physical superiority and his dominance over women in all the ways that are important to him. Of course, he has no respect for the qualities that women have but men lack.

Bravado is a way of covering up embarrassment. Adults use euphemisms to avoid being explicit. We don't say a man impregnates a woman. We say a woman gets herself pregnant. The proactive male role is never explicitly referred to in everyday conversation. The result is that children grow up with no idea where babies come from. Men's sexual references offend women, who prefer to avoid all direct references to intercourse. Movies use sound effects to imply off-screen sexual activity: a regular thumping (of a bed against a wall) and a woman moaning. Men laugh but women are embarrassed.

There are many slang terms for intercourse, which are sexually explicit. Men talk about fucking, humping and banging which describe so succinctly the male urge to thrust into a vagina until ejaculation. Women are the people being humped or banged. Such terms offend women because they emphasise women's role in providing an orifice to be penetrated. Shagging and screwing are used as more mutual terms, implying that a woman may be participating more proactively by assisting with penile stimulation. In an attempt at equality, women have recently starting using 'fuck' to refer to the proactive female role of assisting with male arousal and penile stimulation.

Men are often aggressive and disrespectful towards women. So sex is essentially women's only bargaining advantage. A woman sees sex primarily as a gift that she confers on a man as a sign of her approval. A woman uses sex, to some degree, to control a man. If he is admiring and amenable to her wishes, she offers him the sex he wants. If he is not, she withholds sex. This behaviour naturally tends to anger men and causes them to feel controlled.

One would think that heterosexual men would want to protect and love women. Yet men abuse women, assault them, rape them and even kill them. Strangely, only heterosexual men attack women. Men abuse prostitutes because of their resentment of women in their lives who withhold sex. If women were as willing as the fantasy implies, men would have no reason to harm a source of sexual pleasure. Some men are much more inclined to violence than others. Most men simply find another partner or sexual outlet.

In species where there is a struggle before the female submits to coitus, the male must be physically dominant and capable of controlling the female. In the ultimate act it is the male which more often mounts in back of the female and makes the active pelvic thrusts which effect intromission. (Alfred Kinsey)

Male propaganda: saying women should enjoy sex

Ask a woman in any developing country about sex and she will tell you it is for male pleasure and making babies. Try asking a woman in a developed country the same question and you get silence. Sexual politics is created by men's desire for intercourse. Men will not accept what women say about sex unless it accords with their own view. Specifically, they want to hear that a woman wants intercourse as much as they do. Propaganda succeeds because of sexual ignorance. This bravado silences any constructive discussion.

The male propaganda saying that everyone should enjoy sex is an implicit bullying tactic. Sexual pleasure is about what we are naturally inclined to do. It has nothing to do with what others tell us we should do. A person either enjoys sexual activity naturally (because they are easily aroused) or they don't. Men say that it is normal and natural for everyone to enjoy sex. If a woman loves a man then she should naturally want sex. Men call women who don't want sex 'frigid', which means unloving. By refusing to accept women's sexuality for what it is, men put emotional pressure on women.

Most women assume that it is their fault that they cannot be like men. Women's embarrassment over sex gives men a political advantage. Men assume their greater interest in and knowledge of sexual matters qualifies them to define women's sexuality for them. Even if a woman challenges their view, men react as they are entitled define women's sexuality. The ego of "You obviously haven't met the right man to make you orgasm!" indicates the male perspective. Women's timidity over sex allows men to do this.

Female sexuality only seems complex because men interpret women's behaviours as responsiveness. The interest in female orgasm is a political desire to promote orgasm claims, no matter how ridiculous. Men are clearly not interested in female orgasm as a scientific phenomenon. Most men prefer female sexuality to be an unsolvable mystery rather than discuss any kind of facts or logic. If they approached the topic from a scientific perspective, men would have been willing to accept the research finding that women orgasm by masturbating. It is the obvious explanation for why female orgasm was a mystery for so long. It also explains women's sexual passivity.

Considering the fuss they make about sex, men invest very little effort in trying to understand the female perspective. Men gloat over the pleasure they enjoy and, even worse, boast about the pleasure they think women enjoy. They never notice that their jubilation is one-sided. Women get tired of men talking about eroticism and sexual pleasure without any sensitivity to the fact that women's minds and bodies do not respond in the same way. Male propaganda silences women because of the implied sexual inadequacy.

Some women promote female sexuality because of the money to be made. It's all an act. Our society's willingness to allow women to promote their sexuality, without ever explaining their claimed experiences in explicit detail leads to much of the ignorance about female sexuality that we have today. Women don't eulogise about male orgasm. Neither do men boast about it. It just happens. Some people enjoy the bravado of promoting intercourse as a mutual act. This helps justify why women engage in intercourse. It is assumed that women have a choice about the sexual activity they engage in.

Men are much more active than women in claiming that female orgasm occurs with a lover. This is the political nature of the topic that interests more men than women. Men promote their own view because it is vitally important to them. Porno movies, directed by men, provide all the turn-ons that men enjoy. Men's key objective is the pleasure of intercourse, not a woman's orgasm. Porn acts as an emotional security blanket. By believing that women orgasm from intercourse, men are reassured that it will always be available. Men hope that their belief in female orgasm will cause women to be more sexually willing somehow. But this not logical. The evidence for female orgasm would be women's obvious enthusiasm for intercourse.

Male propaganda far outweighs any attempt by women to put men right. This is for a number of reasons:

- The obsessive interest many men have in discussing sex far outweighs women's extremely low to negative interest in the topic.

- Men are physically and psychologically more forceful than women so they can use brute force to ensure that their view prevails.

- Women want to be attractive to men. They can only do this if they silently ignore men's claims to provide them with sexual pleasure.

- Women depend on men's support to have children. So women have an emotional investment in their relationship with a man.

Female orgasm justifies women's role in an activity that, in truth, focuses on male orgasm. The fact that women's lifestyles are subsidised by their partners, is overlooked. Many women have no chance of being financially independent. Even women who could be independent if they were single, make themselves dependent on a man because they want to have children. Women define their lives in terms of their relationships rather than their own achievements. So sex is the currency of women's relationships with men. There's little to be gained by taking on conflict with a man who is supporting the family. This is why so few women comment on sex.

As the feminist group the Redstockings put it, for many women marriage is one of the few forms of employment that is readily available. (Shere Hite)

Sexual scenarios tend to be biased in men's favour

No one ever admits that sex is biased in men's favour. Accounts of female orgasm are heavily promoted and accounts of harassment, exploitation and rape are hushed up. A woman doesn't need sex. So sex, and all its issues, is a male problem. Sex is foremost a biological male need that some men can satisfy with any woman. We talk of women of pleasure or sinful women. It's not that women are inherently bad (or enjoying pleasure). Their bodies tempt men into illicit sexual liaisons, which lead to unwanted pregnancies and broken marriages. No man is ever going to accept responsibility for prostitution or rape. It's always some other guy. But the result is that women are left to pick up the consequences of men's sex drive. Women accept sex with all its disadvantages because of their desire to have children. They are willing to keep men happy because they need a man's support for the family.

Men are lucky because their personal happiness is easily achieved. As long as they have regular sex, men rarely complain. Sexual pleasuring involves an exchange but not the mutual exchange men assume. Men tend to assume that women's emotional happiness is achieved in the same way as theirs. A woman only has the reward of giving pleasure, which relies on her feeling appreciated by a lover. Men need to be prepared to understand how they can give back in other ways. A man needs to make a woman feel that he cares about her personally, which takes much longer than a few minutes.

Men are much less inclined to consider consequences than women in general. Men don't necessarily feel that a woman's pregnancy has anything to do with them. Semen is harmless while it's inside a man's body. It is only once semen enters a woman's body that there is a problem. It's a woman's role to bear children so when she falls pregnant, it's solely her problem.

Young women get themselves pregnant because they are inexperienced, ignorant or just stupid. The men they have sex with often know better and yet they take no precautions. Of course it's a woman's decision to have an abortion. It's her body. But it takes a man and a woman to create a new life. Why are men not concerned about their own progeny? Why is abortion solely a woman's issue? It is this apparent callousness on the part of men that brings so much negativity to the topic of sex in the eyes of women. Men need to respect a partner who provides them with sexual relief and pleasure.

Sexual scenarios often have negative aspects for women. Women encounter abuse, harassment and pain fairly routinely. Women find men's erotic turn-ons and genital responses both crude and offensive, so men cover up their regular arousal, to avoid offending women. Sexual pleasure, which focuses on male gratification, has negative connotations for women. The sex industry is associated with the exploitation and degradation of women. Women fake orgasm and men take the credit. This is the deceit of sex. It's just bravado on both sides. Only men can put an end to this fiasco. Men are at the root of the deception because of their need to reassure themselves that women want the sex they need. But equally, men know what an orgasm is. Women have little interest in their sexuality beyond using it to manipulate men. Women's lack of responsiveness makes it difficult for them to define their sexuality.

Women complain about the way men express their sexual urges as being too sexually explicit, crude and even obscene. Women prefer to see intercourse portrayed as a lovemaking act. Women's dislike of eroticism and their natural lack of responsiveness mean that women cause much of the negativity surrounding sexuality. But it is equally true to say that men's refusal to accept the reality of women's sexuality is responsible for the taboo. Men want to be convinced that women like sex so that they can feel good about insisting on it. Few people are willing to confront the moral conflict involved in the enjoyment of eroticism and achieving arousal. The issue is that the male penetrator enjoys sexual pleasure while a woman has something done to her that she does not want. This is one of the key reasons why sexual activity (intercourse in particular) and eroticism are likely to remain taboo.

Sex provides men with an emotional reward because of the pleasure they enjoy. If it came from their love for a partner, they would be more sensitive to women's needs instead of focusing on their own. If a man was thinking logically, he would accept a woman's passivity as a sign of her lack of arousal. It is obvious that women are not having orgasms from the stimulation men provide but a man enjoys extending his own arousal. Men continue, not for a woman's pleasure, but to reassure themselves they are not being selfish.

Most women come to the realisation at some point in their lives that sex is primarily a male interest. In this sense, women have to be more worldly than men. Most women do not blame men for being male. They just want men to take responsibility for their own needs. Men need to come to sex with proactive suggestions for bringing some variety to a couple's sex play. It's not a woman's job to provide men's sexual pleasure. Women in long-term relationships know their male partners always want more sex than they are willing to offer. They also know that men are attracted to women throughout the day regardless of any relationship. So women don't always feel that their efforts to please and satisfy their partner's sexual needs are respected. Men need to negotiate for what they want instead of just sulking like a spoilt child. A woman wants a partner she can communicate with. She wants someone who is honest, sincere and a real grown-up who can talk about adult topics.

... she's a person and you should treat her with respect. But seriously, do you want someone to one day bang your daughter if they don't respect her? (Alice Carter)

Sexual insults, bullying and habitual harassment

Young people should understand what makes a positive relationship and what makes a bad one. There are benefits and risks involved in relationships depending on the degree of sexual intimacy. Before we can formulate our own view without being coerced by undue pressure from others, we need a minimum level of maturity, experience, self-esteem and self-confidence.

Children should understand the importance of standing up for themselves. They should be given guidelines for dealing with negative behaviours, such as online and face-to-face name calling. They should understand how actions such as making sexual comments and sharing sexual pictures, either in person or online, may cause shame and affect another person's reputation.

Behaviours that can offend or upset others include sexual insults. These can be verbal, written or communicated by gestures. Name calling is particularly hurtful when a person knows that they belong to a social group that is victimised in society e.g. the disabled, gays, women, ethnic minorities or poor people. The person making the insult has a sense of superiority and confidence from knowing they have the support of the society around them.

Children should be taught when to stand up to bullies and when to ask for support from adults. A bully is not a strong person. A bully feels successful if they are able to victimise someone who is more vulnerable than they are. Teenagers should be informed about the emotional impact and legal implications of different types of harassment and abuse in relationships.

Teenage girls especially can be highly sensitive to remarks made about their appearance. Many women of any age translate eroticism into dirty (disgusting or obscene). This causes women embarrassment and even shame over their sexual role of facilitating male orgasm. Men like to imply that women engage in sex to enjoy their own orgasm as if women have male sexual urges. Women may need support in knowing how to reject sexual invitations or other unwanted intimacy. We all need to think about how we deal with rejection, feeling shame and feeling used. Girls can be just as hurtful as boys.

Today laws protect women against unwanted sexual advances but they are also used against innocent men. Men need to be increasingly vigilant. A man needs to recognise when a woman's behaviour is likely to lead to entrapment. Work situations are particularly sensitive. Drunken escapades and being alone with a female colleague can be unwise for a man. Men need to ensure their comments and behaviour towards female colleagues are exemplary.

Women expect so-called civilised men to restrain themselves. This attitude is evidence that women never experience a sex drive as men do. Women don't understand that it is simply not possible to suppress a true biological sex drive. Men's sexuality needs as much respect as women's does. Young women rely on the protection of society to tease men by behaving in a provocative manner but never having to face the consequences. This is the equivalent of a gazelle prancing around in front of a hungry lion knowing that the lion is not allowed to get at it. Particularly in work areas, such as sales and marketing, the attraction of women's bodies to male customers is used to assist with the company's goals. Any man who attempts a sexual advance is accused of sexual harassment. This sexually provocative behaviour, that women are encouraged to engage in, sends confusing and contradictory messages to the male population. Some men are more likely to assault women than others, who return home hoping their partner will oblige them.

Sexual harassment including stalking is most usually (but not always) perpetrated by men with women as the victims. If men are victims of sexual abuse, they may be reluctant to get help because of the shame of being a victim. Many women put up with sexual harassment because they are too embarrassed to complain or they don't know how to deal with the conflict.

Some men feel compelled to fight to secure personal power and supremacy over male rivals. Most women don't want to get themselves killed. Their goal is survival. Men are more determined and stronger than women. But women also lack the ability to fight as men do. Only a naïve person would suggest that men do not use these advantages to get what they want from women. Most men prefer a woman to be financially dependent on them. Men use this economic advantage to make a woman feel obliged to offer regular sex.

Ignoring what someone says is a form of bullying. One person promotes their own point of view thereby implying the invalidity of the other person's until they give up. Once the second person has been silenced, the first person claims victory. Thereafter the first person concludes they are right because no one objects. When someone is trying to keep you happy or they need your support, they may agree with you just to please you. If someone is receiving money from you, they will agree with almost anything you say.

Men can't understand why women are not more willing to offer intercourse. Men often use any means available to pressure their partner into obliging them. A man may use a woman's love for him to make her feel obliged to give him the intercourse he wants. Men can be frustrated because women control their sexual opportunities. Bullying behaviour comes in various guises. Some approaches are cloaked in sentiments of love or even affection.

Men often feel very angry with women who never initiate sex and too often don't want sex. But this anger has a tone of alienation, guilt, and insecurity: men feel instinctively on some level that sex does not involve an equal sharing, especially when they are having an orgasm and the woman does not – and this puts them on the defensive. (Shere Hite)

Domestic violence and emotional abuse in the home

Domestic violence (violence in the home), with women and children as primary victims, is a major worldwide epidemic. The majority, an estimated 90 percent to 95 percent, of victims in heterosexual relationships are women. It is estimated that at least 3 million to 4 million women are beaten by their husbands or partners annually in the US. About half of all marital relationships involve some form of domestic violence. More than one-half of the female homicide victims in the US are killed by their male partners.

A woman is more likely to be assaulted, injured, raped or killed by a male partner than by any other type of assailant. In the US, battering is the top cause of injuries to women (more incidences than rape, muggings and car accidents combined). Women may also abuse their children. Women are often more inclined to inflict abuse verbally rather than physically. Given the absence of physical injuries, this emotional abuse is more difficult to identify.

Men can be much more dangerous than women because of their inclination towards aggressive behaviour. Some men are even willing to go as far as killing to get what they want. Domestic violence crosses all ethnic, racial, orientation, religious and socioeconomic boundaries. Authorities may be reluctant to intervene when violence occurs between two consenting adults.

In some societies, violent and abusive male behaviour towards a spouse is even condoned because of the belief that a man has the right to be physically aggressive as a means of asserting his authority in the home. Some couples appear to be willing to accept or put up with an atmosphere of constant angry shouting. Crime statistics indicate that men commit many more crimes than women do. Women commit around 10% of all murders but their motives are different. Women are typically motivated by self-preservation. Men dominate jealousy-related killings because of their territorial instincts.

Domestic violence or abuse is a deliberate strategy to control women rather than being an impulsive act. Abuse is a learned behaviour. It is learned from seeing abuse used as a successful tactic of control, typically in the home in which the abuser grew up, but also in schools, peer groups, and the media. The behaviour is target specific. Men, who abuse, don't use this behaviour at work. They use abuse at home as a means of control over their partners.

Abusers often use violence or defence mechanisms to justify abusive behaviours, extreme jealousy and conflicting personalities. Abusers deny responsibility for their actions and they also often deny that any type of abusive behaviour has taken place. They typically present a different personality outside the home than they do inside, which makes it difficult for a woman to describe her experiences to people outside the relationship. Abusive behaviour can include physical abuse (violence directed at causing bodily harm) and sexual abuse (forcing a partner to perform sexual acts against their will). Psychological or emotional abuse may precede or accompany physical violence as a means of control. Economic coercion is used to make a partner dependent on the abuser for money and survival.

Men tend to express their emotions primarily through violence. But equally one has to ask why men have such strong negative emotions towards women in the first place. Couples argue over sexual frequency as well as money. Men use money to get what they want while women tend to use sex. Women are often better at arguing their perspective articulately when it comes to discussing relationship issues. Women talk from their own perspective and the implication is that men are in the wrong. Men either hit out or fall silent.

Sex may be a male problem but women can be sentimental about those they love. Men know this well and they often use a woman's love as a means of bartering for sex. A woman stays with a man because she loves him and she believes he can change. Abusive men often have times when they are charming and affectionate. A woman may try to be perfect so that her partner will show his loving side. Unfortunately, an abuser is driven by his own emotional needs and so continues his behaviour regardless of her actions.

A woman can have intercourse during her period and during pregnancy. No harm is done. Not all women want to. They may worry about being unclean or that intercourse will harm a foetus (only in the case of rape). They may also use their period or pregnancy as an excuse for a rest from the regular intercourse men require. Advanced stages of pregnancy leave a woman less able to defend herself. Medical sources suggest that about 37 percent of obstetric patients are physically abused while pregnant. About 21 percent of women who were previously abused, report an increase in abuse during pregnancy. The risk of injuries to a woman and her foetus increases.

Certain factors appear to place certain women at greater risk. Young women (aged 19 to 29) are most at risk. This age range correlates with the time when men are at their most sexually active and at their physical peak. Separated or divorced women are 14 times more likely than married women to report having been a victim of domestic violence. It is, however, likely that the violence was a direct result of the relationship breakdown. Women who have an excessively jealous or possessive partner are more at risk. Women who abuse drugs or alcohol, or who have a relationship with someone who abuses drugs or alcohol, are at greater risk than average. Men who have witnessed domestic violence between their parents are three times more likely to abuse their own wives than men who have nonviolent parents.

You deserve a man who loves you, respects you, and is attentive to your needs. Don't feel like you have to settle for anything less. (Stephan Labossiere)

Child sexual abuse, incest and paedophilia

Paedophiles blatantly challenge the concept of consent. Paedophilia involves a few men who are sexually attracted to pre-pubescent children. Many paedophiles control their urges and avoid coming into contact with children. Others do eventually act on their urges by exposing themselves to children, watching naked children, masturbating themselves in front of children or touching children's genitals. Oral, anal and vaginal penetration rarely occur.

Most paedophiles who act on their impulses, manipulate children by gradually desensitizing them to inappropriate behaviour. Then they escalate it. In about 60% to 70% of child sexual abuse cases involving paedophiles, the perpetrator is a person who has regular and open contact with the child.

Paedophilia is now categorised as an orientation. Paedophiles are born that way. Paedophilia cannot be cured. A paedophile's dependency on children as a mechanism for sexual arousal is normal for him and cannot be changed by therapy or any other kind of treatment. Treatment involves preventing these men having access to children or ensuring that they are closely supervised. Paedophiles are typically attracted to children of one gender.

A paedophile is clearly attracted to a child as an object. A child does not remain a child for ever. So a paedophile is not attracted to the individual but to the anatomy, the immaturity and vulnerability of a child. Paedophiles try to justify their actions by insisting that a child acted seductively or enjoyed the encounter. This reflects the predator's inability to empathise with the victim. Likewise men say they raped a woman because she was asking for it.

If a man is sexually constrained for some reason (he may be very timid or lacking in sex drive) he is more likely to prey on those who are less able to defend themselves. Some men prey on children not necessarily because it is their first choice but because they know they are more likely to succeed.

Men often consider genital exposure to be harmless because it is a natural male urge. Although there is no physical harm, a non-responsive person still feels threatened by the potential threat and uninvited intimacy. Some men who like to touch others are impotent. They may only want to hold hands. Abusers often start with innocent activity such as hand holding. The situation may seem trivial and so hardly warranting a complaint. A victim may be reluctant to report abuse. The victim may feel that reporting the activity will lead to public exposure over which they have no control. They are likely to feel embarrassed about talking to another adult in authority about such intimate activity. Pride may also cause them to prefer to remain anonymous.

Men rarely appreciate that they are the ones who generally have control in sexual situations. Men may start with pushing for innocent activity but inevitably this leads to a desire for penetrative sex. Children of both sexes and teenage girls do not have the physical strength or the necessary assertiveness to fight off unwanted advances from men. Many children who have been molested never recover from the shame of being involved (even though against their will) in sexual activity that they did not invite or enjoy.

There are sometimes bystanders: people who suspect that a child is being sexually abused but who may not know how best to intervene. Women may know about the abuse but feel afraid or powerless to intervene. They may not be aware of the abuse because they cannot imagine that such a thing is possible. Most women are intensely embarrassed by the crudeness of men's urges and are either unable or unwilling to discuss sexual abuse. Some women even blame the child (a form of jealousy) for tempting a man into sexual activity that they themselves consider to be disgusting and obscene. Children are often silent because of fear or shame. This embarrassment contributes to the social taboo over sexual abuse and the suffering of victims.

When sexual activity occurs between adults and children in institutions, it is called sexual abuse. About half of all child sexual abuse victims are 12 to 17 years old so their abusers don't fall within the definition of paedophilia. Experts estimate that only one in 20 cases of child sexual abuse is reported.

Men are not usually attracted to members of their own family. Incest may occur when men look to a daughter for the sex their wives withhold. There may also be sexual feelings between siblings. Incest is likely to be most common in communities where there is little education of any kind. Many young males do not appreciate that it is not always appropriate to act on their sexual urges, which provide a man with such pleasure. Men are typically oblivious to the fact that the receiver feels none of the same pleasure. There are more likely to be genetic abnormalities in offspring of close relatives. In most countries it is illegal to marry your parent, grandparent, child or sibling.

A few women do have a sexual interest in children but they represent only a tiny proportion of female sex offenders. Sex crimes perpetrated by men are crimes of power over the victim. Female offences can be control-driven but the need for intimacy seems to play a larger role than domination. Women who work as teachers of teenage boys may engage in a sexual relationship with an under-age boy without truly appreciating that it is an illegal act. Most women are looking primarily for an affectionate relationship. They may feel that they have more control over a relationship with an adolescent rather than with a grown man. A third of cases involving women are those who abuse children alongside a male partner. Some of these women have been coerced by their partners by the use of emotional or psychological pressure.

Many small girls reflect the public hysteria over the prospect of 'being touched' by a strange person. (Alfred Kinsey)

Sex without consent is rape regardless of intent

It's important to appreciate that the situation where a man rapes random strangers is rare. These men (called rapists) specifically enjoy the violence of the rape scenario and sometimes rape habitually. Rape relies on an inability to empathise with the victim. Most men's ability to objectivise a lover is not this extreme. Sex education must explain these situations in black and white terms that everyone can understand. Many men have a strong biological drive to engage in intercourse (regardless of the other person's feelings).

The vast majority of rape occurs when a woman knows a man, either casually or because she has or had a relationship with him. These situations are often not clear-cut. Women are often oblivious to the effect that their bodies and apparent sexual availability may have on a man. When a man is aroused, he is in a highly emotional state. He is not thinking logically. A woman's behaviour may cause a man to think that she would welcome his sexual advances. Men say women are 'asking for it' as if men have no choice. A man may feel strong resentment towards a woman (her personally or women in general). He may justify punishing a woman to assert his sexual authority.

A man's right to have intercourse with his wife, is enshrined in law and often makes it impossible for a woman to charge her husband with rape no matter how violent the act. Men may not understand the anger a woman feels at being penetrated against her will. There is physical damage: blood and pain. Women can be badly injured (rendered infertile) or even killed. More importantly there is the psychological violation of the victim's ability to make their own choices. Rape is an act of violation by a man because he has taken something the victim did not want to give. Rape also potentially forces a woman to bear a man's progeny. A victim of rape feels fear when they cannot defend themselves against a man's unwanted assault. They also feel humiliation and anger towards a person who has brutally violated their body.

Most men, most of the time, respect the fact that they only obtain intercourse from a woman who is amenable to offering it. If a man is angry with a woman, he may disregard the usual custom of waiting for her implicit consent. We say that he forces himself upon her. When a man does this, he does it knowing that she doesn't want intercourse. He does it as an act of aggression towards a woman who is refusing to make herself sexually available to him.

The fact that men drug women or get them drunk to have sex, does not lead an objective observer to conclude that enthusiasm for intercourse is shared equally between the sexes. When we are drunk, we are consciously taking a risk. We are still responsible for what goes wrong. A woman makes a conscious choice to risk being impregnated if a man takes advantage of her inebriated state. When our wallet is stolen, it is clear what we have lost. But what has a woman lost by having intercourse when she was so intoxicated that she does not remember what happened? It is rarely her virginity or her chastity. A man has taken his pleasure from her body without her permission. Many women claim rape after the event. They feel they were manoeuvred or pressured into having sex when they didn't want it. Equally, a woman may change her mind half-way through. There is also sex without consent where a woman is silent or ineffective in making her objections. She is too embarrassed, intimidated or frightened to object. Everyone has the right to control what happens to their body. But the role of education is to make sure that women understand the need to respect men's sexual urges. A woman should take the morning after pill after unprotected intercourse.

In many developing countries, the age of legal maturity is set lower for girls than for boys. Without the benefit of an education and a job, many women have little choice but to marry and have children. Girls as young as 10 or 12 are sold as wives to rich and older men. Young girls do not have the maturity to form an emotional attachment to a man. Even a mature woman wants a man to be affectionate and considerate during intercourse. When a child is crying, there can be no illusion that they are enjoying any form of pleasure.

A young man accused of rape suggested in his defence that he had assumed (from watching pornography) that women were supposed to scream. Most men recognise the signals that a woman gives out when she wants sex. She is smiling. The lead-in to sex is affectionate and mutual. During intercourse a woman cooperates. She is not resisting. Women are shown screaming in pornography as a turn-on. In real life women do not enjoy pain or violence.

Women are rarely convicted of sexual crimes. A man can subdue a woman but it is difficult (if not impossible) to force a man into intercourse against his will (when he is not erect). Except for the psychological reward of inflicting shame, a woman has nothing to gain by forcing herself on a man. One woman forced a chained-up man to have intercourse with her. Other cases involved statutory rape, underage sex between teachers and students. In such cases women are looking for a relationship and there is no violence.

It is relatively easy for a man to immobilise a woman and keep her controlled using his body weight. Rape is defined as forced intercourse (vaginal, oral or anal penetration) by an offender. Male rape involves a man receiving forced anal intercourse from another man. The receiver is homo- or heterosexual. Male rape (by other men) is not so common that men take precautions against it. Men are often raped within institutions such as prisons, boarding schools and the armed forces where men are incarcerated without women.

If she's too drunk, she can't give you consent. Also, silence is not consent. What kind of creep tries to have sex with a girl who is so drunk that she doesn't know what's going on? (Alice Carter)

Topic: The sexual mind

Some people enjoy abstract eroticism and fantasy

Sexuality is about our motivation to explore our fantasies both during masturbation alone and during sex play with a lover. Our ability to reach orgasm ultimately depends on what happens in the brain. We tend to focus on the mechanics of sex but erotic pleasure is foremost about turn-ons. Men enjoy the turn-on of penetration as much as the stimulation of intercourse.

A man has three possible sources of erotic arousal:

- Hormonal: including young boys' random and spontaneous erection and the regular erections many men have each morning.

- Physical presence of a partner: this is a response to anticipating possible opportunities for intercourse as the penetrating male.

- Erotic fantasy: those with a creative imagination can make use of imagined opportunities for intercourse as the penetrating male.

Women do not experience hormonal arousal. We can also rule out the second option because of the fact that porn (that is so arousing for men) is censored in every society. So the only option for women is erotic fantasy. But this is evidently very rare given most women's aversion to any form of eroticism. Responsive women effectively put themselves in the position of the penetrating male by using surreal fantasies and by stimulating the clitoris.

How we explore sexual activity both alone and with a lover depends on having a creative imagination. As with intelligence, what we achieve is a combination of the potential we are born with and our motivation to capitalise on it. Our ability to use our imagination allows us to enjoy arousal and orgasm outside the reproductive scenario of intercourse. Some people find this easier to do than others. Due to timidity and embarrassment over discussing sexual pleasuring, few people maximise their sexual potential. Our cultural environment, religious beliefs, the attitudes of the society in which we live and our own personal values all affect our enjoyment of the intellectual aspects of sex. Social restrictions limit men's inclination for promiscuity. Propriety, marital loyalty and family responsibilities are issues.

Orgasm only lasts a few seconds. Sexual pleasure revolves around what happens in the mind. Those who are sexually active assume that everyone responds positively to eroticism. This is far from the truth. There are many people who refer to sex as if they are sexually active when they are not. This is misleading. The most responsive people are having sex rather than talking about it. Perhaps the shame associated with sex (for women) and the desire to conform (to attitudes about what is proper) is too strong. Certainly the average person is not nearly as sexual as we like to think. This certainly includes the vast majority of women of any age as well as many older men.

Eroticism is defined by explicit portrayals (usually visual) of sexual activity or genitals. When someone bends over, the view from behind is provocative to a man. A heterosexual man enjoys the view of an attractive woman's buttocks. A homosexual man responds to the view of a man's behind. Women are not aroused by the same sight because they do not have a drive to penetrate. A woman can admire a man's clothed backside but she has nothing to gain by obtaining it. A woman lacks an organ to penetrate with.

Turn-ons vary according to gender and orientation. The male and female views of what is erotic are very different. An erotically responsive person may not understand that others are not necessarily interested in fantasies. Not all men want to enjoy their arousal through erotic concepts, fantasies and portrayals. Some men's fantasies can definitely be shared. Women can also suggest activities that they enjoy with a lover. We each have the right to privacy. It's a personal decision. Many people don't want to share fantasies.

There is a difference between a man's responsiveness and his enjoyment of erotic turn-ons. The vast majority of men focus purely on opportunities for intercourse. Other men (often the more educated) enjoy fantasies, masturbation alone and foreplay activities with a lover. A man with a creative imagination can obtain release through masturbation alone. He may also want to spend longer enjoying sexual pleasuring with a lover. This impacts on his lover. Women are not always willing to engage in extended sex play.

For a highly responsive man, his sexual responses are a constant biological challenge. A man has no control over these responses. When a man talks about something arousing, interprets a behaviour as arousing or sees someone who arouses him, he has an instant reaction. In the situation where he is not consciously seeking a sexual opportunity, a man can easily interpret the behaviour of those he is attracted to as an invitation. It is difficult to see them as people with their own motivations. For a young man, these feelings are fun. The novelty wears off as a man learns that the feelings never go away.

Many men enjoy eroticism beyond their relationships. Men use porn to substitute for the variety of partners and sex play they do not find in reality. Some women claim to be aroused by porn but they cannot name any explicit turn-ons. If women were aroused by porn, they would want intercourse outside a relationship. They would generate demand for strip-bars and lap-dancing bars. They would heckle and harass men for sex. Women don't do this because men are sexually proactive. A responsive woman uses fantasy to achieve orgasm. But if she openly reads erotic fiction or masturbates, a man always wants intercourse and she loses her opportunity to enjoy orgasm.

We do know that the frequencies of nocturnal dreams show some correlation with the level of erotic responsiveness of an individual. (Alfred Kinsey)

An arousal trigger is either an object or a concept

Some boys and young men can be so highly aroused that they orgasm spontaneously or with little time needed to become aroused. But most adults (and certainly women) need a period of time to build the kind of arousal that leads to orgasm. Arousal arises as an instinctive response to turn-ons, which are objects or concepts that cause arousal, regardless of any relationship or emotional connection. So men can be erotically aroused by a total stranger.

Women tend to find this concept impersonal. Most women want to know a man well and have a sense of emotional connection before they offer a man intercourse. Women are attracted to a lover by emotional factors such as the sound of their voice or their personality rather than their sexual attributes. Women are attracted to men who exude charm and emotional warmth.

Turn-ons work unconditionally. A woman's physical presence represents a sexual opportunity for man even if the woman is not emotionally amenable to sex. This is because men respond to women as objects (body parts) rather than individuals with feelings and choices. Intercourse is a simple pleasure for a man who can insist on taking his pleasure simply by using brute force. A woman cannot. A woman is not aroused by the physical presence of a man because intercourse represents, not a pleasure, but a potential risk. A woman offers intercourse under her own conditions. Most women want to feel confident that a man cares about her personally before offering intercourse.

Each generation of men thinks that women of their generation are more sexual than any previous generation of women. This is because young men are aroused by young women's bodies. But our responsiveness does not depend on how we look. Responsiveness depends on what happens in the mind. Arousal occurs when the mind responds positively to eroticism. Young women are no more enthusiastic about eroticism than older women.

The turn-ons that trigger male arousal are many and varied. Male turn-ons include women's legs, buttocks or breasts. Such stimuli cause arousal rather than orgasm. Otherwise a woman could just show a man her breasts instead of needing to offer intercourse. Orgasm triggers must be much more explicit. Men orgasm from the reality of being a penetrator in penetrative sex. To orgasm alone, both sexes need to focus on highly explicit erotic concepts.

A person needs to be able to block out other distractions in order to obtain the focus necessary to achieve orgasm. The precise thoughts that cause orgasm are highly explicit, personal and often taboo. The concept or the reality of penetrating a lover is the kind of specific turn-on that can cause orgasm. Responsive women use fantasy to focus on the concept of penetrating a lover. Women masturbate to orgasm alone by using surreal fantasies, which are independent of a lover or any relationships in real life.

Many men are turned on by objects that they associate with sex, such as women's underwear. Men talk about women's panties because of the association with genitals and, therefore, with sexual activity. Other men are aroused by sucking on a woman's nipple. Women are bemused by this male fascination with a partner's sexual anatomy and underwear, which they evidently do not share. Men's minds are much more varied in how they use real life scenarios for erotic arousal. Traditionally men have enjoyed "wine, women and song" but there is no female equivalent. Women enjoy relaxing with a book, a non-sexual massage, chatting with friends or clothes shopping.

Some men need a woman to dress up and act out a role in order to obtain their sexual and emotional satisfaction. Popular outfits include house maids, nurses and air stewardesses. Women who work in these lower earning jobs may be more amenable to sexual advances because of the social advantage of obtaining a rich benefactor. Women are not aroused in the same way by the idea of a man acting out different roles or wearing a costume. Some women will provide for a man's unusual needs especially if they are paid.

Some men develop an association between arousal and objects or activities. These result from the way the brain develops and responds to erotic stimuli. As with any arousal mechanism, we have no choice over what arouses us. A fetish is an object that is not directly associated with sexual activity. Men who have fetishes need to have the object on hand or be fantasizing about it, whether they are alone or with a partner, to reach orgasm. A man might masturbate while he holds, smells, rubs or tastes the object. He might ask a partner to wear it or use it during sexual activity. The most common fetish is feet, followed by clothing (often leather or rubber). A fetish, like porn addiction, is not a disorder unless it causes intense, lasting distress. In an attempt to imply equality, some sources suggest some women's willingness to engage in kink and **BDSM** activities is equivalent to having a male fetish.

Women associate sex with a loving act because of their desire for affection. For men, sex can be compatible with violence and aggressive behaviour. A few men even enjoy torture and killing. Men share photographs or live footage (in confidential rings) of real victims (typically women or children) being raped or beaten. There is an adrenaline rush that comes from contemplating an act of aggression and a unique gratification that arises from observing an act of cruelty or violation. The helplessness of the victim causes feelings akin to (but different to) arousal (even in women). Few people are willing to acknowledge such feelings, which contribute to the taboo of sex. They arise from our primitive fascination with observing the gruesome fate of another person. In the past, people watched public hangings or prisoners being butchered. Today, they can watch violent or blood-thirsty movies.

Fetishism is an almost exclusively male phenomenon. (Alfred Kinsey)

Understanding a man's need for erotic turn-ons

For most people, sexual activity whether alone or with a lover is a private affair. We rarely see other people engaging in sexual activity. We rely on fictional accounts from books or movies. Most of this fictional activity involves sociable situations. Masturbatory activities are less commonly portrayed. Men's key focus is penetrative sex. Male erotic turn-ons include a lover's genitals and observing their response to stimulation (especially penetration). Men feel threatened when another man admires their partner because they appreciate the strength of men's sex drive. Men know exactly what is going through a man's mind when he sees an attractive woman.

Men's need for erotic turn-ons has evolved from the fact that intercourse is based on an act of male assault. When a woman is sexually amenable, she has no response due to of her lack of arousal. But equally the vagina is the wrong anatomy - it has zero sensitivity. The only response a woman can have to intercourse (because of the lack of physical sensation) is an unwilling one. For millennia, intercourse often led to a woman becoming pregnant. So women naturally avoid intercourse especially given their lack of erotic arousal. So men's expectation for women to have a response to intercourse is based on a scenario where a woman is resisting the act. This adds to the confusion over how a woman behaves when she is aroused and has an orgasm. She doesn't scream or provide other turn-ons and vocal come-ons.

A man responds sexually to people in the real world. But when a man masturbates, he has to rely on pornography or use his memory alone to conjure up erotic fantasies. This puts a man in a similar position to a woman. Women do not respond erotically to real-world stimuli. There are no naturally occurring triggers such as genitals or sexual activity that cause female arousal with a lover. But a responsive woman can use surreal fantasies to achieve orgasm alone. These fantasies involve appreciating the male view of sex. They allow her to put herself psychologically in the penetrator role.

A man is aroused on seeing a lover and by close body contact. He is aroused by touching and watching a lover undress. He is aroused by stimulating a lover and by being stimulated. For men, even the smallest hint of a cleavage or camel toe is cause for speculation. If women were aroused by a lover's genitals, more men would display their bodies provocatively as a female turn-on. Women go to see male strippers for a laugh rather than erotic arousal.

Women have little interest in visual portrayals of any kind of sexual activity. A tiny amount of porn is produced for women in the mistaken belief that women can be aroused just as men are. If this were the case, women would also use prostitutes, lap dancing and voyeur bars as men do for physical gratification. There are people today who are political motivated to promote the idea that women enjoy eroticism just as men do. But if they did, there would be demand from women in the population, not just political activists. Not only are women not aroused by the idea of male masturbation, they are often disgusted by it. Men tend to keep their masturbatory activities private.

Women are offended by men who whistle at them on the street because, instead of the romantic admiration women enjoy, men refer to their crude and impersonal sexual urges. Unlike women, men do not need an emotional context to enjoy sexual activity. If women were aroused in a similar way, they would understand the male sexual response. Women don't understand how men can want sex with a random unknown person they pass in the street.

A man may say he wants intercourse to last for ever but a woman notices that a man loses confidence if he is taking too long. Perhaps he realises that the woman is waiting for him to finish. A woman knows that he will not be satisfied until he has ejaculated. So she helps him by moving her hips to stimulate his penis or makes encouraging noises in time with his thrusting. Many men expect a woman to fake orgasm so that they can feel fully satisfied. At the most basic instinctive level a man needs to think that what he is doing to a woman is producing some kind of response. He doesn't necessarily need her to enjoy what he is doing. This reflects the primitive penetrative act. A woman screams when she is unwilling such as in the flasher situation.

Some men also need the reassurance of an apparently engaged partner. This is difficult for women to understand. A woman assumes that a man only needs the physical stimulation he can obtain from her body. Women rarely understand that men need assistance with their arousal. Many men don't just want dinner. They want dinner with a show. This emotional reassurance men want (that they are not being selfish), lies at the heart of the dishonesty over sex. A man wants to feel that a lover is pleased by his performance.

A woman feels guilty because she assumes that she is supposed to be aroused by sexual activity with a lover. She feels pressured into making effort but she doesn't see why she should. Providing turn-ons involves even more effort. Many women never appreciate that arousal depends on erotic turn-ons. Even if they do, some women are not comfortable with the deceit of play-acting. No one explains this explicitly because it involves admitting women's lack of arousal. Men are too embarrassed to ask. They assume women should be aroused but they don't raise the issue. They fear their own inadequacy in providing the pleasure that would make sex more mutual.

It is, at once, an interesting reflection of man's absorbing interest in sex, and his astounding ignorance of it; his desire to know and his unwillingness to face the facts; his respect for an objective, scientific approach to the problems involved and his overwhelming urge to be poetic, pornographic, literary, philosophic, traditional, and moral. (Alfred Kinsey)

Only men are aroused by the prospect of sex

Men often vocalise their appreciation on seeing an attractive woman but men are rarely on the receiving end of similar flattery from women. Men never seem to notice that women are not aroused by men's bodies. Many men like to display their sexual interest as bravado. They never notice that women do not admire men for their sexual stamina or technique. To women, men's interest in their anatomy seems crude and basic. Women do not talk about men as sex objects. It is said that women treat men like provider objects.

Men enjoy the sensations of arousal when they look at or come into contact with a women's body. Trains and buses around the world at rush hour provide an opportunity for certain men to grope women's bodies when they are defenceless. Women do not have the benefit of the same turn-ons. So women cannot retaliate by taking the same liberties with a man's body. Women want men to respect the fact that women's bodies are their own.

Some men take advantage of proximity to others to enjoy their own sexual arousal. Other men take advantage of children's innocence and inexperience to coerce them into sexual acts. Women do not do this. This male behaviour makes it much more difficult for men to be allowed to care for children without any supervision. Women are trusted with children's welfare (not just their own) because they do not obtain physical gratification from others.

By thinking about an opportunity for penetration, a man's mental arousal causes blood to flow to his penis. The mental response causes the physical erection that motivates him to complete his arousal cycle by engaging in intercourse. This is an instinctive response. The biological drive is for a man to deposit his semen (containing sperm) within a vagina. A woman lacks a similar drive to ensure that a man deposits his sperm in her vagina. The clitoris is incapable of penetration. Women only ever orgasm when alone.

Humans can remember past events and form associations. If we enjoy a meal, we remember the experience the next time. Even before we sit down to eat, we anticipate the pleasure we will enjoy. Women are just as capable as men of anticipating future pleasure. They certainly respond to the smell of food in a similar way. Men are aroused in anticipation of intercourse because it provides an opportunity to be a penetrator. The pleasures of sex do not impact on women's minds (as they do on men's) because women are not aroused by sexual activity in the first place. There are no erotic stimuli connected with sexual activity with a lover that cause a woman's arousal.

Men are aroused by objects that they associate with erotic pleasure. Even after they have become impotent in old age, men can enjoy fantasies about leggy blondes in suggestive poses. They may appreciate observing young women's backsides as they bend over (interpreted by men as a possible sexual invitation). There is no male equivalent to a leggy blonde. Nor do women ogle men while they proffer their crotches. It is assumed that women become less sexual as they age but no one forgets the pleasure of a turn-on.

Pornography portrays a male view of sex, with visually explicit views of the genital action. As a penetrator, men are aroused by images of nudity (which substitute for a real-life partner) and close-ups of penetrative sex (which remind men of the pleasure they enjoy from penetration). Sex often provides physical gratification for men at the expense of women's dignity and emotional happiness. Pornography makes women feel their bodies have no privacy and no respect. Men's fascination with female nudity makes women feel like face-less, personality-less bodies rather than thinking, feeling people.

Eroticism is defined by male turn-ons: crude and graphic images that cause male arousal. Women consider explicit eroticism to be offensive, even obscene. Even X-rated movies, which are made for adults (over 18 years of age), focus on the upper body contact between lovers rather than genitals. It is assumed that women are aroused by genital activity (just as men are) yet pornography is censored because it offends women. Women are naturally shielded from such images in their relationship with a lover. A woman has limited visibility of her own or her lover's genitals. No one can evolve a response to erotic stimuli they do not naturally experience. Very few couples use mirrors in the bedroom. It is men who enjoy observing sexual activity.

A man does not attract a woman by showing her his erection. Neither does a woman ask to see a man's erection before agreeing to have sex with him. Women are not aroused by genitals and they tend to consider them ugly. Pubescent boys become interested in their own genitals and those of a prospective lover because of their responsiveness. Girls do not experience this sudden increase in sexual responsiveness that boys do at adolescence.

A woman experiences no erotic arousal from sexual scenarios with a lover. Neither is there any physical sensation from intercourse. Consequently, a woman takes little interest in the lower body action of intercourse. She is happy to leave all the genital stimulation to a man. Women describe their sexual motivations in terms of romantic and loving emotions rather than crude sexual urges and erotic responses. Women prefer to see intercourse portrayed as a love-making act rather than as a primitive mating act, which they associate with animal-like activity. A woman hopes that a man cares for her. She is reassured by a lover's display of affection (kissing and caressing).

Most males find it difficult to comprehend why females are not aroused by such graphic representations of sexual action ... The wives, on the other hand, are often at a loss to understand why a male who is having satisfactory sexual relations at home should seek additional stimulation in portrayals of sexual action. (Alfred Kinsey)

Men are aroused by seeing and stimulating genitals

Children of both sexes are indifferent to genitals. They may be mildly curious but they consider genitals to be ugly and smelly parts of the body. At puberty, the increase in male responsiveness causes young men to be fascinated by genitals. For women the connotations from childhood continue into adulthood because women are not responsive as men are.

We say that a woman is sexy if she is attractive to men. It means that a man is aroused by her body or her behaviour. If a man compliments her, it is an opening for a woman to indicate her sexual amenability. A man isn't sexy in the same way. As the initiator, he is assumed to be interested in having sex. Women provide turn-ons to obtain a man's sexual interest or, more often, simply to enjoy being admired. Intercourse relies entirely on male arousal. Women do not need to be aroused to participate in intercourse and so their arousal plays no role in sexual relationships. There is no reason why a woman would be aroused by a penis. A man doesn't have an instinctive interest in the clitoris either. His instincts motivate him to stimulate the vagina. He stimulates the clitoris because of the information he has been given, which implies that orgasm results from clitoral stimulation of any kind.

When a woman is taken by surprise by a strange man (a flasher) displaying his penis, she screams and runs away. This is clear evidence that women are not aroused by a penis. Women consider genitals of either sex to be ugly, hairy and smelly. They are clearly not erotically aroused by them. Yet some women insist against all logic that they are aroused by anatomy as men are. Female arousal serves no useful purpose with a lover. The purpose of male arousal is to make penetration possible. But a woman is never a penetrator.

Most heterosexual men would be interested in observing naked women if they could do so undetected. Men and women use different toilets because women feel uncomfortable thinking that a man might be masturbating himself while watching her relieve herself. Men who spy on women are called Peeping Toms. There is no female equivalent. Women consider this behaviour perverted. Women may be mildly curious to see male nudity if they feel safe from male advances. Men can enjoy watching a woman urinate because of the view of her genitals, which excites them because of the possibility of intercourse. Women are not easy to get into bed but male interest is often guaranteed. A woman has other criteria for choosing a lover.

With a lover, a woman has to engage on explicit genital stimulation with a fully conscious and unaroused mind. A woman experiences no mental arousal with a lover so such situations are social rather than erotic. There is no attraction for her in doing so. She feels the reverse. If she wants to pleasure a partner, a woman does so against her natural instincts. Apart from a woman's desire to share intimacy (love for a partner), there is no reason why she should please her lover any more than a complete stranger.

Most women are embarrassed to name their genitals and sexual anatomy, often considering them to be dirty. Many women prefer to use an applicator to insert a tampon rather than a finger, to avoid having to touch their genitals. During childbirth a woman's skin can tear from the vagina to the anus. Because of embarrassment women often fail to ensure that these tears are dealt with properly and that they heal satisfactorily. Older women often suffer from bowel and bladder incontinence as a result of childbirth damage. Not only are they too embarrassed to ask a lover to look for them but they are not even motivated to use a mirror to look at their own genitals. This aversion to genitals is inbuilt and not the result of upbringing or attitudes.

Men refer to the honeypot to reflect their enjoyment of the pleasure a vagina can provide. Women don't have similar terms of endearment for the penis. It is sometimes called the one-eyed snake because of the opening to the urethra (where urine comes out) in the centre of the glans. Male lovers of men describe fellatio and male ejaculation enthusiastically in graphic terms. Women are repulsed rather than attracted to body function (noises and smells) as men are. Gay men use rimming, stimulating a lover's anus with the tongue. Deep rimming involves inserting the tongue deep into a lover's anus. Filching involves ejaculating into a lover's rectum followed by sucking out and swallowing the semen. Women do not talk of equivalent turn-ons.

Men enjoy talking about pussy juices. Others are turned-on by the idea of a woman urinating. This may be where the male fantasy of female ejaculation comes from. Women are not similarly fascinated by a man's ejaculation. After intercourse, a man's ejaculate flows out of the woman's vagina leaving a wet and sticky patch on the woman's side of the bed. This is because it is typically the man who moves and puts himself on top of her. A woman has to run to the bathroom (cupping her hand to catch any drips) to wash her genitals. She takes no delight in this. It is merely a distasteful inconvenience.

Men are not aroused by breasts if they are nudists or live in cultures where women never cover their breasts. But when women cover their breasts, men come to associate them with sexual opportunities. Straight men can enjoy lesbian sex play because they are aroused by female nudity. If women were aroused as men are, they would comment openly on their appreciation of male nudity and create demand for images of male nudity rather than being offended by them. Male homosexual porn would be freely distributed. Men would also display their sexual attributes for women to enjoy as a turn-on. Men cover up much more than women do because women dislike nudity.

But in all this quantity of pornographic production it is exceedingly difficult to find any material that has been produced by females. (Alfred Kinsey)

The erotic pleasure a man enjoys from sex

Men typically initiate sex and they masturbate much more frequently than women do. If male sex drive only involved a desire for orgasm, then men could settle for masturbation instead of sex. Men have a reproductive or biological drive that means they need intercourse for the best sexual release.

For a man, the action of thrusting into a lover's body produces a strong sense of erotic pleasure and emotional reassurance. This is about being accepted and interpreting the act of penetration as one that arouses a lover. Ejaculation happens but isn't the goal. The fact that a man is accepted as a penetrator is much more emotionally rewarding. Quick or mechanical sex doesn't produce these responses. Masturbation doesn't get anywhere close.

When it comes to an opportunity for penetrative sex, a highly sexed man's arousal is so easily triggered that he has to concentrate on trying not to get triggered inappropriately. Once triggered, a man feels an overpowering adrenaline rush. It's massively exciting and very difficult to resist. A man is conscious of his raised pulse rate and a wave of energy that is indescribable. If we compare the feeling with drinking, it is like feeling the wave of sensation across the brain as the body absorbs the alcohol. A man's sexual response happens much faster and is considerably more powerful. It may equate perhaps more to the intense and instant euphoria of intravenous drugs.

Penetration itself involves a further boost of excitement and adrenaline. The initial entry is exquisite but doesn't last long. It is soon replaced by a soothing and pleasurable experience of being totally enveloped. Some men look for emotional reassurance and sexual acceptance. At this point a partner's subconscious physiological response becomes significant. Through his penis, a man can feel a woman's body responding in terms of pelvic muscle response and the nature of her vaginal secretions changes as he penetrates her. It is amazing how much physical feedback the vagina gives the penis.

These responses a man feels are physical responses that occur within a woman's body. Her body produces vaginal lubrication subconsciously in anticipation of intercourse. But she feels almost nothing either physically or erotically from intercourse. She is not conscious of any mental arousal. A man interprets her physical response according to his own experience of erotic arousal. He is most likely feeling his own sensual and emotional reactions to how he interprets his lover's responses. The fact that a woman offers sex, that she is amenable or affectionate makes him feel loved. But these responses depend on a man giving back in the wider relationship.

A man's sex drive is unaffected by relationship issues. A man is attracted foremost by a partner's physical appearance. He needs to know nothing about a person's personality, whether she is interesting or kind. His prime concern is that she will be amenable to offering him intercourse. A man gives little thought to what a woman might want in return. Some men convince themselves that intercourse is a gift that men bestow on women. When a man can't get an erection, he has no interest in sexual activity of any kind.

A young man tends to be fully absorbed in his own performance. Over time some men come to expect a sign of female appreciation during intercourse. A woman can be a good lover by taking an active role and providing erotic feedback in the form of encouraging noises, verbal sex-talk and by co-operating with intercourse and thereby assisting with penile stimulation. This is the reassurance a man hopes for that his performance is appreciated. A man wants a lover who understands a man's desire to live out his fantasies. Occasionally a man hopes a woman will share his enjoyment of eroticism by watching porn movies together, by indulging in sex play that is more adventurous than intercourse, by exploring the use of sex toys or different sensations and by having sex in different places or in different positions.

Sex is a male pleasure. A man enjoys the sensuality of a woman's nudity and the erotic pleasure of penetrating her body. Men stimulate women because it assists with their arousal. They enjoy sex chat, again because it assists with their own arousal. Women do not respond to the same kind of erotic stimuli that arouse men. So men do not provide erotic turn-ons for women. Men do not dress up in sexy underwear or provide provocative sexual come-ons.

Men can feel ashamed of their urges because women are often offended by the crudeness of the anatomy and the sexual activities that arouse men. Carnal desire includes the crude eroticism of sexual activity with a partner. If a man is behind the woman during intercourse, he has a view of the genital action that optimises his own sexual arousal. A man's desire to enjoy eroticism (the turn-ons of seeing a lover's genitals and the sexual act) is often at odds with a woman's desire to experience intercourse as a loving act.

There is nothing wrong with men's sexual instincts. It is just that women are not aroused in the same way, so they don't understand the pleasure of the adrenaline rush and the sexual release. A man does not see intercourse as a selfish pleasure but rather as an act of worship of a woman's body that arouses him. Ideally intercourse involves full body interaction with a lover who is (at least apparently) in tune with an appreciation of the eroticism of the act from the male perspective. Men want a lover to admire or accept their ability to achieve an erection and to ejaculate. Many men hope for a lover who can enjoy a variety of scenarios and enjoy some erotic fun together. Adventurous sex play for a woman is like playing a game that involves providing the ideal lover in line with a man's fantasies (as portrayed in porn).

"Who wants to have sex for eight hours?" Ask a dude. Ask even a tired dude. No contest. (Joan Sewell)

Women make conscious effort to respond sexually

With all the fiction surrounding women's sexuality, it is important to appreciate that female sexuality has not evolved solely for the purpose of gratifying male ego. Women can't respond in certain ways simply because men would like them to (unless they fake of course). Female sexuality has evolved so as to maximise the chances of successful reproduction. Part of this success can be attributed to women's ability to consciously behave in a way that pleases men. Specifically, women can provide erotic turn-ons that assist with male orgasm, which is the goal of reproduction and intercourse.

Men are naturally more proactive as lovers than women are. Men stimulate a partner because they are aroused by touching, kissing and penetrating a lover's body. Their sex drive focuses them on penetration and the act of thrusting until ejaculation. Women do not have the benefit of erotic arousal. So a woman is not focused on achieving her own orgasm with a lover. She can only make conscious effort to assist with male orgasm (if she wants to). A woman learns that she can excite a man by moving her hips or faking her arousal. This increased male arousal means that a man achieves his sexual release more quickly. This reduces the effort that a woman needs to make.

A woman may be reassured if she can convince herself that she experiences orgasms that reflect male fantasies. But it is vital that other women know that there are no facts or logic to support these fictional responses some women think they have. There's nothing wrong with a woman faking orgasm if her partner expects her to. What a woman decides to tell her lover is up to her.

A dog runs after a ball not because dogs have evolved an interest in chasing balls but because the ball emulates the behaviour of the small mammals that dogs used to hunt for food. When we throw a ball for a dog, it acts as a stimulus that causes the dog to chase after it and perhaps retrieve it. In the wild, the ball is a rabbit and the dog catches the rabbit to eat it. There is a parallel in sex because sexuality encompasses more than reproduction.

Sex play involves a woman throwing the equivalent of a ball for the man. Except, she is the ball! A man wants to emulate the conquest of catching a woman and forcing himself on her. The moans and facial expressions of the porn actresses are based on the resistance scenario. Yet men hope that their wives and girlfriends will provide the same turn-ons naturally. They don't appreciate that the whole thing has to be an act from the female perspective.

When she is a virgin, a woman accepts the stimulation a man offers. A virgin lies inert during intercourse anticipating that something will happen as if by magic. When nothing happens, she can choose between remaining immobile or simulating some kind of enthusiasm. Both social and sexual interaction rely on the active interest of the participants. If a woman lies inert, a man loses confidence in his performance. He interprets her behaviour negatively, even though logically no one can ignore their natural responses.

When a man is a virgin and has intercourse with a sexually experienced woman, she can guide him. But she does not have her own sexual needs. Women have no natural response to consensual intercourse, which provides little sensation. But men seem to need a response from a partner. So an experienced woman moves her hips and makes some noise to help with male arousal. She does this because she loves a man or because she wants to help him achieve his sexual release. She responds because she thinks she should or because she is being paid to act out the part of the proactive lover.

Sex is trivial when a woman is in love but it becomes more onerous over time. Young women are more enthusiastic about sex because of the novelty, romance and ego. There is the hope that orgasm will eventually happen. Men know that platonic love ties women into their relationships. Men often stop providing romantic lead-ins to sex once they have secured a partner.

A man likes to think he has pleased a woman by providing stimulation. Unfortunately, given the sexual inertness of the female body and her lack of arousal, there is little a man can do that provides more than vague sensual pleasure. A woman feels no erotic arousal with a lover, so she can only respond to a partner's initiative. She does this either mechanically (in the case of the prostitute or disenchanted lover) or more ideally because she enjoys demonstrating her love for a partner. A woman has the emotional reward of giving pleasure. For this emotional reward to be effective, she needs to feel that a man cares about her. A woman's enthusiasm dwindles over time because of the effort involved. But she provides sex to keep the peace. She doesn't feel loved, merely used. She stops including affectionate foreplay. Sex becomes a means of satisfying a man's basic sexual needs.

Men tend to look for signs that a female partner is amenable because they get used to the fact that often she is not. A proactive woman may offer when she is in the mood or just to get sex over with. Other women accept a man when he pushes hard enough. Over the longer term a woman equates intercourse to other chores like ironing or washing up. But while ironing, she can watch television. While washing up, she can chat. With sex, there is nothing to do but lie there trying not look too bored so that her partner doesn't take offense. Women offer sex because they know that it is expected. This expectation comes from society (women are expected to offer a partner regular sex), from knowing that men may take their sexual needs (and their income) elsewhere and from women's instincts to care for those they love.

I'm pretty sure he wouldn't be satisfied if we only had sex when I feel like it. I have had to learn it's not all about me. Sometimes I wish it was, but it's not. (Valerie Harris)

Women fake orgasm to reassure men's sexual ego

Faking orgasm provides an easy way for a woman to speed up sex and get it over with as quickly as possible. If a woman lies (by faking orgasm) to a man he finds her hugely attractive. If she's honest then he finds another woman. What do men expect? Some women consider faking to be humiliating and frankly ridiculous. Supposedly 50-80% of women fake. Just because a woman doesn't fake, it doesn't mean she has an orgasm. Many women feel humiliated by the idea of making all that ridiculous and unconvincing noise.

Kinsey's research revealed that some women orgasm by masturbating alone. Previously no one had any idea that women might be capable of orgasm at all. Yet generations of men had no difficulty achieving orgasm from intercourse. The belief in female orgasm with a lover is a modern fantasy that reassures men of women's continuing willingness to offer intercourse. Some women realise that a man's sexual performance is vital to his emotional happiness. If a woman wants to give her lover the satisfaction of assuming that, through intercourse or by other means, he has provided the stimulation that she needs to achieve orgasm, then she is obliged to fake.

The problem with honesty over sex is that a man needs to be aroused by and to feel accepted in his sexual relationship. He relies on erotic turn-ons even if these are only in his head. Woman, who love men, haven't got the heart to disillusion them. Men appear to have an almost infantile need to believe in their fantasies of arousing women. Even if women tell men that sex doesn't provide them with the same pleasure, men don't get it. A man's ego means that for his whole life he can believe (despite all the contrary evidence) that every woman he had sex with wanted it as much as he did every single time.

The fact that every animal in nature mates by the male mounting the female does not persuade him. The fact that women want a relationship, probably a legal one, to offer sex over the longer term does not persuade him. The fact that women have to be paid to have sex does not persuade him. A man never questions why it is the male role to keep a woman happy. This is because it is self-evident what a woman needs to do to keep a man happy. Nevertheless, a man needs to believe that a woman wants sex as much as he does so that he can be reassured of an on-going and regular sexual outlet.

A man assumes that a woman should tell him what he needs to do. It never seems to occur to men that women don't know. Stimulation is easy enough to supply once a person is aroused. The problematic issue is mental arousal. No one can name any female erotic turn-ons. If a woman is unenthusiastic about intercourse, which does nothing to excite her, a man takes this as a personal rejection. Instead of accepting that women do not experience the same pleasure from sex, a man is concerned about satisfying his own needs.

It's pretty cruel to promise someone that they can expect to experience something amazing from something that is, in reality, totally lacking in both erotic turn-ons and physical stimulation. This is the disappointment women face if they approach intercourse with their heads full of the fantasies our society promotes. Saying that women can hope to experience exactly what men do from sex is propaganda spread by those intent on making money.

In some senses, men never grow up. Women have to face the deceit of sex as soon as they lose their virginity. Rather than face their own fears, men pass on the taboo of sexual inadequacy to women. In addition to the other disadvantages of sex that are attributed to women (abortion, prostitution and illegitimate children), women are also labelled as frigid if they do not fake orgasm. Men don't accept that women have different sexual anatomy that provides for childbearing rather than erotic arousal. Neither do women have the mental response to eroticism that men have. This is like blaming a blind man for not being able to see or blaming men because they can't have babies.

Most of the time a woman is only likely to offer intercourse where a man makes all the effort. A woman may offer to pleasure a man occasionally. She may also be willing to let him pleasure her sometimes. A woman needs to be in the mood to be willing to give a man the time to do this. Her generosity is likely to occur sporadically and relies on many factors such as a woman's general state of happiness and the state of the relationship with her lover.

Men are highly aroused by the prospect of intercourse. Many younger men do not offer foreplay because they would ejaculate before they ever got to intercourse. Men much prefer to ejaculate through intercourse. This is natural given the biological precedent (the need for a man to impregnate a woman). A man's dilemma is that he may be too aroused before intercourse to pleasure a woman by stimulating or caressing her. But after intercourse he no longer has the incentive to engage in sexual activity. More mature men actively enjoy pleasuring a woman, which they do before thrusting to orgasm.

The average time a man lasts (from penetration until ejaculation) is only two minutes. Quick intercourse involves least effort for a woman. She only needs to remain in position for the required time. Men who enjoy eroticism like to extend pleasuring by offering foreplay. This need some men have for a woman to be actively engaged makes sex more onerous for women. It is not just the time involved but also the need for a woman to appear to be aroused. A woman may be able to sign over her body to a man's pleasure from time to time. But very few women maintain this sexual generosity over decades. Due to the boredom and invasion of her privacy, even ironing is preferable.

She knows how personally you are going to take it when she can't orgasm, and it makes her dread having sex because she doesn't want to hurt your feelings and then feel even more inadequate. (Sophie Martin)

Why couples don't discuss female arousal

Much of the sexual activity between heterosexuals is carried on without communication. Once intimacy has been established, by kissing for example, a man assumes that he has been accepted as a lover. He increases his exploration of a woman's body. A woman responds by allowing him access to her body. There is no explicit discussion. A man knows what he wants and a woman cooperates because she has no agenda of her own.

There is an advantage in having silent acquiescence. If a person's objection is explicitly acknowledged then it becomes more difficult to ignore. All men want intercourse regardless of whether a woman experiences pleasure, so men prefer to assume that issues with female arousal are a woman's problem rather than an issue for men. Some men enjoy foreplay as a means of feeling that sex is not so one way. But many others do not want to waste time on peripheral activities. They want to get on with obtaining their own release.

Another reason couples don't discuss female arousal is because nothing works. Many couples are unadventurous in bed but even those who try everything do not solve the problem of how a woman can orgasm with a lover. This again is natural because intercourse focuses on male arousal and orgasm by design. For the purposes of reproduction, a woman has to be willing to continue intercourse until a man ejaculates. If women's reason for engaging in sexual activity with a lover was focused on achieving orgasm, then they would stop all activity as soon as they had their orgasm just as men do.

Most of us are insecure about pleasing or performing for a lover. We want to know how we can be good in bed. But men ask, much more than women do, about how they can pleasure a lover. Men believe that they would get more sex if they could provide the stimulation a woman needs for orgasm. Men never seem to wonder why women don't do this for themselves.

Even if a woman is not as sexually proactive as a man would like, talk of orgasm indicates a willingness at least to cooperate with intercourse. Men assume that women who are selling sex do so because they want sex. But women can find sexual partners easily enough. A woman's challenge is to find a man who is willing to offer a supportive relationship in return for sex. Apart from ego, emotional problems and a desire make money, women have no need to go looking for sex. Men always have to seek women out.

Over the longer term, a man comes to accept that his need for intercourse is greater than his partner's. Rather than face constant rejection, he waits for his partner to offer. This puts the onus on a woman to need to plan times when she can reconcile her feelings of being used by a man as a sexual outlet. Over the longer term a generous wife offers when she feels vaguely 'in the mood' just to get the sense of obligation out of the way (until the next time).

A man could ask his lover to explain the specific stimulation she needs to use to achieve orgasm. If a woman is embarrassed, angry or defensive then she doesn't know. Men don't ask about turn-ons because they know that women talk about emotional factors that men do not relate to. Confusingly for men, the suggestions for arousing a woman relate to relationship issues. Women need to be in the right mood for sex. A woman wants a man who is respectful and loving. By definition, these are very different experiences. Men are aroused by sexual opportunities so they fail to appreciate that women only need to be amenable to intercourse not aroused by it. A man can stimulate a woman but he cannot provide the erotic turn-ons that arouse her. Most women have no understanding of the concept of erotic turn-ons. Women are clearly not erotically aroused as men are by real-world triggers.

Many women are disappointed when they lose their virginity because of the lack of sensation from intercourse. Instead of being sympathetic, men cannot accept that a woman's experience could be so different. A man imagines that a lack of orgasm must be easy to solve. He assumes it is just a matter of providing stimulation. He doesn't appreciate that from puberty onwards his mind is full of sexual thoughts. A woman's is not. A woman knows that she is nowhere near being aroused by either the prospect or the reality of intercourse. The fact that a man cannot accept this, makes the subject impossible to discuss. Even if a woman tells her lover that sex does nothing for her, he is undeterred. He sets off on a life-long quest to try to please her sexually. This is the mission of any heterosexual man sensitive enough to realise that his lover obtains less pleasure from sex than he does himself.

But most men simply have no idea what they could do differently. Others are unwilling to explore beyond intercourse, which satisfies their own sexual needs. A man is likely to be cautious. He doesn't want to challenge because he doesn't want to risk losing a woman's amenability. He is similarly happy to accept a woman talking of arousal and orgasm regardless of the lack of evidence. Men's sex drive is emotional and cannot be justified logically.

Women's responsiveness plays no role in sociable activity with a lover. Women are not aroused by talking about sex so they do not have the same incentive to talk about sex, either in reality or fantasy. Even a responsive woman may assume that she feels aroused with a lover despite the lack of orgasm. This is due to the diffuse sensations (increased blood flow) from anticipating intercourse and because she is convinced (due to sexual ignorance in society) that she should be aroused with a lover. Female arousal is largely a subconscious phenomenon. A responsive woman discovers how to use an intense mental focus on surreal fantasies to enjoy orgasm alone.

The average female is not aroused by nearly so many stimuli as is the male. (Alfred Kinsey)

How we know women do not orgasm with a lover

Neither women themselves nor their lovers ever comment on the obvious contradiction over assumptions about the female anatomy involved in orgasm. A woman is assumed to orgasm through intercourse (stimulation of the vagina) in a way that complements the male anatomy. The vagina complements the penis in reproductive terms. A woman is also assumed to orgasm through cunnilingus (stimulation of the clitoris) in a way that mirrors a man's anatomy. The clitoris parallels the penis in terms of responsiveness.

So although men always stimulate the same anatomy (the penis) when heading for orgasm, it is assumed that a variety of anatomy can be involved in female orgasm. The implication is that different women achieve orgasm by stimulating different anatomy. Alternatively, the suggestion is that the same woman achieves orgasm on different occasions by stimulating different anatomy. The mechanism by which orgasm is achieved has to be the same for everyone regardless of sex or orientation. Orgasm involves massaging the blood-flow (resulting from mental arousal) within the erectile sex organ.

We assume that women orgasm because a man knows how to (or is willing to) stimulate her in the correct way. If women were aroused with a lover, they would behave proactively in order to obtain the stimulation they need for orgasm. Women are sexually proactive in pornography because porn actresses are directed to behave in a way that is attractive to men. Men cannot possibly know how to stimulate a woman if she doesn't know herself. We orgasm because of the mental arousal that motivates us to supply (ourselves through masturbation) or obtain the appropriate stimulation (from a lover).

No one ever eulogises about male orgasm, not even men themselves. This is because orgasm ends men's ability to engage in sexual activity and their ability to enjoy the sexual pleasure of the intense sensations of arousal. But when society learned of female orgasm, we did not use our knowledge of the male experience to define it. Instead female orgasm was defined according to the hope that women enjoy pleasure from being stimulated by a lover. Yet, for men, this stage in their arousal cycle equates to arousal rather than orgasm. The reason for this anomaly is that women never reach a point when they can no longer engage in sexual activity or be stimulated by a lover. This is, of course, for the very obvious reason that they do not orgasm with a lover.

The research that identified female orgasm (Kinsey) clearly linked it with clitoral stimulation and female masturbation. This was why female orgasm was not identified by heterosexual couples (or even lesbian couples for that matter). Kinsey's research was unpopular for many reasons. His research highlighted the clitoris (which was obviously considered to be a dead end), which heterosexuals have long showed little interest in. Some men, who enjoy foreplay as a means of extending their own arousal, invest in cunnilingus in the hope of pleasuring a woman. But few women have any use for the clitoris. Even a responsive woman cannot orgasm with a lover.

If female orgasm was common, we would not need so-called orgasm experts to tell us about it. There are no male orgasm experts. Male orgasm occurs reliably. It is not a female fantasy or a turn-on. The words arousal and orgasm refer to women's experience. No one discusses these phenomena for men. If female orgasm were as reliable as male, there would be a similar lack of interest in it. Men's fascination with the idea of female orgasm encourages some women to talk about orgasm with a lover in line with male fantasies. The word 'orgasm' is taboo because of the association with pornography. When orgasm is mentioned men laugh nervously and women say nothing.

No one asks women before they embark on a professional qualification in sexology whether they know what an orgasm is. It is simply assumed that every adult experiences orgasm naturally. Expectations for equality mean that women vehemently defend their orgasm claims when in truth they have no idea what orgasm involves. It would be easy enough to show that these women have no idea what an erotic response involves. But no one ever asks them to provide explicit details. This is partly because of the embarrassment over sex (particularly in the case of women). It is also because men are happy to accept any and every account of female orgasm no matter how unrealistic.

We know that women do not orgasm with a lover because of the enormous political and emotional pressure that is brought to bear to insist they do. Only men talk of sexual pleasure. Most women refuse to comment on the topic. The few women who comment, provide no evidence of enjoying sexual pleasure. Women list various possible body parts as the source of their orgasms and typically cite porn as their means of arousal. Women who say sex is wonderful are probably not even having sex. It's just a mantra that means nothing. They have no idea that arousal involves a mental response. Likewise, the idea of erotic turn-ons is incomprehensible to most women.

The other issue is responsiveness. It is implied that a woman can orgasm whenever she chooses but certainly every time a man does. This is highly unlikely. Even a man cannot time his orgasm exactly to match a lover. Gay men may orgasm in close succession because they are aroused. Women are much less responsive than men and not aroused by real-world erotic stimuli. We know this because no one can name any female erotic turn-ons. If women were aroused with a lover, they and their lovers would know what psychological stimuli, of an erotic nature, cause female arousal and orgasm.

The female's failure to respond to orgasm in her sexual relationships is, nonetheless, one of the most frequent sources of dissatisfaction in marriage. (Alfred Kinsey)

Topic: Masturbation to orgasm

How anyone achieves orgasm when they are alone

Sexuality is about enjoying the responsiveness of our own body through masturbation. Our mind's ability to respond to erotic scenarios (both real and imagined) causes us to investigate our body's responses. Orgasm is a response of the brain. Our minds respond to erotic stimuli regardless of our relationship status and the availability of a partner. A basic characteristic of responsiveness is that we may be able to achieve orgasm by ourselves. Using the hands (or more accurately the fingers) to massage the aroused sex organ, allows us to enjoy the pleasure of arousal and orgasm when we are alone. Humans have used their hands for masturbation since time immemorial.

Frequency of masturbation is an indication of responsiveness. Male masturbation is much more common than female masturbation. Masturbation is most common among men who become adolescent first. Around 99% of such men masturbate compared with 93% of men who reach adolescence later than the average (13 years old). Not every man masturbates but on average men masturbate much more frequently than women (once in three weeks). Some men masturbate many times a day, every day for years.

Regardless of gender, sexual activity that is aimed at achieving orgasm involves continuous rhythmic movements of the whole body focused on the pelvis. Masturbation, for both men and women, simulates the male role in intercourse. Men and women tighten the buttock muscles in a similar way to pressure the sex organ from within the body. Both sexes may also point the toes. Some men stand on tip toe. These subconscious reflexes are a result of the mammalian thrusting instinct. They cannot be used to cause orgasm.

Adults do not tell children how to masturbate. Children and teenagers discover masturbation by themselves if they have the capability. Stimulation is highly likely to lead to orgasm for boys because they are easily aroused. Girls are not automatically aroused (by hormones) as boys are. Even if girls try masturbation, they do not typically achieve orgasm due to lack of mental arousal. Responsiveness involves the brain responding to erotic stimuli. Once aroused the right kind of clitoral stimulation is instinctively applied.

Today because of visual media and a more liberal society there must be few boys who are unaware of how a man masturbates to orgasm. Male masturbation techniques tend to be manual and consistent. But years ago, men still discovered masturbation even without this knowledge from others. Women today are presented with an array of different suggestions for how women are believed to masturbate to orgasm. There is no consistency. The circumstances, the position and even the anatomy varies. A responsive woman learns to masturbate by instinct, just as men did years ago. But when a responsive woman discovers orgasm, she assumes that other women must achieve orgasm in different ways to how she achieves it. She lacks confidence in her own experience because of the conflicting portrayals in the society around her. This so-called knowledge is not a true portrayal of how women achieve orgasm alone. It is sexual ignorance based on what arouses men.

The function of sexual activity alone is the pleasure of the individual. Male masturbation is much more common than female because men are easily and regularly aroused. This constant arousal causes a build-up of sexual frustration that many men like to release through masturbation. A woman is not aroused hormonally, by the visual stimulus of a lover's body or in anticipation of sexual activity. So a woman does not have the same need to masturbate. She never experiences pent-up sex drive as young men do.

Masturbation clearly fulfils quite different functions for men and women. For men, masturbation is usually a poor substitute for sexual activity with a lover. But women only ever orgasm through masturbation. For a responsive woman, orgasm is a simple pleasure but it is not essential to female sexuality.

Responsive women masturbate much less frequently than most men do (once every 3 weeks on average). Few women have the mental response to eroticism that makes orgasm possible. This is natural because female orgasm has no purpose. Orgasm is a male characteristic that is redundant in women. Orgasm represents a relatively minor and occasional pleasure for a woman who is responsive. But she has to make a considerable effort to achieve it.

If a young boy was marooned on a dessert island, he would quite likely experience hormonal erections. But it is unlikely that he would ever masturbate because he would not have the stimulus of another person's body to use as a fantasy. If a young girl was marooned on a dessert island, she would never discover orgasm. She would never be an object of male desire and so a girl would never develop the erotic fantasies she needs for orgasm.

Adults masturbate over the longer term because they can generate fantasies that reliably lead to orgasm. The incidence and frequency of masturbation is related to our responsiveness and to the creativeness of our imagination. The more creative and inventive we are about imagining scenarios, the more likely we are to enjoy solitary sexual activity that relies on our imagination.

A man experiences fantasy as a reflection of the real-world. He imagines a real partner in realistic and achievable situations. But a woman's fantasies are based on unrealistic scenarios quite unrelated to real life. We could try different approaches to achieving arousal and orgasm. But we tend to use the mechanism that works. The techniques of masturbation are limited.

Masturbation may or may not be pursued to the point of orgasm, and it may or may not have orgasm as its objective. (Alfred Kinsey)

How men masturbate themselves to orgasm

Few boys masturbate before the onset of adolescence. Only 10% of boys are masturbating by the age of nine and only 13% by ten years of age. Male masturbation frequencies vary significantly in the population indicating not only a range in responsiveness but also variations in how different men can use their minds to enjoy their arousal cycle from erection to ejaculation.

Boys only start to use fantasies once they have some sexual experience (either alone or with a partner). A boy engages in sexual fantasies (at least to start with) because he enjoys remembering how someone aroused him. He uses his memories (perhaps enhanced over time by imagination) to achieve what initially occurred spontaneously or through physical stimulation alone. For a man, eroticism is inextricably linked to opportunities for penetration. When masturbating, a man imagines graphic activity with a real-life partner.

Men masturbate by emulating the male role in intercourse. Men use the fingers of one hand or their whole fist to vigorously massage the shaft of the penis. Male masturbation simulates intercourse as much as one can by just using a hand. The action of using fingers to massage the skin covering the shaft of the penis rapidly up and down over the glans, stimulates the shaft of the penis in a similar way to intercourse. Men masturbate by using mental images or fantasies that involve fairly realistic opportunities for intercourse.

Men typically stand and move their foreskin firmly and with considerable speed back and forth over the glans (head of the penis). The glans is only stimulated through the foreskin and it is a fleeting movement. Most of the stimulation is directed towards the shaft of the penis, which is where the blood flow is concentrated in the corpora cavernosa. Men may observe their erection as they push their penis downwards and thrust their hips forwards.

Men are usually fairly flexible about where and in what position they can masturbate. Standing is the most natural position for male masturbation, which allows a man to easily tense his buttocks. Men can also stimulate themselves to orgasm when sitting or lying down, with a lover for example. Men have no difficulty being masturbated to orgasm by a lover. Some young men masturbate in public, for example, in front of their same-sex friends.

Men masturbate with their eyes open. A man is aroused by the visual evidence of his own arousal. He typically watches the action of his hand pumping the shaft of his penis. A man may squeeze out some pre-cum liquid to lubricate the glans. As he approaches orgasm, a man raises himself up on tiptoe and pushes his hips forward. This has the effect of tightening the buttock muscles, which pressures the internal erectile organ from behind.

Only 92% of men masturbate. Out of every hundred men, eight men never masturbate. Some boys have their first ejaculation through intercourse. They may never masturbate because they have intercourse sufficiently frequently that they never need the additional sexual outlet. A very small number of men have sufficiently low sex drive that they never feel a need to masturbate. Men masturbate when they are alone. They are typically much less interested in masturbation with a lover. Manual stimulation of the penis tends to be a transitory activity with a lover that rarely proceeds as far as ejaculation.

Men can orgasm through a variety of penile stimulation techniques including intercourse, masturbation and fellatio (oral sex). Men masturbate to orgasm within a minute or less because of the more specific physical stimulation that masturbation provides. Some men choose to masturbate because they enjoy the variety of sexual outlet. Most men would not masturbate if they had an opportunity for intercourse, which is much more erotically rewarding.

Although male speeds to orgasm are quicker with masturbation (than intercourse) the orgasms may be less emotionally rewarding. Masturbation relies on being able to imagine turn-ons. Whereas with intercourse a man has the turn-on of a partner that allows him to achieve the best sexual release. Intercourse has the benefit of providing a warm and wet environment. Men enjoy the arousing sensations of whole-body contact and thrusting that intercourse provides (especially as they age and their hormone levels fall).

Highly responsive and younger men are easily aroused. So men only need to use fantasy to boost their natural arousal during masturbation alone. Some men rely purely on imagination but often visual material is more effective. Masturbation relies on having a creative imagination. The closer a scenario is to real life, the easier it is to create a scenario in one's imagination. Pornographic movies work better than still images. Young men naturally transition to sex with a lover because their fantasies reflect realistic scenarios.

Men's dependence on a partner is reflected in the popularity of inflatable dolls as masturbation accessories for men. Sex dolls are always available. The fact that a heterosexual man can use a sex doll to ejaculate into reflects the active male sexual role and the passive female sexual role. Women do not use sex dolls because they are not aroused by real-world erotic stimuli. Responsive women do not imagine real people or realistic scenarios when aiming for orgasm. They have to use surreal situations and fictional people. This mechanism (that makes men into sex objects) is much more naturally achieved by a man, who can view a partner in terms of their sexual attributes.

In the human male, masturbatory techniques are largely manual. ... Most males carry the activity though to climax as rapidly as is possible, which means it does not ordinarily continue for more than a minute or two. (Alfred Kinsey)

Educated men masturbate more than other men

Masturbation is least common among less educated males (89%). More men who are high school educated (95%) and men who are college educated (96%) are involved in masturbation for at least some period of their lives.

Masturbation frequencies after marriage are highest (69%) among men who are college educated. Only 42% of men, who are high school educated, masturbate after marriage and only 29% of the least educated males.

There is no objective measure of a person's imaginative capacities. But someone who is more educated is likely to be more imaginative because they use their minds and have been exposed to more ideas. Those who are successful academically may have a more active imagination due to increased mental capacities in general. Education is therefore only a guide to the likelihood that someone is imaginative. A good imagination is useful when masturbating because even men need to use fantasy in the absence of a lover.

Kinsey commented on the taboo over masturbation among the uneducated. Kinsey linked male sexuality and education because of the use of fantasy. A creative imagination is an even more critical requirement of female masturbation because women are not aroused by real-world triggers. There are many fewer women (compared with men) who have a mind that responds positively to eroticism. Accurate statistics are difficult to obtain for women's experience due to ignorance about orgasm and how it is achieved.

The vast majority of men see women purely as objects of sexual interest. They may only interact with women on a sexual basis. Such men can obtain satisfaction from making sexual assaults because of the adrenaline of the hunter and victim scenario. They may even enjoy a woman's protestations because of the erotic turn-on of obtaining a response. They may not fantasise about how a woman feels about the sexual scenario because their focus is their own role as penetrator. Such men are much less inclined to masturbate.

Other men (sometimes the more educated) are more sexually timid. They look for the emotional reassurance of obtaining a woman's approval. Such men are much more likely to indulge in fantasies about how a woman might be responding to their attentions. They imagine that she is aroused and that she welcomes their advances. These men enjoy masturbation because of the fantasies that they develop over time around the idea of a female response.

Research indicates that uneducated men seek out prostitutes more than educated men do. Many men's sexual satisfaction is not related to knowing a person. Educated men make more discerning choices over the sexual scenarios that interest them. Educated men look for more sophistication in the woman's sexual performance including her willingness to be proactive with a lover. Educated men also expect a greater emotional connection with a lover. Education causes a person to have an increased sensitivity to the views of others. Educated men are more inclined to accept a woman's desire to spend time getting to know a person before becoming sexually involved.

Men have a biological sex drive but they make conscious choices over how and when they achieve orgasm. A man is also influenced by the company he keeps and the society in which he lives. Sex involves another person, which makes consent an issue. Some women, those who lack confidence, experience or who are less educated, may be less discerning than others.

Alfred Kinsey found that younger generations of women were better informed about orgasm. They were more inclined to say that orgasm was possible with a lover but at the same time they agreed to have sex less often than older women. He suggested that changing attitudes in society and women's emancipation, meant that younger and more educated men were more inclined to take into account their partner's lower desire for sex. As women gain confidence with age and experience, they are more likely to insist on their own preferences for less regular sexual activity with a lover.

Research indicates that less educated men are more responsive than educated men. This means that overall (including all forms of sexual activity) educated men have fewer orgasms on average than less educated men. It is strange that something such as education should have an effect on responsiveness. Responsiveness is an innate characteristic of the human mind and body. It is not determined by environmental factors. We need to differentiate between our potential to orgasm and what we actually achieve. Our responsiveness (orgasm frequency) depends not only on biological factors but also on our motivation to capitalise on opportunities to engage in sexual activity. Men, who are insensitive to women's lack of responsiveness, are more likely than more sensitive men to continue to insist on intercourse.

Less educated men tend to have more intercourse than more educated men. This is because more educated women are more assertive about making their own sexual decisions. They are potentially more financially independent and so have less need to keep men happy. Such women are less inclined to marry and to be asked to marry than less educated women. So less educated men who marry less educated women have an advantage. Men can orgasm easily through intercourse because of the turn-on of penetration. Orgasm is not as spontaneous with masturbation because a man relies on imagination. So a less educated man who relies purely on intercourse is likely to orgasm more than a man who uses masturbation.

Males with the highest frequencies of masturbation are most often those who become adolescent first. These are the males who have the maximum total outlet throughout their lives (Alfred Kinsey)

How women masturbate themselves to orgasm

Women may be mildly curious about genitals but they are not aroused by them. Neither are women hormonally aroused as younger men are. So most women are not remotely curious about masturbation. Female orgasm is rare. So we will never have millions of women agreeing on how they orgasm. The best we can hope for is a scientific justification of women's orgasm techniques. If our motivation to masturbate arises because someone tells us we should, because we buy a sex toy or from a wish to experience orgasm, nothing will happen. We are motivated to masturbate because we feel a sense of excitement in our minds when thinking about an erotic scenario.

Orgasm arises from stimulating the anatomy men and women have in common, the phallus. The clitoris is stimulated in a similar way to how a man masturbates his penis. As for a man, a woman focuses the stimulation on massaging the blood-flow in the corpora cavernosa (resulting from mental arousal) that are located within the body (or shaft) of the clitoral organ.

With other body functions such as urination and defecation when there is a need, our brain makes us increasingly conscious of the need to take action. Men have an instant and urgent sense of needing to take action on becoming aware of their sexual arousal. But a woman never has a biological (or any other) need to orgasm. A woman is never conscious of her physical arousal except when consciously generating it during masturbation. A responsive woman only embarks on masturbation when her mind is responding to a fantasy. The feelings she has in anticipation of sex are quite different. She may be conscious of diffuse sensations, which are probably due to increased blood flow in the pelvis. They are not a result of any mental focus on eroticism and they do not equate to the kind of arousal that leads to orgasm.

The initial catalyst for masturbation is the thought appearing in a woman's mind that orgasm might be possible. There is a mandatory period of time upfront, when a woman has to decide whether she can generate enough arousal for orgasm. This is the most critical and often the longest phase. She cycles through possible fantasies to see if her mind is going to respond. She uses a handful of scenarios from erotic literature. Over time these extracts are reused over and over by relying on memory. She homes in on the aspects of the scenario that she knows from past experience will cause her to orgasm.

One of the first signs of female arousal is a very slight genital response to a woman's mind responding positively to a sexual scenario. When she massages over her glans, a responsive woman feels a slight tingling. She is conscious of a sense of excitement as her genitals become tumescent and an increase in heart rate or breathing. If a woman is not responding, then fantasies that would normally arouse her seem unappealing. She just abandons the idea. She may feel a mild sense of disappointment but no frustration. Female arousal is easily dissipated by real-world interruptions.

While a woman is waiting for a fantasy to provide the tumescence she needs, she lies on her front somewhere comfortable, with her fingers from both hands over her vulva. Initially, she keeps her fingers in position over the top of the glans (protected by the surrounding skin) and moves her hips by shifting her legs alternately up and down while concentrating on her fantasy. A woman holds her breath as she concentrates, followed by involuntary sharp intakes of breath. A woman stimulates herself much less aggressively than the action men use. A man masturbates with rapid (5 times a second) jerks but a woman uses a slower (once a second) rhythmic massaging motion.

A woman masturbates to orgasm by lying face down with her eyes closed. She rubs down over her vulva with fingers from both hands. She cannot easily see what she is doing nor is she aware of the specific anatomy she is stimulating. It is only if she learns of the clitoris that she can appreciate that this must be the anatomy she is stimulating. She masturbates by pressing down over her glans and into the area of spongey tissue immediately below.

Initially a responsive woman focuses stimulation over the clitoral glans. She uses the index and middle fingers of both hands to push the loose skin gently and rhythmically over (the hood of) the glans (either side of the labia) and down towards the vagina. As her erotic excitement increases, she shifts the focus of her stimulation. A woman presses her fingers down rhythmically and firmly into the spongy internal pelvic tissue immediately beside the labia majora (just below the pubic bone), kneading the internal clitoral organ. This second stage of massaging is combined with internal pressure on the clitoral organ, achieved by a hip thrusting motion and by rhythmically clenching the buttock muscles. She uses a squeeze technique, which involves thrusting the pelvis forward. The shaft (or body) of the clitoral organ is squeezed between her hands in front (externally) and her pelvic muscles behind (internally). All of this stimulation is an instinctive response. It is not a conscious behaviour.

A woman's mental focus (which blocks out all awareness of her surroundings) throughout is on the fantasy until she reaches orgasm. A woman imagines a penetrator's excitement, which culminates in an urge to ejaculate. She uses both hands to push down firmly and closes her eyes as she orgasms. Once her mind has tuned into a fantasy a woman can orgasm within a minute or two. While masturbating, a woman makes little noise until her orgasm when she may grunt or pant. Her facial expression is not smiling or pouting. She may grunt or groan depending on the strength of her release.

... a high percentage of all the females who masturbate use techniques which involve some sort of rhythmic stimulation of the clitoris, usually with a finger or several fingers or the whole hand. (Alfred Kinsey)

Women's fantasies are sexually explicit scenarios

A responsive woman's use of fantasies means her experiences do not fit with any of the descriptions of sexual activity that we see portrayed in society. Sexual activity is usually sociable but it is also portrayed in graphic terms. When something happens in your head, it can be purely conceptual. This is probably why women prefer reading erotica rather than looking at images.

A woman experiences orgasm by delving into her subconscious. She has to concentrate on the script she remembers from prior sessions. Alternatively, her mind may be focused on the text of a book she is reading. She cannot be distracted even by a dripping tap. She needs 100% concentration to dredge up enough arousal that enables her to orgasm. Afterwards it is difficult for her to remember exactly what she felt in the build up to orgasm.

While fantasising a woman's mind is focused on some of her most intimate memories or ideas that cause her arousal. Fantasies are concepts that reach into the more instinctive rather than thinking parts of the brain. They may include the idea of enduring pain, of inflicting pain, of being vulnerable, of fearing attack and the mystery of what another person may do to us. Many of these thoughts are like vague dreams and not consciously acknowledged. They are the kind of thoughts that we never consciously admit to ourselves.

When we read, we can imagine the setting, the people and their emotions as narrated by the author. These images are not like focused photographic images. They are more like a collection of impressions or feelings when we dream. They are like echoes of the real world. The scene is presented in terms of the feelings and motivations of the persons involved. This builds anticipation in a way that books do (but movies don't). Erotic fantasies that a responsive woman uses for arousal are psychological, full of anticipation and the idea of others doing things to her. The action focuses on bondage, BDSM and penetration. Ultimately the action of the fantasy escalates her state of arousal so that the climax of the fantasy coincides with her orgasm.

Women who discover how to masturbate to orgasm, understand the need for a source of eroticism. Although they don't respond to pornography in the way that men do, they may be more understanding of men's need for an arousal mechanism in the absence of a partner. Responsive women do not reveal their erotic fantasies because they are private and surreal. Our fantasies represent aspects of sex that we find most arousing and taboo. Even men do not readily admit the explicit and crude sexual images that they need to focus on for orgasm. These are our most private and personal thoughts.

Most men are lucky because they are aroused by body parts and basic concepts, such as a women's sexual amenability. Women use much more disturbing fantasies to masturbate to orgasm. Arousal relies on BDSM concepts and the idea of inflicting penetration on someone. Having a fantasy about a particular activity does not mean that a person wants to engage in that activity for real or that they would enjoy such activity in reality. Nor does a fantasy represent an unconscious desire. This in part, explains why women are reluctant to tell anyone, even a lover, what they fantasise about.

Eroticism is a male portrayal of intercourse. Penetrative sex is arousing from the point of view of the penetrator. Penetrative sex is not arousing for the person who is penetrated by an erect penis (the receiver). A woman needs to be able to identify psychologically with the male perspective in order to achieve orgasm. When a responsive woman immerses herself in a surreal world in her head, she can put herself in the male position psychologically. She does not do this as a result of a conscious decision. It occurs naturally as she explores scenarios in her mind that cause her mental arousal. The experience is strange and inexplicable because it is an instinctive response. It is not a conscious behaviour based on information she has been given.

The concept of penetration is key to achieving erotic arousal. A woman obtains a sexual release from the idea of dominating or doing something to another person. A woman's fantasy focuses on her own body that is being conceptually penetrated as well as the psychology of the man penetrating her. She is not trying to be a man. She uses the psychological technique of emulating a man's proactive role as penetrator. This is not done consciously but occurs as a subconscious response to mental arousal. Women sometimes describe this technique as putting themselves in the director role.

Fantasy is a mechanism for enjoying the sensations of orgasm rather than being an activity a woman engages in for itself. Responsive women use erotic fantasies as a conscious psychological technique for the sole purpose of enjoying orgasm. A woman's sense of release comes from the use of fantasy. Women have a limited menu of fantasies to choose from. This seems to be a result of a natural apathy over making effort to search out erotic material. A woman may have only a handful of fantasies that she uses on a regular basis, some of which originate from when she first started masturbating.

Given a choice a woman finds the romantic scenario much more emotionally rewarding than the erotic. Women may avoid masturbating feeling that it is immoral. This is not so. When we fantasise, we release the subconscious thoughts that are there, whether we consciously admit to them or not. Women may use a constructed rape scenario (these lack the real-world sense of violation) that allow a woman to assume a passive role and to focus on the psychology of the male taking his pleasure from her body.

There is a startling gulf between fantasy and what a woman is really seeking in a sexual relationship and she may find this very disturbing. (Sheila Kitzinger)

The kind of stimulation that leads to orgasm

Regardless of orientation, men orgasm through intercourse, masturbation and fellatio. A man's arousal (in the form of an erection) also gives him a clear indication of the anatomy he wants to stimulate. By contrast women, including lesbians, enjoy more sensual whole-body and emotional pleasures with a lover because of their lack of arousal. This contributes to the confusion over the anatomy involved in achieving female orgasm. Men assume women are aroused and that they orgasm with a lover as men do.

On the basis of our porno education, we tend to assume that a woman can orgasm from different kinds of stimulation applied to a variety of sexual anatomy. Yet men clearly always need penile stimulation. Male masturbation and fellatio both mimic intercourse and involve a similar massaging stimulation of the shaft of the penis. A man can obtain the stimulation of intercourse, regardless of a partner's willingness. But a woman cannot force anyone, especially a man, to provide any form of stimulation. She can ask a man to penetrate her vagina but she cannot make it happen according to her own need. This is significant because we cannot evolve a response to stimulation that we cannot reliably obtain. A woman can buy a vibrator in modern times but this form of stimulation never existed before. All forms of female stimulation by a partner depend on a lover's willingness to provide it.

There is no precedent or justification for female orgasm. Other female animals do not appear to orgasm at any time and female orgasm has no role in reproduction. The only precedent relates to male orgasm, which is required for reproduction because it triggers ejaculation of sperm. Male animals use an insertion method to fertilise the egg within the female's body. Female orgasm can only be explained in terms relative to male orgasm. Female masturbation mimics male thrusting. A woman emulates the male role in intercourse, by thrusting with her pelvis and clenching her buttocks. A responsive woman lies on her front and uses the fingers of both hands to push gently over the glans and towards (either side) of the vaginal entrance.

An adult experiences orgasm (once aroused) by stimulating the erectile sex organ (the phallus). The penis and the clitoris are anatomically equivalent. The sex organs (penis and clitoris) have two corpora cavernosa that fill with blood when the mind is engaged with thoughts of an explicitly erotic nature. The kind of stimulation, that might lead to orgasm, is highly specific and involves massaging the erectile organ or more specifically the blood-flow within the phallus. The phallus must be stimulated from arousal through to climax, by massaging the erectile organ in a firm and continuous rhythm.

A man masturbates by holding his erect penis between his fingers and pulling the skin up and down the shaft. A woman's masturbation technique does not feel so explicitly sexual or genitally focused. A responsive woman pushes down over her vulva while thinking about an erotic scenario. It is a very personal and private experience. When a woman is stimulating herself, her actions are dictated by subconscious instinct rather than conscious thought.

A responsive woman experiences very slight physical arousal when focused on erotic fantasy. She is motivated to massage her vulva because of the tingling sensation from the increased blood flow (tumescence). A woman has little awareness of the specific anatomy she is stimulating. Her focus is on what is happening in her mind. She could not see easily even if she wanted to look. Kinsey reported the external anatomy that women stimulate including the clitoral glans and labia. More accurately a woman stimulates the internal clitoral organ, which contains the corpora cavernosa, by pushing down with her fingers. She pushes the skin down over the top of the glans. As arousal builds, she presses down into the tissue either side of her labia.

Anyone who can orgasm should be able to describe not only the anatomy but also the kind of stimulation that leads to orgasm. Most women are unaware of the location and function of the clitoris. Neither cunnilingus nor a vibrator massage the internal clitoral organ in the correct way. If female orgasm was achieved by stimulating visible and clearly identifiable anatomy such as the clitoral glans, throughout history women would have been aware of the clitoris. If they had been able to use this technique with a lover, then their partners (heterosexual men) would also know about it. Heterosexuals would have discovered female orgasm by themselves. Society would not have needed scientists to tell them about the clitoris or about female orgasm.

The hands are the most natural masturbation tool and everything else is a gimmick. The massaging motion over the glans is similar for both sexes. The main difference is that a woman doesn't have a shaft to stimulate. Her technique cannot therefore mimic intercourse as closely as a man's can. A woman uses a humping motion to thrust her vulva against her fingers. Some women do rub their vulva against a soft object such as a stuffed toy or a pillow. This type of stimulation is not sufficiently explicit to cause orgasm.

Immediately before reaching orgasm, we may cease stimulation. Just like the shove penny game at the fair, we are nearly there and we know that just a little effort can now cause orgasm. Like waiting for a wave to reach us and then riding the wave onto the beach, we wait for our climax to arrive. Once the surge of orgasm starts, we apply firm pressure to have the satisfaction of thrusting as we massage our sex organ and enjoy the pelvic contractions.

The effectiveness of such a technique depends chiefly upon ... pelvic movements and rhythmic contractions of the large muscles (the gluteal muscles) in the buttocks, and of the muscles (chiefly adductors) which are located near the front and inner surfaces of the thigh. (Alfred Kinsey)

How we know that female masturbation is rare

Kinsey concluded that masturbation was not only the quickest way for a woman to orgasm (4 minutes on average) but also the most reliable way (95% success rate). Women's masturbatory activities provided the clearest evidence for female orgasm. Kinsey found that 20% of women masturbated regularly. So his work indicates that around 20% of women may be capable of orgasm. But the percentage of women who do truly orgasm is likely to be much lower than this in the general population. Women are under such pressure to have orgasms that they also assume mistakenly that they orgasm from masturbation. He found that two out of every five women (42%) never masturbate while a similar number (38%) try masturbation but are not motivated to continue. Kinsey's sample included university educated women who are likely to read more and be more imaginative than average. This may increase the likelihood that they discover orgasm (if they are responsive). Kinsey remarked on the taboo over masturbation among the less educated.

Research inevitably involves women who are confident enough to come forward and talk about sex and orgasm. The silence of women in the general population over sex suggests that female masturbation is much less common than this. Reading Shere Hite's book is a tremendous relief to any woman who masturbates. Her work is the only evidence that women orgasm easily alone but that they cannot achieve the same thing with a lover. The fact that her book is largely unknown is clear evidence that few women masturbate.

Shere Hite listed a variety of positions that women reported using during masturbation. Only 5% of the women in her sample who masturbated, did so by lying on their front. This means that the rest (the vast majority) were not actually achieving orgasm. Kinsey noted the technique of lying face down and thrusting with the hips, which only related to a few of the women who said that they masturbated. Kinsey also commented that many women do not use fantasy. Clearly many women are not masturbating to orgasm.

Beliefs about women's presumed orgasms with a lover are based on the stimulation that men provide and a variety of anatomy. Achieving orgasm depends on being able to stimulate the sex organ continuously. Women clearly mistake emotional sensations for orgasm with a lover. Even without mentioning sex directly, there are signs that indicate a person's attitude towards eroticism. Most women ignore or are offended by sexual references, which is a sign that they are not receptive to discussing orgasm. Most women dislike explicit references to genitals and so they say 'front bottom' or 'down there' by which they mean anywhere between their clitoris and their anus. Most women consider the clitoris to be too sexually explicit for a heterosexual woman. Orgasm is associated with women (because male orgasm is so automatic). Both the clitoris and the word orgasm are taboo, being associated with porn more than with women's own sexual pleasure.

Women can be strong in their condemnation of explicitly sexual activity. Many women simply do not understand why anyone would masturbate. Neither men nor women appear to be aware of the fact that before anyone can orgasm, they must first be aroused. Men's arousal is fairly automatic but women have to work much harder at generating their arousal consciously. Most women react with self-righteous disgust if masturbation, genitals or fantasies are mentioned. A responsive woman is inevitably alienated by such attitudes. Female masturbation is so rare that she has no one to compare notes with. Other women react negatively to any talk of sexual fantasies and the clitoris. Men also avoid referring to masturbation for the same reason.

From the universal silence and ignorance over female orgasm, we can conclude that female masturbation and hence female orgasm are rare. Women allow men to portray their sexual responsiveness in completely unrealistic ways without ever commenting. Most women have little confidence in their own experiences so they accept all the fictional accounts, as possibilities for other women, if not for themselves. Few women even know that they have a clitoris, let alone know what to do with it. Men explore the female body as they always have done. Armed with the latest news of the clitoris men convince themselves that, as a new breed of male lover, they provide women with amazing pleasure for the first time in human history.

Some men feel threatened by women's success with masturbation alone. They may conclude that by having orgasms alone a woman is less likely to orgasm with a lover. This is not the case. Women are just not aroused with a lover. The surgical removal of a girl's clitoris (grossly misnamed female circumcision) certainly ensures that she will never discover masturbation. This practise, which is accepted by women, indicates the rarity of female masturbation and therefore of female orgasm. Female circumcision is clear evidence that clitoral stimulation does not cause orgasm with a lover. Men would never eliminate a means of women having an orgasm with them.

Women never comment on the different stimulation techniques and anatomy that are supposed to cause female orgasm. If women knew how to masturbate themselves to orgasm, then more women would realise that intercourse does not cause female orgasm. Also their lovers would realise. Clitoral stimulation is associated with lesbians who cannot engage in intercourse and so tend to engage in more explicit genitally focused sex play.

... certainly, it is easier for most women to be orgasmic during masturbation than during intercourse. ... For most women, masturbation involves stimulation of the clitoris, whereas with intercourse, the clitoris is only stimulated indirectly. (William Masters and Virginia Johnson)

We (not a sex toy or lover) cause our own orgasm

Even when a sex organ is capable of penetration (as the penis is), it cannot cause a lover's orgasm. For a person to orgasm, they must be motivated to obtain the correct stimulation of their own phallus. Men are aroused biologically and automatically; women are not. The physical stimulation involved in achieving orgasm is almost incidental in the sense that it is trivial. Once a person is aroused the stimulation is supplied instinctively. Any woman can buy a sex toy to reassure herself that she can orgasm as she has been told she should. This is not the result of an instinctive urge. Men do not use a vibrator to masturbate because it is the wrong kind of stimulation.

Even men do not orgasm simply by pressing a button. For stimulation to be effective, we must focus on an aspect of eroticism that causes mental arousal. Ironically, it is women's aversion to fantasy that makes a vibrator attractive. A gadget gives women something to do. It is devoid of the dirty associations that women attribute to sexual activity. A gadget is acceptable because it can be accessorized and comes in different colours. Many women find the idea of touching anyone's genitals (even their own) distasteful. By using an accessory, women avoid needing to touch their genitals with their fingers.

Vibrators tend to be modelled on dildos (shaped like an erect penis) which were symbols of male potency in the past. This shape is suggestive of eroticism but also confuses women into thinking that they are supposed to stimulate their vaginas to simulate intercourse. Undoubtedly, a dildo is most useful to men who want to experience anal penetration. There is no obvious explanation for why women should orgasm from the high-speed (powered by an electric battery) kind of vibrating stimulation that does not occur in Nature. Despite all the publicity, few women are tempted to buy a sex toy.

Some women claim to orgasm by stimulating the clitoral glans. Unlike the body of the clitoris, the glans does not become tumescent during sexual arousal, as it does not contain erectile (expandable) tissue. The technique of stimulating the clitoral glans appears to mimic male masturbatory techniques. But this is a false analogy. When a man stimulates his penis, he focuses his stimulation on the corpora cavernosa within the shaft of the penis. The clitoris also has corpora cavernosa but they are located within the internal clitoral organ rather than the glans. The only way to massage this area is to push down into the spongy tissue either side of the labia majora.

Most so-called sexual knowledge is based on erroneous assumptions. There is no research that proves women orgasm through intercourse. Neither is there any research proving that a vibrator guarantees orgasm. A few women boast about orgasm and we believe them. But millions of other women are silent. The sex toy industry (very wisely) never claims that their products give anyone an orgasm. We can deduce that a vibrator does not increase women's enthusiasm for sex. If it did, men would be rushing out to buy one. Vibrators are noticeably missing from pornography. Men prefer to believe that the stimulation that satisfies them, also provides women's satisfaction.

Some women claim to use a vibrator either before or during intercourse. A key question is why a woman would want to masturbate during intercourse. Why would she not masturbate alone without the distraction of a lover who is likely to interrupt? Research indicates that men only last an average of 2 minutes before ejaculating. So a woman would be under considerable time pressure. This activity is neither loving nor sociable and it is difficult to imagine couples engaging in what amounts to parallel masturbation. It's tempting to think that a woman might want to share her orgasm with a lover but this is just because we accept women's role of providing male turn-ons.

Ignorance over the role of mental arousal, means that everyone accepts that women's orgasm difficulties must be due to inadequate stimulation. Perhaps women are reassured by implicitly shifting the blame onto men. Orgasm is promoted as a commodity that can be purchased rather than being an instinctive response. Yet this form of stimulation has only been available recently. The marketing of sex toys has been so successful that many people assume every woman owns one. Many women appreciate that they are not aroused so stimulation is pointless. Women buy vibrators because they do not discover orgasm by instinct. It is also a reflection of the political and emotional pressure on women to say that they can orgasm just as men do.

Responsiveness is a capability that has evolved over eons. That means our ancestors must have had a similar capability. It is not possible for women to evolve a new physiological response overnight. By applying 'the dog and ball theory', we can see that a vibrator does not replicate any kind of naturally occurring stimulation. The stimulation provided by a vibrating gadget is nothing like a thrusting penis or the stimulation of manual masturbation.

For most of our history, there has been no substitute for a penis. Women couldn't just use a random stick because it would be too uncomfortable. If a woman wants vaginal stimulation, there are more than enough men willing and available. Why would she ever need a substitute? In the past witch doctors sold ineffective lotions and potions to an ignorant public desperate for a cure. Today the sex industry thrives on people's embarrassment and ignorance about how orgasm is achieved. If a woman finds a vibrator does nothing for her, she has no one to tell. The marketing of these gadgets is so universal that it's difficult for a woman to question their ineffectiveness.

A rhythmic development of muscular tensions is probably the most important of all the physiologic changes which occur when an animal responds sexually. (Alfred Kinsey)

Women only orgasm when alone not with a lover

Men's drive to penetrate inherently involves another person. But women do not have this hormonal drive that men have. So women have not evolved the ability to be aroused by a man's body because their orgasm does not contribute to the reproductive process. There is no reason why female orgasm should occur during sexual activity with a lover. The circumstances in which women orgasm are much more limited than they are for men. But women are more self-sufficient than men because they do not need a lover.

For men, penetrative sex is more rewarding than masturbation alone. So it's difficult for men to accept that the experience of a responsive woman is the reverse. Men assume that the act of penetration is core to becoming sexually aroused. They do not appreciate that intercourse is only arousing from the male perspective. Intercourse is a mating act that has a social context for a woman. It is not an erotic act. There is no taboo, suspense or sexual arousal.

A man's arousal is evident from his erection. But his mind is also focused on eroticism. He can orgasm fairly easily just by applying the correct manual stimulation. When women stimulate themselves without mental arousal, they never achieve arousal or orgasm. Men may think this strange behaviour but men behave in a similar way despite knowing exactly how orgasm is achieved. Men stimulate a female lover in quite random ways and then assume that she must have had an orgasm. Women get used to engaging in sexual activity with a lover without ever being aroused or having an orgasm.

A woman must be single to discover orgasm. While she is a virgin, a woman can imagine what she might enjoy with a lover. Once a woman has a relationship with a man, his need for intercourse dominates. This is how our sexuality has evolved. Female orgasm is merely a private pleasure for a woman to enjoy alone. Sexual activity is intended to focus on male orgasm.

Any scientific account of female sexuality has to be able to explain why the clitoris was a secret for so long and why most women remain ignorant of its role. The clitoris was unheard of until it was publicised by Kinsey and Hite who were both ridiculed and ignored for focusing on the clitoris. If any form of clitoral stimulation (oral or manual) were to cause female orgasm with a lover, women would have no reason to accept intercourse with all its risks. Men's high responsiveness and women's low responsiveness both contribute to successful reproduction. Sex is an activity that is driven by men's sex drive, which focuses them on obtaining intercourse, and women's willingness to accept intercourse as an activity that focuses on upper body lovemaking. Given women's lack of arousal with a lover, they lack any motivation to engage in activity that might focus on achieving their own orgasm. Hence, the only proactive role available to women involves facilitating male orgasm.

If clitoral stimulation (either manual or oral) provided easy orgasms with a lover, then it is inconceivable that heterosexual couples would not have discovered it by themselves. Women would have told men how their own orgasms are achieved. Alternatively, even if we think every woman in history has been too modest to discuss the details, men would have figured it out.

When a man reaches down between his legs, there's something to grab onto. A woman has nothing. Well, maybe a blip. That's all she has to work with. It's amazing that she manages anything. A woman can only obtain the stimulation she needs for orgasm by lying on her front and pushing down over her vulva while clenching her buttocks. This position is incompatible with interacting with a lover. A male lover would never give her time she needs to orgasm because he is so strongly motivated to thrust to his own. A woman is not aroused with a lover, so she has no incentive to stimulate herself. The sociable nature of sex prevents a woman generating any arousal. With a lover, a woman has no chance of focusing on the fantasies she needs.

A woman cannot stimulate herself to orgasm with a lover because it is impossible for her to achieve arousal when someone else is present. This is how women's sexual psychology works. A woman needs to be alone to experience orgasm, in an environment devoid of distractions. Women's use of fantasy is like meditation. Rather than being fully conscious, a woman is almost in a semi-conscious dream state. This kind of mental block-out is incompatible with sexual activity with a lover. If a woman cannot come up with a suitable fantasy, she can stimulate her clitoris as much as she likes but nothing will happen. If she is interrupted, then the chance of orgasm is lost.

Women's sexual fantasies involve taboo themes and engaging in surreal sexual activity with complete strangers. Real men represent a threat of potential pregnancy. Women's fantasies provide a mechanism for women to turn men into sex objects that can be used for arousal. Women use fictitious men in their fantasies who can be depersonalised rather than being people. As soon as a woman imagines a man she knows, the realities of how she sees him as a social (rather than an erotic) person take priority. The men in women's erotic fantasies are not men they have ever met or who they are in a relationship with. These fantasy men represent male sex drive or an erect penis that is part of a penetrative sex scenario. Women's sexual psychology does not involve visualising real-life opportunities for vaginal intercourse. A responsive woman instinctively uses fantasy to put herself psychologically in the position of the penetrating male. This virtual role is incompatible with the reality of sexual scenarios where she is naturally a receiver of intercourse.

Another important reason why women fake their orgasm is the fear of upsetting their partner. Many men anxiously insist that the woman must have satisfaction. (Rachel Swift)

How we know that female orgasm is uncommon

Orgasm is achieved by stimulating specific anatomy. This is because mental arousal causes the erectile organ (the phallus) to become tumescent. Confusion over the anatomy involved in female orgasm arises on two counts. Firstly women are not aroused with a lover, so they do not focus on obtaining the stimulation they need for orgasm. Secondly, very few women ever masturbate to orgasm. The vagina is assumed to be a sex organ because of men's sex drive and because very few women know how to achieve orgasm.

Women suggest that they are aroused when, in truth, they have no idea what erotic arousal involves. They attribute almost any sensation to arousal. But they cannot explain why they are amenable to sex on one occasion and not on the next. It is assumed that women are aroused either by emotional stimuli (e.g. kissing) or by genital stimulation (e.g. cunnilingus). This is the mystery of female arousal. Men rarely seem to appreciate that it is what they think about, or their senses (foremost sight) respond to, that causes arousal.

It's easy to tell whether a man is aroused because he has an erection. We don't have the same kind of visual evidence of female arousal. We don't know how women are aroused because women themselves do not know. Unless a woman masturbates to orgasm, she has no means of knowing. Even a responsive woman assumes that she should be aroused with a lover, even though she knows that she needs to focus on eroticism when masturbating. If women were aroused with a lover, the erotic turn-ons and the anatomy that needs to be stimulated (to cause orgasm) would be common knowledge.

In any survey or even in everyday life there are many women who are happy to acknowledge that they have never had an orgasm. Other women clearly assume that they are supposed to orgasm through intercourse as well as all the supposed orgasm techniques suggested by erotic fiction. But they have no interest in discussing sexual pleasuring techniques or erotic turn-ons. A person knows when they have had an orgasm. Women's uncertainty over whether they have had an orgasm is clear evidence that they have never had one. If female orgasm were common, there would be significant numbers of women in the general population able to provide explicit accounts of how they achieve orgasm as a response to erotic stimuli. This is not the case.

There's no reason why a woman should experience erotic arousal at any time. Female orgasm has no useful function so it would be strange if it were common. This is why female orgasm was discovered by researchers rather than being a well-known phenomenon in the population. Few women ever ask about orgasm, which is natural because you cannot miss what you have never known. Few women are responsive, so mothers object to girls being told that the clitoris can be pleasurable to touch. Most women associate the clitoris with lesbians or pornography rather than with their own orgasm.

The clitoris was hardly heard of before Kinsey and remains unpopular to the present day. This reflects the difficulty most people have in visualising sexual activity that does not involve a penis penetrating a vagina. Everyone has a phallus, which means that both sexes are potentially capable of orgasm. But intercourse, involving a man inserting his penis into a vagina, dominates our view of sexuality. The biological facts that define the sex education some of us may have had, help to reinforce this definition of women's sexuality. The impression is that female orgasm is just as much part of human reproductive biology as male orgasm (as the trigger for male ejaculation).

Men enjoy exploring a lover's body. Heterosexual lovemaking relies on the man's proactive role in stimulating a woman. It is assumed that women are already aroused (as men are on approaching a sexual opportunity). Yet a woman assumes a passive stance with a lover, only perhaps assisting with turn-ons. Rather than exploring a lover's body, women talk about what a lover is doing to them. Women enjoy a man's voice, his caressing touch and what they interpret as his passion. These are emotional pleasures not erotic stimuli. Gay men talk of sweaty smells, nutty taste of semen, glistening glans, trickle of pre-cum, silky skin of the penis and the hairy skin of the testicles.

Many women insist that lovemaking is superior to self-stimulation. Masturbation depends on a woman's own (rather than a lover's) motivation. It is only a responsive person who appreciates that turn-ons are required for orgasm. Many women are shocked by the idea of fantasies. They never appreciate that a woman achieves the mental arousal for orgasm by using erotic fantasies. Before a person can orgasm, they need a minimum level of responsiveness. Few women enjoy fantasies because they never experience a response to erotic stimuli. Female arousal does not occur naturally. Once sexual arousal has been consciously generated, the stimulation is instinctive.

There is remarkably little interest in knowing the explicit details about the orgasms women are supposed to have. Men only want to hear accounts of female orgasm rather than challenge them. Apparently, there are no scientists who want to improve their understanding or lovers who want to improve their techniques. Women are intimidated by the bravado of others and men are frightened to reveal that their hopes are just fantasies. Knowing the facts doesn't change reality. It simply reveals the deceit. The only reason most people protect the deceit is because they gain some advantage from it. Sadly, it seems unlikely that this emotional situation is ever likely to change.

Also because of its small size and the limited protrusion of the clitoris, many males do not understand that it may be as important a center for stimulation for females as the penis is for males. (Alfred Kinsey)

Topic: How orgasm is achieved

Orgasm is a one-off release of sexual tension

Sexuality is about appreciating what causes us to become aroused and learning how we can achieve orgasm both alone and with a lover. Orgasm is foremost a response of the nervous system. For adults (even premature ejaculators), orgasm is always consciously engineered in a situation where the mind responds erotically and by stimulating the phallus. Spontaneous orgasm (with no stimulation or mental focus on eroticism) occurs rarely. A few boys orgasm (as a one-off) in response to sudden shocks or other triggers. In rare cases (reported in the news) a woman is taken to hospital to have continuous pelvic spasms (a nervous disorder that is reported rather sensationally as orgasm) stopped. These are neither erotic nor pleasurable.

More highly sexed men experience regular morning erections during their most active years as a subconscious and automatic response. This results in a desire to engage in intercourse (because an erection makes intercourse possible) but before they can orgasm, men need penile stimulation. Physical stimulation is only effective because men are already mentally aroused. Mental arousal occurs as the brain responds to explicit aspects of eroticism.

Orgasm involves the brain, the central nervous system, the genitals and the whole body. Achieving orgasm relies on continuous communication between the brain and the erectile sex organ (penis or clitoris) via the nervous system. Initially the penis is flaccid and a woman is unaware of any sensitivity in her pelvic region. As the mind responds to eroticism, messages from the brain via the nervous system build erotic tension in the mind as blood flows to the sex organ (penis or clitoris). If a person's focus on erotic stimuli is interrupted for any reason, then physical arousal is immediately impacted.

A person learns from experience that if they massage their sex organ when aroused, it is usually possible to achieve orgasm. A person focuses their mind on some aspect of eroticism that they know has caused them to become aroused in the past. Once a person is conscious of their arousal, they are instinctively motivated to apply the correct stimulation. Arousal is biological (automatic) for a younger man. Women have to generate sufficient arousal for orgasm by making conscious effort to focus on explicitly erotic scenarios.

As our mind responds to eroticism, blood flows into the corpora cavernosa within the sex organ. The corpora cavernosa are within the shaft of the penis and inside the body of the internal clitoral organ. We gradually become conscious of this physical arousal (tumescence). But the evidence and sensations of physical arousal are much stronger for men than for women.

For a fifth of men (22%) orgasm is primarily a genital reaction while nearly half of men (45%) have some build-up (body tension). The remaining four variations are similar to the first two but can include additional trembling, fainting, frenzied movements, convulsions, collapse, laughter and talking. Female arousal is muted compared with male arousal that leads quickly and easily to orgasm. Female orgasm is also less dramatic and much less intense.

Tension builds as we become increasingly aroused. Heightened mental arousal causes us to lose full consciousness of our surroundings as we concentrate on the thoughts that cause us to orgasm. We use a squeeze technique to massage the corpora cavernosa within the phallus. Manual stimulation of the sex organ from the front is combined with a tensing of the buttock muscles to pressure the internal organ from behind. This massaging motion is continued rhythmically until orgasm. Muscular tension in the pelvic region increases, culminating in a peak that is abruptly dissipated.

Orgasm involves genital secretions from cervical and male glands, tumescence (increased blood flow in the whole body and the sex organ), rhythmic pelvic thrusts, the ejaculation of semen (men only), contractions of pelvic muscles and an abrupt release of nervous energy (sexual emotions) in the brain. After orgasm there is the sensation of blood (accumulated in the genitals) flowing away. Typically, an orgasm is followed by a period of resolution before another one is possible. The sex organ (penis or clitoris) cannot easily return to an aroused state. Some highly responsive young boys can attempt a number of orgasms sequentially with little rest in between. For adults, most of the time, there is a period of at least a few hours before the individual is receptive to being aroused again. In responsive women, this period may extend for weeks. Female sexual tension builds subconsciously.

Some women assert that they have a right to have orgasms but we have no conscious control over orgasm. Responsiveness is a physiological response that arises subconsciously as a result of how our brain responds to eroticism. Arousal is a psychological response that is triggered by the mind. Orgasm is a response to erotic stimuli of a psychological nature. These stimuli may be visual or imaginary but they are explicit images or erotic concepts related to the genitals and most typically penetrative sex. Orgasm can be achieved reliably because we learn over time which erotic stimuli cause us to orgasm.

Orgasm occurs naturally for a responsive person. We have to focus on erotic concepts until first our mind responds and then stimulate our phallus until our body responds. A responsive woman is only aware of clitoral tumescence once she has obtained 100% concentration on an erotic fantasy. She cannot force her mind and body to respond. It will happen only if sufficient sexual tension (at a much lower levels than for a man) has accumulated over time.

Considerable psychiatric therapy can be wasted on persons (especially females) who are misjudged to be cases of repression when, in actuality, at least some of them never were equipped to respond erotically. (Alfred Kinsey)

Orgasm is an instinctive response to erotic stimuli

Orgasm is an instinctive response. That means that even when we have no prior knowledge or experience of orgasm, we are still able to discover it. It has to be that way because otherwise the human race (and other animals) would not exist. We haven't always had books or even word of mouth to tell us about intercourse and masturbation. There is no such thing as an instinct to buy a vibrator and use it to stimulate yourself. This is a conscious behaviour motivated by the advertising slogans of the sex toy companies.

Imagine a boy and a girl who grow up on a dessert island without any knowledge of the outside world. At adolescence, the boy will have erections and may masturbate. If they have close contact the boy will become aroused (have an erection). Without any instruction, he will be instinctively motivated to engage in thrusting activity. He would discover the woman's vagina without knowing of its existence. A girl doesn't have a similar instinct to complement his. She may be motivated to demonstrate her affection if she loves him.

The mind responds to erotic stimuli by causing blood to flow to the genitals in preparation for sexual activity. This causes observable evidence of arousal in the form of tumescence. A man is naturally motivated to explore a woman's body because he is aroused by it. This means that even in the absence of all knowledge of intercourse he would eventually discover it.

Research indicates that when men are deprived of female company they are aroused much less frequently. Kinsey's research found this to be true of less educated men, who cannot substitute masturbation for intercourse so easily. He found that when men are imprisoned (without women) most men experience little arousal. Responsiveness is split into two distinct issues. We have a biological capability but also, we need an opportunity. If a man lacks a partner or has no access to erotic stimuli, he may not be responsive at all. Men work on ships or oil rigs without sexual arousal so long as no erotic stimuli are available (probably unlikely now in the age of the internet!).

Various nervous system responses have symptoms in common with orgasm. These include anger, fear and epilepsy. We can experience a peak of sensation for various reasons. For example, someone could tickle our feet. We may reach a point where we don't want further stimulation. Such a sensation is not orgasm. Firstly, the erectile sex organ is not involved but secondly there is no mental focus on eroticism. Orgasm is defined by the pleasure a person enjoys from the erotic stimuli that cause mental arousal. Female orgasm is often assumed to occur simply because stimulation ceases.

Male orgasm is not an issue because it is usually a given. Men's prime motivation for engaging in sexual activity (alone or with a partner) is their mental arousal. Men's heads (to varying degrees) are full of sexual thoughts.

A man is likely to keep some (less socially acceptable) thoughts to himself out of embarrassment or to avoid offending a lover (particularly a woman). Anyone who has had an orgasm knows that crude sexual thoughts and genital urges are involved. We are embarrassed to admit these urges because they reflect our most private thoughts. This is why we can be sure that women who boast about orgasm have never had one. They are not embarrassed because they don't understand that sexual arousal (and the resulting orgasm) must arise from thinking about something crude. Women assume that orgasm arises purely from emotional sensations and physical stimulation.

What does the word 'blue' mean to a blind person? You can say that it is the colour of the sky. But if they have never seen the sky, then they have no idea what colour means. The same goes for orgasm. It is just a word. Some women assume they orgasm. Others just ignore the concept. It's something that is important to men. Female orgasm is often defined in emotional terms. Yet if women experienced same the response that men do, we would expect these orgasms to have characteristics in common with the male experience. We would expect female orgasm to involve erotic turn-ons and the phallus.

Most women conclude that orgasm (like masturbation) is over-rated because they assume that orgasm involves purely pelvic muscle spasms. Other women believe they orgasm either alone or with a lover but without using any erotic stimuli. This is evidence that they do not appreciate the nature of orgasm. Any adult needs some form of mental stimulation of an explicitly erotic nature to achieve orgasm. Orgasm is a release of sexual emotions. Stimulation of the sex organ is only effective once we are mentally aroused.

If men want women to have a positive attitude towards eroticism or to be willing to engage in more adventurous sex play, then so-called female orgasms that arise without women engaging on erotic concepts of any kind are not going to help very much. It is the mind's positive response to sexual scenarios that causes someone to empathise with eroticism. Our ability to respond to eroticism is what motivates us to engage in sexual activity. Our mental arousal causes sexual tension to build up and be released as orgasm.

We do not discover orgasm because we are given information. Once we have had an orgasm, we may understand the information that we had been given. But the motivation to engage in sexual activity that culminates in orgasm arises in our own mind. Erotic stimuli (that cause the brain to increase blood flow to the genitals) motivate a responsive person to massage their sex organ (penis or clitoris). The stimulation technique we use is instinctive. We could experiment with different masturbation techniques but there's little point. We continue to masturbate as we began because the technique is reliable.

Most males ... are definitely aroused upon seeing things that are associated with sex, and most females are not so aroused. (Alfred Kinsey)

Arousal is psychological and arises in the mind

Sexual arousal arises in the brain and is a form of nervous excitement. In other words, the nervous system is disturbed (more agitated than its normal resting state). Both our breathing and heart rate are elevated due to the brain activity. Sexual arousal occurs initially subconsciously. But at some point, we become conscious of our arousal. Adrenalin causes blood to flow to the sex organ and makes orgasm possible. For men, this mental arousal causes blood to flow to the penis, which is trapped thus causing an erection. A man becomes conscious of his arousal because of the acute physical sensations of having an erect penis. But the penis becomes many times more sensitive than the clitoral organ ever does. A woman does not have clitoral erections.

The clitoris is an internal organ and does not have the same mechanism (the penis has) for trapping blood. The clitoral organ is only ever tumescent. Only once mental arousal has been achieved, does the sex organ becomes sensitive to stimulation in a unique way (that leads to orgasm). The stimulation that leads to orgasm is instinctively supplied (or obtained) and involves massaging the corpora cavernosa within the tumescent sex organ.

A woman has to be anti-social to obtain the focus on eroticism she needs for orgasm. A responsive woman rests her fingers over her vulva to gauge whether her genitals are responding to possible fantasy scenarios. Even responsive women do not experience arousal (during masturbation alone) as a pressing state of excitement as men do (that inevitably leads to orgasm).

Once conscious of our arousal, we typically (especially during masturbation alone) use a conscious mechanism to achieve orgasm. This conscious mechanism involves focusing our mind on explicit aspects of eroticism that we anticipate (from experience) will cause us to become aroused enough to achieve orgasm. A woman keeps her eyes closed when alone so that she can fully concentrate her mind on the fantasy that appeals at the time. Women are aroused by abstract erotic concepts rather than images of genitals and penetration. Women have to make conscious effort to become aroused by using fantasies that have nothing to do with their real-life sexual experiences.

The idea that a man has an orgasm with his head full of non-sexual thoughts (such as work priorities or a sporting event) is unthinkable. His mind is fully occupied by the erotic sights, sounds and sensations of sexual activity with a lover. A man is easily aroused by many different stimuli. Anticipating sexual activity with a lover is sufficient to cause male arousal. During masturbation his mind is focused on a fantasy or visual stimulus such as pornography. A man is motivated to masturbate because of the sexual thoughts he enjoys.

Men think about sex much more frequently and explicitly than women do for biological and hormonal reasons. There are many erotic triggers that cause male arousal in the course of a day: from women in the street to advertising for women's underwear. Men are also aroused by kissing and caressing a lover. There are no similar triggers for female arousal. Women are embarrassed or offended rather than aroused by sexual references.

Women engage in sex hoping that one day something will magically happen. But arousal doesn't work this way. Ideally, arousal is the initial trigger for engaging in sexual activity. But even a responsive woman is rarely conscious of her own erotic arousal. When a partner is present, emotional and social factors dominate so a woman is never consciously aware of being aroused. A heterosexual woman engages in sexual activity because of male initiative. Lesbians have sex because they think they are supposed to or because they enjoy the sense of emotional bonding that comes from sensual pleasuring.

Much prejudice is based on the belief that people can consciously control their sexual responses. It is understandable that women might think this way because women rarely experience responsiveness. Men should know better. No one chooses the erotic stimuli that cause their sexual arousal. Yet some heterosexual men think it should be possible for gay men to be aroused by vaginal intercourse. This equates to telling someone to stop feeling tired, hungry or thirsty. We cannot change our body's subconscious responses.

Men ideally want to ejaculate into a lover's body so their orgasm is typically observed. A man expects his lover to assist with and share his orgasm. Simultaneous orgasm is often claimed to be the ultimate satisfaction. But it is not possible for two people to orgasm as the exact same moment. Orgasm occurs in the mind of the individual at a moment that cannot be predetermined because it is fixed by their individual arousal cycle. Orgasm is private and personal to us. It is a selfish pleasure. A woman may be pleased that a man has been able to use her body to obtain his sexual release but she is not aroused by his ejaculation in the way that a homosexual lover might be. Sexual phenomena are much more vital to men than they are to a woman. Responsive women only ever orgasm when alone. This is because they need a high degree of mental focus on eroticism to achieve orgasm.

Aspects of control and domination, as well as the way a man might negotiate his own pleasure, are all core to arousal. Pain is often used as a conceptual turn-on in erotic literature. We use BDSM (Bondage, Discipline, Dominance, Submission, Sadism and Masochism) for arousal because it involves revelling in the control of others (of doing something to someone else). Typically in heterosexual situations, the man inflicts pain on a woman. Some men enjoy the idea of the role reversal. But in real life, pain is not arousing for the receiver. Spanking is used as a token form of punishment.

Similar situations are recognized in anger, in fear, and in epilepsy – all of which are physiologically related to sexual response. (Alfred Kinsey)

The mental focus required to achieve orgasm

Anyone who masturbates needs to use fantasy for arousal. Turn-ons are erotic concepts or images that motivate us to engage in sexual activity. We enjoy the sensations of arousal that result from exploring our fantasies. Sex involves our enjoyment of mental arousal through an appreciation of eroticism (men tend to use graphic images and realistic physical scenarios while responsive women use surreal and unrealistic conceptual scenarios).

As we know from the male experience (a man needs an erection before he can orgasm), it is no use anyone stimulating an unaroused sex organ. If we are intent on achieving orgasm, we must first be aroused. Mental arousal is what makes stimulation effective. After the first time, we know from experience how we get turned-on. The trigger for orgasm arises in the brain. We have to shut out other concerns and distractions to focus on eroticism. The stimulation that causes orgasm, involves massaging the erectile organ.

Turn-ons are personal to the individual. Only the individual can determine what explicit aspects of sexual activity are arousing for them. Only we can generate the mental focus we need to achieve orgasm. This psychological arousal, when combined with massaging the blood-flow within the erectile organ (penis or clitoris), can result in a release sexual tension (orgasm).

A man is motivated to stimulate his penis from the start of sexual activity because he is already aroused. Having an erection is his motivation for engaging in sex. In order to ejaculate a man must focus his mind on specific (personal to him) and explicit (involving the genitals) aspects of eroticism. Men cannot achieve orgasm while holding a non-sexual conversation for example. Men also need penile stimulation to be continuous until orgasm.

A man knows what turns him on because male arousal occurs regularly. Men are aroused in similar ways regardless of orientation. For young men, arousal is biological or automatic. Men are aroused by real-world stimuli. Men are aroused by sexual opportunities, by nudity and specifically by genitals. Men's minds are easily focused on erotic thoughts when engaging in sexual activity with a lover. Men seek foremost to be the penetrator. A man can be aroused simply by a partner's amenability because he anticipates his own pleasure.

Male turn-ons are relative to the society we live in. Years ago when women covered their bodies, men were aroused by the sight of a woman's ankle. Likewise, the actresses in pornography are not truly aroused or having an orgasm when they make all that noise. So men can be turn on by the noise because they interpret it as a sign of female amenability to being penetrated.

Men achieve orgasm through masturbation much more quickly than a woman does. This is because men are aroused at the start of any sexual activity. The clitoris does not respond to stimulation except in specific circumstances. A woman needs to know how to become mentally aroused enough to achieve orgasm. She needs an environment of absolute privacy so that she can achieve arousal by concentrating her mind on an erotic fantasy.

A woman is not aroused by real-world stimuli (such as male underwear or genitals). Given their much lower responsiveness, women have to work much harder than men do to achieve the mental arousal needed for orgasm. A woman does this when alone by using an intense focus on erotic fantasy. These fantasies are different to the romantic scenarios most women are talking about when referring to sexual fantasies. Even a responsive woman's ability to respond to eroticism is buried deep within her subconscious. A woman has to generate arousal from zero, which takes time. A woman puts herself in the position of the male in penetrative sex, which involves immersing herself in a surreal fantasy. A woman needs considerable mental concentration to focus on the explicitly taboo aspects of sex that arouse her.

Some men (75%) have sex dreams that result in orgasm at some point in their lives. Women rarely have sex dreams but if they do such dreams are romantic scenarios based on the emotional aspects of lovemaking. Even for responsive women, their dreams are focused on vaginal intercourse with men they know. Specifically, these dreams do not focus on women's erotic fantasies or even on the genital stimulation that they need to achieve orgasm.

The psychological environment of dreams is not intensely focused enough to cause female orgasm. Women cannot orgasm when asleep because female arousal (the kind that leads to orgasm) does not arise without considerably conscious effort. Female arousal is achieved by creating an intense mental focus on surreal scenarios that are chosen specifically for their ability to arouse the individual. Even when fully conscious, a woman has to push her way towards orgasm at every stage with studied concentration. At no point is female orgasm inevitable except once it is already happening.

Orgasm, when it is our objective, defines the end of the activity that was focused on achieving it. Stimulation stops for a variety of reasons. Firstly, the point of stimulation is to achieve orgasm. Job done. The sexual tension has been released. Secondly, orgasm coincides with the sense of release and the end of our ability to be aroused by a particular fantasy. The fantasy we have been playing out in our mind has reached its conclusion. Thirdly, our sex organ can no longer be aroused by the same stimulation, which may become uncomfortable if continued. The blood has flowed away from the genitals. We feel relaxed and sated. We know from experience that we have to wait for a period of time before our body will respond in the same way again.

The male is aroused because he has been conditioned by his previous experience, as most females have not. (Alfred Kinsey)

Mental arousal combines with a thrusting instinct

Men can orgasm from non-reproductive activity such as fellatio or masturbation. But men obtain the most satisfying sexual release by ejaculating into a lover's body. So although another person is not absolutely necessary for men to enjoy orgasm, it is typically preferred. So men naturally assume that women have the same preference. But female arousal is not needed for intercourse and female orgasm is not needed for reproduction.

Men's acute arousal (especially with a lover) means that they can be much more flexible in the techniques they use to achieve orgasm. A woman's masturbation technique is not limited by a lack of imagination or a reluctance to try other approaches. A woman learns from experience that orgasm is achieved only in a highly specific way. She can only orgasm by using a meditation technique that involves an intense focus on erotic fantasy. She also has to thrust with her hips and put pressure on the internal clitoral organ (by pushing down with her fingers and clenching her buttock muscles).

The actions of masturbation are subconsciously done and result from a primitive thrusting instinct. The body responds to what is happening in the mind. If a woman's body is capable of orgasm, the clitoral organ responds. She can feel a sense of erotic excitement as blood flows to the genitals in response to what she is thinking about. The clitoral organ becomes more sensitive to stimulation and provides an erotic feedback loop via her fingers.

When a woman masturbates in a position other than face down, she is not responding to sexual instinct. She is consciously deciding to stimulate herself because she thinks she should or because she hopes to discover orgasm. Rather than responding to an instinctive response to erotic arousal, she is just copying what she has seen in pornography or read about in erotic fiction. These accounts are based on what arouses a man rather than being a reflection of how a woman truly achieves orgasm. A responsive woman responds instinctively to the mental arousal that causes clitoral tumescence.

Women's masturbation techniques are not sociable as a man's can be. She cannot orgasm with a lover or with an audience of any kind. Neither does a woman observe herself during the performance. If she is aiming for orgasm, a woman needs to eliminate distractions and block out the physical world to focus on the sensations within her mind and body. A woman shuts her eyes to focus on achieving the psychological arousal that she needs for orgasm.

Just as intercourse represents the natural expression of a man's arousal cycle, masturbation is the natural expression of a responsive woman's ability to become aroused and enjoy orgasm. She enjoys eroticism through fantasy and the feelings that accompany mental arousal. She enjoys the pleasure of achieving a sexual release and the subsequent relaxation. But there is no urgent need, no pent-up arousal or frustration. Nor is there any accompanying sex drive. Given the impossibility of sharing her arousal cycle with a lover, female masturbation is a very private and personal experience.

When a man engages in intercourse, he clenches his buttocks as he thrusts. This is because he is thrusting into the body of another person. The thrust of his groin comes up against a firm obstacle in the form of a lover's body. He can thrust only to a certain point that is defined by the length of his penis. When a woman masturbates, her fingers substitute for the stop of a lover's body. The second and third fingers from each hand are pressed together and down into the spongey tissue either side of the labia minora to provide a firm pressure. This mimics the effect a man has when thrusting into a body, of coming up against a firm stop point. The squeeze technique includes pressing the sex organ up against a firm obstacle just as orgasm is reached.

The kind of stimulation that is required for a woman to orgasm restricts the position in which she can masturbate. Orgasm is achieved by the combined stimulation of fingers, pelvic muscles and body weight on the clitoral organ. This technique is incompatible with a lover or a vibrator. Unfortunately, women's instinctive masturbation techniques do not provide the genital display and presumed invitation to penetrate that arouse men. Being face down, with her hands on her vulva, allows for the freedom of movement needed for thrusting. Men also like positions for intercourse that give them control of thrusting. They stand over, behind or on top of a woman to obtain the internal pressure, which intensifies the physical sensations of orgasm.

A woman achieves orgasm when her mind has reached a peak of arousal determined by the fantasy she is using. She synchronises this mental arousal with both internal (by clenching the buttocks) and external pressure (from her fingers) on the internal clitoral organ. The use of surreal erotic fantasy produces a sense of release including an increased heart-beat and heavy breathing culminating in waves of relaxation. The sense of release is followed by relaxing sensations of lassitude. After orgasm a woman's vulva remains swollen. Post-orgasm, it can be pleasurable to gently stroke over the hood of her clitoral glans as well as the swollen area either side of her labia minora.

Male masturbation acts as a safety valve for men's sex drive. But a woman has no conscious awareness of needing sexual release. A woman does not have the benefit of the external triggers that cause male arousal before men even start on stimulation. A woman has to generate sufficient arousal for orgasm out of nothing. A woman masturbates purely to enjoy orgasm. She is conscious of the potential for mental arousal that makes orgasm possible.

The concentration of stimulation on the clitoris and labia minora in masturbation is a demonstration of the fact that they are the portions of the genitalia which are best supplied with end organs of touch. (Alfred Kinsey)

The male psychology of seeing a lover as a sex object

Unlike emotional attachments, arousal is not caused by a specific person or by a relationship. Arousal relies on being able to see a person, to some degree, as an object. Arousal is achieved when the mind focuses on objects or concepts that a person finds arousing. Arousal mechanisms (erotic turn-ons) involve physical attributes and the psychology of a scenario or a lover.

Straight men naturally see attractive women as an object of arousal. Women may accuse men of being sexist but this is just how male sexual psychology works. Men may suppress their comments, if they accept that women are offended by them, but they cannot change their innate responses. Men can love a partner and still see them as a sex object. Men are not usually aroused by blood relatives because of the emotional significance of the relationship.

Women's nurturing and caring instincts mean that they can empathise with others. Men are more emotionally detached, which helps when they need to use violence against others (hunting or killing) as well as in sexual scenarios. Their sex drive causes men to respond to erotic rather than emotional stimuli. Men, who are natural hunters and have a strong sex drive, cannot afford to empathise with their victims, or with their lovers, as women do.

In the early days of the profession, all the actors were men. Acting was not a safe occupation for women because any woman who put herself on display (no nudity implied) was a target for male advances. Later actresses were associated with prostitution. Women's activities have often been limited due to men viewing them as sex objects. Men have not suffered in the same way. Women do not see men as sex objects but equally women don't want sex in the way a man does. While there are few men who turn down sexual opportunities, the vast majority of women avoid sex outside a relationship.

A woman lacks this male ability to view a lover as a sex object. Women tend to see people purely in a social and relationship context. In a real-life sexual situation, a woman is aware of her lover as a social person she cares about. When masturbating, a woman is aroused by scenarios unconnected with her real-life lover and her sexual relationship. A woman has to envisage imaginary men to consciously generate the equivalent mental arousal a man needs for orgasm. This mechanism does not work in a sociable context.

Women's fantasies are surreal because, in the absence of any sex drive, women need to focus on the more indirect consequences for women that arise from men's sex drive. They are artificial scenarios that put a woman in control of the action. In fantasy a woman can simultaneously imagine herself being the person who is penetrated as well as the penetrator. She can focus on male ejaculation as a means of producing her own release. This role of being a penetrator does not mean she wants to be a man. She retains her female identity but she focuses on the intimacy and eroticism of penetration by a phallus. Likewise, the climax of the fantasy comes from the satisfaction of being in the proactive sexual role and the concept of male ejaculation.

Fantasy is a mechanism a woman uses to focus on a more psychological view of sex by being the object of male sex drive. A woman fantasises about a man doing things to her because men naturally initiate and drive penetrative sex. A woman needs to see herself as sexually attractive and she needs to take pleasure in the knowledge that a man wants her sexually. A woman may enjoy imagining a man's desire to penetrate her body. In her mind she can also be the male who is driving the action and experiencing the pleasure.

Men enjoy sharing their fantasies because they hope a lover will participate in activity that they fantasise about. Women's fantasies are not based on reality. They focus on impossible and unreal situations and people. A fantasy involves imagining impossible or improbable things. Women's sexual fantasies are purely a mechanism for enjoying orgasm. They lack all the practicalities of real life and the crude visual eroticism that men enjoy.

Responsive women discover orgasm because their minds respond positively to eroticism of a highly specific kind. A responsive woman enjoys eroticism through surreal fantasies that do not involve real people or real situations. In her fantasies, a responsive woman focuses on the concept of penetration rather than visual images. She focuses on a man's sex drive to penetrate her body. This is much more explicitly erotic than a romance novel. A sexual fantasy culminates with male ejaculation as a sexual release rather than the graphic images of semen that gay men revel in. A responsive woman enjoys the concept that a man's mind is focused on his need to penetrate her body.

A responsive woman dislikes pornography as much as any other woman. She isn't motivated to see or touch a penis by hand or mouth to enjoy male responsiveness as a gay man does. She is horrified if it is suggested that she might want to participate in one of her fantasy scenarios for real even though such scenarios enable her to achieve arousal and orgasm alone. No doubt from a male perspective, there is no logic to this explanation. Men need to consider how enthusiastic they would be about intercourse if every single time, they potentially risked having to carry a foetus in their belly for nine months as well as being held responsible for the child's daily care for decades. Masturbation is a risk-free way for women to enjoy their own arousal and orgasm. A fundamental characteristic of enjoying sexual pleasure (arousal and orgasm) is that it does not involve being impregnated.

On the other hand, since there are marked differences between females and males in their response to psychological stimuli, it seems apparent that those responses must depend upon some mechanism which functions differently in the two sexes. (Alfred Kinsey)

Similarities between men and women's responses

Orgasm is a basic physiological response of the human body. Just as the same mechanism causes men and women to sneeze, so we also orgasm in the same way. Regardless of gender and orientation, both the anatomy and the trigger are the same. We massage the tumescent phallus and focus our minds on explicit aspects of eroticism. Orgasm techniques are similar whether we are male or female, alone or with a lover, gay or heterosexual.

It is inconceivable that men and women would have evolved a response as fundamental as orgasm through different evolutionary routes. This is where the anatomical precedent comes in. The phallus (penis or clitoris) is always involved in orgasm. The penis and clitoris (only the glans is visible) may not look very similar but they develop from the same anatomy in every foetus (regardless of sex). Whereas the vagina develops from female reproductive glands that every embryo has initially but that wither away in a male foetus.

The penis acts both as a sex organ and a reproductive organ. So men enjoy orgasm (which triggers ejaculation) as part of their reproductive role in intercourse. But for women, intercourse has a purely reproductive function. A woman has separate anatomy for reproductive function (the vagina) and orgasm (the clitoris). Women's reproductive anatomy (the vagina) complements male responsiveness (orgasm ability). Female responsiveness mirrors (or parallels) the male instinct to thrust to orgasm during intercourse.

Masturbation is based on an instinctive thrusting behaviour. This thrusting action is not consciously determined by the individual. It happens because the individual does what comes naturally when they are mentally aroused. Build-up to orgasm involves rhythmic movements of the whole body, focused on the pelvis. The hips are thrust forward, the thigh and buttocks muscles are flexed. This is an instinctive behaviour that puts pressure on the internal sex organ (penis or clitoris). The sex organ (clitoris or penis) is stimulated simultaneously from behind (or within) as well as from the front (by rubbing the loose skin over the shaft of the penis or the body of clitoris).

Sexual activity that is aimed at orgasm is not accompanied by a dialogue. Anyone who wants to orgasm needs to concentrate on the mental turn-ons that cause arousal. During masturbation alone we always need some form of fantasy to achieve arousal. These fantasies need to be explicitly erotic and include aspects of sex that are sufficiently arousing for us to achieve orgasm. Fantasies are based on the personal erotic preferences of the individual.

A woman can enjoy vaginal intercourse but this enjoyment arises from the emotional reward of feeling desired and appreciated for providing a lover with the pleasures of penetration. This is why women vehemently object to the same stimulation with a stranger. The sensations of being penetrated and receiving a man's ejaculate do not cause orgasm. Gay men may offer a lover an opportunity for anal penetration. Stimulation of the prostate gland can cause ejaculation but orgasm usually relies on massaging the erectile organ.

Sociable activity with a lover does not allow a woman the focus on fantasy that she needs to be able to achieve orgasm. Neither can she align herself psychologically with the thrusting role. The position a responsive woman needs to assume is incompatible with intercourse. A woman masturbates by lying face down with her hands on her vulva. This position allows for the thrusting motion and the clenching of the buttocks that is critical to achieving orgasm. Although men are much more flexible in the position in which they can orgasm, they often prefer a position that is above a lover or facing down.

If we want to understand responsiveness, a good place to start is male sexuality. When men engage in intercourse or masturbation, they stimulate their penis rhythmically up until orgasm. It only appears as if men are intent on the goal of orgasm. In fact, men are responding to an instinct to thrust into the vagina (or other body orifice). This thrusting action inevitably ends in orgasm, which ends a man's ability to engage in sexual activity. No one can predict the exact timing of an orgasm. But intercourse stimulates a woman's vagina only while a man has an erection (until ejaculation). No one (not even a man) can orgasm within limits set by another person's responses. Neither can we orgasm with exactly the same frequency as another person.

The idea that women (but not men of course) need a lover with specialised stimulation skills to make them orgasm or give them an orgasm is a fallacy. Orgasm is a specific erotic phenomenon that occurs relatively predictably given the appropriate psychological and physical stimuli. But physical stimulation (regardless of who provides it) is a secondary issue. Mental arousal is much more crucial and must be achieved before physical stimulation can be effective (lead reliably to orgasm). When we become responsive in adolescence (all men but very few women), we discover orgasm by ourselves. Orgasm occurs in the brain as a response to erotic stimuli.

A responsive woman may enjoy resting her hands on her vulva before going to sleep or when she is relaxing alone. There is no sense of sexual arousal, just a feeling of comfort. Men also enjoy resting a hand on their penis even when flaccid. Unresponsive women are often unaware that cursory genital contact cannot cause orgasm. Achieving orgasm involves specific stimulation and a degree of privacy to focus on turn-ons. Mental arousal causes tumescence so that the erectile organ becomes sensitive to stimulation. This sensitivity is considerably heightened for a man. Even when aroused, a responsive woman obtains relatively little pleasure from clitoral stimulation.

The basic physiology of sexual response is essentially the same among females and males. (Alfred Kinsey)

Women mistake emotional sensations for orgasm

Female orgasm is not an issue in sexual relationships because the vast majority of women accept sex for what it is. Such women describe orgasm in terms of emotional factors. For some women this means they accept that orgasm does not occur with a lover. For others, they may assume that orgasm occurs but they assume that it is trivial or implicit. Saying that women orgasm from intercourse means that any woman who has intercourse can believe that she has orgasms and reassure herself that she is sexually normal as defined by her social culture. Either way it makes little difference to women's attitude towards sex. Intercourse relies on a man having an erection and so women can only engage in intercourse by responding to male initiative.

Women's sexuality is portrayed unrealistically in fictional media, both pornography and movies for general release. Yet women never correct these fabrications. Women's arousal is largely subconscious and few women are responsive enough to orgasm. This explains women's lack of interest in their own sexuality and why the male view prevails. The male response to their bodies is the only aspect of their sexuality that most women are aware of.

Being ignorant of what orgasm feels like, some women assume various vague sensations with a lover might be an orgasm. Some women believe they orgasm from intercourse. They may feel mildly pleasurable sensations from the diffuse stimulation of intercourse. These physical or emotional sensations that women feel are all quite normal and do no harm. They are not orgasms because they do not involve a mental response to erotic stimuli. Women's erotica is often associated with themes of humiliation, domination and sadism. Just as with fear or horror, such themes can cause nervous excitement that women might mistake for sexual arousal but they do not cause orgasm. Orgasm is a mental response to explicitly sexual scenarios.

A responsive woman is surrounded by so much fiction that she assumes that other women may experience arousal and orgasm in situations where she doesn't. There are so many fictional stories that no one even recognises a real account of orgasm when they hear it. A responsive woman has no reason to talk about her enjoyment of masturbation alone. It is only women who are trying to be popular with men who promote their stories. Consequently female masturbation, as portrayed in fictional media, reflects fantasies and assumptions rather than how a responsive woman masturbates to orgasm.

Young girls and women can stimulate their vulva, without ever achieving orgasm. Perhaps they are responding to some latent instinct. Maybe they are experimenting. Perhaps they feel that they should masturbate. It could be that they experience some kind of genital itch. They rub it for a while and then finally stop, seeming satisfied. Perhaps the rubbing has eradicated the itch much as it might do in any other part of the body. These assumed orgasms occur outside any erotic context. Women never refer to turn-ons.

Any activity that starts when a child is pre-pubescent cannot be a true orgasm. Ultimately, regardless of gender we can only start to respond sexually once our sexual anatomy (the sex organ in particular) has developed the ability to become tumescent. A woman needs the sexual maturity to respond to eroticism at a much more sophisticated level than a man does. A young man can be aroused by visual images of body parts or genital activity. Girls learn to masturbate later than boys because their fantasies involve a more psychologically complex mechanism. To masturbate to orgasm, a responsive woman needs to think much more explicitly about penetrative sexual activity.

Reproduction relies on women providing a man with an opportunity for intercourse rather than being focused on achieving their own orgasm. So sexual activity with a lover has a social rather than an erotic context for women. Compared with men's acute arousal, women feel much more diffuse feelings of mild excitement. Nevertheless these sensations, whether they are strong or weak, draw our attention to the sex organ. It is only when a responsive woman is alone that she is able to enjoy her own responses.

Anyone who is responsive struggles to understand why someone who has never had an orgasm would say that they have. Women refer to orgasm to obtain approval from others and because they are told that they should orgasm. Few people are ever explicit about what an orgasm feels like and how it is achieved (that it relies on mental arousal). So women have the idea that orgasm is just a nice feeling. They can assume that almost any sensation (especially with a lover) might be what other people are calling an orgasm.

People who advise others about female orgasm or on related issues (such as lack of sexual desire) are never required to explain how women achieve the mental arousal that is a prerequisite for orgasm. It is assumed that women orgasm even though no one can account for any female erotic turn-ons. This is because women don't appreciate that arousal is a mental phenomenon.

Women who know that orgasm is impossible with a lover deserve explicit explanations for why some women can claim what others know is impossible. Female arousal needs to be explained in terms that are compatible with women's behaviours. These arousal mechanisms need to operate as men's do, by providing a psychological erotic stimulus. The physiological process for achieving orgasm as a result of different anatomy being stimulated by a lover in a variety of ways also needs to be laid out.

How do women learn what an orgasm is? Your parents aren't talking to you about it. Where would you learn? I don't know. Maybe they're reporting orgasms just when they're having a pleasurable sensation. (Nicole Prause)

How we know that someone has had an orgasm

Orgasm is a subconscious response but we need to take conscious actions to achieve it. A responsive person knows when they have had an orgasm because they took specific and focused steps to get there. Arousal (and hence orgasm) relies on what happens in the mind. Some women assume they have had an orgasm just by engaging in intercourse. So we need to consider the external signs and behaviours that indicate a person has had an orgasm.

A man only engages in sexual activity of any kind when he has an erection or can be reasonably sure of being able to achieve one. In other words, he must be mentally aroused. His short-term objective may be penetration and the pleasure of thrusting but the apparent goal is orgasm. This is because his desire to engage in sexual activity ceases once orgasm has been achieved.

This explains why sex ends with a male orgasm but never with female orgasm. There is never a point at which women can no longer engage in sexual activity. This is clear evidence that women do not orgasm with a lover. If a woman's motive for engaging in sexual activity with lover was the desire to achieve orgasm, then she would cease sexual activity before even getting to intercourse. Not only would she leave the man unsatisfied and frustrated, but the result would be disastrous in reproductive terms. A woman needs to be willing to engage in intercourse regardless of her own arousal and orgasm.

Achieving orgasm relies on a number of factors. The most critical issue is that an individual must have the necessary responsiveness. Responsiveness is a male characteristic. So men are much more likely to experience orgasm than women are. Further factors include a degree of privacy, a degree of confidence for men in the sociable situation and a relaxed state of mind.

A man can feel secure in a harem because he is the only male. Men fantasise about threesomes: sex with one man and two women. Foremost a man doesn't want any interruptions until he has ejaculated. Women want privacy because of embarrassment. Men need to recuperate before they can be aroused again. In a swinging situation, women can have more partners than men because they are not erotically aroused and do not orgasm with a lover.

Achieving orgasm involves applying consistent stimulation until orgasm and then desisting. The time taken to achieve orgasm depends on various factors including our current state of arousal. But that period of stimulation cannot be determined in advance. We cannot set our watch and demand that someone reaches orgasm at an exact point in time. This makes it very unlikely that lovers can orgasm at the exact same moment as each other.

If we are aiming for orgasm, we want to control our own stimulation. We want to synchronise the stimulation of the phallus with what is happening in our heads to optimise the mental impact of orgasm (satisfaction obtained from sexual release). For adults, achieving orgasm may involve considerable effort. We experience an increase in heart rate and heavier breathing due to sexual excitement. For men, this effect is increased if they have engaged in vigorous intercourse for some time. Female arousal depends on mental concentration rather than physical effort. A woman may tense and hold her breath as she concentrates on her arousal, which adds to her breathlessness.

We do not experience the exact same sensations every time we orgasm. Sometimes the release is more satisfying than at other times. The most satisfying orgasms are those that involve some build up in erotic arousal and culminate in an orgasm that includes strong pelvic contractions, multiple waves of pleasure and a deep sense of release. Factors that affect orgasm quality include: our pent-up need for sexual release, our ability to achieve a mental focus on eroticism and factors such as our general state of well-being.

The feelings that accompany orgasm are unique and do not equate to any other experience. Arousal feels like excitement or anticipation. We feel a slight adrenaline rush. We hold our breath to concentrate on the feelings. Our mind is totally absorbed in what is happening. Orgasm is joyful. Orgasm ideally involves psychological stimuli (conscious erotic fantasy or a subconscious response to eroticism) combined with genital stimulation (of the tumescent sex organ: penis or clitoris) that culminate in a release of sexual tension (called an orgasm) followed by a pleasurable aftermath of orgasm including waves of post-climax echoes and sensations of lassitude.

After orgasm there is a sense of release and relaxation as the blood flows away from the penis and vulva. An orgasm is a release of sexual energy. Following sexual release, we feel sated. We have a similar feeling after eating a big meal but especially if we were very hungry beforehand. We also feel sleepy after a heavy meal. Responsive women masturbate as a means of getting to sleep. The process of achieving arousal clears a woman's head of all other concerns (that may be keeping her awake). She feels totally relaxed after her orgasm. The effect is stronger for men because male orgasm is considerably stronger than female orgasm. This is why men often fall asleep readily after the exertions of intercourse. While women are left wide awake. This is evidence that women do not orgasm from sexual activity with a lover.

Erotic stimulation ... effects a series of physiologic changes which ... appear to involve adrenal secretion; ... increased pulse rate; ... a flow of blood into ... the penis ... and the clitoris; ... often considerable loss of perceptive capacity; increase in nervous tension; some degree of frigidity in whole or part of the body at the moment of maximum tension and then a sudden release which produces local spasms or more extensive convulsions. (Alfred Kinsey)

Differences between men and women's responses

One of the major differences between the way men and women respond in sexual scenarios is that being touched by a lover, is emotionally significant to men. A man takes pleasure in stimulating his penis when alone because he is aroused. But his pleasure with a lover is much greater because of the emotional acceptance of having a lover touch his genitals. Men look for signs that a lover is amenable to sex. A woman's lack of arousal means that any stimulation by a lover has little effect. Being touched by a lover may provide some sensual and emotional pleasure for a woman but primarily when she is first in love. She is likely to be embarrassed by some men's desire to suck on her nipples because of the parallel with suckling a baby. Any manual manipulation of the clitoral glans can be painful or even uncomfortable if not well lubricated. Cunnilingus provides little sensation as does intercourse.

When a man walks down the street with a woman on his arm, he is proud that others may assume that he has a sexual relationship with her. His role is one of command and supremacy. He has obtained her approval as a lover and is the happy recipient of her sexual favours. Other men envy him when his lover is attractive, sexually provocative and demonstrably affectionate.

When a woman walks down the street with a man on her arm, her feelings are quite different. She is happy because she feels emotionally close to her lover. She enjoys her feeling of security at having his protection. She may be proud of his achievements, of his earning ability or just the car he drives. Other women envy her when her lover is handsome, rich and affectionate.

Men need to be aroused by a sexual opportunity. From adolescence onwards many men have their heads full of sexual fantasies on a daily basis. Men have the benefit of both hormonal arousal and the ability to be aroused by many triggers in their daily lives. Highly responsive men are conscious of their arousal and have a strong sense of wanting to resolve that arousal as orgasm. They imagine opportunities for penetration and anticipate the pleasure they will enjoy as a penetrator. They imagine that a lover approaches sexual scenarios with exactly the same degree of anticipation.

A man's sex drive means that he pays little attention to his general appearance. His sex drive focuses his mind on the need to ejaculate through intercourse. He hopes that a lover will stimulate his penis. But a woman has a social (rather than an erotic) focus. She hopes a lover will keep in shape, particularly as he ages, and that he will wear attractive (not functional) clothes. This is a key misunderstanding between the sexes. Each sex hopes the other will provide what they want but fails to give what their lover wants.

A boy's masturbatory activities are a natural precursor to his adult sexual activity. During masturbation, he imagines a real-world situation that later on he is able to realise to some degree. His sex drive focuses his mind on sociable activity with a real-world partner and penetrative sex that can be accounted for on reproductive grounds. Even for male homosexuals, their focus on anal sex is a clear parallel to the reproductive heterosexual act. All male sociable activity centres on stimulation of the penis. Fellatio, anal and vaginal intercourse all involve penetrating a body orifice with an erect penis.

A woman's masturbatory activities do not relate to sociable activity in the same way. They are quite standalone because she does not experience a sex drive to engage in sociable activity, nor is she aroused by real world stimuli. A woman is not normally conscious of her physical arousal. Women can engage in intercourse without being in the least aroused. A responsive woman consciously decides to achieve arousal by using erotic fantasies. Men are highly sensitised because of their genital and whole-body tumescence. A woman undoubtedly enjoys a fraction of the physical and emotional sensations of a man's orgasm. Female masturbation is a personal experience that a woman cannot account for in terms of reproductive activity. Her discovery of orgasm is instinctive but it doesn't make sense. She may be disturbed by the nature of the fantasies that cause her erotic arsousal. This is very different to the emotional sensations that she experiences with a lover.

Most men (especially when younger) are easily aroused and can achieve orgasm in almost any position with a lover. They enjoy different forms of penile stimulation such as oral sex, manual stimulation and penetrative sex. Although male masturbation depends on a manual technique that varies little between individuals, it does not depend on a fixed body position. Some men have had partners but find the erotic pleasures of masturbation, such as in voyeur bars, or using a prostitute can substitute for sexual activity with a lover without having to incur the emotional and financial overhead of a relationship. Even responsive women are not aroused nearly as easily as men or by as many erotic stimuli. Most women are unresponsive. They never masturbate to orgasm because they never discover how to achieve arousal.

Women are not nearly as flexible as men are in the circumstances in which they can orgasm. The position a responsive woman uses for masturbation (to orgasm) is fixed for two main reasons. Firstly, she needs to block out the real world to focus on her fantasy. By lying face down and shutting her eyes, she assumes what feels like a comfort position. It probably feels that way because it is an instinctive position. Secondly, she massages the internal clitoral organ by pressing down into the tissue alongside and slightly below her labia. At the same time, she pushes her hips forward and clenches her buttock muscles. This is almost impossible to achieve in any other position.

The male is aroused at observing his potential sexual partner, as most females are not. (Alfred Kinsey)

Topic: The sex industry

The sex industry focuses on male gratification

Sexuality is about talking, observing or interacting with others in return for payment or other non-relationship rewards. Depending on our personality we may employ a variety of behaviours and attitudes to attract, impress or arouse a potential lover. Sexual contacts are usually a private affair. We are either alone or with one other person. Most people are not comfortable with group sex. This is a question of how we view sexual intimacy. It also depends on whether we enjoy displaying our bodies or being observed by others.

How we express our sexuality depends on our personality. We find some situations and people much more attractive than others. Even the most promiscuous of men are not attracted to everyone. Sex is political. We have sex with someone who impresses us or who is above or below us socially. Sex is about the power to arouse, to seduce and to dominate someone.

Human sexuality is often presented in terms of a relationship. This allows male and female sexuality to be viewed purely through social liaisons and reproduction. Little importance is placed on the massive sex industry because of the taboo over men paying women for sex. Men have a need for sex that is quite independent of any relationship or emotional feelings. Eroticism is defined by male turn-ons and a woman's sexual role is to arouse.

Sexual pleasure is often linked with immorality because of the associations with the sex industry, where women provide sexual services for male gratification. Men can be tempted away from their wives and families in search of sexual pleasure outside marital sex. Both casual sex and prostitution bring an increased chance of catching a sexual disease. The odds of being infected increase if we have penetrative sex with different partners.

Sexually transmitted diseases (STDs) and Acquired immune deficiency syndrome (AIDS) are transferred via the body fluids involved in sexual activity. The more partners a person has (the more promiscuous they are) the more likely they are to catch a sexual disease. AIDS is usually fatal. Drug-users are also vulnerable to catching AIDS. Treatments may be available but some diseases are incurable as well as being inconvenient and even painful. Anyone who contracts these conditions (including prostitutes) must always ensure condoms are used to prevent the disease spreading further.

When a man has no emotional feelings for a woman, he can simply use her body as a sexual outlet. Women are exploited by being led into prostitution or pregnancy by men. Then men vanish without paying for the consequences of their actions. When a woman has no emotional connection with a man, she may offer sex just for money or other rewards (such as a meal). By using their bodies to consciously attract male attention, some women gain control.

All around the world and by every means possible, women have always sold sex to men. If women obtained the same pleasure as men, they wouldn't need to be paid. Yet when it comes to providing sex information to young people no one is willing to be honest and admit any difference between the male and female experience. Men protect their sexual interests and women are embarrassed or ashamed of the trade that they are inevitably involved in.

Women naturally resent prostitutes because they represent a threat, both physical and psychological. Prostitution highlights the male need for a sexual outlet that means little to women. Women prefer to interpret male sex drive in terms of loving emotions and romantic passion rather than sexual lust. Most men are unwilling to admit to using a prostitute because of the social shame and the risk of a partner being offended by the male need for sexual release. Men pay for sex (unlike women) because they do not need an emotional connection to enjoy sex. Many men prefer to have it if they can.

Most people think it is inappropriate to talk about sex in front of children as well as teenage girls. Most women are embarrassed by the erotic fantasies that men weave around female sexuality. In the same way, sex educators typically provide medical and biological facts but carefully avoid talking about sexual pleasure. Most men refrain from making sexual comments to avoid offending women. Even so, few men accept that sex is a male pleasure.

Sex is hugely political. Discussions involve opinions (rather than facts) aimed at persuading people to behave in certain ways. Young women are targeted. Pornographic and exploitative images are readily available to everyone regardless of age at the click of a button. These images are often violent, humiliating and degrading to women. They send confusing messages to men on consent, personal boundaries and women's ability to respond sexually. It is dangerous for anyone to immerse themselves constantly in fictional media. They inevitably lose the ability to differentiate between fiction and reality.

There is no problem in promoting sex to men. But when sex is promoted to women, it needs to be associated with a relationship. For example, 'Love, sex and intimacy' fairs are more acceptable to women because the word 'sex' is softened by the more acceptable words love and intimacy. Women are reassured that they will not be exposed to the explicitly erotic turn-ons that men enjoy. Men learn that women respond to love rather than sex. A man never says "I want to thrust into your vagina until I ejaculate". Women want to hear about a man's sexual passion in terms of platonic admiration and romantic love. So men talk of love and women rarely appreciate that many men assume that sex and love are the same thing. This is, of course, not so. Men love sex but they do not necessarily love a woman who provides it.

The truth is ... this (lap-dancing) is a male form of entertainment ... for men!
(Peter Stringfellow)

Prostitution generally involves men paying for sex

There have always been some women who are willing to offer men sex on demand. But they want to be paid. By far the most common form of prostitution involves women providing sexual services to men. The second most common sexual service is for gay men (4% of the male population). Women usually pay male escorts for companionship rather than sex. Prostitution is least common among lesbians (2% of the female population).

Women are respected for being wives and mothers. They are not respected for being a mistress or a prostitute. Most women are embarrassed by references to the pleasure quarter, which equates sex to a transaction and highlights the function of women's bodies as a sexual commodity for male consumption. Most women would never be a prostitute even if they were well paid. It is not possible to buy the platonic, loving and non-sexual intimacy (based on affection) that women hope for when they love someone.

In the red-light district of any city (often near the train station), women are employed to provide men with sexual pleasure or just sexual relief. Women typically go into prostitution as a last resort or out of desperation. Other women claim to enjoy earning a living by providing men with sexual services.

Women are sometimes forced into prostitution. These situations reflect men's need for sex and women's reluctance to supply it. Men like to assume that women enjoy sex as much as men. But if they did, women would not need to be forced nor would they need to be paid. Sex acts as a massively positive boost to men's sense of emotional well-being. In wartime a man can face even death with more equanimity. A loving relationship is supposed to transform sex so that it becomes to women what it always represents for men. The truth is that women accept sex when they are receiving something else in return. Women want love, a relationship, moral support or just money.

The men who are most likely to use prostitutes are under thirty and those who are less educated than average. Some men pay for sex as easily as they would for a massage. It is likely that many more men would pay for sex if there was no taboo. Cheaper prostitutes do not feel obliged to pretend that they are erotically aroused. Some men find a prostitute unsatisfying because they like to believe that a lover appreciates their lovemaking. Some men interpret a woman's love as emotional acceptance of their sexual needs.

Prostitution is dangerous work and the risk of assault is high. Also some men want more specific sexual services related to a fetish or a perversion. Women in the sex industry provide for these sexual needs, which saves other less worldly women from engaging on the true nature of some men's carnal needs. Much of the violence men show towards prostitutes reflects their frustration at not obtaining the sex they need from their partners. Men can also resent prostitutes because they make money out of men's need for sex.

Male prostitutes ejaculate with a client. So they only work part-time. If women had orgasms with a lover, prostitution as we know it would not exist. Sex involves a woman allowing a man to ejaculate into her vagina, her mouth or her anus. No one can have an orgasm to order but an orifice can be offered at any time. A woman can service men almost indefinitely because she experiences no erotic arousal, no orgasm and has no recovery period. Since men naturally provide most of the stimulation, a woman doesn't need to do very much except perhaps behave appreciatively or fake her orgasm.

In any sexual scenario, men can escape responsibility much more easily than a woman can. Women who sell sex can easily be identified but the men involved can usually ensure that they remain anonymous. A woman is shamed by society for being a prostitute but men are rarely shamed for using a prostitute. Yet women only respond to the demand from men. Most women go into prostitution as a last resort to earn money and sometimes in order to support their children by absent fathers. Some women offer sexual services rather than work in low-paid unskilled jobs. Men make most of the money out of the sex industry by employing low-paid women. Prostitution is a service that allows men to enjoy sexual release with a partner. It is naïve to think that prostitution could ever be abolished. Some men (regardless of their relationship status) will always be prepared to pay women for sex.

In most countries, prostitution is illegal. Holland and Germany are notable exceptions. Some people believe that legalising prostitution equates to condoning the practice of men paying to use women's bodies for sex. Others support decriminalisation, which offers prostitutes (who register) a safer working environment and medical support but in return for paying taxes. Prostitutes have been relabelled sex workers but prostitution is still linked with organised crime, violence, abduction and slavery. The problem is the male brothel owners and male pimps who exploit and abuse women. We have the impression that women are offering nude images, sex chat or sex on the internet but most of this content is posted by men. Most of the money in the sex industry is made by men. Men know exactly what other men want.

We find that about 69 per cent of the total while male population ultimately has some experience with prostitutes. Many of these males, however, never have more than a single experience or two, and not more than 15 or 20 per cent of them ever have such relations more often than a few times a year, over as much as a five-year period in their lives. This means that there is nearly a third (31%) of the population that never has any sort of sexual contact with prostitutes. (Alfred Kinsey)

Women are not respected for being promiscuous

A polite way of expressing some men's enjoyment of promiscuity is to say that they like the ladies. There is no equivalent expression to describe a woman who is promiscuous. The term lady is used as a form of respect that is needed because of the disrespect men often display towards women.

A man defends his honour by fighting and beating an opponent. A woman defends her honour by fighting off unwanted suitors and saving her virginity for a mate of her own choosing. One of the greatest insults a man can use against another man is to assert that his mother is sexually promiscuous.

Women have two key reasons for engaging in intercourse. Some women have sex solely for personal gain without any emotional attachment. They have sex for money or personal ego. The second motivation is, of course, romantic love leading to a relationship. Women do not have sex for sexual release or erotic pleasure otherwise they would pay for sex as men do.

Some women think it's cool to emulate male bravado by suggesting that they use men for sex. Of course, women use men for sex! But women are motivated by ego, by money and by love. Women use men to earn money or for some other social advantage, such as career advancement or marriage. They are not motivated by orgasm or even by sexual pleasure. In this sense women are not sexually motivated. Female promiscuity has nothing to do with a woman's responsiveness. A woman cannot use a man's body to enjoy arousal and sexual release in the way that a man can use a woman's body.

Most women are not willing to offer intercourse to a stranger. They need to feel an emotional connection before offering sex. Various factors, including personality, mean that some women are promiscuous at least initially. Many people don't expect much and are less considered about what they do. Many women have low self-esteem and see sex as an easy way to obtain admiration. Some women cannot stand up to someone with a stronger will or personality. Young women are unassertive. They give in to men's persistent and flattering sexual advances only to find that they are then disrespected by everyone.

Some women enjoy casual sex and are happy to have superficial sexual contacts just for the fun and for the ego. They enjoy being chatted-up or having a romantic dinner. Sex is a small price to pay. They have sex when they choose to. They can go for weeks without sex and no one notices. A wife does not have this luxury. Women who are in relationships with men, have sex with a much greater frequency and regularity than women who engage in casual sex. This is one of the injustices women face. Women who are promiscuous are considered more sexual than women who are faithful.

It has become fashionable to imply that everyone should engage in sexual activity at every opportunity. Some people are naturally more selective than others. We need to choose sexual opportunities that feel right to us personally. Certainly no one should feel coerced by others. The quality of a sexual experience depends on emotional criteria that cannot be guaranteed. Some people are much more sensitive than others. Those who go for quantity over quality often lack self-esteem and see promiscuity as a means of promoting their own personal popularity. They are simply keeping score.

Not every man (particularly if he is married) welcomes an approach from an attractive woman. Women do not typically approach men they don't know. So a man suspects that her motives might be sexual. He may feel pressured by his own assumption that a sexual performance is expected of him. If she can do without the usual need for an emotional connection, any woman can regard sex as trivial. A woman's role is not onerous. Sex will always be trivial to some women who are naturally resented by other women. Logically, given men themselves are tempted by promiscuity, one might expect men to look favourably on promiscuous women. Promiscuity is potentially a sign of sexual motivation. But men don't like women to be too easy to get into bed.

A man wants a woman to be motivated to offer him intercourse but not other men. Yet anyone with a sex drive wants sex with any attractive partner. Men create this contradiction over women's sexual amenability. They don't respect a woman who spreads her legs and offers sex too easily. Yet at the same time they are frustrated when they don't get the sex they want. A man cannot understand why a woman does not want sex when her role is so trivial compared to his own. Men often prefer to marry virgins or modest women who are unlikely to be sexually promiscuous or adventurous because they want to know that they have sole rights to her body as a sexual asset. Over decades, women have sex with a man because they love him, which has nothing to do with orgasm. Men take advantage of a woman's platonic love.

Decent men do exist but a woman has to give out the right signals. Men who are looking for casual sex tend to focus on women who are easy to get. But decent guys are willing to wait a little for sex. They value personality and intelligence as well as body parts. A man who is willing to invest in a relationship wants some reassurance that a woman will be sexually faithful. Intercourse provides men with the turn-on of penetration and the emotional reassurance of being accepted. But a man does not feel privileged to have his sexual advances accepted by a woman if she gives her body to any man.

Many a male... is prone to seek coitus from every available girl, while insisting that the girl he marries should be virgin when he first has coitus with her. It is the male, rather than the female, who imposes this incongruity on the social code. (Alfred Kinsey)

Sex as a competitive sport and erotic entertainment

A woman values a man as a social asset (who has status and experience). But a man values a woman as a sexual asset. A young woman is a trophy because of her attractiveness and her inexperience. A man enjoys knowing that his lover is attractive not only to himself but also to other men. A man enjoys the erotic satisfaction of having an attractive woman choose him as a lover.

There's nothing a woman can do to make intercourse happen. But if she is attracted to a man, she can indicate her willingness. Women complement men's sexuality, not by having a similar focus on their own arousal, but by responding to the fantasies that assist with male arousal. When a woman seduces a man, she can use sexual behaviours that tempt him into wanting intercourse with her by providing erotic turn-ons that cause his arousal.

When a man invests special attention in a woman, she is naturally flattered. All the time he is admiring her or talking to her, in her mind she knows consciously or subconsciously that he wants to have sex with her. She may enjoy rewarding him for his admiration in the hope that he loves her. If he moves on to another woman the following day, she feels betrayed. She has offered him her love and he has trampled on it. For men, sex often seems to be just a basic physical need. Some men have no interest in women as people. They just want the erotic variety and the sense of conquest. Women don't understand how sex can be so important to men and yet so trivial.

Some women use men's sex drive for their own advantage. They indicate that they may be sexually amenable and wait for him to offer dinner, taxi rides and so on. Then they tell him that they cannot oblige him. This can be a dangerous tactic as not all men are gentlemen. But it's also very unfair. Women who behave like this are taking advantage of men's sexual needs.

There are always many more men looking for sex than there are amenable (or apparently amenable) women. Clubs and bars make men pay while women enter for free. Men are asked to bring a partner but single women are welcomed. The imbalance between male demand for sex and female supply is a constant source of frustration for many single and married men.

It used to be called wife-swapping but today the more unisex term swinging is used. People meet up in order to have intercourse with complete strangers. Some people find this extremely erotic while others find it the reverse (impersonal) because of the lack of emotional context. Women enjoy being admired sexually but the prime motivation comes from their male partners.

Both heterosexual and homosexual men can be obsessed with their own performance, and a lover's, as if sex is a competitive sport. However, over time this approach can cause dissatisfaction. Over the longer term, most people derive more contentment from relationships based on an emotional connection with a lover. Non-orgasmic aspects of sex, such as anticipation (by planning sex sessions) and the build-up of arousal, are also enjoyable.

Addictions are characterised by compulsive behaviours. For men, sex addiction often centres on a porn obsession. This causes problems because of the mismatch with reality. Women, on the other hand, use sex to find love. Inexperienced women often think that a man will love them if they offer sex. But men don't necessarily connect sex with love. Perversely men often marry women who are less promiscuous because they value sexual loyalty in a wife even though they may not be ready to offer it themselves.

Rather bizarrely, men are much more interested in female orgasm than women are themselves. If women love sex so much why does any man care what is said about their responses to it? It's the fact that women are not as enthusiastic about sex as men would like that causes men to promote female orgasm. This pressure causes some women to fake orgasm or to profess a false enthusiasm for sex. By promoting the idea that intercourse causes female orgasm, a man can transform his selfish need for sexual release into a selfless desire to pleasure a lover. This male behaviour is a man's way of obtaining sexual permission and emotional acceptance from a female lover.

A man is aroused by contemplating opportunities to penetrate a partner with his erect penis. It might be very different if his sex life involved him being penetrated by a lover. It is not an exact parallel because men have a prostate gland, which can cause anal penetration to be extremely pleasurable. But it might help men to appreciate how women feel, to imagine how they would feel if pornography involved images of penises penetrating men's anuses. How would heterosexual men like to live in a world filled with men looking for opportunities to penetrate their orifices regardless of their amenability?

Straight men would not be so happy to have images of penises constantly in their faces all the time. Just because such images are arousing for some, does not mean that they are for everyone. Images that are faked to give the impression that someone wants to be penetrated are equally offensive. Male homosexuals keep their pornography to themselves but male heterosexuals inconsiderately inflict their turn-ons on women. Women may be sexually subjugated for reproduction but they want respect from a man who is enjoying his own pleasure at their expense. Women don't want to be sent images of men's penises on the internet because they think genitals are ugly.

She can say she had 5 orgasms and you will have no way of proving her wrong. Truth is what man would even want to prove her wrong. We all like to believe that we laid it down right, so who is really going to question it unless it was a horrible performance (act) on her part. (Stephan Labossiere)

The sexual politics of women competing over men

If men and women wanted the same thing there would be no sexual politics. Men and women are at odds because they want different things. Marriage comes with its privileges and obligations. A man's reward is regular sex. A woman's reward is caring for those she loves. Sexual politics involves men and women using sex to manipulate and exploit each other. Men tell women that they can enjoy sexual pleasure to optimise their sexual opportunities. Women tell men that they love sex to get money or relationship rewards.

Women's orgasm claims are just simple mantras, totally lacking in erotic detail. They reflect male beliefs that women orgasm from the stimulation that men provide. Women never refer to turn-ons in the appreciative way that men do. They don't talk about their enjoyment of a lover's body. If their claims were true, they would be sympathetic towards those less fortunate rather than defensive. Instead, they are superior and condescending, basking in the glory of male admiration and male protection from challenges to the obvious holes in their claims. Men are convinced because they want to be.

Women boast about orgasm to impress others and to bolster their own or a lover's ego. Some women like the attention they get, or the money they make, by promoting themselves sexually. They are confident that no one will ever be able to assess their willingness to do more than flaunt their bodies and their bravado. A woman impresses less worldly women with her supposed sexual expertise. She can change the political balance by suggesting that men are sex objects she uses for her own satisfaction. When a responsive woman enjoys orgasm alone, none of the above apply. But other women are threatened because her experience calls their own orgasm claims into doubt.

Kinsey warned of sexually inert spinsters who were commonly found in the educational institutions of his time. He remarked that teenage boys have more orgasms than these women have in their whole lives. What he did not appreciate is that these women are not trying to please men. Very few women are willing to be honest about their lack of sexual motivation. Millions of other women either actively support the male view of their sexuality or passively allow it to prevail. Most women desperately want male approval. Women's most prominent sexual behaviour is their desire to please men.

Men evidently do not get the variety and type of activity they would like from their relationships with women. Otherwise men would not seek out prostitutes and extra-marital affairs as they do. The corollary is that women who are in relationships with men tend to get more sex than they want. This is the eternal dilemma of the heterosexual couple. Women offer sex in return for the emotional reassurance of a man's willingness to support them.

Men compete with each other but they also collaborate. They often join forces to fight a common foe. Women compete with each other singly over men. Women do not collaborate because other women are a threat. Men have extra-marital affairs, maintain mistresses or visit prostitutes. Wives compete with these women who divert men's earnings away from the family.

A young man may be disappointed that his female lovers are not as enthusiastic as he had hoped they would be. But he is pleased that his own experience of enjoying sexual pleasure with a lover matches his expectation. However, a young woman is likely to be disappointed that her experience does not match what she has been led to expect. Women rarely admit this fact but if they do, they are told that there is something uniquely wrong with their sexuality. Very few women ever admit to having the same experience.

There is no reliable source of sex information. Women rarely compare notes compare notes honestly over sex because of politics. So women never know what they can realistically expect from their sexual experiences. In addition, different women interpret their experiences in very different ways. The young and inexperienced often reflect the male view that sex is wonderful. Responsive women are devastated to find that sex does little for them. Many other women are disappointed to find that, despite all the hype, sex is just a male pleasure. But only the positive view is actively promoted.

Many women enjoy displaying their bodies, knowing that men admire them. Men enjoy being aroused by women's bodies but this constant arousal causes sexual frustration. This causes resentment between women because men expect their partners to provide the outlet men need to release their arousal. This is another reason why few women comment on sex. A dress code that is the same for everyone regardless of gender, would respect men's sex drive.

Men are not interested in whether women are capable of orgasm per se. They don't care about the orgasms women enjoy alone. Neither have men welcomed the invention of vibrators. Men's prime interest in female orgasm is as a means of making women more amenable to sexual activity with men. Specifically men want women to respond to intercourse. Men, foremost, want the erotic turn-on of believing that their lover is erotically aroused. Men, who enjoy erotic turn-ons such as breast and clitoral stimulation, may also be motivated to pleasure a woman so that sexual pleasure doesn't seem so one-sided. Men want to justify their need for intercourse in terms of their desire to pleasure a lover. They don't want to admit that a woman is just having sex in order to provide for their own sexual and emotional needs.

Thus, we have two problems: First, the male version of sex drive is what women are unjustly measured by. Second, women are trying too hard to please men who need more realistic expectations of women's sexuality. (Joan Sewell)

Women attract men by sexualising themselves

We wear clothes for protection, for warmth, for decency and also for display. The need to differentiate ourselves depends on our personality. Many women believe it is an essential part of their femininity to display their bodies. As long as there are no consequences (they are protected from male advances), women enjoy the admiration they get. Men don't display themselves in this way. Men display themselves when they have an erection.

A woman has no biological reason for engaging in sexual activity outside her fertile period. A woman may be impregnated if sperm are deposited in her vagina around the time of her monthly ovulation (when an egg is released). Her reproductive capability relies solely on her ability to attract a mate. A man's erection communicates his desire for penetrative sex. A woman is not aroused in the immediate and obvious way that a man is. Even when woman masturbates to orgasm, there are no obvious signs of female sexual arousal.

We can differentiate between erotic turn-ons and sexual come-ons. A turn-on is something that causes arousal. Turn-ons are not always associated with the intention to arouse. Men are easily aroused and they assume women respond similarly. Young men may easily confuse turn-ons (such as a woman's attractiveness) with come-ons (her conscious sexual behaviours).

A come-on is a behaviour that is aimed at causing arousal. A come-on is an implicit sexual invitation. Specifically, a come-on is a behaviour that a woman uses to indicate her willingness to be penetrated by an aroused male. She is explicit about what she says or does so that there is no room for doubt that she is making a sexual invitation. This behaviour is common in pornography. Prostitutes and sexually experienced women provide sexual come-ons which a man interprets (according to male sexual behaviours) as a sign that a woman is aroused and actively seeking vaginal stimulation. Other women may use the simple mechanism of wearing a negligee as a mild come-on.

Some women like to dress in a way that is sexually provocative and that acts as a sexual come-on. But more typically, women display themselves to obtain platonic admiration. Men assume that a woman displays her body because she is aroused and making a sexual invitation. In truth these women are not available. How a woman dresses is a conscious behaviour and not a sign of responsiveness. A woman enjoys the power of knowing that she is attracting attention. Putting on a short skirt, a low-cut blouse and a push-up bra is easy. It is much more onerous for a woman to provide a partner with regular sex.

The colours women wear have connotations. Red lipstick or red clothes are attention seeking and daring. Black and lace are associated with women's provocative nightwear. There are no male equivalents. Other women can be offended by partial female nudity because it is display for male admiration.

If a man waited for a woman to be enthusiastic about sex then he would wait for ever. So many men follow their instincts and take the initiative by making an advance. The vast majority of interaction between the sexes, involves a man admiring a woman. This male admiration gives women power in their relationships and may cause a woman to feel loved. So women allow men to make all kinds of innuendo that they quietly ignore. A man gets used to interpreting women's silence and passivity as acceptance. Women have to be directly rude before most men will accept rejection. This insensitivity comes from having a sex drive and is an almost inevitable part of being male.

Women look at other women for a variety of reasons. Firstly, they look out of curiosity to judge the attractiveness of their own body relative to others. Secondly women want to learn from other women's successful behaviours. Lastly women want to reassure themselves that they are more attractive than others so they can feel better about themselves. Invariably, the message for a woman is that if she is to succeed, she must use her body. That is how she is admired, gets friends and is promoted at work. By believing they orgasm as men say they should, unresponsive women feel better about themselves.

Orgasm is a specific physiological response of the human body. Yet some women think they have the right to define orgasm however they want. Women promote orgasm as if it's a kind of club they can invite their friends to join. We do not choose to be responsive. It's just the way we are born. Responsiveness has nothing to do with being attractive or amenable. We do not orgasm because we wear a sexy dress, pout our lips or spread our legs. Men find this confusing because they assume a sexy-looking woman must be responsive. And yet they know male responsiveness doesn't work that way.

Confusingly, for men, the women who are shouting loudest about female orgasm are the ones who have no idea how it is achieved. But because they are essentially reflecting male fantasies, their claims are very persuasive. This is very natural. But men need to differentiate between what women say and what they actually do. The real issue for men is whether a woman is enthusiastic about investing in a sexual relationship over the longer term. The men, who are most likely to succeed with longer-term sex lives, are those who have invested in the wider relationship by responding to a woman's needs. It also helps if a man takes responsibility for his own sexual needs rather than expecting his lover to provide turn-ons for him. A woman is most likely to offer sex when she anticipates that little effort is expected of her.

Much of this interest in rare or non-existent forms of sexual performance may represent the male's wishful thinking, a projection of his own desire to engage in a variety of sexual activities, or his erotic response to the idea that other persons, especially females, may be involved in such activities. (Alfred Kinsey)

Women are often disappointed with casual sex

We are all living longer due to improved health and lifestyles. So 'til death do us part' is much longer than it used to be centuries ago. Some couples like the idea that they are not bound solely to each other for decades. For most couples this is not an option and adultery is a guilty secret. Divulging sexual infidelities can be unwise. Many people demand an instant divorce.

Women want loyal devotion but men want their freedom. These two aims can cause conflict. If a man's sex life is not meeting his expectations, he may want a more attractive partner or more adventurous pleasuring than his wife is willing to provide. Men enjoy casual sex for the opportunity to experience first-hand the variation in the genital anatomy and sexual behaviours of a new partner. Some men appreciate a variety of lovers much more than others.

Women tend to take male sexual loyalty for granted without appreciating the struggle many men face to avoid temptation (even though many of these temptations do not represent true sexual opportunities). Men experience many more sexual temptations than a woman ever does. Some men want to explore sex with different partners. They feel that having one lover severely limits their sexual freedom, which they see as a basic male right. But as men age, they may appreciate the emotional security of a long-term relationship.

Since intercourse is the default heterosexual activity, it requires no communication. The novelty of casual sex means that a man is highly aroused and wants to have intercourse as soon as possible. He does not want to ejaculate too soon. There is little foreplay, which needs more time for trust and communication to develop. Casual sex focuses on intercourse, which satisfies a man's basic sexual needs and is over quickly for a woman.

In fictional media we see sexually confident woman who expect a man to deliver their sexual satisfaction. This presumed sexual assertiveness on the part of the modern feminist is just a political stance. Men today provide the same they always have, vaginal thrusting until male ejaculation. Women never complain because they don't know what else to ask for. A woman is initially wary of what a man might do during a sexual encounter. She anticipates a man's sex drive to explore a woman's body and initiate intercourse. Equally a woman feels helpless because of her own passivity in approaching sexual activity with no motivation to do anything other than go along with (or to defend herself against) whatever activity a man initiates. Women's lack of arousal with a lover means that they do not have the focus on achieving their own orgasm that men have. Women cannot tell a lover what stimulation they need for orgasm because they don't know themselves.

Some young women find it difficult to say no to male advances. They give in to men's persuasive interest in them but afterwards they have regrets. They resent other women who are disapproving of their behaviour. Most women understand how easy it is to arouse a man, who admires them. They also know that this admiration arises because men want intercourse. A woman who provides sex without obtaining anything in return is not respected. Women are not respected unless they trade sex for a relationship rather than for money. This is a key difference between male and female sexuality. Women have different sexual roles including mistress, concubine, hooker, slut and whore. There are no male equivalents because men are responsive.

Men find that younger, less experienced women are more easily pressured into having sex. Reliable contraception has made more women willing to have casual sex. Lack of confidence and self-esteem lead some women to experiment with casual sex for a time because they enjoy the novelty of being popular with men. Women have sex for fun, for ego or to obtain non-sexual rewards such as material assets or a loving relationship. However, not all women will engage in casual sex, even with reliable contraception. The vast majority of women still prefer to have sex with someone they care about. Women gain confidence with increasing age, experience and social status.

Women obtain none of the physical gratification that makes sex so pleasurable for men. Relatively few women are interested in casual sex with multiple partners. Women do not need sex as men do. Neither does a variety of activities or partners have the same interest for women as it does for men. Women often feel used through casual sex because, without a relationship, they get little in return for providing male pleasure. Women focus on the platonic aspects of relationships: companionship and affection.

A woman needs to trust a man (because some men are abusive) and she wants to know that he is committed to a relationship with her before she offers sex. A woman is attracted by a man's mind as well as his dependable character, his considerate behaviour and his caring attitude. For most women, even the idea of sex is repugnant if there is no emotional attachment. Some women never or rarely engage in sexual activity of any kind (asexual). They never feel the emotional attachment to someone (male or female) that is necessary for a woman to feel amenable to physical intimacy with a lover.

The emotional rewards women receive from their relationships do not depend on sex at all. Women are rewarded by feeling that a partner loves them (by demonstrating affection) and cares about them (by demonstrating an interest in a woman's concerns). These aspects of relationships depend on knowing and liking a person, which takes time. Women appreciate the emotional intimacy and the social reassurance of knowing someone well.

Numerous research studies make it very clear that the people who have the best quality and most frequent sex are married couples. That says a lot about the inadequacies of 'casual sex'. (Les Parrot)

Women have varying degrees of sexual willingness

Human beings are sociable animals. Most of us want to be accepted in our social group. We want to share experiences. We hope to enjoy the company of others. We are reassured by the support of family, friends and a lover. It is also a survival strategy because humans tend to attack those who are different. We often feel under pressure to conform to the expectations of the society we live in. Women particularly try to avoid conflict. Many people have enough challenges in life without trying to tackle unsolvable problems.

Most people never comment on sexual issues. Those who do (a tiny minority) have political motivations and they are rarely interested in facts and logic. Men insist that women love sex as much as they do. In order to attract men, women suggest they are always sexually willing. Most of the silent majority ignores this bravado but many others feel they have missed something. They have the impression that others have better experiences.

Women's behaviour of claiming to orgasm with a lover is just another way that women avoid engaging proactively on the eroticism that men enjoy. A man never challenges because he has what he wants: a woman's implicit consent. Men don't appreciate how easily they can be exploited by women telling them what they want to hear. Who is exploiting who? It probably depends on how clever you are about getting more than you are giving.

Men may be aroused by women's bodies and obtain their sexual release from ejaculating into a vagina. But they don't thank a woman for giving them an orgasm. A man usually obtains his own stimulation through thrusting. In his eyes, a man makes his own orgasm. For much the same reasons, women never boast about their lover's orgasms. Male orgasm tends to occur reliably but a man's implicit or explicit gratitude may cause a woman to feel loved.

A man's own performance (ability to get an erection and thrust until ejaculation) is critically important to him. Many men also want to feel that their efforts to stimulate a lover (through intercourse or other activity with a lover) also pleases a woman. When it comes to sex, a woman's desire to be considered sexually normal is equally as strong as a man's desire to perform in such a way as to please a woman. Men interpret women's amenability to intercourse as an erotic response. This concept was cemented with the discovery that women were capable of orgasm. The term orgasm was ascribed to the pleasure men assumed women must experience from sex.

Heterosexual men are confused by references to the clitoris. Their sex drive (to engage in penetrative sex) focuses them on the vagina. Why does a woman agree to have sex with a man if she wants clitoral stimulation? She can get that by herself or with another woman. A man assumes that a woman is focused on the same act that he is. He overlooks the fact that a woman only needs to be amenable to intercourse rather being driven to obtain it.

Consent is not a natural concept for many men. They only see the male side of sexual attraction. As long as they are aroused by a woman, they can guarantee their ability to stimulate her through intercourse and thus (in their eyes) provide women with sensational pleasure. Just as a man doesn't want to miss the opportunity a hard-on provides so he assumes a woman would not want to miss the opportunity provided by his erection. That opportunity is intercourse. He is oblivious to any reproductive risks or social issues.

Given the background of the anti-social pursuits of others of their sex (rape, sexual harassment, etc.), men equate talk of female orgasm to a green light. When a woman says that she has an orgasm, a man accepts her account no matter how unconvincing it may be. Even so there are complicated conditions that don't apply when men want sex. A woman needs to feel loved and respected. She wants the right to rescind her consent at any time.

Men assume that a woman enjoys sex unless her behaviour indicates otherwise. As long as a woman does nothing to challenge a man's belief in her supposed sexual pleasure (orgasm during intercourse or other activity with him) he feels reassured. The fact that she never talks about sexual pleasure and that she never initiates sexual contact, does not concern him. This is an emotional belief that does not stand up to scientific questioning.

Men's foremost concern is their own sexual opportunities. They don't want anyone saying that women get less from sex in case it puts women off sex. The idea that a woman orgasms every time, allows men to assume a woman wants intercourse whenever they do. Men don't think about female orgasm in logical terms. Female orgasm represents their chance of getting sex. Women often appear to want sex by displaying themselves or claiming to orgasm but very few men ever work out that these behaviours are not a sign of responsiveness. If women wanted sex, they would not hint and suggest, they would initiate sexual activity and engage in sexual assault as men do.

The most basic consent a husband has from his wife allows him to take the initiative and make all the effort involved in penetrating her and thrusting until he ejaculates. Many wives offer nothing more than making themselves available. Prostitutes offer intercourse by default but for a higher price may also provide fellatio. If a man is rich, he may maintain a mistress in addition to his own family, who may engage more explicitly on a man's specific sexual needs and fantasies. Some societies or religions allow a man to have more than one wife, which increases his chances of finding a more proactive lover.

Rather than having sex, many women simply want to LOOK like they are having sex. (Bella Ellwood-Clayton)

Misunderstandings over how orgasm is achieved

The issue of female orgasm with a lover is at the core of sexual politics. Men want to feel valued as lovers. Women want to keep men happy in bed so they get other things in exchange such as love, support and companionship.

The confusion over female orgasm is down to two main factors. Firstly, women's lack of responsiveness means that they have no understanding of what is involved in orgasm. They can happily fabricate stories or embellish their experiences because they are ignorant of what an orgasm is. Their motives for talking about orgasm revolve around reassuring themselves (that they are sexually normal as defined by men), reassuring their partner (that they are sexually willing) or simply making money by being popular. They have no interest in a scientific understanding of true female responsiveness.

The second factor in the confusion over female orgasm, is men's desire to define female orgasm to suit their own purposes. Men know exactly how orgasm is achieved. Yet they accept a definition of female orgasm that is inconsistent with their own experience. Even men cannot achieve orgasm in the ways they propose that women should. For example, men suggest that women can orgasm within random time constraints set by their lover's responses (of erection and ejaculation). They believe in such impossible feats despite the contrary evidence of women's behaviours. For example, men are motivated to obtain the stimulation they need. Men discontinue sexual activity as soon as they orgasm. Women do not behave in the same way as men do because they are not aroused and do not orgasm with a lover.

Men enjoy the pleasures of being the penetrator, including:

- obtaining release from sexual frustration;
- enjoying the pleasures of psychological domination; and
- the territorial pleasures of ejaculating.

Female orgasm is assumed to equate to the pleasure of male orgasm plus all these combined pleasures of a penetrator. If so, how is rape ever supposed to be a problem? It is implied that a man's attitude (abusive versus loving) transforms intercourse from a pleasurable act into violation. Our response to stimulation does not vary according to the attitude of the person supplying it. No wonder men are confused and sexual assault thrives! For a man, it is almost guaranteed that intercourse ends with his orgasm. So men naturally have difficulty accepting that women do not orgasm from the same activity.

Women often describe relationship factors when referring to their arousal. Such feelings to not lead to orgasm. Many women only ever have romantic fantasies, which involve the idea of intercourse but without any close-up genital activity of penetrative sex. A responsive woman achieves orgasm by consciously focus her mind on the explicit detail of penetrative sex. Some women say they stop having orgasms. But no one forgets how to orgasm. Women mistake romantic factors early in relationships for orgasm. Our ability to orgasm does not disappear overnight. Responsiveness slowly ebbs away over years. So when men suffer erectile disfunction this is quite a different phenomenon that is not related to their natural responsiveness.

When aroused a man may exude clear liquid (commonly referred to as pre-cum) from the end of his penis. Tumescence and lubrication of the genitals are a result of the mind and body preparing for sexual activity. A man's erection is evidence of his mental arousal. A woman's body also prepares for intercourse by producing vaginal lubrication. The function of vaginal lubrication is to facilitate intercourse and reproduction. Vaginal lubrication is produced quite independently of a woman's mental arousal, which is evidenced (as men's arousal is) by tumescence of the sex organ (phallus).

Anyone who writes a book or produces a movie can portray women's sexuality in any way they choose especially if it entertains an audience. These sources of erotic fiction have wide reaching impact on general beliefs because they are presented so convincingly. We will never stop men from producing their artistic interpretations of female sexuality. But by providing universal sex education we can help an audience apply some common sense in assessing the fantasy and reality components of what they read and watch.

Our society's portrayal of sex suits those who are looking for emotional reassurance that they can easily please a lover. To some women, the idea that they are supposed to be capable of something that men find so appealing, helps to make them more attractive to men. The suggestion that they can please men so easily validates them or makes them feel good about themselves. But porn consists of male turn-ons produced for men by men. It has nothing to do with how a woman achieves orgasm for herself. It is very easy for any woman, who wants to reassure her lover, to fake an orgasm.

The only reason men care about female orgasm is because they attribute a woman's orgasm to their own sexual prowess. Men interpret claims of female orgasm as evidence of women's enjoyment of intercourse. Some men proudly supply accounts of the orgasms they believe their partners have as a result of the stimulation they provide. Orgasm is a selfish pleasure we enjoy because we are aroused in our own mind as a result of specific erotic stimuli that are personal to us. The stimulation is supplied or obtained instinctively.

The majority of women worldwide do not have orgasms during intercourse: as a matter of fact, female sexual dysfunctions are popular because they are based on something that does not exist, i.e. the vaginal orgasm. (Vincenzo and Giulia Puppo)

Sexual behaviours compensate for responsiveness

We cannot start to understand sexuality unless we differentiate between responsiveness and conscious behaviours. For the most part, our minds and bodies function in similar ways regardless of sex or orientation. We cannot control the level of our sex drive, the erotic stimuli that cause our arousal and the frequency with which we orgasm. Our responsiveness cannot be changed. But sexuality depends, not only on our responsiveness, but also on our personality. Different people employ a range of behaviours according to their personality. Some people view sex as a series of conquests. Some enjoy fantasy and masturbation. Others enjoy exploring sex play with a lover. We consciously choose to engage in fantasy, masturbation and erotic sex play.

Men enjoy talking about the turn-on of a lover's sexual attributes, the sexual pleasure they enjoy with a lover and the satisfaction of obtaining their sexual release. Women do not talk about a partner in the same way. Women talk of love and companionable activities they share with someone they love.

There are different motivations for our conscious sexual behaviours. Some behaviours are motivated by a person's responsiveness. For many men, sex involves enjoying sexual release and the physical gratification obtained from penetrative sex. The most responsive men are more proactive than average in seeking out a partner. Most men, especially the more responsive, are looking for opportunities to be the penetrator in any sexual situation. A woman's physical presence signals a potential sexual opportunity. Men are initially attracted by a person's looks but their goal is obtaining intercourse.

We are all different in the sense that we have a unique set of genes. But saying that every woman responds sexually in a different way is just the result of sexual ignorance. Much of women's sexuality is defined by conscious behaviours, which cause the apparent variations between women. If women were aroused with a lover, they would use consistent stimulation on the same anatomy. In heterosexual relationships, the man is the proactive partner who stimulates the anatomy, such as the breasts and vagina, that arouse him. Even responsive women (who are capable of orgasm) are not aroused with a lover. So women have no reason to stimulate themselves with a sexual partner.

On average men are much more promiscuous than women. Homosexual men demonstrate similar behaviours to heterosexual men. Regardless of orientation, men have a drive to engage in penetrative sex and to enjoy the eroticism of being physically intimate with a lover. Lesbian women are rarely promiscuous. Lesbians have long-term relationships based on emotional attachments. Lesbians enjoy companionable activities and engage in affectionate sex play, such as kissing and whole-body caressing. Orientation determines turn-ons (whether we are aroused by the same sex or opposite sex). It cannot affect the anatomy involved in orgasm. Lesbians stimulate the clitoris during their sex play but this does not mean that they achieve orgasm.

Women's behaviours are determined by their personality and attitudes. This includes their amenability to offering a male lover an opportunity for penetration as well as their willingness to pleasure and be pleasured by a lover. Women might admire an attractive man but if he displayed his erect penis, they would run a mile. Men do not use the teasing behaviours women employ because men are actively looking to engage in sexual opportunities.

If a woman behaves in a sexually provocative way, a man concludes that she has taken deliberate steps to arouse him. He assumes that she knowingly behaves in this way to obtain the intercourse that his erection can provide. He assumes she is happy with the consequences of her actions. Women instinctively want to be admired by men because it is a means of obtaining male protection. Women are often quite unaware of how their provocative behaviour affects a man because women do not have a sex drive. They come to accept that men want intercourse in exchange for offering protection.

When a man stops getting the sex he wants, he stops feeling loved. A woman offers sex initially out of love. But she expects to obtain some benefit in return for offering sex. This benefit is essentially emotional control. She assumes that a man will feel gratitude towards her for providing sex. She expects him to offer gifts, pay the bills or just be considerate of her wishes. If he repeatedly ignores her requests, she feels disrespected. He has taken the sex that he wants from the relationship but he has not been willing to give back what a woman wants. As a result the woman stops feeling loved.

Women's reproductive role makes them dependent on a man's support. So women have to be more amenable than men in general. A woman's behaviour of offering sex is not just generosity on her part. It is also a selfish behaviour because she knows that by offering sex, she will gain more control in the relationship. There is a chance (at least to begin with) that a man will be more willing to please her as a lover. Unfortunately male post-coital gratitude tends to diminish over the years as a man takes sex for granted.

Women's sexual passivity means that they are more likely to focus on pleasing a lover. Most of the time this is not about being sexually proactive. It simply means offering men an opportunity for penetrative sex. Perhaps women's apparent generosity as lovers has nothing to do with them being nice people but is purely a result of a selfish behaviour to ensure their own survival and the achievement of their goal of raising children to maturity.

The problem I've heard most about over the years ... is the problem of mismatched desire ... which is the issue of sex-starved men and reluctant women ... (Bettina Arndt)

Topic: Committed relationships

Men and women's perspectives on relationships

Sexuality is about a sexual relationship, which includes social, emotional and sexual aspects. Long-term committed relationships are vital to supporting families over the decades needed to raise children. Men tend to focus on their sexual needs while most women hope for affectionate companionship.

Sex education should present the different moral and social issues that are raised by different behaviours in as unbiased a way as possible. Sex education is about putting behaviours in context. Teenagers of both sexes need to understand that consideration and respect for a partner are paramount when they engage in any kind of sociable sexual activity, especially penetrative sex.

Throughout human history men and women have faced death in very different situations. Men have died and witnessed the death of others in violent situations such as the military, rescue services, sport, hunting and other dangerous activities. Women more typically died and witnessed the death of others in domestic situations as a result of childbirth or when nursing the old and the sick (often their children). So men and women have different emotional responses because of the different risks they experience.

Relationships are a compromise. Someone has to flex and often this is a woman's role. It is in men's nature to push. It is in women's nature to give way. But it shouldn't always be this way. There is a tendency to expect a partner to put up with or accept behaviour that we would not accept from others. This is wrong. We should treat our lover better than others because we love them. A man demonstrates his love in a way that suits him, which is based primarily on sex. But sex does not satisfy women's emotional needs.

A woman puts up with bad behaviour when she feels there is no choice. A man thinks that if he earns more money and says 'I love you' once in a while, a woman should be happy. Saying sorry is easy. A woman wants to see evidence that a man is concerned for her welfare on an on-going basis. A caring person loves all the time, not just when it suits them. They respond to, rather than ignore a lover. They avoid offending or upsetting their partner. They offer comfort. Men do not have the same instinct to demonstrate this kind of platonic affection towards those they love. This explains why lesbians have the most caring relationships of all. Of course, there is a spectrum of caring behaviours and personalities in both genders.

Men grow up in a world where men have more power and money than women. Men assume that male superiority is the natural order of things. Most women are content with a dependent role that keeps them close to family. Men simply ignore topics such as relationships or family, that don't interest them. The fact that feminists are always trying to emulate men only serves to confirm men's superiority. Men find it difficult to acknowledge that inevitably there must be some areas (such as relationships) where women surpass men. Yet men feel it is humiliating to learn from a woman. Men often lack any natural instinct when it comes to relationships with women.

Here are some ideas:

- Do you regularly ask your partner how she is? Do you take an interest in what is important to her?
- What do you want from a relationship? What does your partner want? How do you balance these demands?
- Where are you? At work, preoccupied, never present, not taking part? How can you contribute to family life?
- Do others respect you? Do you keep in shape, take care of yourself? When did you last talk about issues, such as honesty?

We have two sexes, which complement each other by being different. Men see their personal status as central to how others value them. They enjoy erotic fantasies and genital activity. A man is sexy because he is responsive. Women are emotional. They enjoy love and companionable activities. A woman is sexy because she makes effort to attract a man and fulfil his needs.

Most women only ever engage in sexual activity because they are in a relationship with a man. Almost all of that activity is initiated and driven by their male partner. Women see lovemaking as a demonstration of a man's love for a woman. Many women dislike the idea of any sexual activity outside a loving relationship. They do not understand the need for masturbation or other crude and explicit activities. Women do not have an arousal cycle (a reliable progression from arousal to orgasm) as men do. Women enjoy the emotions that arise from sharing interests and affectionate companionship.

A man who wants a woman to enjoy sexual pleasure is equivalent to a woman who wants a man to wear a dress. Women enjoy presenting themselves in ways that are attractive to men. A woman's reproductive role is to attract a mate and subsequently facilitate male orgasm by offering intercourse. Women look for a man to support a family rather than provide her with turn-ons and sexual pleasure. By insisting that women enjoy sex as men do, men are showing their ignorance of men and women's different sexual roles. A woman can enjoy sensual and emotional pleasure with a loving partner. But a woman does not orgasm with a lover because of our reproductive biology. Orgasm occurs a result of releasing sexual tension but very few women are able to respond to eroticism in way that causes mental arousal.

Work on yourself first so you can be an asset and not a liability in a relationship. (Stephan Labossiere)

The misconceptions that arise from pornography

Pornography provides boys with completely unrealistic images of women's sexuality. The female body is sexualised and objectified (projected in way that causes male arousal). Such images give misleading impressions about women's sexual willingness and availability. This issue needs to be addressed by sex educators if boys are to have healthy relationships and find emotional happiness. Porn shows women doing things that real women do not do. In other words, women are shown as men would like them to be: sexually proactive and enthusiastic. Porn actresses are also portrayed as if they relish all the body fluids that men enjoy including ejaculate and vaginal secretions.

One of the most confusing things about how female sexuality is portrayed in erotic fiction, is the implication that women achieve orgasm by stimulating a variety of different anatomy. Even men cannot achieve this imaginary feat. Equally, we see women apparently achieving orgasm as easily as men do. Without the general all-body tumescence that men have, women have much less sensitivity to touch. Women are shown apparently having orgasms in different positions as well as from totally different stimulation techniques.

In porn, the portrayal of female arousal is based on the resistance scenario. There is an inherent turn-on in the screams, the body straining to escape and the shocked expression of someone being penetrated against their will. A porn actress has an expression of surprise as if she can feel a penis thrusting in her vagina, which she cannot. A woman feels almost no sensation from consensual intercourse. Women are shown tiddling their vulva while facing the audience because this gives male observers the best view. Stimulation of the clitoral glans does not provide amazing pleasure. A responsive woman enjoys orgasm rather than the stimulation that leads to it. Cunnilingus is portrayed as an amazing pleasure when, in truth, there is little sensation.

The problem with visual media is that we don't know what is happening inside a person's head. This is confusing for anyone watching because they assume that a woman is responding naturally to stimulation (rather than acting). Even in erotic literature women are portrayed as if they are aroused by real-world erotic stimuli just as men are but this does not reflect reality.

Pornography gives a completely faked portrayal of women's ability to become aroused with a lover. It also shows women being able to apparently have orgasms almost without end with no recovery time. Responsiveness does not work like this even for men (only rare cases of some young boys).

In porn a woman is shown apparently having almost continuous orgasms during penile thrusting. So-called multiple orgasms have been used to explain how women might do this. Even men enjoy only arousal, rather than orgasm, while they are thrusting. Anyone who has an orgasm does not want to continue with the same stimulation that caused their orgasm. This is the whole point of orgasm: that it releases sexual tension. Women can engage in sexual activity indefinitely with a lover because they are not sexually aroused.

Porn actresses moan intermittently throughout the male performance. They build in some smaller climaxes along the way to bring the man on. It's as if women are aroused and re-aroused on a never-ending basis until the man has had his orgasm. Finally when the man is about to ejaculate, the woman is miraculously also simultaneously satisfied. Ideally, she brings her vocal accompaniment to a final crescendo coincident with the man's orgasm. Porno actresses provide vocal accompaniment as a male turn-on. Men don't have to make all that noise to convince a lover that they have had an orgasm.

Women also offer enticements as a tease. "Come on Big Boy! Come and get me!" Vocals range from "Oh my God!" to "Come on baby. Give it to me!" Porn actresses indicate their sexual willingness by talking dirty or engaging in sex chat. A young man assumes a real woman should provide all the same turn-ons he sees in porn. So some women copy these cries of ecstasy, verbal come-ons and proactive engagement as a turn-on for a lover.

Porn actresses smile or pout. There is a continuous dialogue. They look delectable and their make-up is not even smudged. This is not a realistic portrayal of how anyone achieves orgasm. Anyone who is aiming for orgasm needs to concentrate on the turn-ons and stimulation at hand. Men do not approach sex expecting to need to provide turn-ons for a lover. When a man is heading for orgasm, he may grunt and his face is focussed in concentration.

Men never observe a woman truly having an orgasm so they have nothing to compare porn with. Most women have no idea what an orgasm is either. So although men do not respond in this way, the sounds and images of a woman faking orgasm have become a substitute for the real thing. Women just have to copy what they see in movies or read about in erotic fiction. A woman can provide a male erotic turn-on just by copying the faked orgasms portrayed in porn. Faking also represents a way for a woman to reduce the amount of time that she needs to invest in sexual activity. Hence why faking, and the idea that female orgasm is possible with a lover, is so heavily promoted.

Men are anxious when their penis does not compare well to those shown in pornography. Porn shows men with unusually large (regularly shaped) genitals and a constant erection throughout almost endless sexual activity. Porn actors are chosen for penis size and stamina so that they look good on film. Presumably they also become desensitised over time to the visual turn-ons and the constant stimulation involved in producing a porn movie.

Nothing in porn is real. You need to watch porn knowing that this is all completely fabricated. (Tracey Cox)

Sex as a bargaining chip in loving relationships

When we are single, we can focus on our own selfish needs. But when we have a relationship with another person, we need to consider their needs as well as our own. Sometimes these two demands conflict. Relationships of any kind are an inevitable compromise. Men obtain their prime emotional reward through penetrative sex. A woman wants an affectionate lover who is interested in knowing her as a person and willing to respect her concerns.

To men, sex is almost always a massively positive experience that they like to promote. For women, sex comes with many issues and problems that they have to reconcile. Women cannot understand men's crude sexual urges and responses because they never experience anything similar. By remaining silent, women are able to accept male advances without losing face. Women don't want to discuss their lack of arousal with a lover. It highlights their sexual subjugation and men cannot believe that women are unresponsive.

A man can only engage in intercourse when he has an erection. His sexual opportunities are limited by his own responsiveness. When a man is aroused, he assumes that his partner is also aroused. But even for a male partner, lovers are not always aroused at the same time or at the same rate. Luckily a receiver of intercourse does not need to be aroused. But the pleasures of offering a lover penetration are considerably less than the pleasures the penetrating male enjoys. The receiver of intercourse enjoys only the emotional reward of giving pleasure to a considerate male partner.

Men learn that women are not always amenable to sexual activity. An emotional attachment to a man (and a desire for family) may cause a heterosexual woman to be amenable to intercourse. But no one can orgasm within time limits set by another person's responsiveness. A woman looks for a man who is socially amenable to compensate her for the intercourse she is expected to offer. She wants a man to invest time in companionship and to support her goals by providing a home and helping her raise a family.

Women's behaviours of playing along with male fantasies by cooperating with intercourse define women's sexual role. A woman knows that a man's love is conditional. Once they are emotionally tied in, many women find it difficult to ignore a man's obvious sexual need. After having children, the disruption and unpleasantness of divorce often persuade women to put up with the sexual overhead to keep the family together. Other women are happy to do whatever is necessary for them to benefit from a man's income.

This range of female attitudes is also a reflection of their partner's sex drive and their partner's need for erotic feedback. A man who is happy with a low frequency of sexual activity is much less demanding. A man who is done within a couple of minutes is also easy to please. But men who want regular sex (at least weekly) with a woman's apparent engagement (her appearance of willingness and affection) put a much heavier sexual load on a woman.

A woman offers intercourse on her terms. Intercourse is a privilege that a woman confers on a man as a sign of her approval. Naturally this causes men to feel controlled by women. A man may also come to resent a lover who does not provide the frequency of activity that he would like. A man knows that if a woman fails to offer the intercourse he needs, eventually he would have to find another lover. Nevertheless, he does not consciously equate his willingness to support a woman financially with her willingness to offer sex. Most men willingly subsidize a partner's lifestyle if they are obtaining the regular sexual outlet they need. Men rarely acknowledge this trade especially if they believe the fantasy that women have the same sexual needs as men.

When a married man uses a prostitute, he can be shamed for cheating on his wife. In this respect women's view of sex, as a token of commitment and monogamous love, prevails over the male view. This is probably the effect of boys being raised by women, who dominate in the home. Most men grow up accepting that women consider men's sexual needs to be crude and offensive. The unspoken trade within marriage is that a woman offers regular intercourse in exchange for a man's sexual loyalty. A man's marital fidelity reduces the risk that his earnings will be diverted away from the family.

Most women will not offer sex for money. Most women offer sex in exchange for a relationship. But men pay much more through a relationship than they ever would to a prostitute. This financial support provides women with tremendous emotional reassurance. This is not about manipulation or exploitation. Men and women have a symbiotic relationship. A man's motivation for wanting sex is the erotic pleasure he enjoys. A woman's motivation for offering sex is the security of knowing she has a man's protection and possibly support. A woman also has the emotional rewards of raising her children, which is why most women want a stable relationship.

In the early days of a romance, a man may be caring (willing to comply with a woman's wishes) and companionable (attentive to her concerns). But over time, men come to resent what they call nagging: a seemingly endless list of demands for them to change their behaviour. Men tend to ignore what they see as an attack on their right to behave just as they want to. Relationships involve a compromise between self-interest and pleasing a partner. But a man sees nothing selfish in continuing to expect regular intercourse. A man's focus on his own needs is so intense that he is immune to the deterioration in his lover's attitude, from affectionate to mechanical, resentful and angry.

Too many husbands, on the other hand, fail to comprehend that their wives are not aroused as they are in the anticipation of a sexual relationship. (Alfred Kinsey)

The misunderstandings behind sexual dysfunction

True sexual dysfunctions are very rare. The word dysfunction implies that something is not working properly. In order to define dysfunction, we must first define normal functioning. We also need to specify whether we are talking about reproductive function, erotic orgasm or emotional pleasure.

A woman may feel miserable if she cannot conceive but sexual dysfunction tends to focus on orgasm rather than reproductive capability. Certainly, male dysfunction does not relate to whether a man can impregnate a woman. A man feels life is hardly worth living if he cannot get an erection, which is a prerequisite for a man to engage in any kind of sexual activity. So sexual dysfunction tends to be defined in terms of orgasm or in terms of a woman's willingness to engage in intercourse because both of these are so vital to men's happiness. But it is important to appreciate that women have no need for orgasm and no need for intercourse unless they want to have a baby.

Female sexual dysfunction (FSD) is based on the belief that women should orgasm from intercourse. Media images that portray women apparently responding to the point of orgasm with a lover are so persuasive that women feel obliged to refer to orgasm as if it occurs naturally in their lives. Many women, who never orgasm, assume that they do, just as men say they should.

Every year billions of dollars are paid to the sex therapists by couples who are frustrated when female orgasm doesn't occur as they think it should. Yet the published research findings (Alfred Kinsey) clearly indicate that women are much less responsive than men. In the past women were called frigid, today they are called dysfunctional. Only the terminology has changed. In the past women were told it was their duty to provide sex. Today women are told they should enjoy sex. If they don't, there are still no answers. The idea that women orgasm with a lover is defended vehemently because of sexual politics. Women are under intense pressure from society to offer intercourse and no one sees any problem in threatening women with sexual inadequacy. Whether we believe in the fantasy or not, makes no difference. Men need regular intercourse regardless of women's response to it. Women must offer intercourse to obtain a man's moral or financial support to raise a family.

Men have no idea how women truly orgasm because female orgasm is only achieved when a responsive woman masturbates alone. Neither are men aware of how female turn-ons work because responsive women use surreal fantasies that they prefer to keep private. So men's idea of these phenomena is based on women's behaviours (not their responses). A woman just copies the porn actresses. Some women assume that the sensations of intercourse equate to orgasm. This is why they believe women need a man with a loving attitude to enjoy sex. But emotional factors have nothing to do with orgasm.

When talking about sex, adults often fail to take into account the very different sexual experiences we all have. We may also have very different responses to the same experience because of our different personalities. Most couples accept a man's greater interest and a woman's sexual passivity. Consequently, few couples ever discuss sexual pleasuring. FSD affects responsive women because (knowing what an orgasm feels like) their expectations for sexual activity with a lover are set much higher than others.

Sexologists explain women's lack of response to intercourse in vague terms. They suggest that women who ask questions are inhibited or repressed for some inexplicable reason. They say that men are incompetent lovers who do not stimulate their female lover the right way (or for long enough). These suggestions make couples feel inadequate and cause huge embarrassment. The fact is that the vast majority of people accept their sexual experiences for what they are. They never consider that they might be dysfunctional because they don't expect too much in the first place. Faking orgasm is easy and reassures couples that their sexual experiences conform to social norms.

Other couples seek help because over decades, women get bored of being a receptacle for their partner's semen. The couple's relationship suffers because a man stops getting the sex he wants and a woman feels unappreciated. Couples tend to assume that experts must know answers to questions no one else can answer. They spend money on consulting therapists but either give up or are satisfied that they have done their best.

What we call sexual dysfunction today is really just a mismatch between expectation and reality. Men and women feel inadequate because of the unrealistic media images based on fictional material. The research findings indicated that female orgasm is associated with female masturbation rather than sexual activity with a lover. But this finding is unpopular because few women masturbate and because men want women to respond to intercourse.

Women are not motivated to stimulate themselves with a lover. So it is assumed to be the man's role to stimulate a woman. Given the ignorance over how female orgasm is achieved, women assume that they might orgasm if stimulated for long enough. So women hold their partner responsible for their inability to orgasm because men ejaculate quickly through intercourse. Some men worry that their penis isn't big enough or that they can't maintain an erection for long enough to simulate a woman to orgasm. This is all nonsense. Intercourse is a mating act. As long as a man can ejaculate into a vagina he has succeeded. Telling a man that the act is also supposed to cause female orgasm only leads him to feel inadequate when it doesn't happen.

The way sex is portrayed in the media and in films often provides us with a base of comparison that is not always realistic for the individual. (Andrea Burri)

Premature ejaculation and erectile dysfunction

It's not uncommon for a man to have a problem with erections from time to time. But erectile dysfunction (ED) that happens routinely is not normal and should be treated. ED is defined as difficulty getting or keeping an erection that's firm enough for intercourse. ED is the most common sexual problem that men report to a doctor. Only a quarter of men are impotent by the age of 70. A man still wants to engage in intercourse even when he is impotent.

Here are some ideas to think about:

- Is your lover open-minded? Do you discuss new approaches to sexual pleasuring? Try a change of venue or different positions.

- Try asking your partner what she would like. How much time do you invest in pleasuring her before starting intercourse?

- Have you talked about bringing some variety to your sex life? Try experimenting with different ex toys, porn movies etc.

- What do you do to show that you appreciate your partner? Do you spend companionable time with your partner?

ED can happen when testosterone levels fall, blood flow to the penis is limited or nerves are harmed. It can also be an early warning of a more serious illness like hardening or blocked arteries, heart disease, high blood pressure or diabetes. Men should avoid being overweight and aim for low cholesterol and low blood pressure. They should also do regular exercise, avoid excessive stress, alcohol and smoking. Anything a man can do to ease tension and feel emotionally stable is likely to help his sexual performance.

Erectile dysfunction becomes more common as men age. But it is not necessarily a normal part of aging. There are treatments, which include consulting a specialist who uses a vacuum pump or obtaining one of your own. The pump creates an artificial erection by causing blood to flow into the corpora cavernosa within the shaft of the penis. Another approach is to ask a lover to provide erotic turn-ons to assist with male arousal. By massaging, kissing and fingering his partner, a man may increase his own arousal. A sensual whole body focus also makes his lover feel appreciated.

Premature ejaculation is the most common sexual problem for men. The objective of a mating act is for the male to deposit his semen in the female's vagina. From a reproductive perspective, the quicker the better. Men are often aroused throughout the day. When they have an opportunity for sex with a partner their challenge is to slow down so that they don't ejaculate spontaneously. Some men ejaculate before any foreplay. Others lose control when inserting their penis, while some ejaculate immediately after penetration. Occasionally losing control of ejaculation is normal. Premature ejaculation is only a problem if it happens frequently. Most men sometimes reach orgasm sooner than they'd like. It is common for a man to ejaculate quickly the first time he has sex or if he hasn't ejaculated for a long time. The occasional loss of control doesn't mean that the man has a sexual problem.

Premature ejaculation can be an issue for a number of reasons. Firstly, men want to enjoy the pleasurable sensations of thrusting for as long as possible. Secondly, a woman may want lovemaking (where a man provides sensual stimulation, upper body kissing and caressing) to continue for longer. But men only engage in upper body lovemaking for as long as they have an erection. Some women mistakenly assume that they might have an orgasm if intercourse continued for longer. Any sense of inadequacy would be easily be overcome if a man was prepared to stimulate a woman orally or manually.

The belief, that intercourse can cause female orgasm, is false and puts the responsibility for female orgasm onto men. Men are not responsible for providing the correct stimulation. Women are quite capable of providing their own stimulation. A woman isn't aroused in the way that a man is. She has no sense of frustration if nothing happens. The pressure comes from a man wanting to enjoy his own performance and enjoy emotional acceptance.

Men's insecurities are that intercourse is a simple act but they're not sure what is expected of them. Surely all they have to do is what comes naturally? All the discussion about female orgasm seems to imply that this is not good enough. So what else do they need to do to keep women happy in bed? It's implied that men need to learn special thrusting techniques to help a woman achieve orgasm. A man is also under pressure to delay his ejaculation forever, which is impossible. Men are responsive. Women are not. Women can engage in all forms of sexual activity with a lover almost indefinitely.

If men just wanted sex then they could pay a prostitute. It would be much cheaper. Men seek out relationships with women to feel loved and appreciated. Prostitutes and one-night stands do not provide this emotional reward. Neither can a woman be forced to provide it. It arises naturally. Of course men think it should arise by them providing amazing sex. But if a man is constantly hassling his partner for sex, then clearly a woman does not want sex in the way men do. A man has to provide some of the things that a woman wants. He has to behave in a way that makes her want to please him. Men seem to struggle with the fact that women feel loved (not through sex but) when a man is a charming companion and interested in their concerns. By obsessing about providing a lover with imagined sexual pleasure (that is not sought by women), men effectively ignore women's emotional needs.

Premature ejaculation is the great male fear. The trouble is that coming too soon is a fact of life. (Antony Mason)

Anorgasmia, preorgasmia and vaginismus

Women who masturbate themselves to orgasm are called pre-orgasmic. Rather than celebrate the fact that they experience orgasm, the implication is that women are inadequate because (regardless of any scientific facts or logic) they cannot please a man by having their orgasms during intercourse. Men's sex drive makes intercourse an obligatory activity for heterosexuals. If a woman cannot or will not offer intercourse, a man naturally assumes that there must be something badly wrong with her or that she must be a lesbian.

Female sexual dysfunction is defined according to this male point of view. Even though women themselves rarely refer to masturbation, it is assumed that most women masturbate. However, a woman is not considered to be dysfunctional if she doesn't masturbate. Most men masturbate. But female masturbation is much less common. Masturbation is an indication of sexual responsiveness. Men's main interest in female sexuality focuses on the orgasms they want women to have from the stimulation that they provide.

Men assume that engaging in intercourse is a natural and regular part of women's biological function. Men are meant to penetrate. Women are meant to be penetrated. A man enjoys penetrating a woman, so he assumes she should enjoy being penetrated just as much. Unfortunately, these conclusions do not follow. The carnivore is obliged to prey on herbivores because otherwise it will die. Even though it is the herbivore's destiny to be eaten, the victim does not actively seek out the situation. Many women want to have a family but they do not tend to offer intercourse nearly as often as men would like. Reproduction relies on a woman's willingness to let a man ejaculate into her vagina but not every day, every week or even every month.

Male sex drive naturally focuses men on the female anatomy involved in intercourse. In the most basic terms, a woman's sexual role involves providing an orifice (the vagina) for a man to ejaculate into. A man cannot understand why a woman would orgasm at any time other than when he is stimulating her. What would be the point? The point of female orgasm is a woman's own sexual pleasure. A woman orgasms alone because she can focus on her own arousal rather than assisting with a man's need for release.

Vaginismus is a reproductive issue because intercourse leads to pregnancy. The sexual issue arises because of a man's sex drive. This male need means a man feels rejected when a woman cannot provide him with an opportunity for intercourse even if she has a good reason. A man assumes that if a woman loves him that she will always be amenable to sex. So consent within a loving relationship has little meaning to men. Yet ironically men themselves cannot be persuaded to engage in sex unless they are aroused and have an erection.

Men may be satisfied at least in part with being masturbated by a lover or by receiving oral sex (fellatio). Most women do not want to offer these more explicit forms of genital stimulation. Ultimately men want the optimal sexual release through intercourse. This is the biological drive. Women accept intercourse because it involves them in very little explicit erotic engagement.

Women accept painful sex because it is often implied that a woman is being selfish if she deprives a male lover of his sexual outlet. A woman assumes that it is her personal failing that she does not enjoy sex as a man does. Even during pregnancy or after childbirth it is difficult to persuade a male lover than penetrative sex may be uncomfortable or even painful for a woman.

Women feel guilty because they think it's their fault that they don't orgasm with a lover. They don't realise that every woman is the same. Women are told that they should orgasm naturally through intercourse. This is like telling a blind man that he should be able to see. It doesn't help him to be told what is possible for others (only men). No one can explain why one woman can apparently experience what others cannot. Male fantasies about multiple or easy orgasms intimidate women into silence by implying sexual inadequacy.

The sexual revolution was not about new knowledge. It was about women's new freedom as a result of the contraceptive pill. Also society condoned the promotion of female nudity in public as a result of more reliable policing. But false expectations were set. By suggesting that sex provides women with the same erotic rewards as men, men came to expect the emotional reward of pleasuring a lover. Men and women receive different but complementary rewards from sex. Men's need for sexual release through intercourse, provides women with the emotional reward of being needed by a partner.

Men assume that vaginal stimulation should cause female orgasm. So, of course, some women assume they orgasm during intercourse. Not knowing what orgasm feels like, they mistake sensual pleasures for orgasm. Sex information, that promotes the many ways in which women are supposed to orgasm, causes people to feel inadequate. These fantasies create demand for sex therapy because people want to be reassured that they can experience these feats. A key objective of sex research should be to provide explanations for the behaviours of real men and women. Yet there are no real women (in the general population or even sexologists) who can talk explicitly about these supposed orgasms. This is one of the key failings of sex research today, which ignores the accumulated findings that clearly indicate that female orgasm is experienced by women who are able to masturbate to orgasm.

One of the diagnostic criteria for FSD (female sexual dysfunction) is feeling distressed. But what causes the distress? Is it the condition itself, or is it what you think is expected of you and in turn, what you start expecting of yourself? (Andrea Burri)

The role of relationship therapists and counsellors

Adults are embarrassed about sex because of their emotional insecurities. Our emotional needs include a need to impress, a need to belong and a need to be valued. Some people lack self-esteem, which stems from anxiety. We avoid discussing relationship issues for various reasons. We want to avoid conflict. We don't want to admit that we have behaved badly, that we have said things we shouldn't have or that we were wrong. We may want to continue behaving in a way that suits us but that we cannot justify logically.

Relationships involve a balance of power, with each partner negotiating (even if only by using silent or moody behaviour) to get what they want. We don't want to put ourselves in a position where we might feel under moral pressure (because the force of logic is against us) to consider changing our behaviour just to please a lover. Men worry about losing out on sexual opportunities. Women worry about having to give more than they feel they should need to.

As with all things in life, the less we expect, the more content we are. Most people never question their sexual experiences. Many unresponsive women are not bothered about a lack of orgasm. Others assume there must be a solution. So they pay for therapy hoping for reassurance. But some situations don't have a solution. They are just way they are. We find this hard to accept. Any facts or logic, that might explain why women cannot respond as men want, are ignored because they do not help solve the issue. This search is endless because no one can accept the evidence of their own experiences.

As long as they get regular sex, most men are happy. So sex therapy focuses on relationship issues that are important, if a woman is to be amenable to offering the sex a man needs. Men want women to be enthusiastic about intercourse because it provides them with so much pleasure. Women also want to know how intercourse could be pleasurable because men expect it.

Therapists assume that their work qualifies them as objective observers of sexuality in the population. But a therapist uses counselling techniques to help with relationship issues. Many women tend to talk about their sexual experiences in terms of orgasm but this does not mean they truly have one. Women may provide sexual histories but a therapist cannot easily challenge a paying client. Sex research is quite different. A researcher needs the personal qualities that ensure they can challenge and question. A researcher should be intellectually independent, free from political bias and prejudices.

There is, of course, money to be made by suggesting that there is a recognisable condition that can be treated in some way or a problem that can be solved by a sexual therapist. We are easily persuaded that other couples have discovered something we have not. However, one has to ask why such vital information is not made available to everyone. If such information existed, it would surely not be secret for long? Therapists provide reassurance rather than explanations. Many so-called solutions do not stand up to scrutiny but we are all much too embarrassed to complain.

A woman can conceive without ever having an orgasm. So-called female sexual dysfunctions rely on the idea that women should orgasm from intercourse, yet this belief is not supported by research. The only real evidence (if you can call it that) of women apparently being sexually aroused with a lover comes from erotic fiction. The sexual bravado of a few individuals of both sexes adds to the confusion over how and when female orgasm is achieved (a woman must first be sexually responsive). Women are only thought to be dysfunctional because of a few bogus orgasm claims.

The first misconception is that women have a sex drive. Women are told that they should be driven to want intercourse as much as a man does. This is incorrect. A woman does not have a sex drive. Women do not orgasm with a lover regardless of the stimulation a man provides. A couple needs to understand this. Telling a woman that she should naturally want sex, when she doesn't, means that she can only conclude that she is abnormal or dysfunctional in some way. This causes embarrassment, silence and taboo.

The second misconception to overcome is that a man is not responsible for his partner's orgasm. Some men are motivated to try to pleasure a woman sexually because they assume that if they could succeed, she would be more amenable to having sex. Unfortunately women are not aroused with a lover. The few women who are responsive only orgasm by masturbating alone. Orgasm is a personal pleasure that we create in our own minds. First, a person must be responsive. Next, they need the appropriate circumstances.

Women can never be a penetrator so (regardless of orientation) they are much less proactive than men. Women generally dislike genital display and manipulation. Most women engage in sexual activity only as a response to a man's initiative. Women are essentially on the defensive. They need only to accept a man's instinctive desire to explore their bodies. Some women are motivated to offer proactive pleasuring because they enjoy pleasing a lover.

A woman needs to put conscious effort into sexual activity of any kind (even when she is alone). She has two options with a lover. She can either engage proactively on providing her lover with sexual pleasure. Or she can give him permission to explore her body and allow him to try to provide her with some sensual and possibly erotic sensations that she might enjoy. If she does this, she can assist her lover by giving some encouraging erotic feedback.

To us men, sex is sex. We want it, let's do it, we're done. For many women it isn't always that simple. You need to be in tune with her emotionally if you want to make her more receptive sexually. (Stephan Labossiere)

How a man can have relationship sex more often

Nature never intended men to be monogamous. In every society, men's greater inclination for promiscuity is accepted as a natural and defining characteristic of male sexuality. A woman offers sex to a man because she knows that if she doesn't, he will go looking for another woman. So women's need for male support, has contributed to the high sex drive many men have today. Men are attracted to women regardless of anyone's relationship status. Most men try to be faithful while in a relationship because they appreciate that sexual loyalty is important to women's emotional need to feel loved.

One of the main justifications men have for insisting on regular sex with their wives, is their greater earning power. Many women who have children, feel obliged to keep a man happy while he is paying the bills. This explains why men do not encourage women in the workplace. Women's greater economic independence is not in men's interests. This is evidence that men know they are asking for something that women don't always want to give.

To a woman, an erect penis is a demand for attention. She is expected to provide the sexual outlet a man needs. She may do this in return for a loving relationship. Women ensure that male genitals are censored (banned by law). On social media women also object to so-called dick-pics sent by men who like to send random women photos of their penis. These images are easy for a man to send to any woman via a mobile phone. Women react to such images with anger and disgust. This reaction appears to have no effect on men's desire to keep sending them. Women call this behaviour sexual harassment unless they have accepted it as part of a committed relationship.

Sexual harassment laws are necessary because of men's insensitivity to the female perspective. A man wants to share his erection and his orgasm with a lover because of his sex drive. Men assume that women take the same joy in their erection as they do. But our experience of arousal and orgasm are personal to us. Women do not experience men's sexual urges and pleasure.

A woman is expected to be amenable to intercourse with frequencies related to her partner's sex drive. Yet a woman does not experience arousal on a daily basis. Even a responsive woman only experiences arousal sporadically. A woman may feel some emotional anticipation on approaching new romantic situations. She can enjoy thinking about the companionable time with her lover. She can anticipate being the object of her lover's desire to penetrate her. A woman's vanity responds to a man's interest in knowing her personally. She appreciates his desire to caress her body. She feels pleasure in demonstrating her affection to him and having her affection reciprocated.

Initially a woman approaches sex through romance. She responds to a lover who demonstrates loving behaviours. But over time, a man stops providing these stimuli. Once a man has been accepted by a woman, he relies on her being more amenable than other women. Otherwise he would just go elsewhere. Instinctively a man knows that when a woman is emotionally attached to him, she is more likely to be amenable to sex than any random woman. Marital sex tends to fall into habitual sexual activity that lacks any romantic lead-in. Sex becomes much more functional based on a man's need for regular intercourse. This creates a stark contrast for a woman. She may feel pressured to respond on an erotic level that she doesn't experience in real life. A woman has great difficulty transporting herself from the social world in which she lives and imagining herself in the erotic world of men.

A woman offers a man sex in the hope of being loved. She withholds sex when she is angry, partly to punish him, but also because offering sex to an offensive lover is abhorrent to a woman when she is angry. Men never behave like this because, for men, sex is a commodity or biological need to relieve sexual tension. At a certain level, sex is just functional for men, like urinating. For women, sex is much more dependent on emotional factors.

If a man isn't getting the sex he wants, he has to change the balance of power. A man should back off for a while (for a month or two) and give his partner time to miss his interest in her. He needs to stop hassling for sex. He should wait until she wants him to notice her. He should focus on providing the companionship she values, by investing in activities they can enjoy together. A couple should ban intercourse and focus on other forms of sensual pleasuring. Intercourse is good for two things: making babies and facilitating male orgasm. Intercourse should be used towards the end of lovemaking.

Men often behave badly in their relationships with women. But when a man is asked to change his behaviour, a man thinks a woman is being unreasonable. For a woman, any relationship with a man is a huge investment. She is not looking for turn-ons or sexual amenability. She is looking for a companion she can feel proud of in a social sense. She has to teach him how to be considerate. She has to work on his presentation style.

Men appreciate attractive women but it rarely occurs to them that a woman might also want an attractive lover, both in looks and amenability. Men's top sexual concern is their erection. But a woman approaches sex, aware of her whole body. She feels on show to some degree because she knows that her ability to arouse her lover is vital to intercourse. If she feels out of shape, she may be less sexually willing. A man needs to make a woman feel attractive.

To be fair women are also guilty because she does not feel confident or comfortable to say to her partner, "Hey, sex needs to be about what I want. And tonight it's going to be an all-about-me-night; which means a full body massage and no intercourse. Next time we'll focus on your fun." (Trina Read)

How a woman can interest a man in having sex

Sex occurs much more easily in the early stages of a relationship because being affectionate with each other provides the most natural lead-in to sex. First a woman offers some affectionate interaction by touching or kissing her lover. Her lover communicates his sexual need by kissing back with passion, by touching the woman with an increased focus on the erogenous zones and by indicating his own sexual arousal by pressing his groin against her body.

A man makes love to a woman to demonstrate his sexual admiration for her. A man does not make love to a prostitute. Neither do we talk about a woman making love to a man. Men want sex, not lovemaking. Women engage in casual sex for ego rather than the physical gratification men enjoy. Women don't use male prostitutes in the same way because they hope for a loving relationship and sex comes as a consequence. Many men also don't want sex with a stranger. But a man can enjoy sex without any need for a relationship.

In the early days of a relationship, a couple may explore different approaches to pleasuring. Given women's sexual passivity, it is typically the man who takes the sexual initiative. A man has the motivation to explore a lover's body because he is aroused by doing so. A woman is not. Female orgasm has become a token of women's appreciation of men's attempts to arouse them. This is because most women only engage in sexual activity by responding to a man's motivation rather than their own. Men try different approaches to sexual pleasuring within the boundaries set by a woman's objections. Over time instead of this random and silent approach, a couple may want to invest in more open communication about their sexual pleasuring. A woman could suggest, outside the bedroom, the activities she would like to try or how she would like a lover to stimulate her. If a woman has read erotic literature or watched porn movies, she may identify with the role of giving pleasure.

In a long-term relationship, a woman accepts intercourse because of the inherent authority that comes with a man's sex drive. Male sex drive provides some reassurance of a man's commitment to the relationship and of his sexual loyalty. A woman may feel loved because a man needs her sexually. In romantic fiction a woman is swept off her feet by a man's sexual passion. Women don't need men to perform sexually but they come to expect it. A woman worries that (if a man no longer wants her) perhaps he loves another.

Older women may complain that their husbands no longer want to make love to them. A woman may miss sex but this has nothing to do with orgasm. If she wanted an orgasm, she could masturbate. Instead of complaining about her partner, a woman should offer some proactive pleasuring herself. The person who is most motivated should make the effort. Typically it is the man who is hassling for sex. Anyone who has a less than enthusiastic partner, needs to ensure that they contribute the lion's share of the effort.

Some women are much more proactive as lovers than others. This is related to personality, culture and how much a woman identifies with the female role in erotic fiction. Men like to assume that a woman is proactive because she is herself aroused. This fantasy reassures a man that a woman will be amenable to regular intercourse. Women who invest in their sex life, do so by making conscious effort to please a lover (just as prostitutes do).

A man wants intercourse regardless of a woman's lack of arousal. So women look for information to help them understand how they could enjoy an act that men insist on. This is not about a desire to have an orgasm or enjoy sexual pleasure. This is about women's role in providing male gratification.

If men only wanted an orgasm, they could masturbate. Men enjoy penetrating and ejaculating into a lover's body. Men like having the lights on, using mirrors and a lover who displays herself provocatively. Male turn-ons are crude, graphic and obvious. They can appreciate obvious sexual invitations such as a woman spreading her legs or holding her buttocks apart. Most women are so disgusted by genitals (even their own) and the practical realities of sexual activity that they have no idea what a man responds to.

Women assume that men are automatically aroused. Men need specific erotic stimuli such as female genitalia or sexual activity. A woman can buy sexy nightwear or pornographic videos to watch together naked. A woman needs to project her appreciation of her lover. She can make encouraging comments about her excitement at the prospect of being penetrated by him.

Sex is like a conversation and no one enjoys talking to themselves. A man appreciates a lover who occasionally takes the sexual initiative. He also hopes for an adventurous lover who gives him permission to explore her body. A woman can enjoy this scenario because she abdicates herself from any need to make effort. She can just lie there and enjoy the sensations of being stimulated by a lover even though the feelings do not culminate in a climax.

Humans have sex much more than is needed for reproduction. So, even men are not motivated by a purely biological drive. Our minds are aroused by the opportunity to have sex with different sexual partners or in different scenarios. Few men would walk away from a relationship where they are having regular and varied sex with an enthusiastic and adventurous partner. Men look for a variety of partners because they are bored by marital sex.

The most frequent reason men gave for having sex outside their marriages was sexual rejection by their wives, or the boring nature of repeated sex with the same person in marriage. (Shere Hite)

Why couples struggle to communicate over sex

Sex is most rewarding for a woman in the romantic scenario of a new relationship. In the beginning a man's easy arousal means that sex is fairly effortless for a woman. Decades later it is not necessarily so easy. Over time intercourse can become a mechanical act. It is neither erotic nor loving. This happens in long-term sexual relationships where intimacy is lost. Sexual issues tend to accumulate and need to be discussed. A woman may feel that sex is expected as a regular duty. A man needs to understand the emotional factors that motivate a woman to provide the sexual interaction he enjoys. Sex also tends to become more routine. A woman may appreciate a man who invests in activities other than intercourse that bring some variety to a couple's sex life. A man may need to plan ahead to make sex more varied.

A young man's sexual needs overcome any timidity he may feel in asking for intercourse. But over time a woman's body language becomes increasingly less welcoming and her boredom more evident. The couple stops having sex but they never discuss the situation. If a couple is not having sex, then a man needs to invest in understanding some of the things a woman wants. A man needs to invest in companionable time. For a woman, intimacy involves feeling that a lover cares for her because he takes an interest in her concerns.

Over decades a couple needs to invest in communication to keep their sex life alive. A more experienced man is cautious in suggesting sex play because he anticipates a woman's disapproval. Few women engage proactively on genital stimulation, so men get used to taking the initiative and they assume that the responsibility is theirs. Rather than accept defeat, a man explores his lover's body to find out what she will allow him to do. If a man rolls off after sex and falls asleep, a woman feels he has used her vagina but not given her the affection that she wants. A woman wants a lover to caress and kiss her.

The key reason women (even lesbians) do not orgasm by any means with a lover is that there are no naturally occurring erotic turn-ons that arouse women. This situation must be almost impossible for a man to imagine because he is extremely aroused by sexual opportunities with a lover. A woman's lack of arousal makes it exceedingly difficult for her to contribute to the erotic scenario. Even if she knows that conscious behaviours are called for, she runs out of imagination. A man can help by suggesting the activities that he would enjoy. Any partner who is motivated by sexual activity needs to make it easy for a lover by taking the initiative and driving the action.

Couples don't discuss the turn-ons and stimulation a woman needs for orgasm explicitly. A man looks for emotional acceptance through sex. He links his need to please a lover with her willingness to offer sex. If a woman says nothing, a man assumes she must have had an orgasm. A woman will often stop a man who is stimulating her because she has had enough. Some men interpret this behaviour as a sign that a woman has been sexually satisfied. Most alternatives to intercourse require some discussion. It is difficult to communicate consent or objection to sexual activity midstream. Communication over sexual pleasuring ideally takes place after sex, when a couple can compare notes on what worked and what they might try next time. It requires a much higher level of trust and communication to discuss ways of sharing our sexual fantasies with a partner during physical sex play.

Sex is vitally important to men and thus non-negotiable. As long as a woman is amenable to intercourse, a man assumes she is happy, even if her behaviour indicates otherwise. Men use silence and a show of affection or a couple's daily routine to initiate sex. When sex is not on offer, they then indicate their displeasure by using behaviours such as moodiness rather than by explicit discussion. Rather than discuss what might help to make a woman more sexually amenable, men use emotional pressure to get their own way.

People are selfish. They want something that cannot necessarily be justified logically. They get grumpy or use silence. But having a fist fight over it or tackling the problem head-on is problematic. People are not articulate enough to argue their point well. They are too emotional to be able to express their feelings. So they resort to silence and more subtle means. Silence is a way of avoiding conflict but, by repressing resentments, partners accumulate charged emotions, which makes it even more difficult to discuss sexual issues. Women can open up to others more easily because they have less to feel guilty about. Men like to take more risk than women (alcohol, gambling and sex). A man doesn't want a woman to control how he behaves. But a woman doesn't want a man to control her body and what is done to it.

Many people struggle with being honest about their feelings and motives. Men to feel guilty about their sexual urges because of attitudes in society, which arise because of women who never experience them. Blaming society is a way of avoiding taking responsibility for our own behaviour. We don't want to admit our vulnerability and our need for reassurance. We feel the only way to protect ourselves and retain some dignity is to go silent. We keep private thoughts to ourselves. But over decades, issues arise and these need to be discussed otherwise resentments build up. Men learn that women will often defer to a stronger point of view. Women tend to suggest what they want rather than have a fist fight. Men interpret women's more conciliatory approach as a sign of weakness. A couple has to be very brave to develop more explicit forms of communication. If he's not getting the sex he wants, it's easier for a man to look elsewhere rather than invest in communication.

One man talked about this chasm as 'My own Gulf war ... 6 inches between us in the bed feels like 1,000 miles!' (Bettina Arndt)

Topic: Sexual pleasuring

How to make the most of sexual pleasuring

Sexuality is about enjoying sexual pleasure with a lover. We experience sensual, emotional and erotic pleasure. A sex education should include a description of sexual techniques that may be used to pleasure men and women. These should differentiate between those techniques which assist with orgasm and those which provide sensual pleasure. We orgasm with a frequency dictated by our responsiveness. People of both sexes regardless of orientation have different sexual appetites. Ideally there's a match of intellect, curiosity, imagination, sense of humour and concern for hygiene.

There are three main categories of anatomy. The sex organ is involved in orgasm and the internal genital organs in reproduction. The erogenous zones relate to sensual pleasuring and may include any part of the body. Male and female erogenous zones are similar in anatomical terms. They include the labia or the length of the penis, either side of the labia or the testicles, the entrance to the vagina or the base of the penis, the perineum and the anus. For a man there is also the prostate gland next to the rectum. Both sexes can enjoy being stroked or kissed on the mouth, nipples, ear lobes, neck, back and feet with varying pleasure depending on the individual.

The focus of marriage has traditionally been a social liaison rather than a relationship based on sexual pleasuring. Passion and lust are associated with first encounters and illicit affairs rather than with marital sex. Sexual pleasure tends to be associated with male gratification. Women are more typically in the role of providing sexual services. So sexual pleasure is defined from a male perspective. When we masturbate, we may enjoy the sensations of orgasm but we don't usually talk about sexual pleasure in the context of masturbation. Men obtain sexual relief as well as significant erotic and emotional pleasure from penetrative sex (intercourse) and other activities with a lover. However, women are not erotically aroused with a lover. Women need to make more of the sensual pleasures of sexual activity and enjoy the emotional reward of pleasing a lover. Even responsive women, who masturbate to orgasm, only experience this erotic pleasure when alone.

Some people limit themselves to intercourse. Others enjoy masturbation alone and a variety of sex play with a lover. Some people consider these non-reproductive aspects of our sexuality to be more important than others. Attitudes in society (driven primarily by women's dislike of eroticism) can cause others to feel ashamed of their sexual curiosity. The only prerequisite for anyone to enjoy sexual pleasure is the need for a consenting lover. Some people look for a variety of lovers while others prefer to be loyal to one. Many people (especially women) limit their sexual life to a long-term loving relationship. Other couples find that being attracted to others or sharing their lover with other people, helps keep their sex life alive over decades together.

Marriage and romance are associated with love rather than sex. Yet when a man marries, he assumes that his wife will offer him regular sex. Women can feel pressured especially if a man has specific sexual needs or a high sex drive. In the beginning of a romance, a woman can enjoy the novelty of feeling sexually desired. She may delight in the ease of a male lover's arousal (especially a young man). She has the emotional reward of providing a man's sexual release by allowing him to thrust into her vagina until he ejaculates.

A woman does not experience the arousal that motivates men to stimulate a lover's body. Women have to consciously decide to engage in proactive pleasuring. Many women never even consider offering a lover explicit sexual pleasuring. Others may be aware that other women do this but they see no reason why they should offer. A woman needs a good relationship and a sense of fun to be motivated to pleasure a man. If a woman enjoys reading erotic literature or watching the occasional porn movie, she may understand the male turn-ons that sexually experienced women can provide. She may not be comfortable with providing some of the more exaggerated responses of the porn actresses. She should select behaviours that she feels fit with her personality and the relationship. She can use how she dresses to be provocative, undress teasingly and make verbal invitations or suggestions.

The sensual and emotional aspects of sex operate most effectively when lovers are young and attractive. Intercourse tends to become repetitive and lacking in romantic passion for a woman after decades with the same lover. She needs to feel admired by her lover and to feel that his admiration is worth having. Mutual respect is important for sexual enjoyment as well as enjoying each other's company and sharing interests outside the bedroom.

Alternatively after years together, there may be more trust between lovers. If a woman has an imaginative partner and she herself is willing, a couple may enjoy exploring sex play beyond intercourse. Each partner can take turns and provide sensitive feedback on what worked and what to try next time.

Having an aging body may not be an issue where long-term lovers have invested in their sex life and built a loving and communicative relationship. As she ages, a woman's body changes and becomes more responsive to sensual caressing. Her clitoral glans becomes slightly less sensitive. An older woman may experience a greater erotic response if a man invests in exploring different pleasuring techniques. An older man has more time to spend on sexual pleasuring because his sexual arousal is not so acute. He is able to delay his ejaculation so that he can enjoy more sensual pleasuring.

If a person is not prepared to embrace the needs and genuine desires of their partner, then they shouldn't get into a relationship. People have to understand and be willing to provide what their partner needs more of in their relationship. (Stephan Labossiere)

Sexual techniques that may pleasure a man

Men hope that a lover will enjoy contributing enthusiastically to their intimate time together: sharing fantasies, sex play and affection. Arousing a man is easy, if a woman knows how men respond. A woman can flirt by playing along with male fantasies. These details of sexual activity (that arouse men) have no erotic significance for a woman. She is not aroused either by providing (e.g. fellatio) or talking about explicit genital stimulation. If she has a sense of adventure, a woman may enjoy pleasuring a lover, for fun or for money. For variety, couples can plan some sex sessions with a porn movie. Watching porn while having sex, can add a little spice for both lovers. If the woman lies on a low couch watching, a man can penetrate her from behind.

Most men want to ejaculate through intercourse rather than through foreplay activities. Above all, men enjoy the sensations of thrusting. A man finds that his partner is not always amenable, so when an opportunity arises it is precious. This in itself creates a sense of urgency, which is increased by a man's own arousal. Once engaged on intercourse, men orgasm quickly so a man should offer to pleasure a woman before taking his orgasm. Some men enjoy offering to stimulate a female lover by means other than intercourse because foreplay extends the length of time a man can enjoy sexual activity. A woman can ask her lover to provide the kind of pleasuring she enjoys. Older men may be able to delay ejaculating for 20 minutes or longer.

A good female lover is relaxed about nudity and sexually explicit activities. She is ready to explore her lover's body and learn what stimulation he finds pleasurable by taking guidance from him. A man appreciates a woman who uses explicit language. If she is comfortable providing sex chat, a woman can make sexual references or use erotic language to arouse him. Exaggeration is part of the fun! For men, sex is just one of the simple pleasures of life. Men are much more interested in the variations in a lover's genitals and sexual attributes. They also enjoy experiencing a variety of approaches and sexual techniques. Sadly, none of these aspects of sexual activity hold any interest for women because they are not aroused by real-world erotic stimuli.

A woman doesn't need to fake orgasm or arousal. She can find other ways to be a responsive lover. Intercourse is like an erotic dance where a woman follows a man's lead. A woman can smile encouragingly. She can stroke her lover's groin through his jeans, massaging his penis. Lovers can enjoy deep kissing and sensual touching. Men can have tumescence (increased blood flow and sensitivity) all over their bodies. So a woman can give pleasure by stimulating most parts of her lover's body, such as the feet, neck or ear lobes.

Women need to provide a simulated erotic response (because of their lack of arousal). By making small moans or sighs a woman can assist with her lover's orgasm as well as provide a form of erotic feedback that indicates when stimulation is pleasurable. A woman pleasures a man by kissing, stroking and masturbating him. A man may last 2 seconds. He may ejaculate in her hand. It doesn't really matter. It's the man who is frustrated that he has missed out on the chance of intercourse. There's always another time.

Men tend to initiate sex, so it can be a pleasant change if a woman occasionally offers to pleasure a man. A woman can lick and suck gently on a man's nipples. She can offer to stimulate his penis manually or orally. She can hold his erection and slowly but firmly move her hand up and down his shaft. A woman can use her hand to guide her lover's erect penis into her vagina. Alternatively, she can move her hips over his erection and lower her vagina onto his penis. She can stimulate his penis by moving her hips to his rhythm of thrusting, grasp his buttocks or stroke his balls. She can kiss her lover passionately and simulate thrusting with her tongue. Lying on her back, a woman can lift her legs up and hug them around her lover's back. A woman can squeeze her man's buttocks perhaps pulling him towards her. She can tense her pelvic floor muscles to squeeze his penis inside her. She may run her hands over her lover's back. If pressure on the cervix makes deep penetration uncomfortable, a woman can put her hand between her body and her lover's groin to prevent his penis penetrating her vagina too deeply.

If a woman spreads her legs, when lying face down, she can direct her partner to plant his erect penis firmly inside her vagina. She can then ask him to keep still and try to make him come just through her own efforts. She can reach down and feel the base of his penis. She can knead his buttocks and pull him from behind deeper inside her. She can feel the rigidity of his erection. If a man moves his weight onto his arms the woman can gyrate her hips or tighten her pelvic muscles rhythmically to give him more sensation.

Men don't have a G-spot. They have a prostate gland. The prostate lies at the base of the penis, just below the bladder. The prostate gland is crucial to maintaining erections and it is also involved in the release of seminal fluid during ejaculation. It is quite natural that any man might want to enjoy the sensations of being penetrated. For some men prostate-induced orgasms can be intensely pleasurable. Even if a man does not have an orgasm, stimulation of the prostate can be very enjoyable. A partner can stimulate the prostate through the walls of the rectum (inside the anus). A lover needs to use a well-lubricated finger and ask for feedback. A man can also access his prostate through his perineum (the fleshy part between his testicles and anus). This may involve using some deep pressure, so a toy or massager can be helpful.

Most guys feel like they are always the initiator and that sets up disequilibrium on the passion scale in the relationship. (Les Parrot)

A man wants a partner to make love to his penis

When aroused, men experience rigidity of the sex organ (the penis). But this increased blood flow, although concentrated in the genitals can also affect the sensitivity of other parts of the body (called tumescence). So when sexually aroused, a man may enjoy being stroked and sucked on almost any part of his body, for example: the nipples, around the anus and the testicles.

If a man loses his erection, a woman can slowly lick around his testicles and take his penis in her mouth. She can gently suck on it until she feels it start to harden. Oral sex is an easy way to give any man an erection. She can hold his penis firmly in her hand and use a gentle pumping action to increase his erection. When a man masturbates, he uses a firm stimulation technique. When a woman first masturbates a man, she may be surprised by just how vigorously she can stimulate his penis with her hand. A responsive woman's masturbation technique is firm but more diffuse, slower and much gentler.

Anyone, who anticipates an opportunity for oral sex, should prepare well. The smell of the skin around the genitals and the pubic hair can have a pungent smell in both sexes. The genitals are not the easiest places to clean. There are folds of skin that need special attention. For a man, the area around the glans must be scrupulously cleaned and any mucus washed away. For a woman, either side of the labia should be washed with soap and rinsed.

Men are disappointed when women refuse to offer fellatio. They don't appreciate that women's lack of arousal means the activity is functional and not erotic. Vaginal lubrication may increase as a subconscious response in preparation for sex. Fellatio obliges a woman to put her nose close to a penis. Women are not aroused by genital smells as men are. Most women are disgusted by the idea of putting a penis in their mouth. Some women ignore this instinctive aversion to please a lover. This depends on their generosity and the state of the relationship (it has nothing to do with responsiveness).

Many women refuse to offer fellatio. Women are not aroused as men are by giving or receiving oral sex so they don't understand the erotic significance. Even the idea of consuming semen makes most women want to vomit. Some people consume their own body emissions but we don't usually volunteer to consume someone else's. Fellatio is probably distasteful due to psychological factors. There is nothing unhealthy about semen. It has a slightly nutty taste and, if a woman anticipates a man's ejaculation, can be swallowed quickly.

If a woman doesn't like the taste of semen, she may want to offer her partner fellatio just as a warm-up. A shared bath is a good venue for fellatio (starting with lathering his penis). There are various gels on the market that can be applied to the body (including the genitals) and then licked off. Some men are very reluctant to cease fellatio before they ejaculate. The male sexual objective is to ejaculate into a body orifice. For some men fellatio has little value, if it does not include the satisfaction of ejaculating into a lover's mouth.

Men don't want women to see their flaccid (non-erect) penis because it is usually quite small. Most men want to know that their erection will be appreciated before they display it. Men may also be embarrassed if their arousal is apparent when it is not appreciated. A woman may laugh out of nervous embarrassment. Women are offended if a man other than a lover displays his erection. Women interpret genital display as a potential threat.

A contributing factor to the longevity of heterosexual relationships is that some men (perhaps the majority) look for an emotional connection. They may be tempted by attractive women because of their automatic arousal. But they never seriously consider a casual liaison. Many men are cautious about approaching women. This is partly due to timidity but also to a desire for acceptance. They fear rejection but they also fear being treated with disgust.

A woman cannot understand a man's pleasure in displaying his erection. Neither can she understand the pleasure to be obtained from ejaculating into another person's body. Men's territorial instincts mean that they can enjoy spraying semen or urine. Women are not aroused by physical phenomena such as body fluids. They are typically revolted by such things. Women are disgusted the genitals, smells and body emissions that men enjoy. A woman is offended if a man shows interest in her genitals. She cannot understand why anyone would be interested in such dirty, smelly and ugly anatomy.

A woman has little interest in a sexual advance from a strange man. But once a man is her lover, a woman accepts his need for regular intercourse because she loves him or because she knows it's expected. A woman reacts very little when her lover reveals his erect penis. She doesn't scream but neither does she express pleasure on seeing his erection. Women think genitals are ugly, even those of a lover. But they know men are offended if they say so. This is another reason for women's sexual passivity and silence on sexual topics. They passively acquiesce to men's desire rather than proactively invite it. This makes a strong contrast between pornography and women in real life.

So many women are highly vocal in condemning men's sexuality as crude, obscene and disgusting. Women never experience this kind of negativity from men. Men value the fact that a lover doesn't react in this way. Women may be passive and silent but at least a female lover is not abusive. Men equate this loving or passive behaviour as sexual acceptance and derive a considerable emotional reassurance from it. Being accepted sexually allows men to feel that their sexuality is a positive aspect of who they are as men.

This greater inclination of the human male towards oral activity is duplicated among other species of mammals. (Alfred Kinsey)

How a couple can bring variety to intercourse

Few women provide explicit erotic turn-ons. But most, at least initially, are affectionate. Demonstrating affection involves close physical intimacy and causes male arousal. When a man is overwhelmed by sensations of arousal, he assumes that a woman feels exactly the same responses. He can interpret her affection as a turn-on because, to him, it appears to be a sexual invitation.

For many people penetration is the ultimate turn-on because it is the most intimate act we can engage in with another person. Different positions for intercourse are popular because they allow men to observe their penis thrusting into their lover's body. Different positions also bring women some welcome variety to what is, for women, a very basic and repetitive mating act.

A woman can sit astride a man's erect penis (woman-on-top), using her arms to lift her weight and simulate thrusting in reverse. The position allows a man to enjoy seeing a woman's breasts. He may interpret his lover's proactiveness as a sign of her own arousal. But sadly, women are not aroused with a lover. Women tend to tire of this position which involves considerable effort. It is suggested that being on top allows a woman to obtain the clitoral stimulation she needs for orgasm. This is incorrect. Stimulation of the clitoral glans does not cause orgasm. Doggy style can also feel highly erotic. Rear entry by the male is typical for mammals. Many women object to the position because it accentuates the crude eroticism of intercourse. By highlighting a man's focus on ejaculating into an orifice, a woman may feel like a receptacle for semen.

More proactive couples change the venue for sex on an ad hoc basis. Some people enjoy the risk of being caught or observed in venues such as on public transport or in the cinema. Some men fantasize about having intercourse outdoors or in unusual places. Some people like to watch and others like to be watched. Dogging is popular in the UK, which involves couples having sex (often in the car) in woods that are designated for the purpose so that others (primarily men) can watch. Others may prefer the privacy and seclusion of venues such as a private garden or a remote rural location. Up against a tree (something to lean on) or behind a large bush both work well.

Quickies can be erotic when used in different venues. Quickies often involve a standing position, for example rear entry with the woman bent over a table or in the shower. The woman can support herself against an object (a tree, a table or the side of the shower) or lean over at 90 degrees and rest face down. If a woman usually moves her hips during intercourse (to provide the turn-on of assisting with penile stimulation and have a more proactive role) it can be a pleasant change to have the excuse to contribute no effort whatsoever.

A man can tell a woman what he is thinking as he stimulates her from behind. A man should talk in terms of desire, domination and possession rather than the explicit and graphic sexual urges that men enjoy. A man can stroke the area between a woman's thighs (from clitoris through to anus). He can hold her butt cheeks apart before and as he penetrates her. He can use a hand to hold a woman firmly down as he dominates her (only with her permission!).

A man should change his rhythm of thrusting and depth of penetration by alternating between teasing the glans of his penis in the entrance of his lover's vagina (the most sensitive part) and using longer deeper thrusts. A man can use his body weight to provide a sense of domination. When a man thrusts deeply into the vagina, the base of his penis thumps against her vulva and perineum (towards the anus). The woman may enjoy mild sensations of arousal, especially when her partner's groin grinds into her labia and clitoris.

A woman may appreciate the eroticism of being dominated (from the whole-body contact and his weight) and the psychological satisfaction of being penetrated (from knowing that his penis is deep inside her body). Intercourse provides little internal sensation but a woman can feel external pressure. A man can demonstrate affection by kissing and caressing her.

BDSM involves the use of physical restraints that limit a person's range of motion and the play-acting of submissive and dominant roles by consenting adults. To increase safety, couples use a safe word so that the person in the submissive role can stop all activity. They also discuss in advance what they agree to be the limits on permitted activities. A less risky version involves using light bondage and a blindfold to make sex slightly more mysterious and heighten the sensations of being penetrated and touched by a lover.

For women, sex is a sensual rather than an erotic experience. The rewards of sex are emotional rather than based on physical gratification. Women may enjoy sensual teasing, sexual anticipation and feeling desired. This all takes time, which is difficult for a younger man. Older men, who are less acutely aroused, have more time to spend pleasuring a lover and enjoying their own arousal. Some couples enjoy dressing up or using fantasy role play to play act sexual scenarios. Some couples enjoy spanking and other kink activities. What appeals depends on our personality, our responsiveness (because a person needs to be responsive to appreciate eroticism) and our fantasies.

Women often conclude that men lack imagination when it comes to sex. This is because intercourse is a relatively mundane repetitive act for a woman whereas for a man, penetrating the vagina (with the ultimate goal of ejaculating into it) represents the most erotic situation imaginable. This is natural given men's biological sex drive. Many men have no need for fantasies of any kind because intercourse is sufficient for their sexual needs.

Just as in the human species, it is the male among practically all of the mammals which initiates the ultimate genital union. (Alfred Kinsey)

Sexual techniques that may pleasure a woman

Men engage in sexual activity to release accumulated arousal through thrusting and orgasm. By contrast, even responsive women only generate the kind of arousal that leads to orgasm by consciously focusing on explicit erotic fantasies during masturbation alone. Women (regardless of orientation) are not consciously aroused (in their mind) with a lover and so cannot have a true orgasm. A heterosexual woman is obliged to engage in sexual activity in response to her partner's initiative for years without any arousal or orgasm.

Sex with a new partner most usually begins with kissing. A woman can enjoy passionate kissing but, even as a lead into sex, kissing does not cause a woman's mind to become aroused as it does for men. Men initiate kissing to indicate their desire for intercourse. In deep (or French) kissing one partner inserts their tongue into the other person's mouth. Kissing varies depending on how open the mouth is, how long the kiss lasts and how much movement is involved. Some people dislike too much saliva flowing which tends to happen if kissing goes on for too long. Passion can also be communicated by the firmness of the contact and by combining hugging with a kiss. The most romantic kisses are gentle in the build-up and not too wet.

Young women can often find intercourse painful. A woman's amenability to exploring sex play depends on the pleasure she enjoys without needing to put in too much effort. As she gains maturity and experience, a woman can enjoy the opportunity to explore sex play. This depends on whether a couple has invested in communicating over sex. As she ages, a woman's mind may respond to the more subconscious turn-ons associated with sexual activity and her body may respond more readily to being stimulated by a lover. Mature women may experience a kind of physical climax from stimulation of the entrance of the vagina (vaginal fisting) and through anal stimulation.

Even when a woman knows that a lover can give her pleasure, she is not motivated by sex to the degree that men are. This pleasure is much more vital to her male lover than it is to the woman herself. She also appreciates that her emotional state affects her sexual willingness. She needs to be motivated to give to a lover, which depends on the state of their relationship.

Firstly, a woman needs to feel good about herself. Having sex does not cheer a woman up. If she is unhappy or if she feels stressed (or just out of shape!) she may not feel sexy, which means that she doesn't feel desirable. She needs to be in the right frame of mind to be amenable to sexual pleasuring. Sadly, a woman's state of mind is not necessarily something her partner can change.

Secondly a woman hopes to feel good about her lover and how other people view him. Heterosexual men often assume that it is only women who need to attract a lover. By dressing in an attractive and sexy way, a man can demonstrate his appreciation of the effort a woman makes to be attractive for him. He also needs to invest time in non-sexual intimacy, including spending time together on sociable activities such as talking, so that sex is not the only activity a couple shares. Sex feels most appropriate to a woman once a couple have spent some quality time together. A woman wants to see her partner demonstrate how much he cares about her as a person. The attention he pays her, motivates her to return the favour by pleasuring him.

Thirdly it helps if a woman feels tuned into eroticism This can be quite random. Sometimes a romantic movie might turn her on (make her more amenable to a love-making opportunity). A more reliable approach is to build in some sexual anticipation (such as planning a sex session). If a woman is amenable, she appreciates being flattered by her partner's sexual interest in her. Some women enjoy watching pornographic movies with a lover (that have some story content) to help bring some variety to a couple's sex life.

Female arousal is largely subconscious. Mature women may be aware of vaginal lubrication in anticipation of intercourse but they are not conscious of any mental arousal. There are no erotic stimuli with a lover that cause female arousal. Women use surreal fantasy when masturbating alone to access their subconscious arousal. Sadly, it is not possible (even for a responsive woman) to use this same intense focus on fantasy with a lover.

Men have a sub-conscious response that transports them instantly from a social situation to the erotic world. A woman needs time for her mind to tune into the sensations of being stimulated. Erotic build-up with a partner takes much longer than when using fantasy during masturbation alone. A woman's mind has no conscious focus except the sensations of her partner stimulating her while she thinks about the consequences of his erection.

A woman may enjoy her lover admiring her body and talking about what he wants to do to her. A man can spend time preparing a woman's body for sex. Shaving a woman's pubic hair feels quite kinky and makes oral sex easier and more pleasant for the man. An enema can cause physical arousal (internal tumescence) so that even intercourse is more arousing than normal.

A woman may enjoy using a blindfold to focus on sensations and low-key bondage (tying hands or feet together or to the bed) to heighten the sense of being desired by a lover. Sex toys can be used to tease, bring in some anticipation (of the real thing!) and take the pressure off a man needing an erection. A man can enjoy arousing his lover while a woman enjoys being pampered. The woman should encourage a lover by reacting appreciatively!

Many men think long intercourse is the key to having orgasms during intercourse, but long intercourse is not helpful to women and some females may be grateful to get it over with quickly. (Vincenzo and Giulia Puppo)

A man needs to make sex exciting for a woman

When women see men, they think of sex. You could equally well say that men think the same thing when they see women. But the reasons are very different. When men see women, they become aroused and so they think of having sex. But women are not aroused by men. A woman knows various men may want to have sex with her. But she only enjoys emotional pleasure when she is admired by a man she is attracted to. She knows that if a man finds her attractive, he might invest effort in knowing her. That is a woman's emotional power of being sexually desired that men never experience. For gay men, their responsiveness is likely to drown out more emotional rewards.

Most women realise that men appreciate women who present themselves in a sexy manner. Men have more difficulty understanding that women also want men to behave in a certain way to satisfy their needs. A woman accepts a man as a lover when she considers him a worthy mate and companion. She feels loving towards him when he responds to her desire to care for him. Women's nurturing instincts mean they want a man to be sensitive to the social and emotional aspects of relationships that are important to women. Women do this when they care about a man. A woman stops doing this when a man has repeatedly rejected her attempts to care about his welfare.

Men like to assume that by offering sex, they are pleasing a woman. It never strikes them as a strange coincidence that sex is exactly what they themselves are looking for. Women need to obtain some kind of emotional reward for offering men an opportunity for penetrative sex. Considering their interest in sex, men don't make much effort to bring variety to sex. Men's sexual needs tend to be very simply satisfied through intercourse but this does not make a woman feel loved and appreciated. Men need to make themselves more socially amenable and to take a share of the investment in a couple's sex life if they are to interest a woman in having sex over the longer-term.

Men's needs are obvious. Women's emotional needs are much less obvious. A woman sees sex as a demonstration of male admiration. If a man is not devoted to her from day-to-day then it's not flattering. It's just a man's sexual need. Over time most women tire of providing male pleasure even through intercourse. Many women become exasperated with men's seemingly insatiable sexual needs. If she is financially independent, it may not be worth a woman's while to remain in a relationship if a man is not companionable.

Most women are fairly indifferent to sex. It's a small price to pay for all the benefits that men bring. To begin with at least. Over years and decades the sexual burden increases as sex becomes increasingly meaningless in emotional and romantic terms. Intercourse does little for a woman but it is the easiest way to satisfy a man. By accepting quickies or sex in unusual places (not always as a routine in bed before sleeping) a man allows a woman to be the object of his desire without her needing to make so much effort.

A woman feels sexy when she feels attractive. Marriage and motherhood do not cause women to feel sexy because a woman feels exhausted, unappreciated and unattractive. Being free of children and dressing up for a romantic dinner may help. When a woman is aware of a man's admiration for her, this can increase anticipation and create a more passionate act. When sex becomes expected or mundane, resentment and boredom set in. A man should try to communicate his sexual appreciation in a way that a woman appreciates by complimenting her and talking of his sexual desires.

Some women enhance their own (and a lover's) apparent sexual prowess by faking orgasm to meet expectations from pornography. Other men complain that their partners make no effort to make sex exciting for them. Men never articulate why women should do this because it highlights women's lack of arousal. It is clear that women do not naturally provide the turn-ons that men ideally hope for. At the beginning of a relationship, a woman may take pleasure in her man's erection and the fact that he wants intercourse with her. She may enjoy pleasuring him and engaging in loving and affectionate foreplay. Intercourse provides an opportunity for kissing and caressing. But since women are clearly not aroused, men become more focused on their own delight in intercourse over time and just focus on their own satisfaction.

Many men are disgruntled that their wives do not offer more explicit genital stimulation. Before men expect more, they should ask their partners: "What can I do for you (outside the bedroom) to repay you for the pleasure that you give me?". When it comes to more explicit sexual pleasuring additional compensation is needed. Some women will not provide oral sex no matter what the compensation. Men need to understand that, for a woman, sex is equivalent to a man having to talk about feelings. It is almost impossible. If a woman is just offering her body, sex becomes crude and humiliating.

Romance is associated with the time before a couple has a sexual relationship when each person is still investing in the other. But over time and with the security of marriage, they take each other for granted. Men become self-absorbed in their own importance as the breadwinner. Then they wonder why women don't want to engage in lovemaking with them. Men resent women who are not tuned into the eroticism of sexual activity. Women resent men for expecting regular intercourse without any appreciation that a woman is not aroused by sexual activity with a lover. Naturally there are also men with low sex drives, who may cause a woman to feel unappreciated.

We've got this generation of boys growing up thinking that, you know, women practically faint at the sight of an erection, that women orgasm through penetrative sex, that threesomes are normal. (Tracey Cox)

Only some men are motivated to offer foreplay

There must inevitably be some men who are content with the frequency and quality of sex that their female partners provide. This may be because they are less responsive than the average male so they can better accommodate women's lesser sexual interest. But it is also equally certain that many men are quite oblivious to any of the obvious feedback that women provide. In other words they expect less than other men. Kinsey noted that the majority of men do not need an apparently engaged partner. The sexual act itself provides their full satisfaction. This is natural. Intercourse is a biological male urge. Peripheral eroticism is due to the fertile imagination of a few men.

Both the clitoris and the so-called G-spot were discovered by researchers. It's important to ask why this was. If these mechanisms are as effective as they are claimed to be, why did couples not discover them in millennia of lovemaking? Researchers concluded that the clitoris is key to female orgasm but this has never been unanimously confirmed by heterosexual couples.

Men have always enjoyed groping women's bodies but women complain about this male behaviour. If women were aroused, they might enjoy such activity. The fact that they do not is evidence that men do this for their own enjoyment rather than for a woman's pleasure. Women have never groped men's bodies in a similar way or even stimulated their own with a lover.

A man's sex drive causes him to focus on stimulating the vagina. In reality, given it is a cavity, little of the vagina is stimulated. Typically only the vaginal entrance and the external labia have any contact with a man's body. Female orgasm is a comparatively recent discovery that has simply been assumed to occur as a result of the stimulation men are naturally motivated to provide. Petting was a product of some men being aroused by and so motivated to explore a woman's body as a precursor to engaging in intercourse. With the discovery of the clitoris, the traditional proactive male role of stimulating a woman through intercourse was expanded to include a responsibility for providing the clitoral stimulation a woman was assumed to need to orgasm.

This is the origin of the popular belief that it is the man's role to supposedly give a woman an orgasm. Women's sexual passivity and men's inclination to be sexually proactive (because men are aroused with a lover and the prospect of penetration) made it a natural assumption. But foreplay makes no sense because of the array of female body parts involved. Orgasm is achieved by applying consistent stimulation (specifically rhythmic massaging of the sex organ) up until orgasm. Someone who is erotically aroused is motivated to supply this stimulation themselves. They do not wait for a lover to supply it.

Almost all men masturbate alone at least for some period of their lives. But many women never masturbate. So it is unlikely that they will do so with a lover (apart from providing a turn-on). Some men stimulate a lover's clitoral glans by hand. But if a woman was aroused, she would be motivated to do this herself. The fact that a lover provides the stimulation is an indication that such stimulation is more important to a man than it is to a woman.

If a woman can stimulate herself to orgasm by using clitoral stimulation, why she would do this with a lover? She can stimulate herself at any time. A key issue is understanding how female arousal is achieved. If women were aroused with a lover (by genitals and sexual opportunities), then they would be similarly aroused by portrayals of the same situations in pornography. Pornography would not be censored in every society in the world as it is.

There are two key reasons why a man might want to vary his lovemaking techniques. The first is to increase his own arousal. But Kinsey concluded that the majority of men are not aroused by such activity. The second reason is to provide women with some variety and some sensual pleasures, given intercourse is almost totally lacking in physical sensation and erotic excitement. But there is no natural or instinctive reason why men should do this. The only instinctive behaviour involves men providing the mating act. This is why so many men assume that women should be satisfied, both emotionally and sexually, by intercourse. They assume erroneously that intercourse provides women with the same erotic pleasure that men enjoy.

Manual stimulation of the phallus is a prerequisite for masturbation alone. But the prime reason that men engage in sexual activity with a lover is to enjoy the pleasures of intercourse. Manual stimulation can be used with a lover. A man may stimulate his penis manually in order to obtain an erection. A man may enjoy a lover masturbating him because the idea of someone else providing stimulation arouses him more than self-stimulation. Women touch a lover to demonstrate affection. They want a lover to touch them to know that they are attractive and that a lover wants to enjoy their body. Most women only allow someone they love and trust to touch their genitals. Foreplay does not assist with female arousal but it does bring some variety into a sexual relationship, which becomes incredibly boring for women if it always focuses on intercourse. The pleasure is not so great that a woman insists on it. A woman waits for a man to offer. If she feels in the mood for some sensual pleasuring, she allows him to stroke and massage her body.

The sexual techniques which marriage councils and marriage manuals recommend are designed to foster the sort of intellectual eroticism which the upper level esteems. It depends on prolonged pre-coital play, a considerable variety in techniques, a maximum of stimulation before coital union, some delay after effecting such union, and, finally, orgasm which is simultaneous for the male and the female. (Alfred Kinsey)

Sexual pleasure is defined by sociable activity

Mammals use grooming to connect socially with others. They also snuggle up together for warmth and comfort. Regardless of responsiveness, it can be reassuring to feel the proximity of another person's body: the gentle rise and fall of their abdomen, the warmth and feel of their skin are comforting. The pleasures a woman enjoys from sex, depend very much on the woman. Some women never enjoy sex. Women have little direct motivation to do so, since they are not erotically aroused with a lover. Women of both orientations can enjoy emotional sensations from physical intimacy with a person they love.

Sexual pleasure is defined in male terms as the pleasure obtained from sexual activity with a lover. Men can enjoy both erotic and emotional pleasure with a lover. But the emotional pleasure derives from (is a direct result of) erotic pleasure. Men feel loved because of the pleasure a lover allows them to enjoy (by offering an opportunity for penetrative sex). Men enjoy a tension that comes from arousal that women never experience. Men enjoy the feel, the smells and body secretions of a lover. Women are not aroused with a lover. So emotional factors are much more vital to a woman.

Most people assume a woman should orgasm with lover even though the research findings indicated that most women do not orgasm from sociable activities. The assumption was that women could be helped to orgasm if a lover knew the correct anatomy to stimulate. No one asked why women did not know this for themselves. Today the clitoris remains as obscure as it ever was. Very few women ever masturbate to orgasm but, even for those who do, there are no easy explanations for why they do not orgasm with a lover.

If we are sufficiently aroused (so that orgasm is possible) then it does not matter who provides the necessary stimulation: ourselves or a lover. There may be a turn-on associated with knowing that a lover is stimulating us but the stimulation itself is just that: physical. So if a woman cannot stimulate herself to orgasm then it will be impossible for a lover to achieve the same.

Men find almost any stimulation by a lover to be emotionally significant. Whereas women experience only social and emotional feelings with a lover. The receiving partner (male or female) may enjoy the emotional satisfaction of offering this pleasure to the penetrator (a male partner). Given women are not aroused with a lover, their sexual role is one of pleasuring men. Men come to expect women to provide the sexual come-ons and turn-ons that assist with male orgasm. Women need to use conscious behaviours (such as faking orgasm) if they want to emulate the arousal men expect them to feel.

Once a woman has got a man interested in having sex with her, it's over to him. What happens after that is totally up to him. He wouldn't be there if he wasn't aroused by her body. All that a man needs for orgasm is the stimulation that can be provided by intercourse. So women don't ask about male orgasm or what men need to enjoy sexual pleasure. Ejaculation and post-coital gratitude usually provide enough evidence of male satisfaction. But a man wants some reassurance that his lover has enjoyed his lovemaking.

Women's experience of orgasm does not fall within men's definition of sexual. Almost all male sexual activity focuses on the idea of penetration. Sexual pleasure is assumed to involve interactive activity focused on penetrative sex. Even a woman who masturbates, thinks of masturbation as separate to her sexual relationship. Female masturbation to orgasm (not the genital display of porn) is not erotic from a male perspective. There are no male turn-ons. There is no chase, no interaction and no genital display.

Because of the male experience, it is incorrectly assumed that women should orgasm more easily with a lover than when alone. Masturbation provides women with an opportunity to enjoy arousal and orgasm without the life-threatening risks involved in intercourse (pregnancy and childbirth). Men and women enjoy sexual arousal and orgasm under different circumstances. Women are not aroused by real-world triggers such as the body of a lover or opportunities for penetration. In order to enjoy orgasm, they need to consciously focus on sexual fantasies, which is only possible when alone. Women masturbate to enjoy the sensations of orgasm and sometimes to help them sleep or relax. A woman cannot share this pleasure with a lover. This is not her conscious choice. It is how female sexual psychology works.

The erotic fantasies a responsive woman uses for orgasm alone do not work with a lover. They are quite different to the romantic fantasies some women refer to. They typically involve BDSM and rape. Specifically, they do not relate to a real-life relationship and certainly not activities a woman wants to engage in for real. A woman needs 100% concentration for a fantasy to be effective. The presence of a lover interferes with this fragile arousal process.

Many lesbians have relationships that never include genital activity. A woman may enjoy greater sensual pleasures with a female partner. Men's bodies are firm and muscular. Women's bodies are usually softer and more sensual than men's because of the body fat that their bodies naturally have. Women look after themselves more than men in general so they often both look and smell better. Women often enjoy looking at other women for this reason. But no woman, even if she is lesbian, is sexually aroused purely by sexual anatomy as men are. Women (especially lesbians) engage in relationships to enjoy affectionate companionship. Many lesbians never have sex at all.

What would truly be revolutionary for women's sex lives is to engage with what research has found all along: the best predictors of sexual satisfaction are intimacy and connection. (Debby Herbenick)

Why women do not orgasm from cunnilingus

Men believe that cunnilingus causes female orgasm. But where does this belief come from? It doesn't come from any research findings. Cunnilingus is clearly associated with pornography rather than women's sexual pleasure. Misunderstandings over cunnilingus arise primarily because of the belief that women are aroused by the prospect of sexual activity in exactly the same way that men are. But women can never be the penetrator (only the receiver) with a lover because their phallus cannot penetrate (or impregnate) a lover.

The sight of his erect penis penetrating an orifice is a huge turn-on for a man. But there is no reason why women should ever be aroused by erotic stimuli (such as the availability of a lover) as men are. Before any stimulation can lead to orgasm, we must be mentally aroused. The arousal technique (of using erotic fantasies) that a responsive woman uses to access her subconscious arousal when masturbating alone does not work with a lover.

Kinsey established that the clitoris was the female sex organ. But it has not been accepted as the source of female orgasm even by women themselves. Even with all the publicity the clitoris has had, heterosexual women still have very little awareness of it. Men are aroused in anticipation of penetration partly because of their sex drive but also because of the significant pleasure of penetrating a lover with an erect penis. The clitoris cannot be used to penetrate a lover nor is it an orifice that can be penetrated. Most heterosexual couples are unaware of its existence. Cunnilingus equates to sucking on a limp penis that remains flaccid throughout. If a man was unaroused, stimulating his penile glans might also provide little pleasure.

The penis and the clitoris may start off the same in the early days of foetal development. But later the genital tubercle develops into two very different organs depending on the sex of the foetus. It's not just that the penis is substantially bigger than the clitoris. A man is acutely aware of his penis. Most women don't even know that they have a clitoris. What is confusing is that the clitoris is not immediately pleasurable to touch as the penis is. The clitoral glans has double the nerve endings of the penile glans. This means that manual stimulation of the clitoral glans by a lover can even be painful without lubrication and tends to be irritating or uncomfortable for a woman.

Fellatio simulates the male experience of intercourse. The penis penetrates the vagina (a warm and wet environment very similar to the mouth), which explains why men enjoy fellatio. Men can easily orgasm by penetrating any orifice of the body (mouth, vagina or anus). Cunnilingus also emulates the male experience of intercourse. But the clitoris is not intended to penetrate a vagina. Neither does it have the sensitivity of the penis. The clitoral organ is largely internal and it is only ever tumescent. The clitoral organ never becomes erect, which is what makes the penis so pleasurable to touch.

A man's corpora cavernosa are inside the penis and run the length of the shaft. Any stimulation of the shaft that replicates intercourse (by being warm and wet) is highly pleasurable. Cunnilingus stimulates only the glans of the clitoris, which is not especially pleasurable to touch. A woman's corpora cavernosa are located inside the clitoral organ. Cunnilingus involves providing a wet and warm environment for the clitoral glans but (unlike the penis) the clitoris is not designed to penetrate a vagina or any other orifice.

Female orgasm occurs as a result of massaging the blood flow within the internal organ (not the external glans or the labia). A responsive woman uses the fingers of both hands to firmly massage the internal organ by pressing down either side of the labia majora and squeezing with her pelvic muscles. The sensations of a lover's tongue do not provide the kind of clitoral stimulation that causes female orgasm. So cunnilingus cannot cause orgasm.

The sensations of cunnilingus are quite diffuse and vague so there is little to object to (though many women are disgusted even by the idea of oral sex). A woman may accept a man's desire to pleasure her through cunnilingus even though she knows that orgasm is impossible. Eventually she tires of the activity and stops him, which he may interpret as a sign that he has succeeded in satisfying her or that she has had an orgasm. Women never confirm this.

Some men go to prostitutes specifically to obtain the fellatio they can't get at home. Women clearly do not offer fellatio as a routine part of their relationships. If cunnilingus is so pleasurable for women, it seems strange that they would not offer a lover the same pleasure. Neither do women pay for cunnilingus. Women do not demand or even ask a lover for cunnilingus. Women rarely refer to sexual pleasure. Women are typically embarrassed by references to explicit genital stimulation. Cunnilingus is portrayed in porn as a male turn-on but it still lags behind intercourse in terms of popularity. In general women prefer so-called lovemaking to explicit genital stimulation.

Some men offer cunnilingus because they enjoy extending their own arousal. This male desire to pleasure a woman causes much of the confusion over female orgasm. Some women may accept cunnilingus, if a lover offers, especially if they are aware of the erroneous belief that it can cause female orgasm. Many more men talk about cunnilingus than women ever do. There is certainly no widespread discontent among women that some men are unwilling to provide cunnilingus. Some men focus solely on intercourse.

The male, with his higher level of sexual responsiveness, is the one who is more often interested in making oral contacts, and it is the wife who is more often offended. (Alfred Kinsey)

Sexual pleasure need not always focus on orgasm

Alfred Kinsey concluded that any research that involved making subjective judgements of the emotional rewards of sex activity would make it impossible to compare individual experiences (because of personal interpretation). He chose to use responsiveness as an objective measure of sexual activity. Measuring physical phenomenon is a very natural male perspective on sexual function. Kinsey acknowledged that this quantitative approach meant that his research did not include a more qualitative assessment of sexuality.

Because of their sex drive, men naturally assume that the function of sexual activity is to focus on the genital stimulation that leads to orgasm. They assume that women respond as they do and that women seek genital stimulation above all else. But genital stimulation is only pleasurable if you are aroused and women are not aroused (enough to orgasm) with a lover. There is an aspect of sexual pleasure that is uniquely defined by orgasm. It is the satisfaction of obtaining a sexual release, together with the muscle spasms and relaxing aftermath that go with a good orgasm. Men have a natural advantage because they experience orgasm more commonly than women do. But men lose out in other ways that only women can appreciate.

Men think they're sexual because they have an arousal cycle that ends with grunts and ejaculation of semen. But they miss the enjoyment of sensuality, the emotional pleasure, the needing and the loving, touching and caressing. It's all over in a flash; until the next time. Women's sexuality involves a desire to spend time with a lover enjoying affectionate companionship. When a woman loves another person, she is typically motivated to demonstrate her affection by kissing and caressing a lover's body. She is not aroused by and so not motivated to stimulate a lover's genitals as a man is. But if she knows that genital stimulation gives a lover pleasure, of course, she may offer it.

Sexual activity includes any behaviour that is directed towards achieving orgasm. But if we consider the person giving oral sex and the person receiving (vaginal or anal) intercourse, even though they are not aiming to orgasm themselves, we still call their behaviour sexual. The role of facilitating a lover's orgasm is just as sexual as being the person having the orgasm. Sexual activity (alone or with a partner) can include psychological (emotional and erotic) and physical (sensual and genital) stimuli that may be delightful but that do not necessarily result in orgasm. This issue is vital in appreciating the confusion over female orgasm. Men's easy arousal means that sexual release of pent-up drive is a priority for men. But women don't need orgasm.

When we suggest that a couple spends some sexy time together, the inference is that they engage in genitally focused activity. We tend to define sex and sexy in the way that men understand these words, in terms of eroticism. But women can find spending time with a lover cuddled up on the sofa watching a sentimental film, very sexy. They may also be more amenable to sex after a romantic dinner. A woman does not get the same emotional fulfilment from sex that men do. But that does not mean that a woman cannot enjoy sex. A woman can appreciate many aspects of sensual pleasuring because she has no need to release sexual tension as men do.

A woman feels little physically from consensual intercourse. Sexual activity in general holds little interest given her lack of arousal. A relaxing massage may compensate a woman for being unaroused. Men tend to complain that they are bored by making effort on platonic activity that doesn't arouse them. But this is exactly the same reason why it's boring for women to offer intercourse. For women, quick intercourse is generally a plus. But they may sometimes miss lovemaking, romantic kissing and non-genital caressing.

A woman engages in sexual activity with a man in order to please him. She offers him an opportunity for penetration because she knows that he obtains great pleasure from the activity and it is relatively effortless for her to provide it (if he is intent on his own orgasm). A woman's objective with a lover is to give him access to her body until he achieves orgasm. He may indulge her in a variety of foreplay but none of this activity puts an end to her willingness to offer him an opportunity for penetration. In fact, foreplay only extends a woman's waiting time and she may prefer quick intercourse if she is not in the mood to indulge him with an opportunity to extend his own arousal.

Men approach sexual activity (alone or with a lover) already aroused and so stimulation leads to orgasm. Women are not spontaneously aroused and so stimulation is not a guarantee of orgasm. Therefore, women often engage in sex without ever having an orgasm. A woman accepts that she does not orgasm so she hopes to enjoy more general sensual pleasuring with a lover. For this, two things need to happen. First a man has to work out what keeps a woman happy outside the bedroom. This involves non-sexual intimacy and caring behaviours, including sympathetic listening, taking an interest in her concerns, demonstrating affection giving support, admiration and respect.

Secondly a couple needs to invest some time and effort in their sex life. They should plan a sex session once in a while. A man should invest in some accessories such as sex toys and porn movies. Women are embarrassed by erotic content so a man needs to be patient and willing to experiment. Movies need to have some story content to be interesting for women. On an ad hoc basis couples could also plan some quickies for variety, by changing the venue for having intercourse to the shower or outdoors, for example.

Women, more often than men, report that they find sex to be pleasurable even if they do not orgasm. ... many women enjoy the intimacy that sex provides, the kissing, touching, closeness, etc. (Debby Herbenick)

Appendix

Why sex education is vital today more than ever

Even though adults may have decades of sexual experience, they are often so intimidated by the confidence of the younger generation that they assume young people know more about sex than they do. The young may be the most sexually active but inevitably they are also ignorant and inexperienced. Unfortunately, young people have little interest in learning from their elders.

Given the personal nature of the topic, many parents feel ill-equipped to discuss sex with their children. There is also widespread concern about the easily accessible pornographic content promoted via the internet that is both unrealistic and misleading. So, schools are coming under increasing pressure to educate young people (from as young as 5 years old) about sexuality. Some parents worry that children will be harmed by information that is inappropriate for their age. But it is very difficult to relate to information until we have some practical experience. If children do not understand an explanation they are given, they will simply ignore it until they are older.

Pre-adolescent children (5 to 10 years) should learn about the changes they can expect at puberty. Some boys of this age may have already experienced orgasm and a few have started masturbating. In the absence of a formal sex education, children learn about sex (or rather sexual ignorance) from other children, often older siblings or school friends. Young children have simple questions relating to the world they see around them such as 'Where do babies come from?'. Children mature at different ages and it is important to anticipate the youngest age that children may need information for their own safety. Children should be told what they should do if they are faced with adults (and teenagers) who pose a threat to them (for their own protection).

Most adolescents (10 to 15 years) experience puberty around this age. They should be told about the changes that occur in their own bodies as well as those of the opposite sex. Even if they have no sexual experience, many teenagers have started dating or have had intimate contact with others. For their own safety, they need to be familiar with the issue of consent and to know the basic reproductive facts. Education should provide a foundation on which children can build an understanding of issues that may arise later.

The hormones of puberty tend to encourage emotional beliefs that stand in the way of absorbing the facts and logic involved in a more thinking discussion of sexuality (backed by research findings). To allow children to progress according to their own social and sexual development, they should be introduced to the fundamentals of sexuality early on. This may protect them from the onslaught of sexual ignorance and erroneous information received from other sources (peers, misinformed adults and erotic fiction).

Young people (from 15 to 20 years) will want to know about casual sex and their choice to abstain from sex. Young adults should have access to all the information regardless of their own experience. This will help them appreciate that any population includes very diverse individuals. A broader education may instil tolerance and help them appreciate some of the issues.

Schools (adults who are emotionally detached from the child) can provide an ideal means of educating children in sexual matters. Facts and logical explanations are best absorbed by studying alone. But teenagers can benefit from having a forum for discussing questions, issues and problems, possibly in single sex or smaller topic-focused groups, where bravado is discouraged.

Mature adults (over the age of 20), especially when they have some sexual experience with a partner, tend to assume that they know everything there is to know. Many lessons from younger years may have been forgotten or need reinforcing. Modern fictional media encourage sexual myths and cause people to reject the research findings. As they embark on sexual relationships, young people may be interested to know about issues that arise in long-term relationships. Some issues only arise as we age and gain experience. Long-term relationships (over 10 years) have special challenges (including family and career demands) that are not encountered earlier on.

Wherever someone tries to talk about sex in public, someone else will say it is inappropriate. The result is that there is no intelligent discussion of sex anywhere. Most men only tolerate sexual content that reflects their fantasies. Most women want to censor any sexual reference whatsoever. Another problem is that sexually explicit vocabulary is associated with pornography. A sex education site is obliged to use the same key words and consequently is categorised with pornography. Sex education is so rare that it does not have its own classification on the internet (or elsewhere). So sex education sites are disqualified from raising advertising revenue to fund themselves.

Today there is no forum for an adult discussion of sexuality anywhere in the world. Educators, in schools and elsewhere, lack the sources of authoritative material that they could use with confidence to explain the issues surrounding sexuality. There are no facts or explanations, just the opinions of random individuals who may advise on the topic but who don't necessarily have the relevant experience or an appreciation of the research. A comprehensive source of sex education should provide a coordinated source of comprehensive (politically unbiased) information that schools (or anyone else) can use to inform themselves. At the current date, there is no society anywhere on the planet willing to provide or to promote such information.

Within the last thirty years, parents in increasing numbers have come to realize the importance of the early education of their children on matters of sex. (Alfred Kinsey)

The idea that women are naturally aroused with a lover

The very first time I had sex, I knew that something was up. I felt absolutely nothing. I just lay there wondering what was going on until my partner had finished. I concluded the whole thing was a hoax. But because of the ignorance in our society, the fabrication continued: the bravado of adults in everyday life, the compelling portrayals and accounts of orgasmic women. I continued to doubt the bravado but I didn't have time to figure it all out.

I had been interested in eroticism since teenage years. I wanted to understand what was wrong so I could put it right. When I tried to find answers from sex manuals or therapists, I was advised that I should naturally respond to the physical and erotic stimuli of sexual activity just as men do. I was embarrassed in the beginning because I assumed that I must be missing something very obvious. There was no one who ever hinted at an issue for women. Shere Hite provided the one and only reference to women having the same experience that I had had. Finally, when I had time, I decided to ask women I knew about these orgasms, men think women should have.

What motivated me was the huge discrepancy between my experience and the way women's sexuality is promoted in society. Even today, men are much more likely to contribute to a thinking discussion of sexuality than women ever are. Very few women are willing to comment at all. Women's idea of orgasm has nothing to do with enjoying eroticism or sexual fantasy. So they cannot contribute to a discussion about appreciating and responding to eroticism. In the end, I suspect that men will be core to understanding women's sexuality simply because so few women ever experience orgasm.

Most people, who suggest that women orgasm with a lover, are willing to agree that only some women can achieve this feat. They do this as a way of ignoring the evidence of millions of other women. The inference is that a few select women are specially endowed somehow. The problem with this assertion (apart from the fact that it is incorrect) is that millions of women in the population are made to feel sexually inadequate for no legitimate reason.

No one dares to ask women, who think they orgasm with a lover, to explain how they manage this amazing feat. Women insist on personal privacy as a way of ensuring they never need to provide convincing evidence that they understand what an orgasm is. They accuse men of being perverts for enjoying the details, which prevents men discovering that women have no idea what they are talking about. Even as a woman, I have also been accused of being a pervert for asking for explicit explanations for female orgasm.

It is not a perversion for men to enjoy their own arousal. Arousal is a natural sexual response that is a prerequisite for orgasm. A woman would understand this if she knew what orgasm involves. Women's orgasm claims are not nearly explicit enough to cause anyone's arousal. Men are just looking for emotional reassurance. Most men will support any woman who hints of having an erotic response with a lover. One woman who blogs about orgasm asked me to pay her $25 an hour (plus expenses) just to have a casual conversation. I'm not even looking for turn-ons, just honesty. In decades of talking about orgasm, for the most part there is just a resounding silence.

When I talked to so-called experts, they confidently quoted their textbook theories. But they were incapable of engaging in any logical discussion of the facts. Of course there are men who are happy to eulogise about the orgasms they believe their partners have. But they can't explain them in logical terms any more than women can. No one seems to see a problem in defining female sexuality according to phenomena that no one can discuss in any detail, let alone with the backing of some facts, logic and research findings.

I have never had an orgasm with a lover but I have always worked with my partner to ensure that our sex life fulfilled his needs. I resent women who suggest that boasting about orgasm is all that is required or men who expect women to fake orgasm to satisfy their ego. It's easy to boast about orgasm but women's behaviours are incompatible with enjoying sexual pleasure. Women refuse to answer, they are angry or embarrassed to be asked such personal questions. There are no research findings that prove that women orgasm with a lover. The research indicates that female orgasm is associated with clitoral stimulation during solitary masturbatory activity. The belief that a woman should orgasm with a lover is simply an assumption. And it's wrong!

No one recognises the truth when they hear it. They imply that your experiences cannot be. Orgasm is a unique experience and I am grateful for the pleasure I have enjoyed through masturbation. I back up my work with an explicit account of my experience for the benefit of women who are interested (and any men who can cope with such honesty). I explain the specific erotic and physical stimuli that I have found orgasm depends on.

When I question the feasibility of the orgasms women think they have, they are evidently used to having their claims accepted verbatim. This is wrong. No scientist should be sold on the claims of a few subjects who have so much to gain from promoting fantasies. Orgasm is a response of the human body. Stimulation must continue up until orgasm (not beyond). A person must control that stimulation (i.e. not intercourse for a woman). Orgasm occurs when the brain responds to eroticism by sending blood to the phallus. The phallus is stimulated directly (not through the vagina or the testicles). Men know these facts but most women have no idea how orgasm is achieved. If women experienced sexual pleasure, they would talk about it unashamedly.

Women can use sex to get what they want. Men cannot, as sex is what they want. (BBC blog)

The idea that intercourse should cause female orgasm

If any of us receive a sex education (which most of us do not), the explanations given rarely go further than the basic so-called facts of life. We are told about intercourse and the mechanics of reproduction. If we are really lucky, we are told about contraception and sexual disease. But who talks explicitly about orgasm? Sex is always presented as a mutual pleasure.

In the light of women's behaviours, there are inconsistencies that need to be explained. The rare women who talk about orgasm have no interest in discussing any other aspect of sexuality. Their motivation centres on having their claims accepted. They never provide the explicit detail that might provide evidence of a response to eroticism. Women need to use facts and logic to explain how they orgasm in circumstances that defy common sense.

Only men ever discuss female orgasm openly and confidently. So it's no wonder that sex education and pornography are essentially the same thing. The sexual revolution suggested that men's role included helping a woman to enjoy sex as much as a man does. These fantasies, myths and ignorance cause women and their partners to doubt their own experiences and make them feel inadequate. The vast majority of women never orgasm even alone. The reality of sex is so far removed from how it is portrayed in fictional media that most women prefer to say nothing. Any woman who questions her sexual experiences is told there is something wrong with her. Individual women interpret their experiences so differently that it is almost impossible for one woman to relate to another. Sex education needs to offer rational explanations rather than tell women that they should orgasm with a lover.

Millions of people never comment on sexual topics. We only ever hear the opinions of the highly vocal political minority who are not interested in science or even common sense. They have political objectives which involve asserting that women have the same sexual motivations as men. Men promote this view hoping it will encourage women to be amenable to intercourse. Women promote or accept this view because they are flattered by the male sexual admiration. But women only want platonic admiration. They don't want male sexual advances. This is where the confusion starts.

There are the two contradictory attitudes towards sex that exist side by side in heterosexual society. Officially everyone agrees that enjoying sexual pleasure is part of being a healthy and emotionally well-balanced person. This is the male view that promotes sex as a positive and erotic experience. But men talk much more freely about sex among themselves than when there are women around. Women are offended rather than aroused by the erotic images and crude sexual references that men enjoy. But also what is erotic for one person may be offensive to the next. Men enjoy talking about turn-ons because doing so arouses them. But this talk centres on fantasies rather than reality. Few people, even men, can talk honestly about sex.

Women who otherwise take no interest in any aspect of sexuality, will vehemently defend the apparent responsiveness of women portrayed in erotic fiction. Yet there are no research findings to support these fantasies. Neither are there any logical explanations or facts that build a consistent story. This is why no society provides a comprehensive account of human sexuality. We like to see ourselves as intellectual beings but human beings are foremost political beings. Female sexuality has been defined by men. This is not just because men have set out to persuade women to engage in intercourse. It is also because few women ever comment on the topic due to a lack of confidence in their sexual experiences. The male view is more appealing and can be used to a woman's advantage. This is the deceit of sex. While the silence over sex continues, we will never understand our sexuality.

Many women feel undermined by the sexual images of women that are freely promoted in heterosexual society. These cause a woman to feel like an object of sexual gratification rather than a respected person (like a man). Wherever women are present, sexual content is banned. Even images portraying partial nudity or implied sexual activity cause offense. Women expect men to respect their sensitivities by refraining from making sexual references in their presence. No one is willing to be associated with sexual content for fear of being labelled a pervert. References to a 'dirty weekend' or 'smut' reflect women's perspective. This is the female view that considers eroticism to be disgusting and obscene. Men never view sex or eroticism in a negative light. People avoid being linked to sex-related topics in order to obtain women's approval. In public women insist that they enjoy sex as much as men do. This contradiction means that we cannot confront the issues.

Silence is an advantage in sexual relationships because neither side needs to admit their motives. Women's insistence on privacy means that they are never required to explain how they achieve orgasm. But it is easy to show that most women have no idea what is involved in responsiveness. They are just reflecting the sexual ignorance in the society around them. Yet because of male support, no one challenges these orgasm claims. My work aims to expose this ignorance. I ask couples to explain explicitly how women achieve arousal and orgasm with a lover. I am pointing out that women rarely explicitly talk about sexual pleasure. What we call eroticism is defined by male turn-ons. I am suggesting that women's sexual pleasure depends on emotional stimuli rather than erotic stimuli. My work is necessary because sexologists today promote political ideals rather provide logical explanations.

If you really think about why vaginal stimulation matters so much, it's because it puts the focus on male pleasure. (Emily Nagoski)

About Jane Thomas, the sex researcher and educator

I am Jane Thomas, the sex educator and researcher. I promote enjoyment of eroticism, sexual pleasuring and caring behaviours. I am passionate about combatting sexual ignorance. Please feel free to contact me with your comments! I don't call myself a feminist. I believe that men and women have a right to equal respect. Neither do I think of myself as a sexologist. I call myself a sex writer because I write about sex in the detail necessary to facilitate an understanding of sexual issues. I give those, who are interested, the opportunity to read and consider the consequences of what I am saying.

I have been accused of setting myself up as an authority on sexuality. If I am an authority, it is only because no one else is willing to be explicit. People are offended because I can discuss a topic that most people cannot. They lack confidence in their experiences because of the persuasiveness of erotic fiction. They are unaware of their own ignorance. Some people use bravado to capitalise on this ignorance, which makes it even more difficult for others to speak up. Personally, I think my ability is a result of dedicated hard work over decades. I make my work freely available via my websites to reach as many people as possible. My books are for those who want a hard copy.

No doubt many people object to my directness. I don't have time to be subtle. Given the need for maturity and sexual experience, anyone who wants to contribute to our understanding of sexuality only has a few decades in which to do so. The opposition consists of millions of sources of porn with millions of devoted male followers. This constant propaganda means that any common sense on the topic is guaranteed to be shocking. The battle is endless. I state the facts and logic clearly for all to see in contrast to the lack of the same for the fantasies that are so heavily and widely promoted.

It is natural that people object to what I am saying because I am challenging the ignorance. But they cannot formulate a meaningful response. Above all I advocate tolerance. An uninformed but vocal minority enjoys being unpleasant. They have opinions rather than explanations. They object to any discussion that challenges their beliefs, not because they have any alternative facts or reasoning, but because their beliefs reassure them. The facts can be inconvenient when we have convinced ourselves otherwise. When a topic is political, people engage in persuasive arguments and use emotional pressure to coerce others. But they do it surreptitiously. They don't confront issues head on. They heckle from the side lines or ignore counter arguments. The politically astute don't declare their case. They rely on the fact that people don't listen well. No one notices that pertinent questions go unanswered.

A topic does not go away, just because no one talks about it. I am challenging the universal silence over sex. Some people object when sex is even mentioned. Others have issues and questions. Few people have the ability to question and to accept the facts when it comes to sexual beliefs. Sexologists promote their theories about female orgasm (taken straight from erotic fiction) much the same as others promote religious beliefs that rely on an unquestioning faith. These beliefs are not backed by any research findings. Science is always moving forward. A true scientist accepts that the status quo is incomplete and has the humility to learn. We can never know everything.

My research has involved asking many difficult questions, most of which I have had to answer myself. The answers were always there. Only naivety, ignorance and embarrassment stood in my way. Naturally, my implied inadequacy was embarrassing. But I was also naïve about sexual politics and I didn't appreciate how rare female orgasm must be. Over time I realised that even the most accepted beliefs were not facts at all but just assumptions.

In a world full of manipulation and deceit, someone has to ignore the taboo and speak out on behalf of others. My anger over how I have been treated has fuelled my motivation to help others. I have been infuriated by the promotion of fictitious porno orgasms (based on pornography and male fantasies) that cause so much distress. I am pointing out that these scenarios are simply not realistic. Even men cannot orgasm in these ways. We need stimulation to continue until orgasm is achieved and not beyond. But men want to believe (beyond all logic) that women orgasm from the stimulation that they provide. Women have no idea what orgasm involves. If women were aroused, they would not wait for a lover to supply the stimulation they need for orgasm. We discuss female orgasm because it is elusive with a lover.

My research involves reconciling the research findings with the biological precedents and with sexual behaviours. I explain in explicit detail how I achieve orgasm alone and how I enjoy sexual pleasuring with a lover. I also discuss the bravado, sexual politics and misconceptions from erotic fiction. My work highlights the contradictions inherent in the portrayal of female sexuality today, which reflects fictional media rather than research findings.

Female orgasm is a gift but it feels more like a curse because of the sexual ignorance. When we have an experience, especially such a personal one, we assume that everyone has the same experience. I know that my experience is not unique because of the research findings highlighting the link between the clitoris and female orgasm. I have also been able to draw parallels between the male experience and my own. But understandably few people can accept an experience that appears to be so rare in the population. So I provide explicit detail, together with the research to support my experience.

If you can't explain it simply, you don't understand it well enough. (Albert Einstein)

Jane Thomas's unique approach to sexuality research

We assume that anyone who has had sex knows everything there is to know. The problem with ignorance is that we cannot know what we do not know. In truth, very few people have the necessary intellect, life experience and emotional detachment to understand sexuality. Most people have only prejudices, assumptions and misconceptions. Initially I accepted the bravado as we all do. But after decades, I have concluded that women who boast about orgasm have no idea what an orgasm is. It seems an ungenerous conclusion to draw but none of them can talk about orgasm in explicit detail.

People are called experts just because they have attended a course. But most of these people just pass on what they have been told. Believing that experts can understand what we cannot understand ourselves is part of the problem. If it cannot be explained (at least to graduates) then it isn't scientific. When I first started writing, I thought these so-called experts would support a motivated newcomer. I assumed they would recognise the courage I needed, as well as the uniqueness of my honesty and my ability to be explicit. Afterwards I was amazed that I could have been so naïve to think that they would support me in challenging their emotional beliefs. Anyone, who has the capacity for original thought, doesn't need to be taught. But the creative ability and intellectual confidence required to change the status quo are rare.

My advantage, as a woman, is that my brain doesn't explode whenever sex is mentioned. I don't care about the taboo (the ignorance that categorises my experiences as dysfunctional) that silences so many women. It is quite easy to demonstrate that these orgasms, men assume women have, are fictional. I have been able to challenge the misconceptions with a mind, clear of any arousal or sense of inadequacy. Any woman can appreciate the behaviours she needs to employ in her sexual relationship. But as a responsive woman, I have been able to empathise with the male perspective to some degree. I have realised that female responsiveness parallels, rather than complements, the male experience. A man could never figure out what I have concluded. He would never accept the almost total sexual inertness of the female body.

Most women, who refer to orgasm, are talking about intercourse. They do not understand why anyone masturbates because they only engage in lovemaking (rather than explicit genital stimulation). My experience of orgasm has been more explicit. I can explain the specific stimulation and the erotic turn-ons involved. I did not discover orgasm because I bought a vibrator. No one told me what to do. I discovered the required stimulation instinctively as a result of my own mental arousal. This is what makes my experiences so convincing and highlights the vagueness of other women's orgasm claims. I hope that my work will inspire others to ensure that our understanding of sexuality is based on (biological and behavioural) facts rather than erotic fiction. In an educated society, every adult should have the right to authoritative sex information and the right to ignore it if they choose.

Learn About Sexuality is one woman's attempt to provide sex information that is factual, logical and backed by research findings. Various factors have come together to make me the right person to do this:

(1) I am an attractive and sexually responsive woman;

(2) I am heterosexual, so orientation cannot be used against me;

(3) I have had a communicative and adventurous sexual relationship;

(4) My partner has given me both moral and technical support;

(5) I have had the benefit of the internet to publicise my work;

(6) I am fluent and articulate in the global language of English;

(7) I am familiar with the academic process; I am analytical and organised;

(8) As a maths graduate, I appreciate the value and pitfalls of statistics;

(9) I have had the time and financial resources to work for nothing;

(10) I am motivated to persevere regardless of any opposition.

If we never discuss sexuality then we cannot hope to understand it. Many of the issues need deeper thought than most people have the time for. I try to bring some common sense to the discussion of sexuality. A person needs to be willing to contemplate new ideas with an open mind. I am challenging the assumptions that have been made about women's sexuality, which are wrong. I am not forcing my conclusions on anyone. Those who are interested can draw their own conclusions from my research work. Kinsey's work is a legacy we should treasure. Nothing has replaced the wealth of insightful statistics and logical conclusions from his work. This is a loss my work tries to rectify.

Science that can be defined by physical laws is relatively reliable. But sexuality depends on human nature which is a factor of our survival instincts. There is no commercial or strategic advantage to improving our understanding of human emotions. Our society doesn't reward those who excel in subjects related to the human condition such as sexuality. Many people are reassured by their fantasies and see scientific logic as a personal attack. A researcher must be undeterred by the inevitable emotional and political backlash. Sources, that are selling fantasies to reassure people, can be commercial. Sex education and research involve telling people what they don't want to hear. For this reason, it will always depend on public funding.

All truths are easy to understand once they are discovered; the point is to discover them. (Galileo Galilei)

www.ingramcontent.com/pod-product-compliance
Lightning Source LLC
Chambersburg PA
CBHW070546050426
42450CB00011B/2744